P'yonggang

Ch'orwon

Kumhwa

Hwach'on

Hwachon
Reservoir

Yangyang

Pukhan River

Inje

38th Parallel

Ch'unch'on

25 June

Kangnung

Hangchon River

Seoul

30 June

Chip'yong-ni

Hoengsong

Samch'ok

25 June

4 July

Han River

4 July

Yoju

Wonju

SEA
OF
JAPAN

5 July

4 July

10 July

Han River

t'aek

6 July

Onangju

10 July

34

8 July

26 - 29 June

Choch'iwon

11 - 12 July

21

1 Aug.

5 Aug.

Yongdok

34

15 July

ROK XX 8

ROK XX CAP

ROK XX 3

19 - 20 July

Taejon

25 July

XX 25

ROK XX

Port of Arrival
1st Cavalry Division

24

XX

14 July

Yongdong

No
1 Gun
Ri

Kimchon

Waegwan

XX 1

Pohang

1 Aug.

Taegu

Kum River

Kyongju

26 July

1 Aug.

Tuksong-dong

XXXX
EIGHTH

25 July

27 July

XX 24

XX 24

1 Aug.

Nam River

Naktong River

XX 25

Kwangju

Somjin River

Chinju

27 July

Masan

X 1 Mar.

Pusan

26 July

5 Aug.

KOJE-DO

1 Aug.

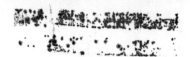

NO GUN RI:

A Military History of the Korean War Incident

Robert L. Bateman

STACKPOLE
BOOKS

Published by
STACKPOLE BOOKS
5067 Ritter Road
Mechanicsburg, PA 17055
www.stackpolebooks.com

Printed in the United States of America

10   9   8   7   6   5   4   3   2   1

Cover photograph courtesy of the U.S. Army Military History Institute
Cover design by Wendy A. Reynolds

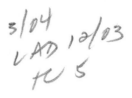

Library of Congress Cataloging-in-Publication Data

Bateman, Robert L.
  No Gun Ri: a military history of the Korean War incident / Robert L. Bateman.
    p.; cm.
Includes bibliographical references and index.
  ISBN 0-8117-1763-1 (alk. paper)
  1. Korean War, 1950–1953—Atrocities. 2. Massacres—Korea (South)—Nogæn-ni. 3. Nogæn-ni (Korea)—History. 4. Korean War, 1950–1953—Campaigns—Korea (South)— Nogæn-ni. 5. Korean War, 1950–1953—United States. 6. United States. Army. Cavalry, 7th. 7. Korean War, 1950–1953—Mass media and the war. I. Title.
  DS920.8 .B27 2002
  951.904'242—dc21
                                                                2002019736

TABLE OF CONTENTS

LIST OF ILLUSTRATIONS

FOREWORD

THIS IS A VERY READABLE AND HARD-HITTING BOOK THAT GIVES A FASCI-
nating and detailed account of what really happened at No Gun Ri in July
1950.

What impressed me most as I got into this riveting work was the
author's diligence as he pursued every possible lead in his search for the
truth. In those few spots where he could not definitely pin down a fact or
facts, he cautions the reader right up front.

Before Bateman gets into No Gun Ri, he details the woeful status of
1950 training, readiness, and discipline in America's short-handed army of
occupation in Japan. Included also is a description of the pitiful, poorly
armed South Korean Army. It's sad to read about that and the resulting battle casualties.

The heart of the book is the compelling coverage of the No Gun Ri
story and factual details on the AP's star "witness-participant-machine gunner," who actually was a mechanic far to the rear and not in the action at all.

The decision-makers who awarded the Pulitzer Prize for investigative
journalism to the Associated Press, and the AP writers for its story on No
Gun Ri, should study this book for its scholarly account of that tragedy.
Indeed, this is a book that will be studied by soldiers, historians, and journalists for years to come.

Harold G. Moore
Lt. General, U.S. Army (Ret.)

ACKNOWLEDGMENTS

IN ANY WORK OF HISTORY ONE INEVITABLY ACCUMULATES CONSIDERABLE personal and professional debts. Peers who reviewed the manuscript, archivists who helped find obscure documents, and friends and family. For their help and advice, and their tolerance and guidance, I would like to thank everyone I came in contact with during my work on this project. If I neglect to mention anyone it is not because I didn't appreciate your help.

For their help in the archives, both in finding the primary sources of this history and in their sage advice about these documents, I am indebted to Richard Boylan and Dr. Timothy Nenninger of the National Archives II facility in College Park, Maryland. For the same services at the U.S. Army Military History Institute at Carlisle Barracks, Pennsylvania, and the archives and special collections of the United States Military Academy, West Point, New York, I thank David Keough and Alan Aimone respectively.

Several historians, journalists, professional editors, and professors of journalism helped review all or part of this work. Their observations, insights, cautions, and encouragement helped me create a work beyond what I might have achieved alone. In this group I want to thank Professor Carol Reardon and Professor (Emeritus) Stanley Weintraub of Penn State, Professor Elizabeth F. Loftus of the University of Washington, Professors Marsha Frey and Linda Frey, whom I had the pleasure to meet while at the U.S. Military Academy, and Professors Elizabeth and Michael Norman of New York University. Among the dedicated journalists and journalism editors who provided crucial insights were David Crook of *The Wall Street Journal*, Joseph Galloway of *US News and World Report*, David Cay Johnston of *The New York Times*, Richard Pyle of the Associated Press, Konstanty "Corky" Siemaszko of the *New York Daily News*, and Glenna Whitley of *Dallas* magazine. Although I know not all of them agree with the results of my research, they were all polite, helpful, and a credit to their profession in every way. My editor at Stackpole Books, Edward Skender, talked me through many points that just were not clear in the initial drafts. I thank him for his patience and understanding as I wrestled with the manuscript. My good friend Mitchell McNaylor, who wrote the initial draft of chapter one, was a bulwark against depression, a constant source of new information and sources, and a useful foil to my various hypotheses. He helped me maintain balance. For this I thank him from the bottom of my heart.

Obviously this work could not have happened without the help of the veterans. They are too many to mention individually here, but it was only with their assistance, patience, and advice that this project made it past the first four pages.

B.G. Burkett and Ralph Zumbro provided much practical advice unattainable from conventionally trained academic historians or professional journalists about the limitations of both.

There is also my family. They suffered for my obsession with this work, for while the writing and research is both a challenge, a pleasure, as well as a burden for me personally, all that they generally got out of the deal was the burden. So to my wife Deborah, my daughters Morgan, Ryann, and Connor, as well as my parents Ursula and Robert, I say once again, thank you and I love you.

Finally, this work is dedicated to the memory of Cyril "Rick" Rescoria, who served with 1st Platoon, B Company, 2nd Battalion 7th Cavalry in Vietnam in 1965 and 1966. Rick died on September 11, 2001 in the same manner in which he had lived—saving others.

INTRODUCTION

---

*How people prepare for and wage war, and the organizations they
create for that purpose, are in fact closely related to the ways in
which they deal with the other, more peaceable aspects of life in
society.*

—David B. Ralston,
Importing the European Army

THIS IS A STORY ABOUT TWO TRAGEDIES. THE FIRST IS A POTENTIAL MISUSE
of the power of the sword; the second is a misuse of the power of the pen.
This book analyzes the events that occurred around a railroad overpass, near
the small village of No Gun Ri in South Korea, in late July 1950, three
days after the arrival of an American army infantry regiment at the very
beginning of the Korean War. At that time and in that place, it appears that
at least some American soldiers opened fire upon a group of civilian
refugees. This much of the story is generally agreed upon by everyone—
participants, victims, reporters, and historians. Fifty years later, we find an
American news organization trying to reconstruct events from those days in
that place, implying among other things that an unreported war crime, a
massacre, had occurred. For its work, it won the Pulitzer Prize for journalism, for a story based upon evidence provided by people who were not
there, people who were impersonators, and people whose motives for saying that they were there were not reported. Placing these events in context
and developing an understanding of them beyond the simple elements of
who, what, and when is the purpose of this book.

This book is organized into two parts. The first part is the history of
the events of July 1950 and specifically the actions of the 2nd Battalion 7th
Cavalry Regiment of the 1st Cavalry Division that led to the incident at
No Gun Ri. The second part addresses larger questions of how the media

and the military relate to each other, how history is written versus how journalism is conducted, and why one cannot substitute for the other. In essence, it is the story of the story.

Writing this book has not been an easy or enjoyable experience. I am a professional infantryman, a soldier in the United States Army, trained as a paratrooper, a ranger, and an air assault trooper. By a sheer coincidence, the army assigned me to a regiment that is arguably the most famous military unit in American history—the 7th Cavalry. This is the regiment of George Armstrong Custer and the Little Bighorn, the unit that chased Pancho Villa in Mexico, the unit that fought through the Phillippines in World War II and participated in the first major fight of Vietnam in the Ia Drang Valley. In modern times, it is a part of the 1st Cavalry Division.

From the very beginning, I determined that I would learn the history and heritage of this proud regiment. History, written as heritage, can motivate and cement the men in an organization from a loose conglomeration into a unit. Military history can also be used to help train officers, sergeants, and soldiers about the realities of combat. Both reasons contributed to my motivation to learn.

I read everything I could about the 7th Cavalry. Most of these writings centered on the performance of the regiment and its most famous commander in their battles against the American Indians in the nineteenth century. The scholarship of many of these books was generally less than optimal. The battalion commander, then Lieutenant Colonel Timothy Lynch, loaned me a few books on the regiment from his personal library. These books recounted not just the Little Bighorn but the whole history of the regiment up through the Korean War. Here was history written, without blinders, by men who had been there. The author of two of these books was a veteran of the 7th Cavalry, a man whom I would come to admire and for a time consider one of my personal heroes. A man named Edward Daily.

Edward Daily was a combat veteran of the Korean War. According to the biographies printed in his two books, he won a battlefield commission to lieutenant in the darkest days of the Korean War. He was taken prisoner during a battle along the Naktong River but escaped and evaded his captors a few weeks later to rejoin his unit. For that, he earned a Distinguished Service Cross, the nation's second highest award for valor. He wore several Silver Stars and three Purple Hearts, and had fought throughout the war as a combat leader at the company level. If ever there was a man from whom one might learn the lessons of history, a man who could teach us something about the realities of infantry combat and battlefield leadership, Edward Daily was that man.

I met him on a mild November afternoon in 1994 just outside Lieutenant Colonel Lynch's office. Fort Hood, in central Texas, can have blister-
ing heat well into the fall, but this day was perfect. A slight man, Edward
Daily looked nothing like his age. His narrow frame and the energetic
enthusiasm he exuded when he burst forward to take my hand in both of his
fit a man in his prime, not in his waning years. His face was long and thin
and bedecked with one of the widest smiles I have ever seen. The shock of
curly blond hair atop his head cemented him in my memory forever.

Daily was the perfect guest. He was always asking questions, forever
fascinated with the answers, and always ready with a pithy comment or a
parable of combat relevant to the situation at hand. For every question I
asked, he had an answer. The author of one of only two books that recount
most of the regiment's history, he was the expert on all things "7th Cav." At
the time we met, he was the past president of the 7th Cavalry Veteran's
Association. He knew people I had only read of; men who were heroes
from the pages of history were "Mike" and "Joe" to him. Edward Daily
was the perfect veteran.

That night, I was planning to attend an officers' call, a gathering of all
the officers of the battalion at the officers' club. There we would drink
beer, tell lies, and make fun of ourselves and each other. Although these
officers' calls were generally private affairs, I was confident that nobody
would object to me bringing such a distinguished veteran as Edward Daily.
I was right.

That night Daily was our honored guest. He was introduced with a full
description of his feats of combat and heroism by the battalion commander
himself. Lieutenant Colonel Lynch gave him one of our battalion coins
(about as high of an honor a battalion commander can give), and most
every officer, respectfully introduced himself to Daily. He was the center of
attention and interest.

Though we regularly exchanged cards, phone calls, and letters, I only
saw Daily one more time when he visited Fort Hood again in November
1995. A new battalion commander was at the helm by then—Lieutenant
Colonel Duane Rackley—and many of the other officers of the battalion
were also new. A somewhat abbreviated, though similar, situation was
repeated, with Daily the hero of this officers' call as well.

In 1996, the army selected me to study for a master's degree in military
history, which would be followed up with an assignment as an instructor of
military history at the United States Military Academy at West Point, New
York.

Ed Daily and I stayed in touch during those years, exchanging Christmas cards and the occasional phone call. Although my thesis focused on the

army in the years between World War I and World War II, in the back of my mind I kept thinking of expanding upon the knowledge I had gained from the many veterans of the 7th Cavalry. Daily helped me by providing phone numbers and names of, as well as introductions to, veterans of the regiment. As I slowly developed the tools of a historian, I drifted away from the study of my former unit towards broader questions of military history. But always in the background remained the idea of a project—writing a complete history of the regiment, or at least its history in the past fifty years. Central to that proposition was my old friend Edward Daily.

Then came No Gun Ri.

In September of 1999, the news wires, papers, and television blared the news of a massacre, heretofore unknown, that took place during the opening days of the Korean War. A copyrighted Associated Press investigative report told a story of American soldiers herding hundreds of South Korean refugees into a railroad underpass at a place called No Gun Ri. Those same soldiers, according to the AP story, then turned their machine guns on the refugees at point blank range under the orders of their officers. Estimates varied, with the overall suggestion being that between 300 to 400 unarmed civilians were killed, with only a handful surviving the massacre. The alleged No Gun Ri massacre occurred in the opening days of the war, as the American forces were reeling backwards towards a defensive perimeter around the southern South Korean port city of Pusan.

I picked up on the stories quickly for the unit accused of committing these atrocities was my own 2nd Battalion of the 7th Cavalry Regiment, and a central figure emerging from the smoke was Edward Daily, the keeper of the 7th Cavalry's heritage.

I needed to know more about No Gun Ri. Too many questions were piling up in my mind about the accounts given in the papers versus the accounts that I was collecting from the veterans that I knew. The training in skepticism I received in graduate school made me suspicious of the recent reports, and my academic historian's antenna was picking up disturbing conflicts in the evidence at hand. The news stories I heard did not jibe with what I knew as a historian about the Korean War and the 7th Cavalry and, almost more importantly, with things that I knew as an infantry officer.

In April of 2000, the team of investigative reporters who broke the story of No Gun Ri for the Associated Press won the Pulitzer Prize for investigative journalism. This shocked and disturbed me, because at that point I had determined that there were major problems, not only with the way that the story had been researched, but also with the very evidence presented. In the course of trying to make sense of the material I had acquired, I told what I knew to several friends and a few superiors. I informed the honorary colonel of our regiment, retired Lieutenant General Harold Moore, and another friend I had met through the 7th Cavalry Association, reporter and historian Joseph Galloway. These men were the coauthors of the military classic *We Were Soldiers Once . . . And Young,* a book about the fighting by two battalions of the 7th Cavalry that took place in the opening days of the Vietnam War. I also talked to another friend, one of the coauthors of my first book, *Digital War, A View from the Front Lines,* a reporter named Edward Offley, then a reporter for the *Seattle Times-Intelligencer.*

I told them about the problems I saw with the reporting done by respected elements of the American media, and I looked to their wisdom and experience to help make sense of the conflicting evidence I was collecting. These men, whose opinions I valued, also happened to know something about the media. Over the course of months, as I asked my friends their opinions on the archival evidence I uncovered or the veracity of a veteran's story quoted in the AP report of the massacre, I taught them a tiny bit about the processes and tools of the historian. At the same time, I learned from them a great deal about how media organizations and reporters approach information.

Within a month after the AP received the Pulitzer Prize, my historical research and the solid investigative journalism of my journalist friends revealed significant flaws in the reporting of that prize-winning story. It now appeared that the AP won the Pulitzer Prize for a story in which fully one quarter of its mentioned sources on this side of the Pacific had not been at No Gun Ri or were not members of the 7th Cavalry at that time, but who were nonetheless feeding the AP and other reporters what they wanted to hear. Even more damning to the reputation of the Associated Press story was the fact that several of the veterans they represented as having witnessed or taken part in what the journalists all but called a massacre said they were misquoted or that their words were taken out of context. By late May 2000, editorials in such major newspapers as *The Wall Street Journal* and such magazines as *Newsweek* began calling the foundations of the story into question. The general tenor of these editorials was, "How can the Pulitzer Prize stand upon accounts which are at best hearsay, and at worst pure fiction?"[1]

This book shows how the *story* of No Gun Ri diverged from the *history* of No Gun Ri, and how one man above all managed to fool the major news outlets of the world with his fictional account of a horrible massacre. That man was Edward Daily.

This is a story of what actually happened as well as why and how it happened. Unraveling the past always requires the skills of a detective, but doubly so in a case when so many of the accounts contradict one another and when sensitive national interests and professional reputations are at stake. I believe that I have come as close as is humanly possible (without having actually been there at the time) to reconstructing the events of those long-ago days. As you will discover, I also have some theories about why this happened. But first, a few cautionary notes must be considered.

The first of these is that this book focuses primarily upon the American side of the story. While the first tragedy happened to South Korean civilians on July 26, 1950, it cannot reasonably be argued that it happened just because they were refugees. The fact is there were South Korean guerillas (not North Korean infiltrators as some have assumed—a significant difference) among the refugees killed that night. No solid evidence exists that the refugees knew of the guerillas in their midst, and consequently I focused largely upon those who fired at the refugees, not on the legitimacy of the refugees themselves.

The second caution is that there are still some gaps in the evidence I have acquired about the incident at No Gun Ri. One gap relates to the question of exactly how many civilians were killed and by what means. Without an unbiased contemporary (circa July 1950) account or any historical or modern physical evidence that anyone was killed (the lack of bodies is a problem), the best I can offer is an estimate based upon an historical analysis.

In the first part of this book, I generally avoid casting blame for the massacre upon any one individual. Media accounts from 2000 and 2001 suggest that higher-level orders to shoot civilians resulted in the shooting of refugees at No Gun Ri. The answer is far more complex than simply stating, "Officer X gave the order." No Gun Ri was not an isolated event. In fact, evidence uncovered during my research suggests that there was no single large deliberate massacre as alleged, bur rather dozens of small shooting incidents involving several U.S. units and civilians that took place throughout the region in the last weeks of July and the first weeks of August 1950. And rather than deliberate acts of wanton cruelty, these shootings were the inevitable by-product of poor training, poor communication, and inadequate readiness for war. In short, a series of decisions made well before the war by people in Washington, D.C., with the best of intentions but with damned little foresight, resulted in situations where desperate and ill-trained Americans attempted to accomplish near-impossible missions.

Dig below the wreaths and laurels laid during wartime, and one often discovers a disappointing layer of military history. What happened at No Gun Ri has happened before, and since, and tends to happen more often when the troops and the officers involved are not fully trained. Poorly trained soldiers lack discipline. Poorly trained officers result in poorly led men. In this case, the ill-trained troops at No Gun Ri are the logical result of national decisions made in the period following the end of the Second World War. In that day and age, we believed that nuclear weapons would make the infantryman obsolete. Money flowed to research and development for missiles and other, cheaper solutions to guarantee the freedom of the United States. The army took a budgetary backseat and endured cut after cut in funding and force structure.

When an administration assigns numerous missions to the army and dictates a force structure to accomplish them but does not supply the funds to accomplish either, the proficiency of the army naturally decreases. The money to accomplish the mission must come from somewhere, and prior to the Korean War, it came out of the training budget. When training decreases to certain levels for long enough, events such as those that occurred at No Gun Ri happen.

Understanding No Gun Ri means understanding how history is recorded. The quote at the beginning of this introduction encapsulates the philosophy of what is now known as the "new" military history. That there is a new military history is somewhat ironic, since military history is arguably the oldest form of history. Notwithstanding the traditions of ecclesiastical accounts, many of which contain vast amounts of military history as well, accounts of war and human conflict have fascinated mankind since the dawn of literacy. Indeed, one could argue that military history extends even further back, into pre-literate times, as the subject of many of man's first etchings and sculptures.

Since this book is also about a journalistic misrepresentation of military history, it will be helpful if the reader knows a little of how history is written and organized. Quite obviously, there are many examples of good history and bad history. Within the field of military history, however, there are also several distinct genres. I would be remiss if I began telling the story of the events that occurred near No Gun Ri, South Korea, in the summer of 1950 without first explaining these genres. The process of researching and writing history is especially relevant when we get to the second part of this book. This book has a purpose—to educate and explain. Without some understanding of how a series of events become history, the reader may not have the tools to critically evaluate what is set before him or her in this book.

In the United States, the fascination and interest in military history have only recently begun to gain favor within the American academic community. Historian Ronald Spector spoke to the point when he said, "Few professional historians could or wished to concentrate primarily on the history of war."[2] The general academic distaste for military history may stem from Americans' aversion to the concept of a standing military force, or it might reflect an increasingly closed academic culture that does not reflect the interests of mainstream America. The caveat to this statement is the academic studies conducted on what are generally considered massacres, to which it now appears that some would like to add the events that took place in South Korea in late July 1950. Before defining exactly what constitutes a massacre, let's examine the question, "What is military history?"

Until recently, most military history was not written by historians, academically trained or otherwise. Instead, military history has often been written either by the participants after the fact or by those attempting an analysis of the military for the military. Some of this comes into play in this history.

Writing more than 150 years ago, Baron Antoine Jomini, Swiss military theorist and historian of the Napoleonic era, identified three types of military history: pure military history, which focused on the exact details of a particular action without analysis; campaign history, which adopted a slightly broader view and was used to discern lessons from the actions; and political-military history.[3] Other more recent historians have also noted several subfields.[4]

Similarly, academic studies by social scientists or psychologists explore the human experience through combat. The classic psychological and sociological World War II study, *The American Soldier*, established the importance of this subfield. More recent books that attempt the same fusion of history and human psychology are David Grossman's *On Killing* and the even more recent *Achilles in Vietnam* by psychiatrist Jonathan Shay.[5] Finally, one of the most useful studies, reported by academic historian Samuel Watson in his book, *When Soldiers Quit, Studies in Military Disintegration*, brings forth six specific case studies of "incidents" in military history, and creates a framework and theory for understanding these events.

One specific type of military history—history written for the military—plays a major role in our understanding of the events of No Gun Ri. This type, generically known among academics as military-utilitarian history, is characterized by the fact that it is sometimes written by members of the military with little to no formal training as historians. It is also history with a purpose and, therefore, contains a higher than normal potential for misuse. The military focuses on its own history for several reasons, the first of which is the development of esprit de corps among its members. We will refer to this as regimental history, although the phenomenon also includes histories of units from companies through divisions.[6]

The armed forces have long recognized that a sense of martial heritage contributes to a unit's cohesiveness and may serve as the glue that initially brings the members of a unit together. There are hundreds of examples of this. The focus of these works is not necessarily a full and accurate account of the past deeds of a unit, but rather only upon its successes. The obvious exception is the history of the 7th United States Cavalry Regiment, which for various reasons tends towards a celebration of the unit's defeats, most notably that of the Little Bighorn. This history is then used to socialize the members of the unit, and help them develop a sense of belonging to a unique unit.

As this book points out, the regimental histories of the 7th Cavalry have, at least in this case, become a central feature in later academic histories. Consider that the published regimental histories of the 7th Cavalry in Korea were used as historical background for many of the initial news reports about No Gun Ri that appeared when the story broke in 1999. Two of these books—*Of Garryowen in Glory*, by Melbourne Chandler and *Skirmish, Red, White and Blue*, by Edward Daily—were penned by central actors in the events that occurred in South Korea in July 1950. Chandler was, in 1950, the commander of one of the two companies most directly involved at No Gun Ri. Edward Daily, the same man who has gone on record, on television, and in print, as having turned his machine gun on the civilians under the now-famous railroad bridge at No Gun Ri, was in fact, not even at No Gun Ri.

I did not write this book with the aid of the army, and arguably it was written despite the army. The Department of the Army Inspector General's (DAIG) office, acting as the United States Review Team, conducted a rigorous investigation of the events at No Gun Ri shortly after the Associated Press story broke. The inspector general had no idea initially that I, an army officer, was doing his own personal investigation into the events. On two specific dates in late 1999, I offered the DAIG information about my own research. The office did not directly respond or comment on my material other than to politely pass down a "thank you." When some of the material I had discussed with my friends Joseph Galloway, who was then with *US News and World Report*, and Edward Offley, who had moved to *Stripes.com*, an Internet military news outlet, appeared in the media, I was ordered to stop my personal research. The army did not want me "contaminating" the memories of the veterans. For this reason, a large gap occurred in the periods of my interviews with veterans. Although frustrating for me, the army was correct in asserting that its investigation took precedence over mine.

As a result, this book is not a product of the United States Army. I wrote this history independently, and my conclusions and observations are entirely my own and do not represent the position of the Department of Defense, the United States Army, or the United States Military Academy. In some aspects, my views differ significantly from those the army inspector general eventually published in January 2001, the executive summary of which is an appendix to this book. Specifically I maintain that armed South Korean guerillas *were* among the refugees on July 26, 1950, that these guerillas fired upon U.S. troops from the vicinity of the railroad underpass, and that the guerillas were subsequently killed and their weapons taken during an exchange of fire with portions of the 2nd Battalion 7th Cavalry. With evidence supporting the role the guerillas played in No Gun Ri readily available, any speculation as to why it was not used in the inspector general's report commissioned by President William Clinton and his secretary of the army is up to the reader. The opinions and interpretations in this book are entirely mine. I am writing this book in spite of the somewhat ironic pressure applied through phone calls to some of my superior officers to suppress this story. In the end, I leave it to the reader to determine into which category of military history this book should fit.

PART ONE

The History

CHAPTER 1

War Clouds Gathering

IN EVERY WORK OF HISTORY, THERE IS ALWAYS A SOMEWHAT ARBITRARY point at which the author must start the story. But without a broader context, one does not have history; one has merely an account. Weaving the events of the main story into a wider tapestry is the true work of history. Therefore, this story must begin with some understanding of how the Korean War came about.

In 1946, the United States was the sole nuclear superpower. America's industry had begun to accommodate the millions of returning veterans released by the end of the Second World War, and life in the United States was slowly returning to normal. In the political arena some traditional American views also began to reassert themselves, one of which was a reluctance to maintain a large standing army.

The nuclear monopoly enjoyed by the United States in the immediate postwar period allowed for a massive reduction in the armed forces. At that time, the main threat to the American way of life lay in the communist Soviet Union, and to confront this monolithic enemy, many inside Washington bought into the idea sold by the proponents of the soon-to-be-independent U.S. Air Force that nuclear-armed airpower could hold the frontiers. Yet this strong reliance on nuclear weapons placed America in an awkward position: What sort of provocation, short of a Soviet invasion of Western Europe, could possibly merit a nuclear response?

Initially the question was barely considered. As the Soviet threat gelled over the next few years, the issue was discussed, but minds conditioned by two total wars did not grasp the potential havoc of more limited ones.[1] The discussion became more complicated when America lost its nuclear monopoly in 1949 and the United States faced the threat of Soviet atomic retaliation. Moreover, few outside the highest circles of government realized how few atomic weapons actually existed in American hands, making the threat of Soviet nuclear weapons all the more real for those guiding the nation. Any American president willing to employ nuclear weapons now risked enormous civilian casualties. Yet how else could our nation contain the violent spread of communism?

Paul Nitze, head of the State Department policy planning staff, when faced with this challenge in early 1950, came to the conclusion that America needed a larger conventional force to meet the challenges of the Cold War. In a policy statement that became known as NSC-68 (NSC standing for National Security Council), he argued for the development of just such a force—funded by a large increase in military expenditures. NSC-68 was strong, yet even that forceful document failed to motivate the administration to act on increased funding for the military.[2] Logic, apparently, does not a budget make.

Few today remember the seriousness with which the Soviet threat was perceived in 1950. Although a mere flicker of time (from a historian's standpoint) has passed since the fall of the Soviet Union, the Cold War has already become something of a mirage for some. Yet despite the fears that swelled at the time, America initially followed that curious dichotomy of public policy and military policy that is unique to democracies. While politicians at home banged the drums of anticommunism, these same leaders simultaneously oversaw the castration of the very forces that could protect the world from communist expansion. In the early phases of the Korean War, American goals directly suffered from the army's lack of preparedness and poor performance. This then is the first layer of the foundation to understanding why No Gun Ri happened.

America had traditionally followed a general policy of studied indifference to the external politics of the world until thrust by the weight of international affairs to join one side or another. The admonition of George Washington to avoid foreign entanglements resonated through the first century of American history. Even the nation's quasi-colonial experiences following the Spanish-American War were marked almost immediately with a sense of regret. Not until the very real threat of the Soviets, as witnessed by their post-WWII takeover of Eastern Europe, and the realization that the United States alone stood in a position to oppose them was America pushed into a new era of international leadership. This era of American involvement in the world might be marked as starting in 1947.

In his address to Congress that year, President Harry Truman called for $400 million in aid to Greece and Turkey, which were then struggling with a Soviet-backed insurgency. In an effort to prevent a Soviet presence in the eastern Mediterranean, he also sought authority to deploy civilian and military personnel to those countries. His action alerted the American people to the growing Soviet threat, and although historians disagree on the specifics, it is not unreasonable to believe that Truman hoped this would lead to support for a moderate increase in conventional military forces.

At the conclusion to his remarks, Truman proclaimed: "The free peoples of the world look to us for support in maintaining their freedoms. If we falter in our leadership, we may endanger the peace of the world, and we shall surely endanger the welfare of our own nation."[3] This was the politics of reality sold to the American people under a label that historically appealed to Americans—a moral crusade. In his statement, which became the foundation of what was known as the Truman Doctrine, the president planted the seed for what would later flower as the U.S. Policy of Containment. His message set the precedent that whenever communist forces threatened the free peoples of the world, the United States would provide military, economic, political, and diplomatic aid.[4] The Greece-Turkey Aid Act passed the House and the Senate, and Truman signed it into law on May 22, 1947.

The Truman Doctrine's underlying message was that while Americans would confront communism worldwide, Europe was seen as the geopolitical center of gravity for confronting the Soviet Union. The budget available to the Truman administration to accomplish its goals was a pittance compared to the largesse of the war years. It focused on the defense and recovery of Europe, and in conjunction with this, the slow development of conventional military forces. The Pacific, and specifically Korea, lay fairly low on the list of American foreign policy and defense priorities.

By the time the Japanese surrendered aboard the USS *Missouri* at the end of World War II, Japan had ruled Korea for thirty-five brutal years. During the period of Japanese occupation, Koreans had long been denied important jobs and were withheld from any kind of education in their own language or about their own history and culture. Although educational levels did increase overall, a largely illiterate population dominated by Japanese masters existed outside the cities. Japan exploited Korea with devastating effectiveness. Industry in the Korean peninsula wore out from overuse during World War II; banks charged Korean customers higher interest rates, sometimes as much as twenty-five percent higher, than that for Japanese customers; wages were low, and Koreans were subject to harsh and racially bigoted Japanese laws. Yet all of this failed to eradicate the fire of Korean independence. Two indigenous factions developed underground during the Japanese occupation. The first was the provisional government, led by Kim Koo and Syngman Rhee, and the second was the Korean communist faction, which bore very strong ties to the Soviet and Chinese communist movements.

Both factions gained some degree of autonomy and power after the surrender of Japan in 1945. In an effort to prevent the complete Soviet occupation of a peninsula so close to Japan, the United States proposed a joint occupation of Korea. While serving in the Operations Division of the War Department General Staff, future Secretary of State Dean Rusk played a crucial role in Korean history. Part of his job was to assist Assistant Secretary of War John J. McCloy in his duties as a member of the State/War/Navy Coordinating Committee (SWINK). The job involved weighing in on a broad spectrum of policy issues. In the closing days of the war, these men determined the fate of Korea. Rusk relates:

> During a SWINK meeting held on August 14, 1945, the same day of the Japanese surrender, Colonel Charles Bonesteel and I retired to an adjacent room late at night and studied intently a map of the Korean peninsula. Working in haste and under great pressure, we had a formidable task: to pick a zone for the American occupation. Neither Tic [Bonesteel] nor I were Korea experts, but it seemed to us that Seoul, the capital, should be in the American sector. We also knew the U.S. Army opposed an extensive area of occupation. Using a National Geographic map, we looked just north of Seoul for a convenient dividing line but could not find a natural geographical line. We saw instead the thirty-eighth parallel and decided to recommend that.[5]

In this way, the superpowers divided Korea. However, the division of Korea was not set in stone, because it required the concurrence of the Soviets. The Russians, for reasons of their own, not only concurred but did so almost without exception. Some of this might have been related to their understanding of the situation from a military, political, and social point of view in Korea. For whatever reason, the Soviets agreed to the division, and the stage was set for a North Korean client state.

Kim Il Sung, the man who became dictator of North Korea, was trained by the Soviets starting in 1939 or 1940. Two years later, he was assigned to an all Korean unit tasked with training communist cadres for what would become the North Korean People's Army, the NKPA. Over time, he became a captain and eventually commander of a battalion. In October 1945, Kim and his fellow officers were transferred to Wonson in Korea, where they would dominate communist Korea for decades to come.[6] The following January, Kim became the chief of the North Korean branch of the Korean Communist Party. Over the next few years, he consolidated his position and eventually became the first prime minister of the Korean People's Democratic Republic, the North Korean communist state that was officially established on September 9, 1948.[7]

As in China, though on a far smaller scale, the end of the Second World War did not bring peace to the Korean peninsula. Arguably, at least two factors were at work in that time and place. The first, the ideology of communism, certainly struck a chord with the Korean peasants who had labored for decades under a harsh totalitarian foreign rule where the line between the haves and have-nots was hard and fast. To a far larger number of South Koreans than the current government of South Korea would like to admit, communism seemed like a viable alternative.

The second factor fostering dissent in South Korea centered on American intervention. In the second week of September 1945, the XXIV Corps of the United States Army arrived in Inchon to begin the occupation of Korea. Among the thousands of soldiers and officers who landed was a round-faced bespectacled infantry colonel in charge of the XXIV Corps intelligence section. His name was Cecil Nist.

Born in Ohio in 1900, Nist arrived at the United States Military Academy at West Point, New York, exactly one week before the end of the First World War. He was a member of the second freshman class in November 1918, the result of the realization that West Point would have to double its classes to make up for the horrible toll the war on the western front was having among the young officers of the American Expeditionary Force. Nist and his classmates did not have the benefit of upperclassmen to learn from since all the other classes had been graduated and rushed into active service in response to the casualties. In response to the desperate need for officers on the western front, that fall West Point had been cut to a one-year school. Then the war ended, and a new superintendent fresh from command of a division in France arrived in West Point to shake things up. He was a brigadier general named Douglas MacArthur.

Nist was an average cadet during his time at the academy. He ran on the cross country team, raised no ruckus, and graduated in 1923 near the middle of his class of 260. Thereafter, his military career was equally undistinguished. Commissioned as a second lieutenant in the infantry, he served in a demonstration unit at West Point, then a few years in the canal zone of

Panama, before becoming a post exchange officer at Fort Missoula, Montana. It was seven years before he was promoted to first lieutenant.

By the time of the Second World War, Cecil Nist had become a staff officer with little experience leading troops in the field. Although he was assigned to command two different infantry regiments during training in the states, he was pulled from the command of each before either was deployed to a combat theater. Assigned first to the 77th Infantry Division and then to the staff of the XXIVth Corps in the Pacific, Nist never saw infantry combat as a commander. During the years when his classmates and peers were rocketing upwards in rank, some to division command, Nist held a position behind a desk.[8]

In 1945, this less-than-impressive West Point graduate played a central role in establishing the future of Korea. His assessment of the South Korean situation set the framework for later U.S. policy on the peninsula. Nist's analysis of the situation that his XXIVth Corps found in the fall of 1945 was summed up in a report sent to Washington one week after his arrival:

> Southern Korea can best be described as a power keg ready to explode at the application of a spark.
>
> There is great disappointment that immediate independence and sweeping out of the Japanese did not eventuate.
>
> [Those Koreans who] achieved high rank under the Japanese are considered pro-Japanese and are hated almost as much as their masters . . . .
>
> All groups seem to have the common idea of seizing Japanese property, ejecting the Japanese from Korea, and achieving immediate independence. Beyond this they have few ideas.
>
> Korea is completely ripe for agitators . . . .
>
> The most encouraging single factor in the political situation is the presence in Seoul of several hundred conservatives among the older and better educated Koreans. Although many of them have served the Japanese, that stigma ought eventually to disappear. Such persons favor the return of the provisional government, and although they may not constitute the majority, they are probably the largest single group.[9]

Following recommendations based on Nist's observations, the United States found itself supporting a group which, although conservative, was also largely associated with the hard years of the Japanese occupation. Peasants in the countryside were swayed by the evidence of their eyes.

For most peasants, Syngman Rhee, the leader of the U.S.-backed provisional government, was in faraway Seoul. More than that, he had not spent his entire life in Korea. Given the right spin, it is not too difficult to see how many South Korean peasants could perceive Rhee as still another figurehead Korean propped up by yet another foreign power. For the average peasant, north and south of the thirty-eighth parallel, communism seemed to offer a chance to improve their stations in life, to gain control of property, and, perhaps most importantly, to have an all-Korean Korea. Even more damning for Rhee's early government was that officers and soldiers who had previously served in the army or security forces of Imperial Japan were retained. Especially detested were those Koreans who served in the police force under the Japanese, suppressing their countrymen with brutal efficiency for their Japanese rulers. Being drafted into the Imperial Japanese army could sometimes not be avoided, but the police were all volunteers serving the Japanese, and their methods, supported and encouraged by the Japanese, were brutal. As the indigenous tools of Japanese oppression, they were doubly detested. Among those who served the Japanese in this role was a young Korean named Chung Eun-Yong from the southcentral Korean village of Chu Gok Ri.[10] Eun-Yong, who plays a role later in this book, joined the Japanese-controlled police in 1944, and when Rhee came to power, he transferred to the new national police force where he was stationed in Taejon.

Even as late as 1949, with the rebellion then raging, Rhee was asking the United States for additional arms and support for a unit of 20,000 Korean veterans of the Imperial Japanese Army.[11] In the eyes of many South Koreans, Rhee's incorporation of men who had served the Japanese emperor under arms was one of his most egregious faults. How could Rhee turn to Koreans who had been the symbol and the very real hammer of Japanese oppression in those long years of occupation?

Very strong and very real class divisions in the Korean society in the late 1940s added to the rebellious thoughts and actions of the Korean peasants. For centuries, the Korean *yangban* landowning classes held on to their positions atop the power heap of the country. When change was absolutely unavoidable, they showed a tendency, over time, of adjusting just enough to stay in power.[12] In the context of the immediate post-World War II period, this class tied its survival to the fortunes of the political right and the power of the police state that South Korea developed.

Within this context, Rhee's actions, and those of his national police, fueled the opposition to the U.S.-backed South Korean government. Time after time, the national police used the brutal methods of its old masters to suppress its fellow countrymen. When food riots broke out in the southern city of Taegu, the police responded with bullets. The people reacted, killing policemen, and chaos ensued locally.

Communist guerillas who infiltrated the south across the then-permeable border added to the already complex mix of southern-born labor activists and indigenous communists as some parts of the rural south reached the point of rebellion.[13] For all intents and purposes, South Korea was in a state of civil war.

Outright guerrilla warfare broke out in South Korea in late 1948, most visibly on Cheju Island off the coast of the mainland. In one of the most violent acts of suppression by even a nominal democracy in modern history, Rhee sent his nascent armed forces and the national police to suppress the rebellion. The national police, a small unit of which was led by Chung Eun-Yong from Chu Gok Ri village (whose actions within the police force had resulted in his meteoric promotion from recruit to police lieutenant in just four years), did its job efficiently. In a crushing campaign, Eun-Yong and his peers in the police force killed between 27,719 and 30,000 of their fellow South Koreans. Officially they destroyed more than 39,000 homes in the process, and wiped out all but 170 of the 400 villages that existed on the island prior to their arrival.[14] Some of the communist guerilas, however, made it to the mainland where they joined with others of like mind.

By early 1949, the U.S. Central Intelligence Agency estimated that between 3,500 and 6,000 active and armed communist guerilas were operating in the mountains in the center of South Korea. Equipped with captured Japanese weapons as well as such American weapons as the M1 Garand rifle taken from South Korean military and police forces, these rebels were strongest in Chŏlla and Kyŏngsang provinces.

In the spring of 1950, the disaffection of the Korean peasantry met head-on with American cultural ignorance. *The New York Times* carried reports from Walter Sullivan who was in the hills of South Korea when he ran across a mobile movie projection team from the United States Information Services. In an effort to counter communism, this jeep-mounted service brought color movies to remote villages, some in the area around Yongdong. Moving pictures of the United Nations Security Council in deliberation and tourism shots of the wonders of Yosemite National Forest were shown to South Korean peasants who had no electricity or running water.

The South Korean government was far more direct in its response to communism. An American who worked in the regional hospital of the area during this Korean-on-Korean warfare said, "Guerilla warfare was around us all the time. We had many commies as patients. [The police would] keep an eye on them, grill them and when they had all possible information, take them out and stand them before a firing squad. This wall was near the hospital. We could hear the men being shot."[15]

The guerillas operated in classic form. Rather than directly confront the southern government in strength, they raided and ambushed and harassed while they built their own strength. Their protected bases were off the main routes, mostly in the mountains that run down the spine of the Korean peninsula in the south. In this mountainous terrain, the guerillas would hold villages and be supported from them. From their home bases, they could sally out to conduct raids and ambushes on the main roads. These armed guerillas were natives of the territory; they were not infiltrated North Koreans. Only some sixty North Koreans could be confirmed as having made their way into the South. While the North did provide significant support to the guerillas near the border and to a lesser extent to those operating on the coast, the majority of the communist guerillas were South Koreans.[16]

In the midst the South Korean communist guerilla territory in the mountains, off the main road running between the small cities of Yong-dong and Hwanggan, were the villages of Chu Gok Ri, Im Ke Ri, Sot Anmak, and No Gun Ri. By their own admission, many of the villagers were at the very least sympathetic to the guerillas, feeding them and providing supplies and shelter at times. Some of the guerillas were local men from the villages themselves.[17]

To counter the various rebellions, riots, and resistance, Rhee had at his disposal forces that were initially little more than a paramilitary police force. Advised by the U.S. Korean Military Advisory Group (KMAG), Rhee retaliated with a vicious counterinsurgency program across the rest of the peninsula. Washington viewed the counterinsurgency operations as a litmus test for the Republic of the Korea: If Rhee succeeded in wiping out the guerillas, then the United States could feel confident that it was not backing another Kuomintang,[18] the Chinese Nationalist Party that had been recently defeated in China's civil war.

The New York Times correspondent Walter Sullivan, who observed the guerilla war firsthand in 1950, concluded that the war revolved around the staple of the Asian diet—rice.[19] According to Sullivan, at least half of the average peasant's crop went to various official organizations of the South Korean government, a requirement that was unlikely to engender great support for Rhee's government in the countryside.

For three years, a sporadic and bloody guerilla war raged through the mountains of South Korea. An ugly and protracted fight, the war was waged with a form of ruthlessness that Americans generally find alien. Whole divisions of the Republic of Korea (ROK) army were deployed in a brutal war of suppression against an indigenous communist-inspired rebellion aided by a sense of alienation from the Rhee government. One American diplomat, writing about the counterguerilla operations in South Korea, described what he called "unusual sadistic propensities" on both sides: "Signal atrocities have been reported, indicating mass massacres of village populations, including women and children, accompanied by looting and arson. In some cases the army has been guilty of revenge operations against guerillas which have brought down vengeance on unarmed villagers . . . ."[20] At the epicenter of some of this activity were those same villages of Chu Gok Ri, Im Ke Ri, and No Gun Ri.

By the fall of 1949, the rebellion was largely suppressed on Cheju Island although fighting continued in the mountains of the mainland. As late as October 1949, the American ambassador in Korea would write to the U.S. secretary of state that the guerillas had lost as many as a thousand men in fighting in Chŏlla and Kyŏngsang provinces in the preceding three months. The ambassador, who was not a military historian and apparently knew nothing of guerilla doctrine, took this loss as a sign that the guerilla threat was waning.[21]

Thus was laid another corner of the foundation for the events that later occur at No Gun Ri.

A key point that has been uniformly overlooked in every modern news story about the events in and around No Gun Ri as well as by the official report of the Department of the Army Inspector General is the fact that *No Gun Ri and the other villages in the area were at the very center of communist guerilla activity during the warfare that occurred in South Korea from 1948 to 1950*.[22] In one map created by the American army's Korean Military Advisory Group (KMAG) in 1949, Yongdong and No Gun Ri were placed in the center of a shaded area depicting areas with the highest communist guerilla activity. KMAG's analysis that communist guerrillas were most active in and around No Gun Ri and other villages in the mountains was right on the mark. Captured North Korean documents later confirmed these earlier assessments. Chu Gok Ri, Im Ke Ri, and No Gun Ri were at the center of the guerilla territory.[23]

By the winter of 1949–50, guerilla operations in the South had largely subsided, although the historical record remains unclear whether counterinsurgency or bad weather was the cause. Overall some estimates place the number killed in this largely unknown war at around 100,000. It could be argued, in the light of later events, that although the fire had been put out, embers still smoldered. After June 1950, guerilla warfare returned to the area when some of the estimated 27,000 communist guerillas emerged from the mountains to take up arms against United Nations forces. Communist guerilla operations would continue throughout the war, waged either by indigenous sympathizers or bypassed North Korean forces.

More conventional hostilities were also a part of a low-level war between the two Koreas as fighting rippled along the border. As early as 1947, raids and counter-raids across the border had begun, and by June of 1949, heavy fighting had flared up again, which continued into August of that year. When compared with later events, most of these actions were fairly small scale—a platoon here, a company there, and, in some cases, a battalion making an incursion into the north or the south. Both sides were testing the strength, abilities, and resiliency of the other side, and both sides were more than willing, if they had the power, to unify the peninsula by force.

By 1950, although both Rhee in the South and Kim Il Sung in the North wanted war for their own reasons, Rhee found himself hamstrung by his ally, the United States. It is now known that Kim Il Sung finally attacked South Korea only after receiving a go-ahead from Soviet Premier Josef Stalin. Recent scholarship stresses the fact that North Korea invaded with the aid of the Soviet Union and the tacit approval (but not the fore-knowledge) of communist China.[24]

Such was the state of affairs in the Koreas, but it is only part of the story. The events that took place in 1950 were also the result of the conditions that existed in the United States and in Japan before the Korean War.

When North Korea invaded South Korea on June 25, 1950, neither the Republic of Korea Army nor the United States Army was prepared for war. The U.S. Army stationed in Japan served primarily as a constabulary force rather than a deterrent to any potential thrust from global communism. Years of restricted army budgets, as well as a focus upon the governing and reconstruction of the nation of Japan, fully occupied the skeletons of the four divisions stationed in Japan between 1945 and 1950.

As a result, the Army was paying more attention to form than function. Although part of the blame for this situation lay with the Congress, some blame must be cast on the decisions made by the chief of staff of the time, Omar Bradley, and the commander of the Far East Command, General of the Army Douglas MacArthur. As a result, most U.S. units in Japan were woefully ill-prepared for war.[25]

Units stationed in Korea and Japan in this period were undermanned and suffered a high turnover rate.[26] As any business will attest, efficiency and effectiveness increase in direct proportion to the stability of the work force. What is true in business is doubly so in the military. The constant transition of soldiers in and out of units decreases cohesiveness and proficiency at larger tasks. Even if the Far East Command and the Eighth Army possessed a full contingent of soldiers and a lower turnover rate, the duties involved in the occupation of Japan simply did not allow a focus on preparing men for war. This fact, as we will see, resulted in contention among the veterans themselves.[27]

Until 1949, new recruits in the U.S. Army were sent to an eight-week basic training program before receiving further training in their units to gain full proficiency as soldiers. This system was a remnant of the Second World War when the division managed much of a soldier's training. Starting in March 1949, the army recognized this deficiency and switched to a fourteen-week training cycle that gave recruits enough skills to go directly to their units, unless their particular branch, such as armor or artillery, required further training.[28]

Many believe that another contributing factor to the decline of the armed forces was the severe blow to military discipline that resulted from an internal review conducted by a panel known as the Doolittle Board. Named after the senior officer of the board, General James Doolittle, this panel was called to address charges that many officers and noncommissioned officers had abused their power vis á vis their subordinates during World War II. Instead of holding army officers to a higher standard of behavior, or attempting to impose discipline upon the ranks, the Doolittle board revoked much of the military's power to enforce discipline. The board's report had a crippling effect upon morale and, some believe, on military order. To this day, the Doolittle Board's action rankles many veterans of both wars.

In the months leading up to the Korean War, both General MacArthur and Secretary of State Dean Acheson stated publicly, albeit indirectly, that the United States did not foresee intervening directly in Korea. In his famous speech, "Crisis In Asia," Acheson described the U.S. Pacific defense perimeter as running from the Aleutians, to Japan, through the Ryukus, and then to the Phillipines. Diplomatic historians have since argued about what Acheson actually meant by his remarks and how Josef Stalin of Russia, Chairman Mao of China, and Kim Il Sung of North Korea interpreted them.[29] Yet if these communist leaders had carefully followed the statements of the secretary of state, they would have heard Acheson's ominous warning three weeks before the Korean War began:

> The future of events in Southeast Asia, in Korea, and in Japan as well as in China are of great importance to the security of the United States. Our policy is and must be devoted to doing everything within our power to prevent the further spread of communism.[30]

The Korean War should be viewed on two levels. First, this war was the first of the indirect struggles between the global superpowers of the communist-bloc countries and the United States fighting each other through client states. Second, the war extended and intensified a civil war between the two Koreas that had existed for years as a guerilla struggle.

For some incredible reason, given the situation in South Korea, by early 1950 the United States had removed all of its combat troops from Korea, without providing Syngman Rhee's army enough muscle to defend itself.[31] A military vacuum opened in South Korea when neither the U.S. Army in Japan nor the Republic of Korea Army was capable of acting as a credible deterrent to a North Korean invasion. As historian Geoffrey Blainey points out with clear reasoning in *The Causes of War*, "Wars start when both sides believe they have more to gain from fighting than not fighting and at least one side believes that their forces are significantly superior."[32] While seemingly obvious, this single salient point is often clouded by the obfuscating nature of modern diplomacy.

In the end, however, American diplomacy gave no clear indication that the United States would defend South Korea. The policy of containment was neither well established yet nor fully credible; American military aid had not provided South Korea with the means to defend itself; and finally, America had stood on the sidelines in 1949 as mainland China fell completely under communist domination.

Who could therefore believe that the United States of America would defend the less important South Korea? Certainly not the soldiers of the 7th Cavalry Regiment comfortably stationed in Japan.

CHAPTER 2

In the Land
of the Rising Sun

HISTORY IS FAR MORE THAN THE MERE RECITING OF EVENTS. GOOD HIS-
tory seeks to convey understanding of events and the people who influenced them and lived through them. Naturally then, understanding the
events of the summer of 1950 requires some understanding of the people
who lived in that time. Just as we today are the products of our history, so
too were the men who went to war in Korea in 1950. In seeking some
understanding of the events and actions of the men of the 2nd Battalion of
the 7th Cavalry Regiment, we need to know more about them as a group,
about their organization, and about the contributing factors that made the
unit what it was in July 1950. The place to start is with these men—the
unique product of an America of the preceding decade.

America was a nation of youthful hope in 1940. The impact of World
War I upon the population in Europe did not apply to the United States.
By 1940, the nation was pulling out of the Depression, buoyed in part by
the war in the rest of the world. Men were back to work, and the economy
was recovering. The news and entertainment medium of choice was the
radio and, to an almost equal extent, the movies and newspapers.

Clustered around the family radio, young boys of ten or so years of age
often received their daily dose of information, education, and entertainment in one sitting. Listening to the broadcasts of Edward R. Murrow in
the summer of 1940 as he reported on the Blitz against London by the

German air armadas of Herman Goering, they might imagine themselves there among the East Enders or as aces in the Royal Air Force. These same boys listened spellbound a year and a half later to the first reports of the Japanese sneak attack against the United States at Pearl Harbor. For these boys, it was an exciting time. War, much as they might wish otherwise, would not touch them personally. They were eleven or twelve, with the cares and perceptions of that age, and to them, the onset of war meant the beginning of a great adventure.

By the time they were twelve, they could not wait for the weekend matinee so that they might actually witness the exciting newsreel footage of the first American offensive in North Africa. These twelve-year-olds learned the litany of heroism, and lionized the leaders who took America from the depths of near defeat to the heights of glory: Generals Patton, Eisenhower, MacArthur, and admirals like Nimitz stood securely upon Olympus; Audie Murphy and Gregory Boyington held the mountain upon their shoulders. There was death there, but the death these youths saw portrayed on the silver screen in the 1940s was not the death seen in films and television today. It was not the death that Steven Speilberg brought home in such graphically realistic visions in the 2000 film *Saving Private Ryan*. Death on-screen during World War II was discrete and did not offend the senses: a man grabbed his chest, said his final lines to his buddies, and died almost peacefully. It was the glorious death of the ubiquitous John Wayne, holding on to the last against the oriental onslaught in *Bataan*. In 1940s' Hollywood, death was clean and the wounded did not scream pathetically as exploding artillery delivered its volley of pain. For the young men who grew up watching these films, war was something of glory, of honor, and it involved a clean fight against a clearly defined and evil foe.

We should remember that.

THE MEN

For the majority of the boys of 1940, the Second World War was not immediately personal. Demographics alone point toward this observation. For the most part, they were not the sons of men who went to war, of men who might, in rare circumstances, convey the true horrors and tragedy of war. A boy of ten in 1940 most likely had a father who was twenty-eight or thirty. By 1942 when the draft for WWII really took off, these fathers were either beyond the target age of draftees, or they occupied legitimate economically important positions that protected them from the draft, thus effectively preventing their service in the front lines. While a certain percentage of these boys may have had older brothers who served, more often it was an uncle or cousin who bore the weight of the fighting in the Great

Crusade. Arguably, this personal distance, combined with the relatively closed-mouth nature of male society at that time, resulted in a skewed perception about war for these boys in their socially formative years.

In 1945, when the Second World War ended, the boys who were the soldiers of 1950 were, on average, between thirteen and fifteen years old. America, in their eyes, was the supreme nation. It had never lost, never been bested upon the field of battle except under the most incredible odds. In their eyes, in all wars at all times, America emerged victorious. They were, as we are, the product of their times.

When they enlisted in the army in 1947 through 1950, they found validation to their culturally and historically formed opinions, which answers, in part, the unstated question of "Why did they join?" To understand more requires some framework to put form to facts.

Military historian John Lynn of the University of Illinois suggests three distinct forms of motivation relevant to the military.[1] While some soldiers might offer one reason for serving in the military, they might give a different reason when queried on why they stayed in the military, and yet a third reason (or set of reasons) when asked why they fought. Lynn categorized these as "enlistment motivation," "sustaining motivation," and "combat motivation." His sophisticated analysis went a long way towards explaining some of the seemingly contradictory evidence found in the phenomenon of military motivation. Obviously, to begin the process, a soldier must join in the first place. In the absence of a major draft, this issue is especially important. After World War II, there was no draft, and enlistment in the much reduced forces of the United States was entirely voluntary. Only in 1948, in an effort to boost extremely low enlistment numbers, did the United States Congress authorize a limited draft.[2]

Enlistment motivation may generally be categorized into economic, patriotic, and adventure seeking. Most of the boys of 1940, socialized in a nationalistic and hyperpatriotic society, could fall into this second category of motivation. Economics, or the desire to advance to a higher economic plane through the potential offered by the G.I. Bill, also contributed to many a soldier's reasons for joining.

Francis Baylock was typical of the soldiers of the 7th Cavalry Regiment after World War II. He was raised in semirural Connecticut during the Second World War, where none of his primary family members participated in ground combat during the war. Without a male role model to explain to him the realities of warfare from the infantry's perspective, his motivation to enlist encompassed two of the three categories laid out by Lynn. Baylock remembers, "I enlisted because, well, I think that we couldn't find much to do here in the States. Me and my buddies, four of us, decided to enlist together. We went to New Hartford, about twelve miles away, because that was the nearest induction center. I was working as a paint sprayer in a factory until then. We were looking for excitement, I guess, and I thought that I might go to college afterwards, so I enlisted for three years."[3]

Baylock surely got his fill of excitement. After his basic training, he went to Tokyo where he was assigned as a machine gunner in the heavy weapons company (H Company) of the 2nd Battalion 7th Cavalry Regiment. Baylock considers himself lucky. A few short months before the war began, he was selected to attend radio operator's school, which he did while the unit was still in Japan. When the war in Korea broke out, he was in the communications platoon at battalion headquarters. He survived the war intact, while most of the men in his old platoon would not walk out of Korea whole, if they walked out at all.

Another soldier of the 7th Cavalry, Marvin Daniel, had motivations that also split between economics and adventure. Raised in Salem, Virginia, he would return there after the war. After his basic training, Daniel went to Japan and was assigned to the first platoon of E Company in the 2nd Battalion 7th Cavalry Regiment.[4] Daniel recalls, "My home was right here in Salem, less than a mile from where I live now. I joined when I was seventeen. Jobs weren't that plentiful, and I felt that it would be one way to do some traveling."[5]

John De Borde had somewhat different motivations. As with many young men his age, he was too young to make it into "The Big One" so De Borde enlisted as soon as he could. He recalls, "To me there was this feeling of patriotism, I guess you should call it. We were kids, then World War II happened, and if I coulda got my dad to lie for me, I'd have signed up, you know? Because you wanted to do what your Uncle Sam needed. You wanted to do what he wanted you to do. I think that many, we all, carried a little bit of World War II in us. Of course that all goes away pretty fast once you get shot at."[6]

Leonard "Buddy" Wenzel was born in Englishtown, New Jersey, on Halloween night 1930, and raised in South River, across the river from New York City. He too had little concept of the realities of war. Although Wenzel's grandfather was in the famous "Rough Riders," the volunteer cavalry unit commanded by Theodore Roosevelt during the Spanish-American War, he died when Wenzel was just eight. Wenzel's oldest brother, Albert, had been in World War II as a medic. He served in a rifle company during some of the hardest fighting in Belgium near the end of the war, but he never talked about it with his younger brother. Like most of his enlisted peers, Wenzel was raised in an America that hadn't yet experienced the post-war middle class boom. Hard working, even as a child,

Wenzel helped support his family. For him, joining the army was both an escape from his home situation and an honest and honorable way to earn a living for a young single man.

Says Wenzel, "My mother and father broke up when I was thirteen. I was going to school, but I had to do a lot around the house 'cause I had to take care of my sisters. My father died three years later when I was sixteen. My mother was living with a guy, and when my father died, she moved in with him. I just couldn't handle that so I got my mom to sign my papers and let me sign up. I joined in August 1948. I thought about enlisting in the navy, but I changed my mind. I had a couple of friends of mine that were talking about joining the army to go to the 1st Cavalry and so they talked me into it."[7]

In many ways, the army that these boys joined as they grew into young men between 1946 and 1950 was not, except in name, the same one that destroyed Nazi Germany and conquered Imperial Japan. These boys, of course, had no direct way of knowing this. To understand how it was different, one needs to understand a little of how the army was organized, trained, and operated between 1946 and 1950.

ARMY ORGANIZATION IN 1950

The way the army was organized plays a unique role in the second of Lynn's motivational trio, sustaining motivation. It is also necessary to understand the situation at No Gun Ri.

Modern armies are hierarchical in nature, the foundation of which rests upon the individual soldier, the lowest-ranking being the private. Privates, who generally have no direct responsibility except to know their military specialties and follow the orders of the leaders above them, are usually the newest, least experienced, least trained men in the army. Upon enlistment, each private is generally trained to a minimum standard that includes use of his individual weapon and any specialized equipment called for by the duties of his position and understanding the generic customs and courtesies of the military profession. With these basic skills under his belt, a soldier is sent to a regular unit where his training continues until such time as it is needed in war. Once sent to a major unit, usually a division, somewhere around the world, a soldier is further assigned to lower and lower level units until he comes to rest at the building-block element of the army, the squad.

A squad of soldiers contains between nine and fifteen men depending on the type of squad required to fill the needs of different types of units. An engineer unit has smaller squads, while an infantry unit has larger squads. The size of a squad is also determined by the military doctrine in effect at the time. In 1950, an infantry squad was authorized nine men.[8] These men operated entirely on foot, their basic weapon a rifle, with only minimal special equipment. The primary variance in infantry squads might be the members' weapons. A squad from the regimental reconnaissance platoon, for example, contained three jeeps with three men assigned to each jeep. Each jeep mounted some heavier weapon, usually a machine gun.

Sergeants, the men who led these squads, were (and still are), the backbone of the United States military. This was no less true in 1950 than it is today. Yet the role and responsibilities of American sergeants were somewhat different than they were in armies elsewhere in the world. By the unique set of circumstances that is U.S. history, the American sergeant assumed a position of greater responsibility than a man of similar rank might have found in any other nation's army, partly due to the uniquely egalitarian nature of American society and, by lesser extension, the United States Army.[9]

America has, until quite recently, relied almost exclusively upon the concept of the citizen-soldier as the defender of the nation. That is not to say that the nation's armed forces have always been conscripted, far from it. Prior to the Cold War, the United States customarily maintained a small military during peacetime, assuming that in time of need it would fill the ranks with volunteers, reservists, and draftees. To field an effective force required competent junior leaders, and the sergeants were expected to fill this role.[10] Throughout the first century of the nation, as the United States expanded from one coast to the other, its army was stretched out along a moving set of frontier posts, establishing a federal presence and effectively serving as a constabulary force.[11] This dispersion meant that there were never enough officers to go around. Accordingly, in modern parlance, the practical result was "empowerment." American sergeants became vested with the *de facto* (and somewhat later *de jure*) ability to issue orders and make decisions on a local scale.

Sergeants are "noncommissioned officers," or NCOs. They have the power to issue orders, although not technically in their own right, as this power is derived from the commission of the officer under whom the sergeant serves.

By the mid-twentieth century, however, due to what sociologists now refer to as "expert power," American sergeants issued orders of their own, and their orders were obeyed. The sergeants were recognized as professionals. They knew what they were doing based upon a long service that encompassed training, education, and perhaps combat experience. Sergeants led the men and served as the interface between the enlisted soldier and the officers. An analogous position in civilian life might be that of the shop foreman in a factory. This analogy should not be taken too far, however, as very few shop foremen hold the equivalent power to make life-and-death decisions.

Without sergeants, it is almost inconceivable that a modern American military unit could accomplish its tasks.

Each squad has a leader, who is usually a sergeant with several years of experience. In the infantry of 1950, this squad leader had another junior NCO to help him control the squad. This assistant squad leader usually was a brand new sergeant or a corporal.

In an infantry unit, which the 7th Cavalry was at this time, four squads combine to make up a platoon. Platoons are the lowest level at which one might find an officer in the infantry. Of the four squads of the standard infantry platoon in 1950, three were known as rifle squads. These squads were armed with the standard rifle, the M1 Garand, and the Browning automatic rifle, known as the BAR, a hefty weapon weighing more than twenty pounds. With a magazine capacity of twenty rounds of ammunition, the BAR was the bridge between the standard rifle and the heavier fire-power of the machine gun.[12] The fourth squad, called the weapons squad, contained somewhat heavier weapons that provided more firepower, but made the men less mobile than the soldiers of the other squads. According to the army Table of Organization and Equipment (T/O&E), the weapons squad consisted of six men under the leadership of a seventh, the squad leader. This squad, made up of two teams of three men apiece, carried two light .30-caliber machine guns. Each team had a gunner, an assistant gunner, and an ammunition bearer. In addition, the platoon headquarters had four men assigned as anti-tank gunners equipped with bazookas.[13]

In combat, the men of the weapons squad served as a base of fire, meaning that it was their job to fire a lot of bullets towards the enemy. A good base of fire has a high volume of fire; the latter is generally considered more important than accuracy.[14] Combat experience taught modern armies that putting out this volume of fire has the effect of forcing the enemy to take cover where it cannot readily move or react to the actions of the rest of the platoon. This combination of fire and movement is the basis of infantry tactics at the platoon level. The heavier weapons of the weapons squad could pin down an enemy both in the offense and defense. In the defense, the weapons squad would generally be dispersed and used to strengthen the line where needed. Both offensive and defensive concepts are simple to explain, yet require years of practice to execute competently for one simple reason: Warfare, at least since the close of the nineteenth century, has not been fought standing up upon broad open plains. Men dig in and fight from ground level in modern war.

In ground combat, perspective is everything. To illustrate this principle, try the following experiment. Go out to a seemingly level portion of ground with a friend. Find an area where you can see for at least two hundred or more yards in a straight line. Separate from your friend by a few hundred yards and both of you lie down on your stomachs. It is unlikely you will be able to see each other. Remember then that this is a flat and apparently featureless table. In infantry combat, a rise and fall of one or two feet across a few hundred yards is enough to become a militarily significant terrain feature in the eyes of the men lying flat nearby. The area masked by terrain that cannot be observed and hit with direct fire is known in military terminology as the dead space. Keep this simple observation in mind when considering the terrain of Korea. Knowing how to position three squads and the machine guns on even the simplest rolls of the ground requires experience. To lead the platoon, the army therefore paired experience with education.

In control of the platoon was a team of men, a matching of the most experienced sergeant of the platoon with the most junior officers of the army. The platoon sergeants were usually, or at least were optimally, veterans with between five to fifteen years of experience. Becoming a platoon sergeant was not easy. This man was also, by virtue of the time required to attain his position in peacetime, usually the oldest man in the platoon. Platoon sergeants were responsible for running the platoon in day-to-day activities. They ensured that the weapons were clean, food and ammunition were on hand, and discipline was enforced. The platoon sergeant had, in the words of military sociologists, both legal and referent authority. He was the master of his profession at this level. His officer counterpart, however, was another story.

Second lieutenants are the most junior officers in the army. The running joke in the American army, (which has a long tradition of thumbing its nose at authority, even its own), was that the only difference between a private first class (pay grade E-3) and a second lieutenant (pay grade O-1) is that the PFC had at least been promoted twice. In 1950, some second lieutenants came straight to their respective units in the army directly from their source of commissioning. They were all graduates of the United States Military Academy at West Point, the Reserve Officer Training Corps (ROTC) at a civilian college or university, or the Officer Candidate School (OCS) at Fort Benning, Georgia.

Platoons generally run just fine without the presence of a lieutenant, albeit at something less than the potential peak efficiency. The experience of a competent platoon sergeant could keep the platoon going, yet where

else could junior officers gain field experience to become competent leaders at higher levels? Where else but at the platoon would a junior lieutenant
learn through example and experience how to train and lead a company,
the next level of command?

One of the primary purposes of having officers at this echelon of command is that these lieutenants represent, through their commissions, the
authority of life and death. Lieutenants are educated specifically to ensure
that they and their men obey all orders that are legal and disobey those that
are not. It is a role that some junior officers, most famously Lieutenant Calley of My Lai and the Americal Division in Vietnam and Lieutenant Kerrey
of the navy's SEALS and the village of Than Phong in Vietnam, did not
adequately internalize. Lieutenants are to know the difference, for example,
between a free-fire zone (which is a measure for controlling indirect fires
such as artillery, not a carte blanche for killing people with direct fires or
knives) and an order to "kill everyone" in a village or an area. The first is a
legitimate means of controlling fire from aircraft and artillery; the second is
an illegal order.

Infantry companies in 1950 had four platoons, just as the platoon had
four squads. Three of the platoons are rifle platoons, while the fourth was
designated the weapons platoon. The weapons platoon had mortars for
indirect firepower and larger direct fire weapons such as the 57-mm recoilless rifle or a bazooka.[15] This platoon filled the same role as the weapons
squads did at the lower level—either providing heavier firepower intended
to pin the enemy down while the company maneuvered in the attack or
supplementing and strengthening the line in the defense. The indirect fires
provided by the mortars were tactically important since their smaller burst-
ing radius made it practical to call in indirect fires closer to friendly troops,
as close as fifty meters in extreme circumstances (though 200 meters was
preferred). Only with this type of weapon could the infantry place fires on
the dead space in front of friendly positions that was mentioned earlier.
Artillery filled the same role further out from friendly troops, but the mortars, because they belonged to the company, were the quickest to respond
and usually very accurate if the crews are adequately trained.

Companies are commanded by a captain (O-3), an officer with at least
three or four years of experience, who is assisted by the company first
sergeant. Like the platoon sergeant, this man was the senior noncommissioned officer of his company. Within his own company, a first sergeant
holds near god-like power in the eyes of the junior soldiers. John De Borde
joined the 1st Cavalry Division in Tokyo in 1948 as a private. He recalls his
former first sergeant this way, "On Saturdays, you see, we had these orga-

nized athletics, you know, to keep the guys busy and out of trouble. Anyway, we would set up this ring, a boxing ring. Then First Sergeant Kelly would say that if you wished, he would get in the ring, he would put the gloves on. Well, he was a big guy. Needless to say, after a few weeks, nobody wanted to do that again. I saw him pick up a guy, with his pack and rifle and everything, and haul him to his feet and get him going again. Nobody ever dropped out or missed training with him around. He would get everyone there."[16]

First sergeants commanded the respect of their soldiers in all sorts of ways, from the trappings of their rank to their personality and personal reputations. The first sergeants were expected to be father, mentor, coach, and disciplinarian to the enlisted men and junior NCOs. Sergeants' training creates new sergeants among those who pass muster.

R. C. "Snuffy" Gray recalls when he first arrived in Japan and met his first sergeant, "I arrived in the 7th Cavalry on the 27th of December 1945. I was in the company of a legend, First Sergeant John T. Gwin. He was returning to F Company, which he'd been with all through World War II. He busted my butt; I mean he trained us. He was on us. He rode all of us from buck sergeant to staff sergeant to sergeant first class and platoon sergeant."[17]

If the first sergeant was seen as the brawn in a company, then the commander was the brains. Together these two men formed a command team that led the company. While a platoon may operate perfectly well without a lieutenant, the same could not be said for a company. It was really at the company level that one started to coordinate extensively, to plan and issue complex orders, and to orchestrate the various weapons of the arsenal available to U.S. combat units. This required professional knowledge, and the captains provided that knowledge.

The company commander was assisted and supported by a second-in-command, usually a first lieutenant (O-2). This executive officer, known in the military as the XO, ensured that the more complex logistic requirements found at the company level were taken care of. This officer coordinated the movement of the company by any means other than on foot and controlled the logistics of the company headquarters. His proximity to the company commander (CO) ensured that in the event of the commander's death or wounding, another officer who was familiar with the unit and the tactical situation was available to take the reins immediately.

All together, five companies made a battalion. In 1950, the 1st Battalion of the 7th Cavalry Regiment was made up of the rifle companies, designated by letters A, B, and C, the heavy weapons company (D Company),

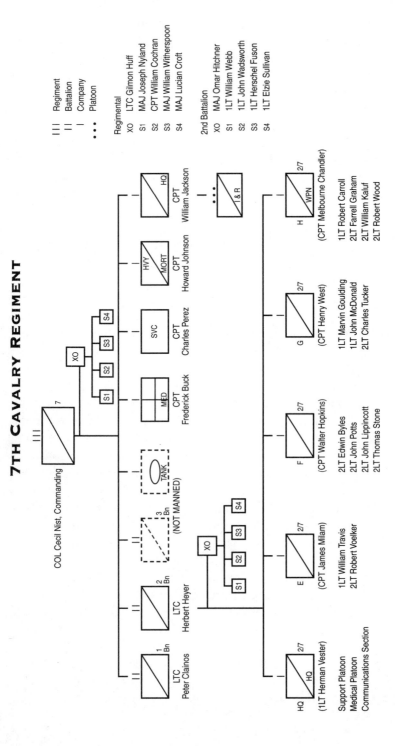

7TH CAVALRY REGIMENT

COL Cecil Nist, Commanding

|||	Regiment
||	Battalion
		Company
• • •	Platoon

Regimental
- XO LTC Gilmon Huff
- S1 MAJ Joseph Nyland
- S2 CPT William Cochran
- S3 MAJ William Witherspoon
- S4 MAJ Lucian Croft

2nd Battalion
- XO MAJ Omar Hitchner
- S1 1LT William Webb
- S2 1LT John Wadsworth
- S3 1LT Herschel Fuson
- S4 1LT Elzie Sullivan

1 Bn — LTC Peter Clainos

2 Bn — LTC Herbert Heyer

3 (NOT MANNED)

TANK (NOT MANNED)

HQ 2/7 (1LT Herman Vester)
- Support Platoon
- Medical Platoon
- Communications Section

E 2/7 (CPT James Milam)
- 1LT William Travis
- 2LT Robert Voelker

F 2/7 (CPT Walter Hopkins)
- 2LT Edwin Byles
- 2LT John Potts
- 2LT John Lippincott
- 2LT Thomas Stone

G 2/7 (CPT Henry West)
- 1LT Marvin Goulding
- 1LT John McDonald
- 2LT Charles Tucker

H 2/7 (CPT Melbourne Chandler)
- 1LT Robert Carroll
- 2LT Farrell Graham
- 2LT William Kaluf
- 2LT Robert Wood

MED CPT Frederick Buck

SVC CPT Charles Perez

HVY MORT CPT Howard Johnson

HQ CPT William Jackson

I & R

WPN 2/7

XO — S1 S2 S3 S4

NOTES: 1. Each line company (E, F, G, H) should have had lieutenants: an executive officer, three rifle platoon leaders, and one weapons platoon leader.
2. Although called cavalry, the regiment was organized under army TO&E 7–11N, *Infantry Regiment*, of 20 December 1949.

and the headquarters section. The 2nd Battalion 7th Cavalry Regiment consisted of E, F, and G Companies as the rifle companies and H Company as the heavy weapons company. While the structure is much the same as at the lower levels, the weapons company operated somewhat differently at the battalion level. With both direct and indirect fire weapons, the weapons company had three platoons, one each of machine guns, mortars, and 75-mm recoilless rifles that gave the battalion its heavier firepower.[18] The platoons of the heavy weapons company rarely operated as a single cohesive group in combat, except when in the rear or in garrison.

When a battalion was deployed in combat, with several hundred men stretched across kilometers of land, it was deemed impractical for the commander of the heavy weapons company to attempt to command his men. Dispersed by platoon or section across the entire battalion front based upon an assessment of where the enemy was most likely to attack, it would be nearly impossible for one man to visit, let alone control each of his elements under the stress and hazards of direct ground combat. Therefore, elements of the heavy weapons company operated under the direct control of whatever line unit they were attached to at the moment. The commanders of D and H Companies, therefore, generally focused on technical training when in garrison. When the battalion deployed to combat, this officer was the jack-of-all-trades, providing security for the rear area of the battalion, coordinating actions in retrograde operations, and serving as the fire support and air support coordinator for the entire battalion.[19] With a direct line to his own mortar platoon and the responsibility to effectively bring to bear assets from outside the battalion (such as artillery fires), the weapons company commander was a busy man under the best of circumstances. Fire support coordination, however, was a complex mission.

William Hoffman was a second lieutenant with the 7th Cavalry in the summer of 1950. He was assigned to H Company that August. Fifty years later, he recalls with frank clarity how his heavy weapons company planned and plotted the indirect fires of the mortars: "We didn't have a fire direction center. Heck, we didn't even use the plotting boards; we were too dumb for that. I mean, we were untrained in using them. What happened was that the forward observers (FOs) for our mortars came out of the mortar platoon and they went up and lived with the [infantry] companies. They called azimuth and distance and since the FOs knew where the mortars were we'd fire a few rounds. When the rounds impacted, he'd say 'drop so many' or 'add so many [meters],' and then he'd adjust the impact from there. These FOs were strictly for our fires; there were artillery FOs for the artillery and other stuff. Stan Bush [an artillery second lieutenant with the

77th Field Artillery Battalion of the 1st Cavalry Division] was one of the guys I remember working with back then."[20]

Battalion command was also a team effort between the officer and his staff. At this level, the officer was a lieutenant colonel (O-5) and the senior noncommissioned officer was a sergeant major. The battalion command team was the first level in the chain of command to be supported by a staff in which each section had clearly defined roles and responsibilities. The S-1 was responsible for personnel issues, while the S-2 was the conduit and filter for all intelligence reports about the enemy. The S-3 handled the plans for the battalion (both in training and combat), drafted the orders that moved men and equipment from place to place, and kept track of the general situation throughout the battalion's area. The final regular staff section, S-4, was the supply and logistics cell. These four elements, all led by officers, made up the brains of the battalion. Several specialized platoons, such as the medical platoon and the communications platoon, also served directly for the battalion at this level, fulfilling the combat support functions that kept the battalion operating smoothly.

According to the military doctrine of the day, three rifle battalions combined to make up the next higher echelon formation, the regiment. In addition to these three battalions of infantry, a regiment might also call upon the services of some portion of the divisional artillery. Regiments were commanded by colonels and supported by additional combat support elements. Organic to the regiment was a medical company, a service company for maintenance and communications support, and a staff. Finally, the regiment could call upon its own pocket artillery in the form of a heavy mortar company of 4.2-inch (107 mm) mortars, a tank company (In 1950 none of the regiments had their organic tanks), and an intelligence and reconnaissance platoon. This platoon, commonly known as "I and R" (abbreviated I/R) came equipped with eleven jeeps: three jeeps apiece for each of its three squads plus one jeep each for the platoon sergeant and platoon leader. Each of these vehicles mounted an air-cooled, .30-caliber light machine gun, and several radios.

In 1950, the 7th Cavalry Regiment was a part of the 1st Cavalry Division. Despite the misleading name, however, the 7th Cavalry was organized and manned as a conventional "straight-leg" infantry regiment, and the 1st Cavalry Division was an infantry division.

Understanding the organizational structure of the 7th Cavalry Regiment, just as understanding the motivations of the men who make up the organization, is critical to making sense of No Gun Ri. But learning the unique history of the 7th Cavalry is just as important.

THE DEAD HAND OF
GEORGE ARMSTRONG CUSTER

Military history can be a strange thing. The fact that it is made up of five different sub-genres suggests little agreement even among those who follow history closely. Of the five types mentioned in the introduction, regimental history—that is, history written or passed down orally within the unit for the unit—applies to the 7th Cavalry's history. Military units preserve their own legacies in a history that assists with the second of John Lynn's military motivational categories, "sustaining motivation."

In the United States Army, for much of its history, soldiers identified the most with their regiment. While many Americans today may be able to name one or two of the divisions that make up the modern U.S. Army, far fewer people who have not served in the army will recognize the identities of the subordinate units. Modern media reports rarely venture below the level of the division and almost always seem to confuse the terms when they do.[21] So, while most Americans may have heard of the 82nd Airborne Division or the 1st Cavalry Division, few are familiar with the subordinate units, where most servicemen focus their attention.

For most of America's military past, the regiment was the largest permanent organization of the United States Army. While the army fought in larger formations (divisions, corps, and armies) during the Mexican War, the American Civil War, the Spanish-American War, and the First World War, these large units were temporary formations created during and for these specific wars. Not until the period between World War I and World War II did the U.S. Army adopt the division as a permanent organization. The 1st Cavalry Division, for example, was not permanently formed until the early 1920s.[22] Regiments, therefore, attracted the most attention and were the natural focal point of allegiance for soldiers.

A soldier arriving in Japan in 1946 or 1949 and assigned to the 7th Cavalry Regiment was coming into more than just a unit. He was entering the pages of history. Moreover, he was frequently reminded of this. In the 7th Cavalry, these young men, barely out of their teens, were to become a member of a unit not only with a history within the army, but a regimental history dripping with tradition and heritage.

The 7th Cavalry, formed by an act of Congress in 1866, was created specifically for the challenges of the Great Plains of the American frontier. From its beginning, the history of the 7th Cavalry has been linked to the history of its most famous battle and commander, Lieutenant Colonel George Armstrong Custer.[23] Custer was commissioned at the bottom of his class in 1861 as the Civil War started. Through brash courage, some might say to the point of foolhardiness, he won engagement after engagement and became the youngest general officer in the Union army with brevet (temporary wartime) promotions to brigadier and later major general in the volunteers. Some of those same personality traits may well have contributed to his defeat and death on June 25, 1876 at the Battle of the Little Bighorn where five of the twelve companies the 7th Cavalry Regiment had at that time were wiped out.

For most of the men in the 7th Cavalry in 1950, the Custer legend was a familiar tale. A romanticized version of the story appeared in most grade-school history texts during this era, a version that made the most of the martial heritage of the United States. (Remember that one of the purposes of military history has traditionally been to socialize young people to want to serve in the military.) In fact, for much of America, the legend of Custer's "heroic" Last Stand was near the apogee. The 1941 classic war movie *They Died With Their Boots On*, became the undisputed history of this battle. Now these young men, many of whom had seen the film, found themselves in the very unit that had been immortalized upon the silver screen. They were the new soldiers of the 7th Cavalry, and with this, came a host of traditions designed to remind them of their martial heritage and indoctrinate them into the culture and ways of the army.

Each soldier identified closely with the regiment. Every man wore the regimental crest upon his uniform. When passing an officer, the men saluted and rendered a greeting that echoed the regimental motto of "Garryowen." The song "Garryowen" (from which the unit takes its motto) was played every time the unit passed on parade.[24] The long dead hand of Custer rested heavily upon the unit, bonding the men in a common identity. Those serving with the 7th Cavalry knew that their unit was different, their unit was special, their unit was, at all times, heroic. This mindset may have helped to remind them of what their true function was supposed to be at a time when occupation duty in Japan did little to reinforce the realization that the ultimate purpose of an armed force is to fight and win in war.

LIFE IN JAPAN

Between the end of the Second World War and the beginning of the Korean War, the 1st Cavalry Division consisted of three regiments of infantry.[25] Stationed primarily in and around Tokyo, the division served first as an army of occupation before shifting slightly towards its new role as a forward-deployed element of American combat power. As an occupation force in the immediate postwar era, the division was there to show American power, to impose the terms of the surrender document, and to remind the Japanese people who won the war in the Pacific.[26]

Occupation forces traditionally have the lowest priority for military resources. This was the case in 1947 when the army was faced with the conflicting signals sent by the U.S. Congress, which, according to law, establishes the size of the army.[27] In a separate action, Congress also determines the money that the army receives. As has frequently been the case throughout the majority of U.S. history, these two did not match each other during the postwar years, and the underfunding of the army between 1946 and 1950 proved to be a near disaster.

During this time, Congress believed that the military was in the good hands of the professionals. The United States had, after all, just recently won the biggest war in history. Therefore, when determining the national requirements for defense forces, Congress was satisfied to establish the number of divisions on active duty and leave it at that. The division was the lowest echelon that generally attracted attention because combat forces below that echelon did not have a sufficient support structure to fight independently for any length of time. Unfortunately, when Congress decided that ten divisions were sufficient for fulfilling America's international roles, it did not provide the funds to fully man, maintain, and train those ten divisions.[28] Our uniquely American system of government contributes to this under funding. A congressman who votes to reduce the number of divisions on active duty may be called to task for being "soft on defense," but one who accepts the number of divisions but votes for a smaller defense budget is viewed "fiscally prudent." The "hollow army" syndrome—much form and little substance—results.

Unlike Congress, the Pentagon cannot indulge in deficit-spending. When told to accomplish the dual directives of keeping ten divisions on the rolls and spending only enough to properly maintain approximately six, the military tried its best. Army leaders prioritized the divisions, allocating men and material to each in accordance with their relative importance. With an aggressive Soviet Union staring across the inter-German border from behind the newly named Iron Curtain, that equation was not a terribly difficult one to work through. The four divisions of the Far East command took the budgetary ax right across the throat.

1st Cavalry Division records indicate that the response to the budgetary crisis in the army was to reduce the army of occupation in Japan to little more than a skeleton force not even worthy of the title "cadre." Each regiment of infantry was reduced to two battalions, where the number of men assigned also fell to perilously low levels. The regimental tank companies went away, and training slacked off. Without enough men to accomplish even the occupation mission, the division found it impossible to fulfill that requirement and also find the time to train. Yet America, arguably, was unaware of the true state of her forces.

In postwar Japan, not one of the four U.S. divisions stationed there would have been rated as combat ready. With frequent turnovers in personnel, all of the regiments in all of the divisions were short of men, not just in key positions, but across the board. All of the units suffered from the effects of inadequate training areas and insufficient resources to train at levels higher than the squad and platoon.

As one of the three regiments of the 1st Cavalry Division, the 7th Cavalry was fairly typical. Instead of the three battalions required for a regiment to accomplish its wartime missions, it had only two. Even this measure, designed to ensure that at least the remaining battalions would be near full strength, could not counter the stingy congressional budget. In January 1948, for example, the regiment was authorized a total of 102 officers and 2,640 enlisted men of all grades.[29] Yet actually standing in the ranks at that time were 48 officers and 298 soldiers.[30] *This means that only forty-seven percent of the authorized officers and a bare eleven percent of the needed enlisted strength were even assigned to the unit, let alone available for training.* Effective training for modern combined arms combat was essentially little more than a pipe dream. Yet with no looming combat duty, life in the 7th Cavalry was fairly pleasant in those days. This was an army of occupation after all.

Don Donnelly epitomizes the typical private in Tokyo at that time. As a young soldier, he started out his career in Guam but soon after was transferred to Tokyo and the 7th Cavalry where he was assigned to the I/R platoon. He recalls that life in the 7th was a soft duty, especially since the regiment was stationed downtown.

Donnelly remembers some aspects of life in Tokyo as particularly amusing: "Oh, Lord, it was a blast. We were right downtown, something like 'Skashima.' It was the old Japanese Merchant Marine Academy building. We used to play. I remember a couple of weeks we spent practicing constantly, practicing marching and parading for the Joint Chiefs. MacArthur wanted to show off his troops. We were like his pets. I mean just about everybody in Japan was in that parade."

Of course, not all of a soldier's time was spent polishing, guarding, and parading. Tokyo offered a soldier many a distraction once the duty day was done.

Donnelly explains: "A lot of it was off limits, and those were the fun parts. The I/R platoon, we had a place in the off-limits area. One thing I found out, we'd go into these little saki bars, and we'd get to drinking with these guys, these Japanese guys with these rubber boots up to the middle of their calf. Of course all of these guys, every single one, well none of 'em ever fought the Americans. They always fought the Chinese or something else. Of course all of the girls, they would sit down next to you and say, 'I love you, GI, you buy me drink?' I never did have a steady girlfriend; I guess all I had were those girls I'd meet on the weekend."[31]

Naturally all of this was against regulations in 1950. Yet many of the veterans recall their periodic brushes with military justice as one vast game of tag or cops and robbers. Fifty years later, they certainly don't express any inordinate amount of shame for their escapades or their escapes from the military police.

One veteran, who prefers that his grandchildren not know everything about "gramps," recalled Tokyo this way: "These off-limits bars, I remember one that had this tiny little bandstand. You'd be in there drinking and having a good time. There were girls all over, uh, 'social workers,' y'know, and then all of the sudden they'd holler, 'MPs come! MPs come!' and they'd have places all over to hide you. Some would go to a house next door, some in hiding spots in there. The MPs would get there, and they'd see like a bunch of half-full glasses all over and just these women in there alone. Then they'd leave and the women would bring you right back in."

Another veteran of the battalion, H. Norman Matthias, started off in G Company. He too recalls an easy, if rowdy, life in postwar Tokyo, "I used to go down to this off-limits place downtown. There was this one Japanese woman there, she used to call me her Baby-Face. She took real good care of me, you know? A girlfriend, if that's what you want to call them, would cost you about twelve dollars a month in those days. I used to bring her toothpaste and soap and stuff. See, at that time a carton of cigarettes would cost you ninety cents, and you could sell it for about ten dollars on the black market. We'd go down to the geisha-street, and you could get a quart of cold beer for about thirty yen. The rate was 360 yen to the dollar as I remember at that time. Anyway, you'd get drunk as a skunk . . . but there was a fight every night down there. Fights everywhere. Either versus the GHQ [general headquarters] pukes or the airborne, but we were fighting all the time."[32]

Those soldiers restricted from leaving McKnight Barracks could turn to the officially sanctioned form of entertainment, the enlisted men's club aboard an anchored sailing frigate unofficially christened the USS *Garryowen*.

"The Garryowen Club was this ship, or boat, but it had like a concrete bottom. As you know, on a ship the doors aren't very wide. Well, nobody would really go there, on post, unless you couldn't get a pass. Lots of beer and bad apples together. We'd stay away from there because somebody would get in a fight and then you might get trapped in there, because two guys could close down one of those doors."[33]

Don Donnelly recalls the regular routine for soldiers on pass. No soldier ever wants pass to end, and like young men throughout history, Donnelly and his pals would do everything to stretch out their time.

"When we got our passes, like on the weekends, you used to have to be back in the barracks that night. It was really rare for anyone to get an overnight pass. We'd be down in town, in Tokyo, and we'd take the trolley. We had these little chits we'd use, like money, for that. You had to be in by midnight, or eleven or something. We'd look at our watch, somebody would, and yell, 'Oh, shit!' and we'd all go piling out of there and into a trolley or whatever. 'Cause if you weren't back in, then you had to pass by the MP barracks, and they'd close the gate and you'd get this ticket. When that got back to the company, you'd get in trouble. It was like they always got some, but not everyone, like just enough to make the rest of us hustle."[34]

As occurred in postwar Germany, a bustling black market existed in Japan as well. Even five years after the end of the Second World War, Japan had not yet fully recovered to its prewar state, let alone become anything like the modern economic powerhouse that it is today. In the 1940s, American soldiers could buy price-controlled items at the post exchange and sell them, illegally, to Japanese citizens at whatever price the market would support.

Donnelly further recalls, "Then there was the black market. It was like a two-way game really. You had the American GI and Japanese entrepreneurs, and they're always thinking of ways to screw the opponent. Back in those days, you could buy a carton of cigarettes in the exchange for something like sixty cents I think. The Japanese would buy your cigarettes for maybe a thousand yen. What, it was like 360 yen to the dollar, so you made a couple bucks. Then some guys hit on the idea of taking a razor blade and slicing open the wrapper from the edge, and taking out about six of the packs and stuffing something else in there. Sell that and you made twice as much. But the Japanese were on to it too. They'd take the carton and hand you a thick wad of yen, and you'd get back and see that the front one was a hundred yen, then scrap paper, more scrap paper, and the last one was another yen. That went on all the time; it was like a game really."[35]

Life in Tokyo was not the most rigorous duty ever encountered by American soldiers. Parades, inspections, and guard duty made up a large part of the daily and weekly cycle of the 2nd Battalion of the 7th Cavalry. The role of a police force, while often necessary, is not considered the primary function of the army. To fulfill its primary function—fighting wars— an army required training, a commodity that was in short supply in the Land of the Rising Sun.

In Japan in the late 1940s, the "old army" had come alive again. Many of the pre-World War II traditions, both good and bad, were resurrected.

Although perceptions about what made an effective leader and what it meant to be a real soldier were somewhat modified by the experience of WWII and the facts of living in an occupied Japan, many uniquely American aspects shone through the army at this time. An emphasis on sports, especially football, was a part of this. Soldiers and officers, especially officers who were former players on the legendary West Point Army football teams of '44, '45, and '46 (during which Army won two national championships and never lost a single game), found themselves assigned as football players, to the exclusion of all other duties they might normally fulfill, including training for war.

In the 7th Cavalry, the coach of the regimental team was Lieutenant Herschel "Ug" Fuson, a West Point officer originally from Kentucky. Fuson's older brother had been killed in combat during World War II the very year that the younger Fuson entered the United States Military Academy. One of the outstanding linesmen of those championship teams, Fuson was a large but quiet man. His soft-spoken manner and overflowing good will made him popular with enlisted men and officers alike. But once he arrived in Japan in the summer of 1948, Fuson spent very little time actually training as an infantry platoon leader. Instead, he was immediately assigned to the division football team, where he played a whole season of games against teams from other army divisions as well as the Marine Corps and the newly created United States Air Force.

Among Fuson's teammates was Lieutenant William West, who like Fuson was a member of the famous army football teams at West Point. Arriving in the summer of 1948, West was nominally assigned to the 8th Cavalry Regiment as a platoon leader, while in reality his priority assignment was as a football player on the division team.

West recalls, "When we got to Japan in July '48, I was immediately assigned to the division football team for the majority of the year. Though I was assigned as a platoon leader in the 1st Battalion of the 8th Cavalry Regiment which was at Camp King, I lived at Camp Drake in the barracks with the 1st Battalion of the 5th Cavalry Regiment and played football. One day a classmate of mine, a friend from West Point gave me a call and asked if he could play. I told him, 'OK, but when you get up here, we play to win and that means no women, no drinking, no nothing,' and he says to me, 'My God, then what the hell are we living for?' [That classmate was future four-star general and U.S. Secretary of State Alexander Haig, who also served in the 8th Cavalry Regiment.]

"That team was pretty impressive. Among the guys on the 1st Cavalry team were Dick Pitzer [USMA '46], Ug Fuson [USMA '47], and Tom Lombardo [who had been the Captain of the West Point team in '44] as the coach. I remember we played the air force, and a team down in Kyoto, and then at the end of the season, I was the captain of the army all-star team against the air force all-star team in the first-ever 'Rice Bowl.' That didn't end until January when there was a 0-0 game in an all-ace game. But otherwise we had a winning season."[36]

Despite the diversion of football, the "old army" way still shone through, the utmost one of which was the way that discipline was enforced. The soldier of this period—not an age of political correctness—was not likely to have his "feelings" or "emotions" considered during his tenure with the army. While the potential abuses of power by commissioned officers were greatly curbed by the previously mentioned Doolittle Board, the noncommissioned officers (NCOs) continued to run things according to the "old ways" for some time to come. Snuffy Gray remembers how it was, "In 1948, I got pulled out of F Company and up to regimental headquarters to be the operations sergeant. Needless to say, I'm not the greatest pencil pusher. They were having trouble down at 2nd Battalion headquarters, so they sent me down there. Well, I used to be a pretty nasty bastard as an NCO. I don't believe in that court-martial stuff if a guy screws up. If a guy screwed up hard, I'd smack him around a few times and he wouldn't do it again. One time I did this, and the company commander and the chaplain wanted to look into it. They wanted a full investigation and they wanted to get me court-martialed. Well, the regimental sergeant major, John T. Gwin, went and made a phone call straight to General Chase [the 1st Cavalry Division commander at that time] and Colonel Kerr, the chief of staff. The very next day, there were orders cut that sent me back to the states to keep me from being court-martialed. You see? That's the way the army worked back then. Those that could took care of those that would."

Gray would continue this behavior for several years. Once stationed back in the states, he ran afoul of "official" army policy again.

"One day we were out at Cape Cod training ROTC cadets, and I had this buck sergeant give me some static so I pulled him away and knocked the hell outta him. And now they were gonna court-martial me . . . again. But now the sergeant major there gets me a three-day pass to cool off, and this was in conjunction with a weekend. So, I went and saw General Chase at the Pentagon while I'm on pass. By the time I got back from that three-day pass, there were orders for me to be discharged, reenlisted, and immediately assigned to the 7th Cavalry! I got back to Japan and the 7th Cav in January 1950. Gwin knew I was comin' and sent a jeep and a trailer to pick me up shipside. I never even went through the repo-depot [the replacement detachment for the division]. They took me straight to the 7th Cav headquarters. From there, I went over and took over the regimental recon platoon."[37]

Gray later left the ranks of the noncommissioned officer corps he so loved and became a commissioned officer "the hard way," through a battlefield commission.

West also remembers discipline problems in the ranks: "When football season was over that year (February 1949), I went down to D Troop, 1st Battalion 8th Cavalry, at Camp King, which was north of Tokyo. I stayed with them until the next football season. This was my first troop duty, but we would have as many as twenty to twenty-five AWOLs a day, and that was out of a company of about a hundred. We were short on NCOs, we had that AWOL problem, and out there at Camp King, I spent an awful lot of time as a defense counsel in special courts-martial. I led the calisthenics every morning, but most officers didn't do that exercising. I remember some of the higher-ranking officers were a little pissed off when we marched past their quarters at 0600 in the morning and were sounding off as we marched past. There were also problems with alcohol. There was an awful lot available, and it seemed it flowed pretty freely. One of the things that a newly arrived officer used to do when he first got to a new post was to pay a courtesy call on his new battalion commander. My battalion commander, well, when I first paid my courtesy call on his quarters when I arrived, he answered the door so drunk he didn't know what I was doing there."[38]

READINESS AND TRAINING

Central to any analysis of the behavior and actions of the American forces sent to Korea in the summer of 1950, and specifically to the readiness of the 2nd Battalion of the 7th Cavalry, is a study of the training that the soldiers conducted prior to the war.

This topic has proven sensitive for the veterans and the U.S. Congress as well as the military leadership who bridged the gap between the two. Nothing illustrated the level of frustration brought out by the 1999 investigative news stories of No Gun Ri better than the outraged E-mails and message postings that flew across the Internet and on the web pages of the alumni association of the United States Military Academy. The graduates of West Point, some the contemporaries of the officers who led these 1950 troops, exploded in fury at the initial Associated Press version of the story of No Gun Ri in late September 1999. Many of these men objected to the reporters' lack of explanation of how poorly trained these soldiers were at the time. These men, retired leaders of tens of thousands of American soldiers, have the combined experience of centuries of military service to validate their opinions. Standing in stark contrast to the opinion of these professional officers were the opinions of the men who were actually there.

Almost all the veterans of the 2nd Battalion 7th Cavalry initially denied the idea that they were poorly trained. Many claimed that they had excellent training, that they were well prepared, and in fact objected to any assessment claiming that they were not prepared.[39] How then to resolve these conflicting views?

The answer lies, as it often does when working in oral histories, in evaluating the veteran's point of view at the time that his memories and opinions were formed. The majority of the men interviewed for this book were enlisted soldiers at the time that they served in the 2nd Battalion 7th Cavalry. To the average officer who blamed No Gun Ri on the poor training of soldiers in 1950, training really refers to collective (larger unit) training, which is the responsibility of the officer corps. Thus, any shortcomings in collective training stand out to the former officers as a lack of training.

War is a complex act even at the tactical level. It involves the coordination of forces on the ground and the integration of direct fire (rifles and machine guns), indirect fire (mortars and artillery), and external assets (such as airpower), all of which must be orchestrated to work together. The ultimate design is to inflict violence upon a moving and intelligent enemy across difficult ground, what is referred to as combined arms operations, and accomplishing such requires a lot of training.

Merely moving a large body of troops from one spot on the ground to another, at night, without lights, requires a significant amount of practice. Add to this the need to control those men to ensure that none of the subordinate individuals or units get lost or separated, coordinate artillery flares to light the way, and fire high explosives to suppress the enemy. Consider that all of this is done at night, in the woods, by the faint light of a red-lens filtered flashlight, while people are trying to kill you. These type of complex tactical operations fall to the officer corps, which also must coordinate the material and logistics support that keep a modern combat force operating in the field. Learning how to do this from a book is one thing, but practice is a prerequisite for success.

In the nineteenth century, a Prussian military theorist named Carl von Clausewitz explained the justification for large unit training quite succinctly. He used the then newly developed idea of *friction* to describe how a million tiny mishaps, none significant in their own right, could collectively affect implementation of the best-laid plans. Friction might be introduced in a million ways. A resupply convoy loaded with ammunition may get bogged down at a stream-fording site because the convoy leader did not know the bridge was washed out. A lieutenant leading the first platoon of the battalion column may get lost, leading the whole column down the wrong road. Either situation has implications far beyond those few men directly involved.

Similarly, mere mechanical failures may be a source of friction. The wheel on a vehicle might fall off at a tight passage on the road, holding up the entire column of a hundred vehicles, or a batch of illumination mortar rounds may be defective, leaving infantrymen in the dark when under attack at night. What may appear as minor events in comparison to the grander scheme of things often has a cumulative effect in the intricate ballet of coordinated combat actions. Without combat experience, units have little ability to remove much of the potential for friction. In the end, only through constant and repetitive practice at progressively larger and larger unit levels might friction be reduced. This is how officers look at the requirements for training.

The soldiers, on the other hand, are often unaware of these larger issues. For many junior enlisted men, training might mean training in their own individual soldier skills or training on their personal or crew-served weapons. In the eyes of these former enlisted men then, if their equipment was well maintained, if they had ample opportunity to practice at the levels with which they were familiar—the squad and the platoon—then they considered themselves "trained." As a minor caveat to this second opinion, when the soldiers train at the squad and platoon level, the sergeants as the squad leaders benefit from the training as they learn how to reduce the friction at their level of expertise. The NCO corps then is the critical glue linking the actions and the plans of the officer corps to the actual execution of the missions by large bodies of men.

With these observations in mind, let's turn to an evaluation of the training of the 2nd Battalion 7th Cavalry in the years and months preceding their deployment to Korea in July of 1950.

Simply put, the battalion, as such, did not train very much.

Here we find our analysis bumping up against the realities of the budgets and priorities proscribed for the forces in Japan in the immediate postwar era. In reality, Japan was a second-string assignment in terms of resources. With the massive demobilization of the immediate postwar years, the army found that it had to choose between full modernization and minimal troop levels, or less modernization and slightly higher troop levels. International politics and the burgeoning realities of the Cold War in Europe dictated the latter. As countless military scribes have noted, one cannot be strong everywhere at once. If the United States was going to commit to the new North Atlantic Treaty Organization in any meaningful way, it would have to short the forces elsewhere. Japan was that elsewhere.

All of this is not to suggest that the men of the 2nd Battalion 7th Cavalry did not train at all. They trained considerably and, from the point of
view of an enlisted soldier in 1950, they trained completely. They trained
on individual marksmanship, they maintained their personal equipment at a
high level of polish, and they trained at the smallest echelons—the squad
and the platoon. Often their training, although it involved marching out by
companies, devolved to the lowest echelon of the squad as there was simply
not enough room to set up meaningful training for larger units anywhere
near their base at McKnight Barracks in downtown Tokyo.

Before John Lippincott retired in 1979 as a colonel, his final assignment
was as project officer for the new National Training Center. Just before that
assignment, he was in the Pentagon as readiness officer where, ironically, he
oversaw the collation of the unit status reports submitted by the army.[40] In
1950, he was a second lieutenant, the third platoon leader in F Company,
2nd Battalion 7th Cavalry. He remembers the training this way: "Our
training was certainly lacking in that we never really did anything above the
platoon level. We could do small unit tactics. I mean, we trained at the
squad and platoon, and we were pretty proficient at that, but beyond that
we were sorely lacking."[41]

John Potts was also an officer in the same company with Lippincott,
where he led the second platoon. By modern standards, Lippincott and Potts
were somewhat unusual in that they both had prior enlisted experience.

Potts explains: "I enlisted in the coast artillery in '42. From there I was
shuffled to an antiaircraft unit; then after that I was reclassified again as an
engineer and went to more training for that. I finally got sent over to
Europe as an engineer in '45, where I never saw any combat. I was discharged in October '45. After I got out, I worked for a little while, enrolled
in college, got married. But by '48, it was getting to be a bind, trying to
meet work and college and family. I had joined the reserves some time
back, and they'd kept reminding me that I could come back. I ended up
going back on active duty when they announced this program where, if you
had two years of college and at least a year of active duty, you could attend
OCS [Officer Candidate School] and get commissioned."

With his background as an enlisted soldier during World War II, Potts
was in a very good position to assess training. Training, however, did not
take up the majority of his time.

"I arrived in Japan in late June '49 and was assigned straight to F Company, 2nd Battalion 7th Cavalry. Mostly the time there in Japan was boring.
I remember all the additional duties, things that every lieutenant does,
inventorying the exchange, inventorying the medical supplies . . . . One

time I remember taking my platoon up to the Bank of Japan and guarding I don't know how many tons of gold."

For all that, Potts does note that there was periodic training.

"We had some training. Just after I arrived we went to Camp McNair up on the slopes of [Mount] Fuji. Because I had some demolitions training, I got pulled from my platoon and they made me the range officer to take care of unexploded rounds and charges and the like. I didn't train with my platoon at all in that time."[42]

On the enlisted side, John De Borde started the war as a private first class. A mortarman in G Company, De Borde rarely had the chance to actually shoot his assigned weapon with the exception of the times that the battalion deployed to the training area in the vicinity of Mount Fuji. He recalls his training like this: "Captain Hank West, [notably, one of the few combat experienced officers in the battalion at the time] our CO, about three times a week, he would take us out. We would run out to this island. It wasn't an island really, but that's what we called it, more of a peninsula really attached to the mainland. Anyway, we trained out there, you know, squad, platoon tactics. When we went to Korea, G Company out of that battalion was probably in the best shape of any of them. That island was about five miles away. I was in mortars. To train, we would set up and basically practice the fire commands and details about the mortars. We had the 60-mm mortars. I can remember twice we went up to Mount Fuji; that was where you could train with ammo. You couldn't shoot ammo on that little island."[43]

Marvin Daniel was a private in E Company in 1950. He remembers the same spit of land but not quite in the same way. "When we got to Japan we didn't do a whole lot of intense training. We had this island we'd go out to; it wasn't like war games or anything. It seems like one time I fired a rocket, and it was a blank. We'd stroll out, or march, or whatever you want to call it. The most intense training that I recall, we were going through a procedure of loading airplanes. We would practice getting on them and tying everything down and all. We got in our trucks and went down to the airfield, and then a heavy rainstorm came and they called the whole thing off. It was rained out."[44]

"Snuffy" Gray recalls training as even less intensive. With the battalion throughout most of the years of the occupation, he was therefore present at the lowest points. He remembers, "We didn't have meaningful training in those days. There was no one to train with and nowhere to train, right? We'd put all but a few of the vehicles, the ones we were using, up on blocks. We'd go into the arms rooms and swipe at, I mean we'd clean, the

M1s that were there, and we'd wipe down the mortars, but nothing in all that much detail, y'know?"[45]

All of these men recall their training well. They remember feeling that they knew their jobs as best they could, and they remember the endless repetitions of certain training events. But none of them remember training to any significant degree above the platoon level. In a few instances, men of some of the companies recall establishing a stationary "company defense" during a training event at Mount Fuji in the year before the unit deployed to combat. This, however, was a static event. The men settled into their perimeters and dug their fighting positions. They established interlocking fires in a notional sense with the units to their left and their right, but they did not "fight." No force-on-force training occurred, and no ammunition supported such an event beyond the lowest levels. In the end, while individuals may have become proficient at their skills as riflemen, the crucial training required for movement and coordination, the training that creates competent officers and noncommissioned officers, and competent larger units, was sorely missing.

Combined arms training, the training of multiple branches of the army such as infantry with artillery or artillery with armor, was nonexistent for the U.S. troops in Japan. Alan Brister was a second lieutenant who experienced firsthand the field artillery training while in Japan in the 1st Cavalry Division. After enlisting in the army in 1944, he served four years as a soldier before he went to Officer Candidate School in 1948. When he arrived in Japan as a new lieutenant in September of 1949, he went to the 77th Field Artillery Battalion, one of the three artillery battalions of the 1st Cavalry Division, at Camp Drew in Koizumi, Japan. (At the time all of the artillery battalions had only two of their authorized three batteries.) Brister would later serve as an artillery forward observer (FO) with the 7th Cavalry. He recalls, "Each firing battery has three FOs. The idea being that each battery sends one of its FOs to the rifle companies of the battalion being supported. A Battery sends their FOs to the first battalion of the infantry regiment, B Battery sends theirs to the second battalion, and so on. You have a quarter-ton [jeep] with a quarter-ton trailer, a staff sergeant—his title was recon sergeant—then you have a radio operator and a driver. So you have one officer and three enlisted men. We used the SCR–300 radio, and we also had these walkie-talkies, but they were all but useless. You would dismount the radio from the vehicle, put the battery pack on it, and you'd carry it on a backpack frame. My calls for fire would go to the field artillery battalion fire direction center [FDC]. Unless that FDC was overloaded, they would handle that mission. You had two frequencies you worked on: the command frequency and the fire direction center frequency. The regimental heavy mortars had their own FOs; they were sergeants from that company. I didn't get involved in firing the 81s and the 60s.

"As far as training goes, well, there was only one area in Japan, on the main island, where you could do live fire with artillery. The result was that that range was very much in demand, and you didn't get much time on it. I think we made maybe two trips for training to Fuji. It was strictly artillery training; we never worked with the infantry at all."[46]

The ubiquitous football program also had an impact on training. In the summer of 1949, the interdivision competition was scrapped in favor of an increased emphasis on competition inside the regiments. Once again, those officers who were former army football players found themselves suiting up in pads and helmets with full football squads rather than leading rifle squads in training. Lieutenant (later captain) William West of the 8th Cavalry recalls: "That August when I was called down to headquarters to be the head coach of the 8th Cavalry team, they had done away with the division-level teams. Fuson was the coach of the 7th Cavalry team. I remember one night that Ug came by my room with two of his other lieutenants and said, 'Now take it easy on us, Woo-woo.' They were teasing me because they had inherited the division champion team from the last year. Fuson said to make it fair, he himself would not 'suit up' for the game. He knew I wouldn't suit up because medically I wasn't supposed to be playing football. Then when the game comes who's leading them onto the field but Ug Fuson. I had had some head injuries at the academy and so I wasn't supposed to play. I told my men what the first three plays Fuson would run would be, and that's what they were, right on schedule, and even with that warning, the 7th got the first touchdown anyway. Anyway, I told my guys to go get my uniform from the barracks and I suited up. It was a tough game but we won, 14–7."

West recalls how football affected his military career: "At the end of the season, the new division commander, Major General Gay, came to the division championship and sat on my team's bench. My team won, and there was a big party that night to celebrate. I was sitting at the head table next to General Gay, and we talked a lot that night. The next day my battalion commander called and said, 'Bill, General Gay wants you to come and be his aide.' So that's how I became his aide in January 1950; I was with him through the whole war."[47]

A final observation on the nature of the 2nd Battalion 7th Cavalry deals with the complex issues of combat unit effectiveness, the idea of unit cohesion, and the role of leadership in both of those.

Simply stated, numerous military historians and military sociologists believe that the combat effectiveness of a military unit is often directly related to the cohesion of that unit.[48] The specifics of this term will be explored in more depth at a later point, so suffice it to say now that "cohesion" is a somewhat tricky term. While implying a unit that "sticks together," this explanation of cohesion within the context of a military unit is not nearly complete. A host of factors goes into this idea of cohesion, and some, such as a sense of unit identity, were present in the 2nd Battalion 7th Cavalry at the time. Others, such as a shared history of rigorous unit combat training, were not. One of the most important factors—the role of stable leadership—is even more intangible.

The role of leaders is important, psychologically, for the men in a unit. Good leaders, be they officers or enlisted men, can help a unit overcome great obstacles. Good leaders engender a sort of synergy within their units so that the abilities of the whole is greater than the abilities of the sum of the men within the units. It is an ideal, a tough one to attain in peacetime. It requires motivated leaders and must be accompanied by difficult unit training. As was mentioned, little to no large-unit training was conducted by the battalion prior to the war. But possibly more important than that, there was no stability within the leadership.

John Lippincott, the second platoon leader in F company of the 2nd Battalion 7th Cavalry, remembers, "I know that in my company we were pretty well staffed on officers. In F Company, we lacked an exec (executive officer) and the fourth platoon leader. I would say that each company was about the same, about four officers. Before we left, battalion did not have an S-2. We had a major as the S-3 and a first lieutenant as the adjutant (S-1). The F company commander we had when we went into combat was Captain Walter Hopkins, but we had several before that. When I first got there, the company commander was a first lieutenant, Loren Dubois. He rotated out, and we had Captain Andrews. He was selected to command MacArthur's Honor Guard, so then we got Captain Birch. He commanded, what, four months. Then he rotated out right before the war broke out. We got Hopkins. I think he came in as a normal rotation officer from the states. So what was that, four commanders in seven months?"[49]

Such was the status of the majority of the 2nd Battalion of the 7th Cavalry when news of the North Korean invasion arrived in Japan.

CHAPTER 3

A Distant Thunder

The Ambassador in Korea (Muccio) to the Secretary of State
CONFIDENTIAL   NIACT
SEOUL, June 25, 1950 - 10 A.M.
[Received June 24 - 9:26 P.M.]
  According to Korean Army reports which partly confirmed by KMAG field advisor reports, North Korean forces invaded ROK territory at several points this morning. Action was initiated about 4 A.M. Ongjin blasted by North Korean artillery fire. About 6 A.M. North Korean infantry commenced crossing parallel in Ongjin area, Kaesong area, Chunchon area and amphibious landing was reportedly made south of Kangnung on east coast. Kaesong was reportedly captured by 9 A.M., with some 10 North Korean tanks participating in operation. North Korean forces, spearheaded by tanks, reportedly closing in on Chunchon. Details of fighting in Kangnung area unclear, although it seems that North Korean forces have cut highway. Am conferring with KMAG advisors and Korean officials this morning re situation.
  It would appear from nature of attack and manner in which it was launched that it constitutes an all out offensive against ROK.

MUCCIO[1]

THE TWENTY-FIFTH OF JUNE 1950 WAS OVERCAST AND RAINY IN THE AREA north of Seoul. Along the main invasion corridor heading into the city from the thirty-eighth parallel, the soldiers of the Republic of Korea (ROK) 1st Division were largely under some form of cover from the rain, when a different sort of rain began to fall. These South Korean troops heard the first booming echoes as whole battalions of North Korean People's Army (NKPA) artillery fired the first salvos of the Korean War. Because sound travels generally in straight lines, they most likely heard the howitzers before the first of the shells came down in and around their positions along the thirty-eighth parallel. The first elements of North Korean infantry followed

45

closely behind their artillery support. What Americans and most of the world would come to know as the Korean War had just begun.

The ROK army was, in 1950, woefully unprepared to meet the onslaught of the NKPA. Technically the South Korean army had only existed since the formal declaration of statehood in 1948, a little more than eighteen months earlier. With its American benefactors reluctant to provide additional equipment, the South Korean army's strength was capped in terms of manpower at a mere 65,000. (Add in the national police, and this number increases a degree, but only in infantry strength.)

Assisted in understanding their U.S.-supplied equipment by only a smattering of American technical advisors, the army of South Korea was barely beyond the level of a police force when forced to confront the NKPA. The ROK army did not have any artillery beyond a thin veneer of units equipped with the 105-mm howitzer. Its soldiers had no 155-mm howitzers, no tanks of their own, only a few antiaircraft weapons, and no anti-tank weapons, making them desperately short on firepower when compared to the average modern combined-arms division.

Despite the beginnings of a professional officer corps (the South Korean military academy had just graduated its first batch of officers), the ROK army lacked leaders prepared for combined-arms warfare. The army's work against guerillas, especially in the preceding twelve months, had prepared its soldiers for that sort of conflict, but guerillas don't have tanks and close air support.

In short, the South Korean army in the summer of 1950 was in a sorry state to repel a conventional invasion by a modern combined-arms force. By design, South Korea was not given significant amounts of weaponry—not because it was unavailable, the United States had surpluses by the ton—but because it was feared that Syngman Rhee would invade North Korea if supplied with enough equipment to do so.

Some historians argue that rather than a war between states, the Korean War was a civil war between different parts of the same nation. While there is a certain simple appeal in this approach to understanding the war, it neglects the very real role of the external actors in both the North and the South. In the end, it comes down to a question of "How long must a state exist before it is a nation?"

Those who argue that this was a civil war believe the United States actually increased the suffering because its intervention changed what would have been the "natural" course of events (a North Korean victory, one presumes). Yet these historians ignore the fact that the United States had done what it could to prevent such a war by not providing its ally with offensive weapons. Such was not the case in the North. As is now known from the recently opened archives of the former Soviet Union, not only did the Soviets supply the North Koreans with offensive weapons, they also trained them on how to use them and stayed with them right up until the moment of contact.[2] Without this external aid, this "civil war" would never have flared into the war of aggression that it became in June 1950.[3]

Unlike the South Korean army, the NKPA had some of the most modern equipment then available. Its artillery, mortars, tanks, and aircraft came from the factories of the Soviet Union. Purchased or given as gifts, these weapons gave the North the combined arms capability that was lacking in the South. The shells that the NKPA hurled at the ROK army came in several calibers supplied by the Soviets: Medium weight 76-mm and 122-mm shells from towed and self-propelled howitzers and mortar rounds ranging from 61 mm up to 120 mm. To reply to this steel rain, the South Koreans had a grand total of ninety-one U.S. Army surplus 105-mm howitzers, along with 60-mm and 81-mm infantry support mortars. Outgunned from the beginning, the South Koreans had little chance in the counter-battery contest.[4]

In the air, a one-sided fight also ensued. The South Koreans had no air force worthy of the name when the first of North Korea's World War II-surplus YAK fighters swooped down across their airfields. The YAK fighter had been one of the designs the Soviets had used to break the back of the Germans in the Second World War. First flown in the spring of 1943, the YAK was a formidable fighter aircraft in the summer of 1950.

The YAK fighters were among the best piston-driven fighter airplanes in the world at the time. With one 20-mm cannon firing through the spinner of the propeller as well as two 12.7-mm machine guns mounted on the centerline above the engine, the machine had a considerable punch. With a top speed of just over 400 miles per hour, the YAK's combat radius (the distance you can go out and get back to your base) of more than 500 miles ensured that these fighters could range across almost the entire peninsula with ease. Their presence in those opening hours of the war demonstrated beyond any doubt that this was an operation backed by the Soviets.[5]

In contrast, the Republic of Korea had twelve L-4 and L-5 light observation planes and six T-6 training planes they had recently purchased from Canada. This was not exactly a balanced equation.[6]

It was on the ground, however, that the heaviest punch came. Artillery is one method, aircraft another, of inflicting punishment upon the opposition through the use of high explosives. But to take ground means moving across that ground, and the ultimate purveyor of power on the ground is the tank. In those desperate opening hours of the war, only the NKPA had tanks in Korea, and they were among the best tanks in the world at that time.

The Soviets had supplied North Korea with just under 200 tanks prior to the start of the Korean War.[7] The most common type provided, the famous T-34 tank that had beaten the Germans, was no longer a "cutting edge" design by 1950. But its basic weapon system had been so well engineered when first created, the tank still stood up well when compared to just about any other tank available to the American allies. Moreover, since the Russians built more than 35,000 of the tanks during the war, they were not particularly stingy about supplying them to their allies.

A number of innovations went into the original T-34s. First, and perhaps most significantly, was the introduction of sloped armor. Although a common feature now, at the time this was an innovation. The sloped armor provides an increased chance that rounds impacting the armor will ricochet rather then penetrate it. The Russians thus increased the "apparent thickness" of the armor to a shot taken from ground level.

The second innovation, an adaptation really, was in the suspension of the tank. Although originally an American design, the Russian suspension on the T-34s the North Koreans used was actually two design generations removed from the Christie suspension of the 1930s that the Soviets first copied from an American design. Regardless of the origins of the system, the fact is that the suspension of the T-34 made it a highly mobile and fast vehicle. The 500-horsepower diesel engine, coupled with a set of extremely wide tracks (a design feature created with the mud of the Russian steppes in mind), gave this tank a maximum road speed of more than thirty miles per hour. All together, not only could this weapon system pack a serious punch with its 76-mm high-velocity cannon, the T-34 could get that cannon where it was needed across just about any sort of terrain.

Relatively light, the T-34 was considered a medium tank. To an infantryman on the ground, however, a tank of any size is a formidable threat. Against this weapon, the ROK army had exactly zero American-supplied tanks and, for all intents and purposes, no other effective antiarmor weapons.

The NKPA launched its combined arms attack soon after the initial bombardments. Some revisionist historians argue that this attack was not intended as a full-scale invasion designed to unify the nation. Regardless of it intent, military reality makes it impossible to coordinate a spontaneous attack by multiple divisions of troops across a 150-mile-wide front without months and months of planning. Attacks across that sort of frontage do not "spread" from a limited area (such as the Ongjin peninsula) spontaneously, and only a neophyte unfamiliar with the realities of the military logistics required to support a broad front offensive would suggest otherwise. What fell on the ROK army on June 25 was a large coordinated and well-supplied assault.[8]

Ten NKPA divisions, as well as several independent brigades, took part in or supported the attack.[9] Arrayed against this were four of the eight ROK divisions—the 1st, 6th, 7th, and 8th—as well as the 17th Regiment, which was stationed on the exposed Ongjin peninsula at the outset of hostilities.[10] Of the other four divisions, the ROK Capital Division was based in Seoul, while the 2nd, 3rd, and 5th Divisions were deployed throughout southcentral Korea to continue operations against the strongholds of communist guerillas in the mountains of South Korea. The 2nd Division, in Taejon, had been specifically aiming to reduce the grip of the civilian-based guerillas in the area between Yongdong and Kumchon, that is to say the area around No Gun Ri, until the North Korean attack caused them to redeploy northwards.

Given this disparity in forces, it is little wonder that the war began so disastrously for the ROK army. Within hours, the NKPA had major gains all across the front even though individual units, in particular the ROK 1st Division, managed to hold the line far longer than might reasonably have been expected. However, as the units on their flanks were destroyed or forced to retreat, those that held out, managing the best defenses, became victims of their own success when they were surrounded by enveloping NKPA forces.

The ROK 1st Division was practically destroyed when the line of retreat it might have followed in an organized manner was closed by the North Koreans. Although the ROK 1st Division was pressed hard by the NKPA 6th Division in its defensive positions at Kaesong (roughly thirty-five miles northwest of Seoul), it held on. To its east, along the direct north-south route to Seoul, was the 7th ROK Division. This unit was initially pushed back, but was pulling itself together for a counterattack on the twenty-sixth of June. To do so, the 7th ROK collected all its forces together, assuming that a reinforcing division (the 2nd ROK, coming up by rail and road from Taejon) would fill the void it left to the east. This was a poor assumption, or at least an ill-timed action, as the NKPA 3rd Division got there first, and the 7th Division found itself cut off from the capital when the NKPA swept south, almost unopposed, to the city of Uijongbu.

The 7th ROK Division, which had made gains in its northward counterattack, found itself overextended. Now deeper into the noose, and with the reinforcements it had been counting upon gone, the division was forced to abandon what little heavy equipment it had and escape cross-country to the west and hopefully move south from there. The beleaguered

ROK 1st Division now faced a defense of Munsan, along the Imjin River, against potential attacks from three directions. If the division failed, the prospect was a fighting withdrawal to the south, capped by a major river crossing.

In the opening days of the Korean War, the ability of news reporters to get to the front was limited only by their ability to hitch rides and get access to the relatively few means of communications on the peninsula. Those reporters who got to Korea in the first days and weeks of the war had absolutely no restrictions imposed upon where they went, what they saw, or how they reported what they witnessed. With no censorship in place at the time, stories in such newspapers as *The New York Times,* the *New York Herald Tribune,*and *The Washington Post* and such news magazines as *Time* and *Life* reflect the utter horror of combat that some reporters experienced. Censorship, such as it was, was self-imposed, and in the first days of the conflict, this was done with a fairly light touch.

The first four American reporters to reach Korea landed at Kimpo airfield on the south bank of the Han River, a short distance to the west of Seoul, on the afternoon of June 27. These reporters—Frank Gibney from *Time,* Burton Crane of *The New York Times,* Marguerite Higgins of the *New York Herald Tribune,* and Keyes Beech of the *Chicago Daily News*—arrived in Seoul just ahead of the North Koreans. What they found was a scene of chaos. The U.S. Korean Military Advisory Group (KMAG) was in the midst of a change in leadership, and the head of the KMAG had been vacationing in Japan at the time of the North Korean attack. The main body of the KMAG advisors was attempting to reoccupy its headquarters in Seoul, which it had earlier abandoned based upon the many confusing and, in some cases, conflicting reports flowing from what passed for a front in the first days. The situation maps in KMAG headquarters showed multiple conflicting reports on the locations and status of the ROK forces and very little reliable information on the NKPA.

Beech, a U.S. Marine Corps veteran of the battle for Iwo Jima, was especially well qualified to describe the confusion he found. The other reporters, perhaps most notably the pioneering woman reporter Higgins, were also veteran correspondents who had experienced the normal chaos that even successful military situations present to the untutored eye. (Higgins had actually arrived inside the compound of the Nazi concentration camp at Dachau, outside Munich, Germany, ahead of Allied troops. Despite the accidental nature of her advanced position there, one could hardly doubt her credentials to serve as a combat correspondent from that point forward.) By nightfall on the twenty-seventh, all four reporters were inside Seoul. Higgins had been separated from the other three when she was ordered to accompany the KMAG senior advisor Colonel Sterling Wright, while the others stayed with his subordinate, Major Walter Greenwood.

Greenwood's comments to Beech are the best evidence that the United States, in general, and the KMAG in particular, did not expect a North Korean invasion, despite postwar accounts and revisions to the contrary. Greenwood's version of events of the first two days of the war illustrate this point as the KMAG officers took no special precautions to evacuate their own families from the city, which was less then forty miles from the area of potential North Korean attack. Right up until the actual attack, these American military advisers apparently did not have the slightest clue of the impending threat to their wives and children.

Greenwood explained to Beech: "I told my wife it was nothing to worry about. I had breakfast as usual and went down to the office. Mary Logan [his wife] wanted to know if I'd be home for lunch. She and Sally— Sally is eight—and I were going out to take pictures that afternoon. It wasn't until eight-thirty Sunday morning that we knew it was a full-scale invasion. By daylight Monday morning Mary Logan and Sally were on a fertilizer ship, with all the other women and children, bound for Japan . . . . Altogether we put 682 women and kids aboard a freighter that had accommodations for ten or twelve passengers."[11]

At some point late on the night of June 27, the KMAG phone network flashed the news to all KMAG members: the South Korean defensive line had not held; the North Koreans were in the city—evacuate immediately.

With no time for a planned or organized movement, most members of the KMAG headquarters managed to get into one of two columns, but these took time to organize. The group of three who that had been staying with Major Greenwood had the best chance at escape over the Han River bridge in a jeep Greenwood gave them when the news arrived in the middle of the night. Instead, they headed for ROK headquarters to try and assess the situation. It was a near-fatal decision. At headquarters, they ran into another KMAG staff officer, Major George Sedberry, who confirmed the impending loss of Seoul and recommended that they leave immediately for the city of Suwon, twenty miles to the south.

Because of their delay, the reporters got caught in the middle of the Han River bridge, just short of the span that was, unknown to them, packed with demolitions. It was now roughly sixty-eight hours after the beginning of the North Korean attack. Beech, Crane, and Gibney were stuck in immobile traffic in the middle of the bridge. Packed in between refugees on foot, civilian and army trucks, oxcarts, and a host of bicycles, they probably could have made it across faster if they had been walking.[12]

At quarter after two on the morning of June 28, 1950, the ROK army blew up the Han River bridge and abandoned Seoul to the North Koreans.[13]

Gibney and Crane were both badly wounded by the shattered windshield glass that was blasted into their jeep by the explosion just in front of them. Beech managed to get both his injured fellow journalists out of the jeep and off the bridge. A few miles away, Higgins, with a column of about sixty KMAG vehicles still in the city, saw and heard the blast as well. The reaction of the chief of KMAG was unequivocal; he roundly condemned the ROK for blowing up the bridge with its own troops still on the north side of the river and most of the city still in its hands.[14] How many people were killed by the detonation can only be estimated, but one thing seems sure, it was done far too early from both humanitarian and military points of view. Trapped on the north side of the bridge with the river to their backs were elements of two ROK infantry divisions.

In Japan, there was initially little indication that Sunday, June 25, 1950, was different from any other Sunday. The first man to get the word on Korea was one of the members of that 1949 division championship 8th Cavalry football team, a young West Point graduate on duty at MacArthur's headquarters in the Dai Ichi building in downtown Tokyo, a lieutenant named Alexander Haig.

"I was MacArthur's duty officer that day, not the headquarters you understand, but MacArthur's personal duty officer. He had a separate headquarters up at SCAP [Supreme Commander Allied Powers]. Anyway, the call came from Ambassador Muccio to MacArthur, and I took that call and passed it on to General Almond. I was a first lieutenant, and I was aide to the chief of staff to MacArthur, General Ned Almond. I remember it was just before noon when the operator called. I answered the phone, and she said that the ambassador to Korea is on the phone, so I took the call. Ambassador Muccio gets on the phone, and he made it very clear to me that this was not a false alarm, that there were massive tank formations coming down the Uijombu corridor and another coming down the coast. I said, 'I'll get this word to General MacArthur and the chief of staff immediately,' which I did."[15]

In the American army of 1950, Sundays were the one and only true day of rest. The soldiers normally worked all week and cleaned their barracks and equipment on Saturday for the traditional weekly inspection. Only after this noontime ritual might they take off and spend the next thirty-six hours or so as they saw fit. Unless on a special pass with permission to head out into the countryside, most of the men of the 2nd Battalion 7th Cavalry spent their days off in and around Tokyo.

Private Marvin Daniel was typical in this regard. The young man from a small town in Virginia spent most of his time off in town. On June 24, his company commander, Captain Milam, released the company after the customary Saturday inspection, and on Sunday morning, June 25, Private Daniel was, as were many of his peers, enjoying a lazy walkabout. He had heard nothing back at the barracks to indicate that this day would be different, nothing that might foreshadow the great changes about to take place in his life. News of the war came to him with the sound of bells.

"I first heard about the war when I was wandering around downtown [Tokyo]," Daniel relates. "The newsboys carried these tiny little brass bells with them. When there was an Extra [edition] or some major news story, they would ring these little bells. You'd hear them all over. That's how I first heard about the start of the war."[16]

Don Donnelly of the I/R platoon was downtown that morning, too. He remembers it this way: "I was in this soda fountain-like place, it was run by the army, and you could use chits there to buy things like this awful ice cream, a bunch of dehydrated stuff that they tried to fix up. Anyway, word came out, and this was on a Sunday, and somebody says, 'North Korea invaded South Korea,' and we said, 'Where's Korea?' We had absolutely no idea where this place was, or what it was. I don't remember if it was that Monday or if it was later, but the thing that made us worry was when they had this mandatory muster. That meant they called out everyone, everywhere. No matter what sort of detail you were on, you reported to your main unit. That's when they started calling out names. Our sergeant was one. They called him, and he got his bags and left. Never saw him again."[17]

Unlike Donnelly and Daniel, some soldiers were in training that morning. Johnny Theodore was the younger brother of a combat infantryman of the Second World War. Raised in Grand Rapids, Michigan, Theodore stood five feet eight inches tall and weighed 127 pounds in 1950. He knew something of what he was getting into because, unlike many of his peers, his older brother had seen extensive combat with the 101st Airborne Division in World War II. Although Theodore had absolutely no technical training prior to joining the army, it appears that for once the Army personnel system managed to fit a round peg into a round hole. Theodore, who tested extremely high on a technical aptitude exam during his initial training, was assigned to become a radioman. On June 25, 1950, he was at one of the technical schools the army runs to teach special skills. This one was located well to the south of Tokyo.

Theodore recalls that the announcement of war was somewhat blasé: "I was in radio repair school there in Japan. It was a long way away from

Tokyo, and except for the time we went training up on Mount Fuji, it was the only time I left Tokyo. We were all in a classroom . . . a lab or something like that, with radio parts spread out over the tables when somebody came into the room and announced that the North Koreans had invaded South Korea. I remember that my first thought was, 'So what?' It just never entered my mind that this had anything to do with me. I was just a few days from going home, back to McKnight Barracks that is."[18]

Other soldiers were also working to improve themselves that afternoon. Jim Kerns was nineteen with his twentieth birthday just a little more than a month away. He was born and raised some twelve miles from where he lives today. For him, the Korean war was an interlude. Both of his older brothers had served in the navy, so he did not have a solid grasp of what he was in for in the army. His father, however, did have some words of advice when he first joined: "My dad was in the First World War, in the infantry. He'd lost a part of his hand in France. He never really talked about it; all he ever said was, 'Don't go in the army.'"

It was advice that the younger Kerns did not follow, and so he found himself in Japan in 1949. By the spring of 1950, Kerns was trying to make the best use of his time off by attending classes offered by the University of Maryland as an extension course. Classes could only be offered during the limited time that the soldiers were guaranteed to be off duty, and that meant Sundays.

"I was in class that day. It was a history class, and I was sitting in the center of the room when this captain comes in and tells us, 'Gentlemen, return to your units immediately. All classes are cancelled.' Somebody asked him why, and he said that North Korea had invaded South Korea. I'm not sure but I think this was at around, maybe, eleven o'clock."[19]

Russ McKinley was a private in the weapons platoon of G Company, where he was a mortarman. In the spring of 1950, he could be described as nothing short of the icon of an American midwestern boy. Blond headed with blue eyes, he stood just half an inch short of six feet tall and weighed in at a taut 160 pounds. On June 25, McKinley was doing his normal routine of Sunday mornings taking it easy in the barracks. "I was in a dayroom somewhere in the barracks, just shooting pool, when Sergeant Secrist came in and said that North Korea just invaded South Korea and I said, 'Where in the hell is that?'"[20]

Norman Matthias learned about the start of a war that would change his life in a similar manner. Although he had started out in G Company upon arriving in Japan, by the spring of 1950 he had moved over to the ammunition and pioneer (A&P) platoon. In addition to bringing the ammunition forward to the front in a battle, this platoon does most of the engineering work in an infantry battalion. In that role, Matthias worked for the battalion, although his platoon was part of the headquarters company. Matthias recalls, "I was on a guard, walking post on guard duty at McKnight Barracks, when a guy walked up and said, 'The Reds have invaded Korea,' and I said, I don't know if I said it out loud or what, 'What the hell do the Russians want with Korea?' I think the guy said something like, 'Nah, it's the North Koreans.' I really didn't know where Korea was exactly, and I sure didn't know that there was any sort of problem over there before this."[21]

All over Japan, the soldiers of the American Far East Command learned the news, yet few outside of the privileged circle of MacArthur's command group understood what this would soon mean to them.

Within days, it was blindingly obvious to even the most militarily obtuse observer that the armed forces of South Korea did not stand a chance of holding their own against the onslaught of the modern forces of the North Korean People's Army. Without significant artillery resources, an air force, or even antitank weapons that could stop the T-34 tank, the infantry of the South Korean army could do little but reel back to successive defensive positions. The collapse came quicker in some places than it did in others. MacArthur himself made a trip to the peninsula, stopping in Suwon on the twenty-ninth of June, to examine the state of affairs and attempt to get some first-hand information on the situation. What he found was grim. Despite the commitment of U.S. Air Force fighters and medium bombers, North Korea still had too much combat power for the shattered ROK army to hold. As early as June 27, American air and sea assets were committed to the South Koreans, but MacArthur's trip confirmed that to hold South Korea America had to commit soldiers on the ground. At the time, only 8,000 ROK soldiers could be fully accounted for, although estimates by June 30 centered on as many as 25,000. MacArthur had already been confirmed as the commander, and the day before, an advanced command (ADCOM) group arrived at Suwon to set up operations. MacArthur's visit was brief. He surveyed the scene, met with some of the journalists who had earlier escaped Seoul, and returned to his headquarters in Japan. At 0457 (Eastern time) on the thirtieth of June, President Truman authorized General MacArthur to commit one regiment to combat and further stated that he would make a decision on two full divisions later that afternoon.[22]

The first American ground forces committed to Korea (their story is well covered elsewhere and so will not be dealt with in any great depth here) were alerted and ordered to move to Korea almost immediately on June 30.[23] The understrength, battalion-sized task force, which was commanded by Lieutenant Colonel Bradley Smith, consisted of troops from the

1st Battalion 21st Infantry Regiment of the 24th Infantry Division. Smith had just two rifle companies (B and C), some headquarters and communications soldiers, a platoon of 75-mm recoilless rifles and some 4.2-inch mortars (only two of each were actually brought along), and an initial force of just over 400 men.[24] Smith's force arrived in the southern Korean city of Pusan on July 1 and by the next day was in the general vicinity of Osan, roughly twenty miles south of Seoul.[25] They would not be emplaced in their final position until three in the morning on the fifth of July.

While defending P'yongt'aek on July 3, the men of Task Force (TF) Smith witnessed just how dangerous uncontrolled airpower really was, to friend as well as foe. A flight of F-51s from the Royal Australian Air Force's No. 77 Squadron banked over and made multiple strafing runs against a South Korean ammunition train that had pulled into town. The men of TF Smith could do nothing about it. The entire area had only one radio set that could contact planes in flight and one man qualified to use it. The accuracy of the RAAF's shooting had disastrous results. Not only were the train and its load of ammunition destroyed, but the pilots continued their strafing runs, killing or wounding several residents.[26]

The Australian air force did not run wild through the skies alone. From the very outset, the U.S. Air Force also demonstrated little understanding of the situation on the ground, and little ability to get it right. The USAF's disdain for the close air support mission shone through in the allocation of assets it sent forward with the original ADCOM party sent into Suwon on June 28. Among those who landed and established a headquarters for Allied command in South Korea was a USAF lieutenant colonel named John McGinn. To form a tactical air control party (TACP) that would control and direct aircraft for the entire Korean peninsula, McGinn had with him a total of two jeeps equipped with VHF equipment instead of a complete air-ground coordination team with the ability to bring in accurate fires from aircraft across the front. To his credit, Lieutenant Colonel McGinn apparently did a yeoman's job on his first two days on the ground. In addition to establishing a temporary ground control station for Allied aircraft at Suwon, he took it upon himself to find the ADCOM headquarters and determine what targets might be in the general range of his radios. (McGinn's radios, which were insufficient to reach back to Japan, could only be used to talk to aircraft already in flight and somewhere in the general vicinity.) Over the next several hours, he did his best to direct the fighters as they approached the area, hoping to guide them on to the enemy over ground that he could not see himself and thus avoid allied troops that he had never actually seen.[27] But at least McGinn was there, and he was trying. The near criminal negligence was that he was the only one on the whole peninsula equipped or trained to perform this mission.

This situation was only a symptom of a larger problem with close air support in Korea, especially in the beginning phases of the war. Much more of the problem had to do with decisions made at the highest echelons of the USAF, decisions about the proper use of aircraft and the aircraft designs themselves.

On May 31, 1950, the U.S. Far East Air Force (FEAF) had a total of 1,172 planes on the books. Some of these were in storage, while others were what is generally known as hanger queens. Only 553 of these aircraft were in the hands of operational units. This included 365 of the oldest USAF jet fighter, the F-80 *Shooting Star*, 32 of the newer F-82s, and 25 of the reconnaissance variant of the *Shooting Star*, the RF-80. Another twenty-six aircraft were the World War II veteran B-26s, the *Marauder* medium bomber. The remaining aircraft were either heavy bombers, such as the B-29, or transport aircraft, such as the C-54. Unfortunately, this force structure included no aircraft designed for, or suited to, close air support of troops on the ground, although an argument could be made for the twenty-six B-26 *Marauder* aircraft.[28]

FEAF's most numerous combat aircraft, the F-80, was designed exclusively for air-to-air combat. Each was armed with six .50-caliber machine guns and had wing ports for rockets, but none for bombs. With its internal fuel tanks, the plane had a range of one hundred miles, just enough fuel, if operating from Japan, to get to the southern tip of Korea and turn around. (Two 165-gallon external drop tanks on the wing tips would later be added to give the plane a range of 225 miles.[29]) These plane ranges were calculated assuming high-altitude and therefore fuel-efficient flights, not low-level ground-support missions.

On top of the inadequate, inappropriate airframe for the close air support mission was the lack of training among the pilots. Most had never fired rockets in training, at best using only subcaliber simulations. The sole unit trained to conduct ground coordination for USAF aircraft attacking in close proximity to friendly troops was the 620th Aircraft Control and Warning Squadron. This squadron had only conducted limited training with U.S. Army troops in Japan in the months and years preceding the war. This training centered on using ad hoc teams to form temporary tactical air control parties and playing out canned scenarios in what might more accurately be described as a capabilities demonstration and not true joint training. While partially a function of the nature of training in Japan, the lack of priority assigned to the close air support mission by the USAF leaders in Japan and the air force overall is brought home by the fact that the F-51, the old "Mustang" of World War II, was retired without a suitable replacement.[30]

As far as USAF pilots were concerned in the opening days of the war, if it was on the ground and it was in Korea, then it was a target. The courage of the pilots, who proved willing time after time to press home dangerous attacks against the North Koreans, was not in question. They were flying blind as the inevitable result of the USAF leaders' reluctance to assign pilots to the unglamorous but absolutely necessary role of ground coordinators for close air support missions. (These attacks put the pilot close to the ground when he is placing munitions near friendly troops as opposed to flying at higher altitudes deep behind enemy lines.) Many Allied soldiers, not to mention thousands of civilians, would pay the price for these air force leaders' reluctance to use ground coordinators. In 1950, The USAF believed that deep attacks were the solution to all situations on the ground. (Deep attacks, taking place well behind enemy lines, do not require an air force liaison on the ground to radio to the pilots so that friendly troops are not attacked. They are also often safer for the pilots.) Task Force Smith, like many of the U.S. forces early in the war, did not have any USAF liaison.[31]

If Lieutenant Colonel McGinn had been on the ground somewhere in that area, or if a tactical air control party had been available to TF Smith, the Australian attack might not have happened. Unfortunately, when the ADCOM pulled out of Suwon on the evening of June 30 for a safer location to the south, Lieutenant Colonel McGinn went with them, taking his valuable radios.[32] Gone were the only radios in South Korea that could direct attacking Allied aircraft, and with no radio communication, more attacks occurred against South Korean soldiers and civilians well behind friendly lines.[33]

The Australian attack was not the only case of "friendly fire" from the air observed on July 3. Farther to the north, American fighters also attacked Suwon, roughly sixteen miles south of Seoul, firing on ROK soldiers. The ROKs had no antiaircraft weapons, but managed to damage one plane badly enough with massed rifle fire that the pilot had to land nearby at the now-abandoned Suwon airfield. Upon landing, he was met by an American advisor to the ROK army and ROK officers, none of whom were pleased about the attack on their own troops. One American officer in Suwon reported at least five Allied air attacks against friendly troops, just on July 3. He wrote to a friend later, "The fly boys really had a field day! They hit friendly ammo dumps, gas dumps, the Suwon air strip, trains, motor

columns, and KA Hq [Korean Army headquarters]." On the highway leading into Suwon, USAF fighters attacked friendly troops again, strafing
thirty South Korean trucks. An estimated 200 ROK soldiers were killed by
friendly fire. The number of civilian casualties attributed to the lack of
USAF ground liaisons has never been calculated for this area.[34]

Meanwhile, in Japan, things were moving as well.

At 0230 hours on June 27, the officer on watch at the 1st Cavalry
Division headquarters entered an unusual order into the log: Eighth Army
headquarters had asked the 1st Cavalry to supply 732 enlisted men and 15
officers to the 24th Infantry Division.[35] The timing and the scope of the
transfer made this request unusual. Despite the protests of some wartime
leaders in postwar accounts, this request showed that the Far East command
was indeed caught by surprise by the North Korean attack and subsequently underestimated what it would take to reverse the fortunes of war
then playing out upon the battlefields of Korea. Removing so many soldiers
from a division that was already thousands of men under the authorized
strength, effectively gutted the division forced to provide these men.[36]
Making matters worse, mostly NCOs were requested.

In executing this directive, the 1st Cavalry Division headquarters made
decisions that would exacerbate the problem for the two battalions of the
7th Cavalry Regiment. The regiment would have to give up 168 men,
almost all of them sergeants, to the 24th Infantry Division. Gone in an
instant were the men who provide the backbone to a unit in combat. Gone
were the majority of enlisted leaders with previous combat experience, and
gone were the men with the technical skills that were won at such a high
cost on the battlefield. The regiments of the division complied fully with
the order, and on July 1 the NCOs of the 1st Cavalry departed for the 24th
Infantry Division. The very next day, the division was ordered to prepare to
move to Korea itself.[37]

At McKnight Barracks in downtown Tokyo, the soldiers reacted to the
news with more than a little confusion and exasperation. Private Norman
Matthias in the ammunition and pioneer platoon noted that the packing list
was designed for something other than sustained infantry ground combat.

"We had to pack everything up. I remember we was gonna take only
two sets of khakis with us, supposed to be for the parade. I had to get my
buddy Dick to sit on my footlocker to help me close it, it was so packed. I
had to sell my damned shotgun that I just bought; I only got $10 for it."[38]

Over in G Company, Private Russ McKinley, a mortarman from Ohio,
noticed (how could one not) the sudden absence of NCOs. His platoon
sergeant, the man who had brought him word of the start of the war and

who had directed their training through all the squad and platoon training, the man who was the centerpiece to their cohesion as a combat force, was not there.

"Then Sergeant Secrist is just gone," McKinley recalls. "We had no real sergeants, and somehow, I'm not sure how this happened, but somehow Jimmy Reed is the platoon sergeant." Jimmy Reed had been in the army only a few weeks longer than McKinley.[39]

Private Don Donnelly in the intelligence and reconnaissance (I/R) platoon learned of the unit's call to Korea during a restricted briefing given to the platoon by the regimental intelligence officer. Recalls Donnelly, "The first indication that we might be going, the Cav that is, was this day when the S-2 and a couple of his guys brought us into the gym there at McKnight. They said to us, 'This is not official, and we don't think we're going, but here's a bunch of maps [of Korea] and language stuff.' We got to look at this stuff a while before the official word. It was kind of ironic, all this secrecy stuff, because all the Japanese knew where we were going. Secret mission, ha! The Japanese knew because they were loading up all the ships."[40]

Private First Class Alfred B. Clair of Portsmith, Virginia, joined the army in the fall of 1948. Immediately after basic training, he shipped out for Japan and the 7th Cavalry where he was assigned as a rifleman in F Company, 2nd Battalion 7th Cavalry. By the summer of 1950, with less than two years in the army and little more than basic training under his own belt, he became the leader for his squad. He recalled that some of the men thought they might deploy by air since the only real battalion-level training that the 2nd Battalion 7th Cavalry had conducted in years had been an air mobility exercise some months before. This idea was dispelled when the marines arrived at McKnight Barracks.

Clair explains, "The marines did a great job with what they had to work with. The training was conducted in four phases. First we had classroom work to show us what the LCVPs [landing craft] looked like and how landings were conducted. Next they took cargo nets and draped them below the second floor window of the post chapel. This would simulate the unloading from the transport. The third phase took place at the swimming pool. We would jump from the board wearing full field gear and rifle. Finally they took us out on the drill field where they had staked out an area roughly the size of the landing craft. The stakes were tall, and they used tape to simulate the top of the boat. They taught us in no uncertain terms to keep our heads below the top of the boat and how to climb over the sides to get out. Although all this sounds very organized, it really wasn't. Overall this training was haphazard at best."[41]

John De Borde in G Company remembers the shock that went through the battalion when the experienced NCOs were taken from the unit. Recalls De Borde, "Even First Sergeant Kelly [the first sergeant who used to challenge the company in boxing] got shipped over. We lost our first sergeant! This was what got everybody scared. We were sending everybody over to the 24th [Infantry Division]. Keplinger—he was a sergeant first class—took over for Kelly. I remember he came to us in Japan as a shell-shocked veteran of World War II. From there we found out, all of a sudden, we were going. Then all of the sudden we're climbing down these cargo nets that are rigged up to the side of McKnight Barracks. We're practicing unloading stuff, getting down into boats."[42]

Robert "Snuffy" Gray was one of the few NCOs not taken to supplement the 24th Infantry Division. As the platoon sergeant of the I/R platoon, he probably managed to dodge the bullet of transfer out of the regiment solely through the intervention of the regimental leadership. From his perspective, when word of the transfers came down, it was sudden and without warning or precedent. He recalls, "I was pretty much amazed by it. Tony Sotosanto was the personnel sergeant major. When we started losing people, I went to regimental headquarters to see if I was on the list and he said, 'I can't tell you.' So I went to Johnny Gwin [the regimental sergeant major] to see if I was on the list and he said, 'Goddammit, if I want you to know, I'll tell you! It's none of your goddamned business!' Well, as soon as I found out I wasn't on the list to go over to the 24th [Division], and that we [the 7th Cavalry Regiment] were probably going ourselves, I went down to Tokyo Ordnance Depot where I had some good friends. I walked out of there with four machine guns."[43]

As the leader of the regiment's only organic reconnaissance asset, Gray was not above the law, but one might consider him to have been one of Orwell's "more equal pigs." Since the I/R platoon often operated independently, his experience was slightly different than the rest of the men in the regiment.

Donnelly, as one of the soldiers under Gray, remembers many of the same events. "We're driving down, at like three in the morning, and we're going down to Yokohama. Most of the equipment was already loaded because we went down on buses. The 24th [Infantry Division] had gone over there, and we didn't really know what had happened to them. As far as we were concerned, they were kicking ass and taking names. Then right before we landed, they pulled us aside, our platoon, and briefed us that we might be making an assault landing. Man, I did not like hearing that. A little while later, we got the word that the Korean 1st Division, or 2nd, or something, was holding and we'd just be unloading. We got there and started down the nets because it was pretty shallow for the ship to come in and they wanted a quick turnaround. Well, I can't swim, never could, and I'm carrying something like a hundred pounds of gear. That's when I started praying that this wouldn't be an assault. I started thinking about what I'd seen on the newsreels back when I was a kid, and I'm thinking, 'Oh, please don't let this be an assault; don't let us get shot at. Well, we landed OK, and we moved in from the shore a little, and we were all thinking, 'Hey, this is cool.' I mean I'd been gearing up to get shot at, and instead there's people all around and stuff, civilians, and everything's like, well, normal. We moved in a little and set up and stayed that night. The next day we mounted up with the regimental commander and escorted him around while he looked at positions."[44]

Gray describes his experience; "We landed there just a while after daybreak, and there was this lieutenant there sitting on the hood of a jeep and he said, 'What took you so long?' When we got there we [the I/R Platoon] unloaded and we followed the lieutenant. We set up there and waited for the rest of the regiment to get there, and they got there later in the day. Later that night, we got orders, and we moved out with the advanced element of the regimental headquarters to conduct a recon for defensive positions up north."[45]

With no time remaining for any combat training, not even basic skills training such as cross-country land navigation or night operations, and certainly no opportunity for the battalion-level exercises it never practiced, the 2nd Battalion 7th Cavalry would go as it was.

Russ McKinley of G Company remembers that evening: "The last night before we left, somebody went out and got three or four bottles of scotch. About six of us went up on the roof of McKnight Barracks. We were locked in, see. We couldn't go out. Anyway, we sat up there and drank, and we weren't really scared yet; we were sort of nonchalant."[46] On July 18, the regiment moved to the docks and departed for Korea.[47]

Although the officers of the regiment knew barely more than the soldiers about the situation, they tried to build morale as best they knew how. Private Johnny Theodore, as a radioman in the battalion headquarters, was arguably in a position to know more about the real situation than many of the lieutenants of the battalion. Theodore recalls life aboard ship: "We'd play cards, talk, and smoke. I remember it was tough getting enough guys to play pinochle. We were in a sort of limbo. We'd had a few short days of amphibious training, enough to know that we didn't know enough. But I wasn't too worried 'cause I figured that the line companies were going in first and they'd take care of whatever it was before we got there. Especially I had a lot of faith in G Company. Captain West had a reputation as a real good one, a great trainer. I remember, as we were climbing down the cargo nets, specifically thinking, 'Boy, what if we weren't doing this in a harbor' . . . We didn't have our radios at that time, so it was an easy climb down."[48]

Several soldiers recall a pep talk aboard ship. One veteran of the battalion remembers, "We were all on deck; we'd been doing exercises. This officer, I don't know if it was the battalion commander or the brigade commander or what, but he gets up on this stage up by where the screen was set up. This was as we were pulling out of the harbor on the first night; they were going to show us *She Wore a Yellow Ribbon.* He gets up there and said something like, 'The 24th and 25th are over there, and when we get there, we're gonna kick ass, and we'll be marching in Seoul in ten days.' He said they've only taken eight casualties so far . . . ."[49]

On July 18, 1950, when this officer made that statement, the 24th Infantry Division was fighting for time, and its life, in Taejon.

Once the 7th Cavalry got to sea, the regiment found itself at the mercy of nature as two typhoons prevented the ship from making port in Korea. Former Private First Class Al Clair recalls, "When the weather first turned bad, we were lining up for chow. The ship was pitching so bad the food was thrown to the decks, making them very hard to walk on. Another of the problems that went from bad to worse at this point was seasickness. Some of the troops were in pretty poor condition. I had grown up in Virginia on the Chesapeake Bay and had been on rough water enough to get past seasickness. I slipped into the galley and was able to fill my soft hat with boiled eggs, a loaf of bread, and a tin of peanut butter. With that, I moved back to my bunk and stayed there because moving anywhere at that point was not exactly easy."[50]

The regiment landed at Pohang-dong on July 22, 1950, eight days after the rest of the division and two days after the fall of Taejon.[51]

CHAPTER 4

Erosion

JULY 20 TO MIDNIGHT, JULY 25, 1950

MASS IS ONE OF THE BYWORDS OF MILITARY DOCTRINE AND THOUGHT. A military unit achieves mass by concentrating its soldiers and weapons fires, and any other effects those soldiers can bring to bear, at a specific point against the enemy. Although it sounds simple, mass can be fairly difficult to coordinate. The antithesis of mass is dispersion.

A second touchstone of military operations is simplicity. Moving hundreds of men across the countryside is far from simple. Accordingly, the military deliberately seeks simplicity as a means to counteract any tendency towards the complex, which leads to confusion, which leads to dispersion and possible defeat. The army refers to mass and simplicity as two of the principles of war. At the very outset of its experience in the Korean War, the 7th Cavalry inadvertently violated both of these fundamental concepts, which compounded its misfortunes until, at one point, barely one half of the regiment could be considered combat-effective. All of this happened before the regiment even met the main body of the North Korean People's Army.

Upon arriving in Korea, the 7th Cavalry immediately split up, thus violating the first principle of war. The 1st Battalion went north of Pohang-dong to bolster the defenses in that direction, while the 2nd Battalion and the remainder of the regiment went west towards the rest of the

1st Cavalry Division. Because the two battalions were separated by roughly a hundred miles, they could not combine their forces to achieve mass. The difficulty of controlling both battalions across that distance made simplicity, another of the principles of war, little more than a dream at regimental headquarters. From the very beginning, the 7th Cavalry rolled a set of snake eyes, its second since word of the war hit in Japan. It was not able to enter combat as a full three-battalion regiment as dictated by doctrine, and now it would not even meet the enemy as a two-battalion regiment. Instead, each of the battalions of the 7th Cavalry, already understrength before the first shot was fired, would have to come to terms with the fact that each battalion was effectively alone.

At the battalion, company, platoon, and even individual level, this confusing situation was further exacerbated by the wild and uncontrolled rumors floating through the units. Had the soldiers known the real score, however, things might have been even worse. In one of the few cases in American military history where the rumor of a disaster was only exceeded by the reality of the situation, the 2nd Battalion was heading west toward a front line of battle that was nearing the point of disintegration.

Even as the men of the 7th Cavalry had been loading their transports on July 18, and riding out the typhoons that kept them from landing until July 22, things were falling apart for their brothers-in-arms already ashore in Korea. While the 7th Cavalry Regiment was still at sea, the 24th Infantry Division was defending Taejon as dearly as it could manage. But by the time the 7th arrived in port, the 24th Infantry Division had lost that city, and its commanding general, and was doing what it could to slip through the lines of the newly arrived 1st Cavalry Division in its position near Yongdong. The 24th Division was wrecked at that point. It was combat ineffective and scattered. This sacrifice was not borne equally across the 24th Infantry, as some accounts mention numerous examples of men just "slipping away" from the front lines for the perceived safety of the rear areas.[1] The men who did not break—the ones who stayed with their units or rejoined them as the fighting continued—were the battered survivors who later passed the newly arrived soldiers of the 2nd Battalion 7th Cavalry on the railway siding as the newly arrived soldiers moved towards the front lines for their own baptism of fire.

By July 20, the situation had so deteriorated that the division commander of the 24th Infantry Division, Major General William Dean (a contemporary of the recently appointed 7th Cavalry regimental commander, Colonel Cecil Nist) had been seen leading a small group as it attempted to break out of Taejon. They never made it.

Major General Dean had already been credited that day with leading a team that destroyed a North Korean T-34, the fourth tank of the day that he had set out to find, in the house-to-house fighting for the city. Despite some serious efforts to escape and evade capture by the North Koreans, Dean's odyssey came to a halt almost a month later when he was captured on August 20.[2]

The losses of the 24th Infantry Division during those first days of the war had not been entirely in vain. By making a series of stands, even if unsuccessful in stopping the North Koreans, the 24th Division did slow them down. After the fall of Taejon, the division ceased to exist as a viable combat force for a period of time, but it did manage to buy the most valuable commodity there is in combat—time. While the 24th Infantry Division had been fighting in the streets, two-thirds of the 1st Cavalry Division and most of the 25th Infantry Division had time to cross the straits, land, and move forward into battle positions in Korea.

The first two regiments of the 1st Cavalry Division to land in Korea were the 5th and 8th Cavalry Regiments. Both landed at the eastern port of Pohang-dong on July 18. The landings, although unopposed, were rushed and created mass confusion on shore for some time until the officers of the division and the regiments managed to get things straightened out. The regiments (both consisting of only two battalions each) took several days to unload, reorganize, and move out to their assigned positions. At the time, higher command levels began to realize that the 24th Infantry Division could not hold the line in Taejon and that the next defensible position was behind the Naktong River. The United States Army was already in a general retreat, although the soldiers themselves were not aware of this. As the 5th and 8th Cavalry Regiments moved forward, it appears they believed that their mission was to hold the line indefinitely.[3]

No one in either of these regiments was aware that they were moving into an area that as recently as three months before had been referred to as a guerilla stronghold. Nothing in the G-2 records of the division or the individual logs of the regiments suggests that anyone had even the slightest awareness that Yongdong was at the geographic center of a region where a South Korean communist insurgency had been raging for years before their arrival.[4] The soldiers and officers knew nothing of the armed South Korean communist bands who lived and fought in the area between Yongdong and Waegwan, a region that had been declared "pacified" only ninety days earlier. They did not know that some of the villages in the area were considered hostile by the South Korean government. They did not know of the brutal and bloody repression that the South Korean army and national police had waged against these same villagers, their own citizens, for years before the arrival of the U.S. Army. They would learn this on the ground.

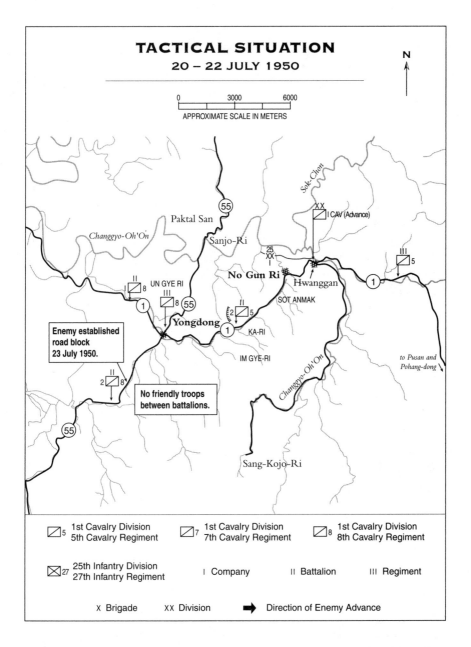

TACTICAL SITUATION
20 – 22 JULY 1950

0   3000   6000
APPROXIMATE SCALE IN METERS

N

	1st Cavalry Division 5th Cavalry Regiment		1st Cavalry Division 7th Cavalry Regiment		1st Cavalry Division 8th Cavalry Regiment
	25th Infantry Division 27th Infantry Regiment	I Company		II Battalion	III Regiment

X Brigade   XX Division   ➡ Direction of Enemy Advance

As the 5th and 8th Cavalry Regiments moved up and online, they were hit fairly quickly on both their flanks and in areas they considered the "rear." In trying to defend the small city of Yongdong from a superior enemy force to their front, they found themselves attacked from unexpected directions as the enemy appeared to be already behind them. The main force of the NKPA was in Taejon, to the northwest, reorganizing after its capture of that city. Yet already some attacks hit the Americans from every point on the compass, from inside the Yongdong lines and from areas to the east. Just a few miles to the east of Yongdong, about a one-hour walk for an infantryman, are the villages of Chu Gok Ri, Im Ke Ri, and No Gun Ri.

TACTICS, TECHNIQUES, AND PROCEDURES

In some ways, the American army of 1950 was the victim of its own success and cumulative history. The situation that the regiments of the 1st Cavalry Division found themselves in that summer was not one they had prepared for or even seriously considered. The military history of the preceding forty years had, almost overwhelmingly, contained battles that might be described as linear with fronts and flanks and a rear area, all fairly well defined with a well-developed set of expectations that governed behavior.

Obviously the military lessons of the First World War centered around the need or ability to break open the front lines of the enemy defenses. With a fairly stable line and no flanks in the theater in which the American Expeditionary Force fought, life in the rear areas was relatively risk-free. Units on the front line were in almost constant contact with those forces on their left and right, and if not, they were struggling to gain that contact.

In the Second World War, the most successful military operation was an attack that gained a deep penetration and exploited it. Yet except for a few glorious weeks in 1943 (in Sicily) or a few months in the summer of 1944 (in France), the Pacific and the European theaters of operation saw little of these successful attacks. Instead of the American blitzkrieg style of Lieutenant General George Patton, military actions more often followed the plodding straightforward attacks of General Omar Bradley. Only in that rarest of military operations, the exploitation, might a unit ride hellbent-for-leather and leave the covering of its flanks to airpower. American ground doctrine focused, appropriately enough in most situations, on the front. The underlying assumption was that units as small as a division would not operate beyond a distance from which they could support each other.[5]

In 1950, the American army was not prepared, doctrinally or organizationally, to conduct combat operations in its rear area. Security behind the front lines was the job of a thin screen of military police units that existed to control traffic and collect stragglers. Both in American doctrinal manuals and in practice, no combat formations were deliberately held off the front line to engage partisans or infiltrators, a concept now called rear area security in army parlance.[6] This is understandable considering the United States Army had not confronted a partisan or guerilla threat since the Philippine insurrection at the turn of the century. Not since then had the army faced an opponent in a conventional battle to its front (at times) and as a guerilla force on its flanks and rear. In 1950, only one American soldier on active duty could even remember those days, and that soldier—Douglas MacArthur—was not then on the peninsula. The regiments of the 1st Cavalry Division had to learn the lessons of rear and flank security on their own—the hard way.

Initially the 1st Cavalry Division's 5th and 8th Cavalry Regiments were hastily posted in a fall-back position through which the remnants of the 24th Infantry Division could pass on its way to safety to rest, reorganize, and refit.[7] As these 1st Cavalry Division units moved forward towards their battle positions on the front line (such as it was), the commanders and staff of the regiments received reports through both the intelligence and operations channels of another threat that the United States Army did not adequately address in its doctrine or training—the use of infiltration tactics by the enemy.

In modern U.S. Army field manuals, infiltration is defined as one of the five forms of maneuver available to military units.[8] In an infiltration, forces move covertly through enemy lines to attack positions in the enemy rear. Commanders may use infiltration to attack lightly defended positions or stronger positions from the flank and rear, to secure key terrain in support of the main effort, or to disrupt enemy rear operations. Infiltration is accomplished by breaking a formation up into its smallest possible components and slipping between or around the opposition's main defensive positions.

Although the U.S. Army defines infiltration, U.S. troops at the time did not widely practice it at the tactical level. Special units such as the U.S. Army ranger battalions of World War II or similar commando elements such as the U.S. Marine Corps raider battalions were trained for this type of operation, but most regular army forces did not even consider it. The American doctrinal definition of infiltration is significant because it says something about American beliefs about the nature of war. The American version of infiltration does not incorporate the idea of deliberate individual deception, but that is obviously another way of passing through enemy lines undetected. During the Second World War, a German operation conducted as part of the overall Ardennes Campaign in December 1944 (the Battle of the Bulge) took advantage of this by sending a column as well as separate teams of volunteers through American lines dressed in American uniforms and using American equipment. In some cases, English-speaking German soldiers carried the deception as far as they could, resulting in chaos behind the lines for a battle-hardened American army. In the summer of 1950, with the situation much looser and the Americans far less saavy in combat, enemy infiltration became the bugaboo of the United Stated Army.[9]

In Korea, American soldiers faced another problem that compounded the first. During the First and Second World Wars, Americans never had to deal with a large-scale exodus of refugees through their lines. During World War II, the problems of mass movements of displaced civilians did not occur in the American experience until after the war. No huge mass of French civilians clogged the roads in an effort to pass through American lines; they waited at home to be liberated. Until British and American forces were quite close to the Russian lines, no German refugee columns attempted to pass through American lines in an effort to avoid the Russians. When that exodus finally occurred, the U.S. and British lines had been stationary for some time. The environment in Korea was quite different.

By the time the 1st Cavalry Division arrived, tens of thousands of Korean refugees had voluntarily packed their belongings and taken to the roads to avoid the North Korean advance.[10] Their motivations for taking flight are too many to address here. What matters from a military context was their effect on operations. This mass exodus southward flushed civilian refugees onto the battlefield in numbers the Americans had never before experienced. This exodus caused only half of the chaos on the battlefield, for it was the unique combination of both enemy infiltration and fleeing refugees that would prey on American fears.

FEAR AND MILITARY REALITY

Even today the mention of the North Korean use of infiltration tactics is something that almost always elicits an angry response from an American Korean War veteran. It was seen as an underhanded and unfair way to fight, and in the eyes of some soldiers, practically criminal. According to international law, these veterans are justified in their outrage. When a soldier takes off his uniform and puts on civilian clothes to impersonate a civilian with the purpose of moving behind enemy lines, he is considered a spy. Aside from the issue of false colors, in war espionage is a crime punishable by death. (The issue of partisans and their entitlement to the protections of international treaties covering combatants is complex and related but beyond the scope of this work.) Thus the American reactions are somewhat understandable, but the emotions tell a slightly different story.

Americans had faced duplicitous infiltration before, but in interview after interview with war veterans, a crucial difference is noted in the perceptions of both situations. Why such ire is evoked in the Korean context goes beyond mere racism. Interviews with veterans of the World War II Battle of the Bulge seem to indicate that the attitude towards infiltrating Germans in that battle was one of anger, but not deep outrage. There was fear, but not true panic. If one word might describe the collective emotions felt behind the lines for the majority of the Battle of the Bulge, it might be excitement. Fear was obviously the fuel for that excitement, but the overall attitude was upbeat after the crisis of the first two weeks passed. This attitude can be tied directly to the perceived mission and intent of the German infiltrators. Almost from the outset, it was known, or rumored, that the Germans sent saboteurs intent on misleading Americans and causing confusion behind the lines. In the eyes of the common soldier and officer, the only direct threat these Germans represented was to the soldiers' supreme commander. Although morally condemned, this German infiltration was seen as a legitimate military ruse.

In Korea, that same sentiment of moral outrage appeared, but added to it was another very powerful combustible—fear, and in some cases, panic. Almost from the beginning, combat reports of American troops in contact with the North Korean People's Army told of large numbers of North Koreans disguising themselves as peasants and slipping through the lines to attack Americans from behind. As time passed and combat reports flowed in, a picture emerged that cumulatively suggested that whole units of North Koreans were using this method to get behind American companies and battalions and cut them off from support or attack them from the rear. This perception fueled the emotions of the soldiers of the 7th Cavalry Regiment, although ironically the actual number of infiltrators was probably quite small, anywhere from several dozen to a few hundred. To understand why, one needs to understand how military units combine "fire" and "movement" to achieve "maneuver."

Understanding why the North Koreans were probably not widely using infiltration as a form of maneuver at this point in the war requires an understanding of their viable alternatives and what fits the evidence available from the combat reports of the time. United States military doctrine recognizes five distinct forms of maneuver: frontal assault, penetration, envelopment, turning movement, and infiltration.

A *frontal assault* is a direct attack across a broad front designed to destroy the enemy by main force. Generally, this is the simplest but the most costly form of maneuver. One trades complexity for speed, and while speed may save lives in the long run, few frontal assaults are bloodless.

A *penetration* is an attack in depth (an attack with many units in support) but with a very narrow front designed to cut through the enemy lines and create two assailable flanks in its line. Flanks are always easier to attack, and if the enemy has its flanks well protected, it might be easier to pierce its line and create two new flanks. This is also, however, generally a costly operation.

An *envelopment* is a movement around one or both flanks of the enemy, followed by an attack against one or both of those flanks. This movement is complex, requiring significant movement as well as coordination with some force to "pin" the enemy in position while the main force moves to the flank. The payoff, however, can be high. People unfamiliar with military terminology might think of envelopment as a "flank attack."

A *turning movement* is similar to an envelopment in that it goes around the enemy. This movement is used when the enemy is in a very strong position and the attacking army has the luxury of time and well-trained troops. The objective is to get the enemy to leave his entrenched positions, to "turn him out" by making his position untenable. To do this, one moves all the way around the enemy main forces to his rear areas or to significant terrain on his flanks that might dominate his main line. This maneuver forces the enemy into an untenable position, where he must now attack (being on the tactical defense is generally an advantage, all other things being equal) or leave and move to somewhere where his lines of communication and supply are open. This movement has succeeded if the enemy has moved out of his strongly prepared positions without either army suffering the massive casualties that a frontal assault on those positions might entail.

Infiltration, the final form of maneuver, is the most complex and accordingly requires the highest level of training, motivation, and skilled leadership. Examples of this form of maneuver successfully used by large formations in war are very rare. To conduct an infiltration, the commander divides his forces into the smallest possible groups, which slip through the enemy lines along routes of limited visibility or routes not covered by the enemy (or in the North Korean example, by blending with the refugee columns). These small units then make their separate ways to an assembly area, reunite, and begin combat operations in the rear areas. The potential hazards to a unit attempting this type of operation almost always outweigh the potential benefits. The North Koreans most likely recognized this as well. Moreover, they had alternatives.

During the American and ROK retreat to the Naktong River, units at the battalion, the regiment, and even the division level only sporadically managed to connect their positions to those of the allied units on the flanks. American units operated almost alone, sitting astride the narrow corridors that represented the high-speed avenues of approach to the successive positions the American and ROK occupied. The situation of the two battalions of the 8th Cavalry Regiment upon their initial deployment demonstrates this separation. Covering a frontage of roughly 1,200 meters per battalion, the two battalions were separated by more than ten kilometers of unoccupied space. Together, these two battalions represented the front line of the 1st Cavalry Division, yet calling such unsupported outposts a front line is almost a contradiction in terms.

Initially neither unit had any contact on its left or right, and both were so far forward of other friendly units that they were effectively deployed into small tactical islands. The succession of positions that the 24th Infantry Division tried to hold in the weeks before the arrival of other American troops was scarcely better. Despite this, all the battalions of all regiments engaged in those first desperate weeks often acted as though they did have friendly units on their flanks. Their positions were uniformly oriented in one direction, to the front, which was usually defined as perpendicular to the road leading from the last known positions of the NKPA. The obvious solution to this neat tactical situation was for the NKPA to go around the Americans, either in a narrow enveloping attack or in a more roundabout movement resulting in a turning movement. After all, why risk destroying your unit in a piecemeal infiltration when you can simply march around the enemy and achieve the same effect?

These alternate forms of maneuver (envelopments or turning movements) almost always resulted in the establishment of North Korean blocking positions behind the American line. Simply stated, the North Koreans conducted little direct infiltration of main forces, preferring to walk a few miles out of their way to get around the undefended and unobserved flanks of American units and set up behind them. It was that simple. These tactics, however, only served to reinforce the Americans' belief that massive infiltration was occurring through their lines, so focused were they on their traditions and doctrine of linear warfare.

This is not to say that infiltration did not occur. Enough prisoner reports prove that North Korean soldiers were in fact slipping through the front lines dressed as civilians. Numerous photographs of disguised enemy soldiers can be seen at the National Archive. It is in the purpose of these infiltrations that the American tactical intelligence failed the soldiers of the infantry regiments so miserably. Infiltration, despite the risks that close contact with large numbers of armed enemy soldiers confers, is useful for gathering intelligence. Soldiers dressed as civilians, regardless of their classification as spies or scouts, can get very close to their targets. They can move near or through the enemy positions and, with a little skill (or a radio), report back to their headquarters exactly how the enemy's defenses are organized.

Such information is invaluable for commanders at the tactical level. Modern training exercises seem to confirm that the side that wins the "information fight" will win the main force battle that follows, other things being equal.[11] The infiltrations that took place along the front in Korea in July 1950 were not generally conducted by soldiers of the main body of the North Korean army. What infiltration that did occur was conducted by small groups of specialists, primarily for the purpose of reconnaissance and sniping.

An account that has worked its way into almost every single secondary-source history of the war provides the best description of infiltration by specialists. The version of this story most often repeated involves a civilian woman who appeared pregnant and her male companion who were attempting to pass through American lines. At an American checkpoint, they were stopped and searched, along with other civilians in the group. At that point, the searchers discovered that the pregnancy was not real, and that the bulge covered by the woman's clothing was actually a two-way tactical radio. The woman immediately confessed that she was North Korean and was sent to observe and report on American positions and call for artillery fire on them. Based on the time that this story first surfaced in the G-2 and G-3 channels of the American forces, the report appears to have originated in the 8th Cavalry Regiment.[12] Women in combat? Faking pregnancy? It would be difficult to deliberately create a situation that would have been interpreted by American males of 1950 as more duplicitous or underhanded.[13]

This report flashed up the chain of command and then down through the command network to the regiments and battalions and companies within a day and was subsequently repeated through the ubiquitous channels of soldier gossip as well as officially told to each regiment reporting on the line. Although the report doubtless had a foundation in fact, the problem was in the interpretation. Because these warnings of infiltration (coupled with the apparent evidence represented by the woman prisoner) occurred as several fresh American units found themselves blocked by forces to their rear, many of the battalion and regimental intelligence officers interpreted the warning to mean that enemy soldiers were sneaking through the lines *en masse*. Added to this were reports of disguised enemy soldiers passing through the lines, throwing off their disguises, and opening fire at point-blank range upon unsuspecting American soldiers behind the front.[14]

One possible explanation that would match both the documentary evidence as well as the memories of the veterans—an explanation that has been, apparently deliberately, ignored—is that South Korean communist guerillas are responsible for these infiltration attacks.

Imagine that you are a young American soldier in the summer of 1950. You have a high school degree and a slim grasp of the geography of the region where you are stationed. Your life is fairly well defined by the routine of duties in garrison in and around Tokyo. During your time in Japan, you conduct a few tactical training events, but a large amount of your time is spent in activities that would earn any unit the semi-derisive title of palace guard.[15] You deploy to Korea in a chaotic manner, and now on the front, word comes down from your platoon leader to be aware that the North Koreans are infiltrating through the lines disguised as peasant refugees. What is worse is that you can hear heavy fighting occurring some miles away and you learn that an American unit is surrounded somewhere out there. Day after day, you watch as thousands of civilians pass right through the center of your lines. At night, sporadic bursts of gunfire can be heard from the rear. The next day, the private in the position next to yours tells you that the gunfire in the rear was actually an attack on the supply trucks and that is why the meals are late. Whether true or not, that information is gospel to you and becomes part of your later memories. Still later, another soldier—this time a radio operator from the company head-quarters—confides that he heard over the radio that the attack was the work of "people in white" armed with American guns. (The traditional garb of the South Korean peasant was white on white.) None of the non-commissioned officers who trained you are with you. The platoon leader later tells the platoon through the squad leaders, men who had been privates just a few weeks earlier, that the attack was not serious and that it was American soldiers repelling some enemy soldiers they had seen on the hills nearby. As the sun falls, another group of people in white, people you assume to be civilians, pass through the lines, more gunfire is heard after the sun sets, and you begin to reach some conclusions. The obvious one for most soldiers was that combat soldiers were slipping through the lines and directly attacking units in the rear once they got through.

These soldiers were unaware of the vicious South Korean-on-South Korean war that raged through these hills weeks before. They did not know that the South Korean army and national police had conducted retribution attacks on villages suspected of supporting the communist insurgents just miles away. They had no idea that a few weeks before their arrival in the area between Yongdong and Hwanggan that, on the day the war started, an entire South Korean division was stationed in Taejon and conducting operations against rebels operating in that very region.[16] These guerillas were, almost by definition, armed with American or old Japanese rifles captured from the Republic of Korea, or national police forces, or perhaps a Russian-made weapon smuggled south across the border. By the nature of who they were, these guerillas were more often than not dressed in the traditional clothing with the traditional color of the Korean peasant—white.

Such was the tactical situation as the 1st Cavalry moved into position for the first time.

THE 360-DEGREE FIGHT

One main corridor runs north to south through South Korea, reaching from Seoul in the north to Pusan at the bottom of the peninsula. Since its initial commitment near Osan to its final rout in Taejon on July 20, 1950, the 24th Infantry Division conducted a series of delaying actions down this main axis. Only the deployment of the 1st Cavalry Division and the 25th Infantry Division brought some, albeit a temporary, pause in the suffering of this beleaguered unit. To provide that relief, the initial plan was to have the 5th Cavalry Regiment of the 1st Cavalry Division deploy to the west of the small city of Yongdong, followed by the 8th Cavalry Regiment. The expectation was that these two understrength regiments, each with only two understrength battalions, could delay the North Korean People's Army for a short period, long enough to allow further Allied reinforcements to arrive.

By this time, the eventual shape of what would become known as the Pusan perimeter, or the Naktong River line as it was also called, was already known to higher headquarters. Since the loss of the Kum River line farther to the north and the subsequent fall of Taejon, planners in Tokyo had concluded that only one more significant barrier could stop the North Koreans from reaching its final objective of Pusan. That barrier was the Naktong River. No other physical barrier would provide the American, ROK, and U.N. forces the advantage needed to allow them to consolidate their strength enough to prevent a NKPA victory.[17]

In war, the most difficult task a commander must accomplish is building the collective fighting spirit and will of his unit. Commanders at all levels struggle with this leadership challenge. A lieutenant or a captain may have a solid grasp of the pulse of his unit; however, as the size of the formation increases so does the difficulty in assessing morale. Military history is replete with examples of units that logically should not have won. In most of those cases, it might be more accurate to say that the lesser side did not so much win as the superior losing side beat itself. Morale means a lot, and a commander will do all he can to bolster it. The Naktong River, shallow and fordable at many spots that exceedingly dry summer, represented the sort of morale-boosting barrier that higher-echelon commanders knew was needed. Stretching the NKPA out over another fifty miles would also help, especially since MacArthur was now well beyond merely conceiving his plan for an amphibious landing on the coast in the rear of the North Korean lines. He was, in fact, in the planning stage for what would become Operation Chromite, the landing at Inchon.[18] The soldiers on the ground, however, had no idea what was taking place, and as far as the soldiers of the 1st Cavalry were concerned, they were supposed to hold the line right where it was, west of Yongdong.

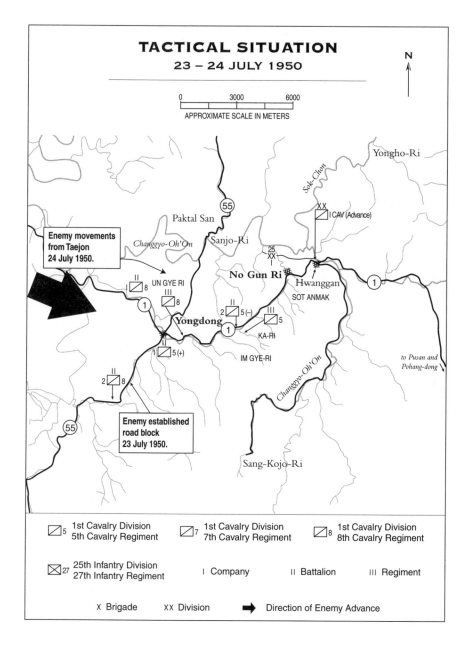

TACTICAL SITUATION
23 – 24 JULY 1950

N

0   3000   6000
APPROXIMATE SCALE IN METERS

Yongho-Ri

Sok-Chon

55   ICAV (Advance)

Paktal San

Enemy movements
from Taejon
24 July 1950.   Sanjo-Ri

Changgyo-Oh'On   25
                              XX

No Gun Ri   Hwanggan   1

UN GYE RI   SOT ANMAK
I   8

III 8
1

2   5(-)   III
                       5
Yongdong
1   KA-RI

1   5(+)   IM GYE-RI   to Pusan and
                                               Pohang-dong

2   8   *Changgyo-Oh'On*

55   Enemy established
            road block
            23 July 1950.

            Sang-Kojo-Ri

	1st Cavalry Division 5th Cavalry Regiment		1st Cavalry Division 7th Cavalry Regiment		1st Cavalry Division 8th Cavalry Regiment

5   1st Cavalry Division   7   1st Cavalry Division   8   1st Cavalry Division
         5th Cavalry Regiment   7th Cavalry Regiment   8th Cavalry Regiment

27   25th Infantry Division
     27th Infantry Regiment   I Company   II Battalion   III Regiment

         X Brigade   XX Division   ➡ Direction of Enemy Advance

Although the original plan for the defense of Yongdong had the 5th
Cavalry Regiment taking position first, for various reasons of communications and a transportation problem, the 8th Cavalry Regiment stepped out
first. Leapfrogging out of their spot as the division reserve west of Hwanggan, the two battalions of the 8th Cavalry established blocking positions

along the two major roads leading into Yongdong from the northwest and southwest. At the same time, because the regiments of the 24th Infantry Division had been ejected from Taejon with such force and were in a state of near total disarray, they had little solid information to pass to the two regiments of the 1st Cavalry Division then in country. On the east coast at this time, ships carrying the 7th Cavalry Regiment arrived at the port of Pohang-dong. It was July 22, 1950, and the 1st Cavalry Division and its two engaged regiments (8th and 5th) was about to receive another baptism of fire.

The area around Yongdong is characterized by generally rolling hills, building to more mountainous terrain as one moves to the east. Yongdong itself is situated on relatively flat terrain, although the city is dominated by nearby hills up to 3,000 feet high. This rolling ground, although not quite as mountainous as the Rockies, is steep enough to earn that appellation from any soldier who climbed up and down them in those opening days of the Korean War. This terrain also limits the number of routes a conventional force may take into Yongdong. With a mission to cover both routes, the commander of the 8th Cavalry Regiment divided his regiment. With no way to make the forces available stretch across the miles to cover the gap between the two battalions, let alone to cover their flanks, both battalions deployed astride the roads. Orienting the majority of their soldiers in one direction, both battalions sent small outposts to their flanks to protect their main line from an enveloping attack. Thus two American battalions found themselves deployed as virtual islands in a hostile sea, waiting for a wave of North Korean regulars to smash into them.

The second regiment of the division, the 5th Cavalry, arrived with its two infantry battalions before the defense was fully engaged, but that almost did not matter. The initial tactical deployment of the battalions of the 8th Cavalry was so fundamentally flawed that additional resources—unless they were whole divisions—could only help extricate those who had preceded them.

Taejon, about twenty miles from Yongdong as the crow flies, fell on July 20, 1950. Reconnaissance elements of the North Korean divisions that took the city were well beyond Taejon by the time the last Americans pulled out of the city. After a major fight, any military unit is likely to be disorganized and in need of reconstitution, but the Americans, retreating in defeat, were even more disorganized. Every second an attacking army delays to gather strength means time that the defender has to collect his wits, establish a defensive line of increasing strength, and add combat multipliers, such as improved defensive positions, minefields, obstacles, and similar military

2nd Battalion 7th Cavalry soldiers off-duty in downtown Tokyo, Fall, 1949.
(ROBERT ROBERTS)

Soldiers from G Company, 2nd Battalion 7th Cavalry in downtown Tokyo, New Year's
Eve, 1950. In the 1950s Army, the uniforms never came off, even when off duty.
(ROBERT ROBERTS)

South Korean refugees streaming away from the fighting in late July, 1950. This photo was taken somewhere between Yongdong and Kumchon by an officer of the 8th Cavalry who was with Team Field. (RICHARD COHEN)

In the opening days of the war, young South Korean peasants were suspected or dragooned by everyone. Americans feared they were North Korean infiltrators. South Korean National Police feared they were communist guerillas. Both the North and South Korean armies pressed them into service, forcing them into the front lines with little or no training, sometimes at the point of a bayonet. (RICHARD COHEN)

In their flight from advancing North Korean armies, South Korean families loaded every possible item their wagons and A-frames could hold, not knowing when, or even if, they might ever return to their villages. (RICHARD COHEN)

This was the typical flood of South Korean refugees allied forces witnessed in the early weeks of the Korean war—about 25 refugees stretched out along 100 yards of road. A group of 400 refugees would stretch along more than a mile of road, placing the people at the tail of the line hundreds of yards from any fire directed at the front of the column.
(RICHARD COHEN)

The 57-mm recoilless rifle was one of the only antitank weapons on hand in the 2nd Battalion 7th Cavalry in the summer of 1950. (U.S. ARMY MILITARY HISTORY INSTITUTE)

A 105-mm light howitzer in action against North Korean troops, somewhere in Korea July 22, 1950. (U.S. ARMY)

Major (then Captain) Henry West, commander of G Company, 2nd Battalion 7th Cavalry was the only officer with combat experience in the battalion at No Gun Ri. He regularly took his company to a small peninsula in Tokyo for training. (ROBERT ROBERTS)

Leonard "Buddy" Wenzel of the 7th Cavalry, Korea, 1950. His M1 semi-automatic rifle had only a limited magazine capacity of eight rounds. (U.S. ARMY MILITARY HISTORY INSTITUTE)

Edward L. Daily. (AP/WIDE WORLD PHOTOS)

A machine-gun team from Company E, 2nd Battalion 7th Cavalry, firing on a North Korean patrol along the far shore of the Naktong River in late August 1950. (U.S. ARMY)

Near legendary chaplain Emil J. Kapuan of the 8th Cavalry Regiment about the time that he earned a Bronze Star medal for valor on August 2, 1950 for saving men while under enemy fire near Kumchon, Korea. (RICHARD COHEN)

Former first sergeant, now Second Lieutenant Robert Gray (left), after receiving his battle-field commission early May, 1951. He is pictured here with Second Lieutenant Edward Fussell who replaced him as a platoon leader. (ROBERT GRAY)

works, to his defense. These combat multipliers often mean the difference between defeat and victory.

Despite the need for speed in follow-up attacks, the NKPA did not stage any main force attacks immediately. Not until July 23—three full days later—did the first North Korean forces begin probing the positions of the 8th Cavalry Regiment west of Yongdong. At that time, the 7th Cavalry Regiment was still unloading in Pohang-dong.

The 5th Cavalry Regiment deployed both of its battalions closer to Yongdong that day. One battalion covered the northern approaches along secondary roads into Yongdong, while the other battalion served as a reserve force. When the first attacks came on July 23, the 1st Battalion 8th Cavalry reported being under continuous fire, though this tapered off by eight o'clock that night. With no significant number of casualties that day, the battalion did not appear too shaken by this contact. These beginning attacks provided the battalion with a gradual introduction to combat, especially when compared to the experiences of the battalions of the 24th Infantry Division that preceded them. With no massed attack, no terrific barrage, the 1st Battalion 8th Cavalry did not receive any rude shocks at the beginning of its fighting—that was reserved for its sister battalion to the south, the 2nd Battalion 8th Cavalry.

The 2nd Battalion of the 8th Cavalry Regiment was located approximately two miles south of Yongdong, along the highway that heads southwest from Yongdong towards the small city of Muju. The battalion defenses were oriented perpendicular to the highway, but the battalion commander, Lieutenant Colonel Eugene J. Field, apparently also intended to cover his flank to the northwest in some fashion. Exactly how he planned to accomplish this is unknown because on July 23, before the enemy hit his troops in their defensive positions, he ran into an enemy blocking position on the road behind his battalion. Field, who was en route to a coordination meeting at regimental headquarters in Yongdong, instead became one of the first casualties of the regiment.[19] Without so much as firing a shot at an identified enemy soldier, one of the four battalions available to the division was now already cut off from the others.

Nothing in the reports or with interviews of surviving members of that battalion indicate one way or the other exactly who the enemy was that established that blocking position in the rear on the first day of combat. Reports filed at the time assume it was the NKPA. While it may indeed have been the most advanced elements of the NKPA, it appears far more likely that it was an element of the local communist guerilla force. Although estimates of the enemy's size behind the 2nd Battalion 8th Cavalry range from platoon to company, most likely the strength of the enemy force was closer to a platoon. The message traffic that passed between the battalions and regiments, also suggests that these were most likely not North Korean troops, but rather indigenous guerillas. Their method of operation— ambushes and a blocking position, which they abandoned when pressed by an American combined-arms attack—was a tactic frequently used by the insurgents in this area. The enemy employed small arms (only rifle and machine-gun fire were reported during this fight), something the North Korean regular army was not likely to do, and the size of the force suggests a domestic communist force, not a lead element of the NKPA.

The 8th Calvary's apparent clash with local guerillas occurred about five miles from the villages near No Gun Ri.

Once word spread, the prospect of guerilla warfare heightened the soldiers' fears and increased their distrust of the civilian population. The operations logbook for the 5th Cavalry provides a good snapshot of the radio traffic between the battalions around Yongdong.

> *23 July: 1150: "Shamrock 6: Advise very close screening of refugees passing through the 5RCT (regimental combat team) area. From indications forward, many are armed.*

> *1230: "Sent a patrol to check 3 men headed towards enemy lines."*

> *1405: "Report of attacks on 8th Cav and troops believed to be filtering into the area; these are both civilians and NK troops."[20]*

From July 24, 1950 forward, the pressure felt by the American troops increased steadily. At that point, one part of the 7th Cavalry was sorting itself out on the dockside at Pohang-dong a hundred miles away and another was already moving forward to become the 1st Cavalry Division's reserve at Hwanggan. The other battalions and regiments of the division were engaged in a fight not just to their front, but in every direction inside and around Yongdong.

7TH CAVALRY TO THE FRONT

The elements of shock started appearing not long after the 2nd Battalion of the 7th Cavalry set foot on the Korean peninsula at Pohang-dong on July 22. Before ever arriving at the front, the soldiers, like many generations of green troops before them, had to contend with the almost obligatory verbal harassment from the newly minted combat veterans leaving the lines. It happened outside Manassas in the Civil War, along the roads leading up to the trenches in the First World War, and in all theaters, at all times throughout the Second World War. For the men of the 2nd Battalion, it started on the train ride from the port of Pohang-dong to the 1st Cavalry Division assembly area at Hwanggan on July 24. The harassment did nothing to help prepare the men of the 2nd Battalion 7th Cavalry for combat, but it did serve to shake loose a few nerves among them.

The G Company mortarman John De Borde remembers it this way: "We were, well, we didn't really know where we were going. We got on the train, and it went. We weren't thinking big thoughts; we just thought, 'Hey, here we go,' but we were real casual about it. I remember as we passed through the Korean villages that the Koreans were giving us this hand waving in a circle signal as we passed. I still don't know what that means. Most of the time on the train, we were laughing and joking; hey, we were gonna win the war here. We didn't know. We just didn't know."[21]

Headquarters Company radioman Johnny Theodore remembers that first train ride clearly as well. From his point of view, it was fairly unremarkable, but in his memories, the first of the psychological "inputs" were felt that will culminate later on the night of July 25. "It was a sort of small passenger train that we got on that morning. I remember at some point when we were passing by a road and we could see these guys from the 24th, and these guys looked ragged. I mean, they were skin and bones, like they hadn't eaten and were tired, dead tired. I remember one guy, as we were going by, sort of tossing his ammo clips to us, not in a mad way, sort of in a depressed, 'Here, you'll need this' sort of way."[22]

Most of the soldiers recalled that at some point in their trip they encountered veterans of the 24th Infantry Division's Task Force Smith returning from the fighting around Taejon. The men of the 24th Infantry Division, who had a rough time of it, were the first combat soldiers the men of the 2nd Battalion 7th Cavalry saw. The image of these battle veterans shook their composure and gave them their first inkling that perhaps this war would not end in a parade through Seoul in two weeks' time as some of them had been told to expect. According to Norman Matthias, a few of the soldiers he encountered from the 24th Infantry Division were over the top in their stories. "There was a quartermaster unit there waiting for us that morning. I can't tell you how happy we were seeing those Eighth Army trucks there. We loaded up, and they took us to our first position. We're dug in, the whole battalion, in kind of a circle in a field right next to these railroad tracks and a station. This was somewhere around that Pohang place. Then some of us got on a train, passenger cars. At some point, we pulled into a switchyard, a train with guys from the 19th Infantry [Regiment, 24th Infantry Division] pulled in going in the opposite direction. We started talking across the cars, and they started telling us these horrible stories. One guy said, 'Goddamned T-34s blew us a new asshole up at Taejon.' They said the only thing that stopped 'em was a 155, the 105 wasn't worth a goddamn against them, and I started wondering what we were getting into. These guys looked bad, all worn out, like they were gaunt, you know? Like they hadn't slept in a week. The train finally stopped; there was no station or anything. We got out, climbed down an embankment, and then just waited there for a while."[23]

It was an uneasy introduction to the area. Many, if not most, of the veterans recount similar tales, unremarkable in that this sort of thing happens in every war, but in this case it was telling because it may have contributed to what happened to the unit the next night.

The twenty-fourth of July also saw the beginning of heavy contacts between the regiments of the 1st Cavalry Division on the frontline and the NKPA around Yongdong. In an effort to relieve the 2nd Battalion 8th Cavalry in its cut-off location, the 1st Battalion of the 5th Cavalry moved from its position as the reserve, through Yongdong, to occupy hills on the southwest edge of town. At the same time, some of the first American tanks to arrive in Korea, the light M-24s of the 71st Tank Company moved into action to help break open the route to the 2nd Battalion 8th Cavalry. These initial efforts were unsuccessful. The men of the cut-off battalion, now under the command of the battalion executive officer, were simultaneously attempting to maintain their watch to the southwest, cover their exposed flank in the hills to the north, and attack towards the "rear" (northeast) to open the route back to Yongdong.

While this action was occurring south and west of the city, the NKPA approached from the northwest, the direction of Taejon. The attacks against the 1st Battalion 8th Cavalry started at dawn with mortar and artillery fire falling on its position and followed soon afterwards by conventional frontal assaults by the NKPA.[24] The battalion held up well, and during the course of that defensive fight that morning, Second Lieutenant Daniel Mahoney earned the Silver Star Medal for gallantry in action while holding his section of the line in A Company, 1st Battalion 8th Cavalry.[25]

Artillery spotters operating from light aircraft reported formations of the enemy due north of Yongdong, but nothing could be done directly to deal with this threat. The divisional artillery was having problems of its own as things heated up inside the city despite the fact that the 1st Battalion 8th Cavalry still nominally held the line four miles to the northwest.[26]

Despite their position in a presumably protected area behind the frontlines, the two howitzer battalions defending Yongdong were attacked at noon that day by infantry forces that had either slipped through the admittedly porous defenses around Yongdong, or had come from Yongdong itself. This attack resulted in the loss of a howitzer, the retreat of both artillery battalions, and the use of an infantry company from the reserve battalion (G Company, 2nd Battalion 5th Cavalry) to help extricate the remaining guns.[27] Added to all of this was a building sense of panic among the soldiers as rumors and facts mixed and filtered through the grapevine.

Master Sergeant Harry Carmack of the 8th Cavalry Regiment told a reporter from *Newsweek* who visited that day something about the nature of the soldiers and the fighting around Yongdong: "These kids are fighting like hell, but they're green and they act it. Last night I had an outpost on that hill over there—five kids. They were sure they were being surrounded and wanted to withdraw. I wouldn't let them. They got panicky. Two of them just took off. Last night I also lost a lieutenant. A kid got nervous and just started blasting away with a machine gun. He didn't hit anything except the lieutenant. And just to make it a perfect day, I lost another god-damned lieutenant who was killed inspecting a mine he had laid himself."[28]

Inside the immediate vicinity of the city, the engineers of the division also learned that the perception of safety associated with being behind the front was just an illusion. One squad of engineers from Company C of the 8th Engineer Battalion found itself pinned down by automatic weapons fire that afternoon. They were only relieved when reinforcements from their company came forward under the command of a lieutenant from the company and conducted an infantry-style assault on the enemy guns.[29]

On most soldiers' minds appears to have been a fear of enemy infiltration. This anxiety was exacerbated by the discovery of the bodies of American soldiers who had their hands tied behind their backs and bullet wounds in the back of their heads, a message that traveled quickly through official and unofficial channels.[30] Very quickly, everyone knew that this was a different kind of war. Even the Catholic chaplain of the 8th Cavalry began carrying an M1 carbine, saying at this point, "If it's a question of a North Korean sending me to heaven or me sending him someplace, I'm not prepared to go to heaven right now."[31]

Then at 1000 hours, an excitable staff officer from the 8th Cavalry, serving as a liaison to the division headquarters, passed the following message over the phone to his regiment: "No refugees to cross front line. Fire everyone trying to cross line. Use discretion in case of women and children."[32]

Because the message was by telephone, and from its own liaison officer at that, only the 8th Cavalry recorded hearing the order. This order does not appear in the message logs of the 5th Cavalry or the regimental diary of the 7th Cavalry or in the logs of any other unit in the division, including the division's own message log. It may be that the 5th Cavalry liaison officer was not present, or that he was just less excitable than his counterpart from the 8th Cavalry, but the effect is the same: The 5th Cavalry liaison officer did not pass any such order to his regiment, nor did any other unit in the division receive any message that resembled what is recorded in the 8th Cavalry log.[33] At the time, the 7th Cavalry had no liaison officer at division headquarters, but even if it had, the regiment would never have received an order sent by telephone because the 7th Cavalry regimental headquarters was on the road en route from Pohang-dong to Hwanggan at 10:00 o'clock on the morning of July 24 and had no working phones at the time.[34]

No better evidence can be found that such an order was not passed by the 1st Cavalry Division to the regiment, or further down to the battalions, than what took place in the 1st Battalion 7th Cavalry later that night.

The 7th Cavalry Regiment was split up upon arriving at the port of Pohang-dong. The 1st Battalion had moved earlier in the day northward from the port city, where it established a line of defense to protect that crucial town from an attack along the coastline. Spending their first night on the line, these green troops were more than a little jittery. When outposts to their front reported a large body of people moving down the road towards them in the darkness, some sections of the line opened fire. At that point, Second Lieutenant Francis Malony, a platoon leader from D Company, led a patrol forward into the darkness against what they believed to be enemy troops in front of their main line of resistance.

Maloney was apparently a cautious man, not prone to losing his composure, even when leading a night patrol against an unknown enemy for the very first time in his life. He ordered his men to hold their fire as he went forward alone. The initial fusillade from the main line had hit something in front of the lines, and the sounds of the wounded suggested to Maloney that this was not an enemy force as initially believed to be. Not wanting to risk his soldiers, Maloney went forward alone, ordering his men to hold their fire. Instead of North Koreans, he found a group of ROK soldiers escorting a large group of civilian refugees. One ROK soldier and one of the civilians had been killed by the burst of gunfire from the battalion's main defensive line, but the rest of the group appeared OK. Maloney moved his patrol forward and made contact with the group, then personally led the group through battalion lines to a holding area in the rear. The group was searched and released in the morning.[35]

When the 7th Cavalry arrived near the division command post in Hwanggan later that day, it received a written order from the division headquarters that contained six specific instructions for dealing with civilians in the area around Yongdong and in South Korea in general. This order was explicit:

(a) No school, shops or industries will be operated except those essential to the war effort.

(b) Movement will be permitted daily from 1000 to 1200 hours.

(c) No ox-carts, trucks or civilian cars will be allowed to operate on the highways.

(d) No fields will be worked.

(e) Municipal authorities, local police, and national police will enforce this directive.

(f) Armbands will be worn by essential personnel such as municipal authorities, police, doctors, midwives, railroad and telephone personnel.[36]

Back at Hwanggan, 1st Cavalry Division Commander Major General Hobart Gay could only focus on one thing—time. The defense of Yongdong had to last long enough to allow the full division to land in Korea and deploy its understrength regiments. Although some contemporary news reports suggest that Gay planned on conducting limited attacks immediately, postwar interviews contradict this assertion. Gay knew that his forces were not yet ready to conduct an attack, let alone a division-size attack. Indeed, even the planned defenses were falling apart, largely because of the difficulty of trying to get the forces to coordinate and act in unison while each was fighting its own battle in small penny-packets across the entire Yongdong area.[37]

Gay also had trouble with one of his regimental commanders, the newly arrived colonel of the 7th Cavalry, Cecil Nist, the same officer who had been G-2 of XVII Corps in 1945. When Gay wanted fire-breathing commanders, what he got in Nist was a staff officer masquerading as a commander, a man more concerned with not being held responsible than he was with taking charge and inspiring soldiers in combat.

When Nist arrived in the vicinity of Hwanggan, near the division headquarters, he was well in advance of his own regiment. The only forces he had on hand in the immediate vicinity were elements of the 2nd Battalion and the regimental advance party that had come ahead with him in a vehicular convoy.

At the time, there was a sense of panic in the division headquarters after reports of enemy ground attacks on the artillery in the rear, large bodies of enemy infantry moving past Yongdong to the north, and a roadblock that had suddenly appeared behind 2nd Battalion 8th Cavalry. The panic is somewhat understandable, considering that only four days earlier the division commander of the 24th Infantry Division, Major General Dean, had gone missing when his division was overrun in Taejon. Therefore, it was the division staff's view that 1st Cavalry Division headquarters was threatened.

When Colonel Nist arrived at the division command post in Hwanggan with the wheeled vehicles of the 2nd Battalion, the heavy mortar company, and his jeep-mounted infantrymen from the regimental I/R platoon, he had with him the only friendly infantry units within five miles of the division headquarters. One can well imagine the sense of relief the headquarters felt when these infantrymen arrived. Nist was ordered to form a provisional rifle company from the men of the 7th Cavalry that he had on hand in the event that they might be needed to defend the division headquarters from an imminent attack.

Cecil Nist responded like the staff officer that he had been for so many years.

Instead of immediately complying with the orders given by division, he dodged the issue. Since Gay himself had not given Nist the order, some room existed for noncompliance. Although Nist did issue instructions to form the available men into a provisional two-company force, he also covered himself with paperwork.

Nist wanted to make it clear, in writing and for the record, that he could not be held responsible for the 7th Cavalry's potential degradation in combat power if his headquarters personnel were used as riflemen. Significantly, Nist did not personally confront the division commander with his reservations. He did not go to Major General Gay and protest his orders, or even call Gay on the radio to request clarification of the orders. Instead, he complied, in a halfhearted manner, and then relied on a paper trail to cover himself from potential future blame. Nist wrote a formal protest to the division that can only be considered as a classic piece of CYA.

4. I have no wish to fight the problem, however I feel that I must point out the following simple facts:
   a. That if this force is employed there will be no Headquarters Company, 7th Cavalry (Inf.) since I have taken every available man including communications personnel in order to give the maximum fire power to my provisional forces.
   b. That I have irreparably crippled the 2nd Battalion because I have stripped their motor section of drivers, heavy machine guns, recoilless rifles and ammunition in forming the provisional force.

5. My present CP is in the assembly area, 3 miles west of Division Advance.

6. If the 2nd Battalion becomes available before it is necessary to commit my provisional force, I urgently request that I be authorized to reconstitute my regiment under TO&E.
NIST
CO—7th Cavalry (Inf)"[38]

His fears were allayed later that afternoon when the train bearing the majority of the 2nd Battalion 7th Cavalry arrived near Hwanggan. Nist would not have to form his provisional rifle company, but he had already demonstrated his colors to the division. Cecil Nist was not a fire-breathing commander spoiling for a fight. While unwilling to confront the division commander himself with an opinion or protest, he was more than willing to try to get out of assignments given to him by the division. In short, he looked like a fellow who would not follow an order that was even slightly out of the ordinary without covering himself in writing. This suggests that any other future orders that were out of the ordinary would also elicit a protest, or at least a note of nonconcurrence, from Cecil Nist. The reproduction of Nist's memorandum, both in the division G-3 log and in the 7th Cavalry's regimental war diary, indicates that Nist had the document saved and read into the record verbatim, for posterity, for much the same reason as he wrote it in the first place.

By the end of the day on July 24, the shape of things to come was already apparent. The next day would be more of the same, only worse, as the pressure from the main body of North Korean infantry began to press against the defenses of the 1st Cavalry Division in earnest, and the pressure of combat on untested troops began to take its toll. The next day would also be the first day on line for the men of the 2nd Battalion 7th Cavalry. But first, that night, they suffered their first casualties. It would be incorrect to characterize these deaths as the battalion's baptism of fire, because these casualties were self inflicted.

The soldiers of the 7th Cavalry received their basic load of small-arms ammunition while still aboard the transport ships in Yongil Bay off of Pohang-dong. Despite the jitters that accompanied their unloading there, the soldiers' first night ashore passed fairly easily. The night of July 24 was different. Although still miles behind the front, the regiment assumed a defensive posture, with perimeter guards and tactical security measures such as reduced-noise and increased-light discipline. Unfortunately, since live ammunition and full nighttime security were new experiences for the soldiers of the 7th Cavalry, they were more than a little nervous. As a result, the first casualties of the regiment in Korea fell to the guns of the regiment itself. Soldiers looking out in the dark at the shrubs and trees around them became trigger happy, as inexperienced and poorly trained troops often do in their first nights in a combat zone. Second Lieutenant Alan Plummer of F Company, who was misidentified by the sentries that night, was killed outright. Another man, Private Sanderlin, was wounded and evacuated.[39]

As stated earlier, higher headquarters knew no viable defensive line was available to the American and ROK troops short of the Naktong River. This information, while common knowledge at 1st Cavalry Division head-quarters, was not widely disseminated to the troops for obvious reasons. American and ROK troops had to buy time, and the higher command acknowledged that the needed time would come with the trade-off of land. To buy that time, the Americans had to prevent the North Koreans from pushing through the defensive line, otherwise the whole situation might deteriorate into a precipitous rout. As the pressure throughout the Yong-dong area increased over the course of July 25, the division sent orders to withdraw, with the first two regiments of the 1st Cavalry Division pulling back in sequence through a blocking position a few miles to the east of Yongdong. The blocking position was to be manned by the 2nd Battalion 7th Cavalry, since the 1st Battalion was still a hundred miles away, in a posi-tion north of Pohang-dong port.

The first rule in war is that no plan survives the first contact with the enemy. This rule came true on July 25 as the plan for an orderly disengage-ment and withdrawal from Yongdong slipped into a chaotic swirl of men, material, and refugees headed east and northeast along the road to the next town, Hwanggan. (Although the general route from Seoul to Pusan is northwest to southeast, this stretch of road runs east and northeast.)

The tanks of the 71st Tank Company managed to blast open the route for the 2nd Battalion 8th Cavalry to extricate itself (or more accurately, enemy opposition melted away once faced with the prospect of armor and massed artillery fire then falling). At the same time the 1st Battalion 8th Cavalry managed to pull through the city and head east with little delay. But not everything went smoothly.

As the 2nd Battalion 8th Cavalry was moving back toward Yongdong from its original positions two miles southwest of the city, it was hit again by the guerillas who had disappeared when confronted by the tanks of the 71st Tank Company.[40] In a classic example of light-infantry guerilla tactics, the enemy apparently allowed the lead elements of the battalion to pass before opening concentrated small-arms fire on the main body of the battalion. The column halted as troops dove from their trucks and took cover on the lee side of the road. Two lieutenants from E Company earned their pay that morning by leading charges up the hill towards the guerilla positions. The citations for the Silver Star medals for valor awarded to Second Lieutenants Mabry E. Cain and Robert S. Wood read nearly identically. Their prompt actions in leading their platoons up the hillside succeeded in dislodging the guerillas long enough for the rest of the 2nd Battalion 8th Cavalry to move out of the kill zone.[41]

As the 2nd Battalion 8th Cavalry closed in on Yongdong, friendly forward observers called fire so close to the American troops that shells intended for the enemy landed on part of the 16th Reconnaissance Company (the divisional reconnaissance unit), which was holding the route open at the edge of the city, wounding four more soldiers.[42]

Meanwhile the 1st Battalion 8th Cavalry pulled out smoothly from its positions far to the northwest, despite reports of enemy armor in the area. At 0600 on July 25, observers reported ten enemy tanks entering the western edge of Yongdong.[43] The light tanks of the 71st Tank Company were no match for the Russian-made T-34s.

To cover the final withdrawal once the 2nd Battalion 8th Cavalry pulled through the former enemy position to its rear, the first platoon of the 71st Tank Company and F Company, 2nd Battalion 8th Cavalry stayed at the outskirts of Yongdong. They attempted an envelopment of the ambush but became misoriented south of Yongdong. Now they were almost immediately cut off from behind as North Korean T-34s entered the city from the northwest. What happened to this composite unit over the next three days sounds like a miniature version of Xenophon's march. Leadership for the composite unit fell to the commander of F Company, Captain Terry Field, with the help of two other captains from the staff of the 2nd Battalion 8th Cavalry, Richard Cohen and Harold McNess. F Company was never given any specific title or designation. For lack of a better descriptor, this group of isolated infantrymen and tankers will be referred to as Team Field. Tuck Team Field, in its isolated position to the southwest of Yongdong, away in memory for the moment.[44]

Team Field was not the only company cut off from behind that afternoon. The 5th Cavalry Regiment also lost its F Company, perhaps due to missed communications, but more likely as the result of a lack of practice in such a complex operation. The 5th Cavalry Regiment had never trained at the regimental level on a tactical problem such as this. An unfortunate sequence of errors resulted. As the 5th Cavalry Regiment began to pull back from its position in and around Yongdong, more and more reports poured in from aerial observers about concentrations of enemy forces directly to the north of Yongdong.

The act of pulling back through successive positions while in contact with the enemy, leapfrogging backwards as it were, is called a retrograde. A successful retrograde, the most complex operation that a tactical unit can attempt, depends upon constant communications, well-disciplined soldiers, and skilled officers who had practiced the operation in peacetime maneuvers. In a retrograde, one part of the force provides cover for the other half of the force to move to the rear where another line is created, allowing the first to disengage from the enemy and leap back to yet a third line. A major part of a retrograde operation is ensuring that supporting fires do not land on the constantly moving lines, but are placed on the enemy moving into former friendly locations. Leaders must also make sure that their own soldiers are aware of all that is going on around them so that they can allow the friendly forces to pass through their lines yet stop the enemy who might be right on their heels. The 5th Cavalry Regiment was not the only unit that never trained for this sort of operation at the regimental or battalion level. Training records and interviews suggest that none of the units in the 1st Cavalry had trained in retrograde operations in Japan. A complex operation, difficult and sometimes awkward even when done right, a retrograde is not something that the U.S. Army considered at the top of its list of things to train on before Korea.

In Yongdong, two units at two echelons were attempting simultaneous retrogrades. Not long after the 0600 retrograde of 2nd Battalion 8th Cavalry, the 5th Cavalry Regiment started its own regimental-level retrograde. To establish one of the successive lines needed in this maneuver, the 5th Cavalry found itself throwing one company from the 2nd Battalion on line with one of the 1st Battalion. A Company, 1st Battalion, was already in position on a ridgeline when F Company from the 2nd Battalion tried to move up onto the ridge and tie in on the right end of A Company. At this critical instant, the North Korean infantry launched an attack. If this sounds confusing on paper, it was certainly doubly so on the ground.

Either through a mistake of land navigation by the company leaders, a mistaken map coordinate given in its orders, or just bad luck, F Company veered slightly too far to the right (north) in its climb up the ridge. It moved over the ridgeline and found itself under almost immediate attack by NKPA infantry flowing in over the hills from the north and west. Contact with the company on its flank was lost. No radio traffic came from the unit at all, and from the volume of fire and soldiers who escaped, F Company appeared cut off and surrounded.

At the same time, A Company, 1st Battalion 5th Cavalry, was slightly to the south along the same ridge, where it too was under attack throughout the morning. At 1000 hours, that battalion was ordered to pull back.

Now with pressure from the front, no units on its northern flank, and the rest of the regiment that had been on its left moving steadily east according to plan, F Company from the 2nd Battalion found itself as the second American unit to be cut off and surrounded that day. Their situation, however, was more dire than what the 2nd Battalion 8th Cavalry experienced the day before. Unless something was done quickly, F Company would be alone, as the rest of the division pulled out. In the end, the 5th Cavalry suffered heavily: The 1st Battalion's A Company took heavy losses, and only twenty-six men returned to friendly lines from the ill-fated F Company of the 2nd Battalion 5th Cavalry.[45]

Everyone at that point also seems to have forgotten about Team Field.

At the same time, no small amount of bad blood developed between the battalions of the 5th Cavalry regiment as the two battalions accused each other, over the command radio net, of abandoning one another. Friendly fire from one battalion reached out and hit units of the other. The retrograde actions of the 2nd Battalion 5th Cavalry prompted the 1st Battalion of the same regiment to accuse it of exposing its flank to the enemy by pulling out too quickly and without warning.[46] The arrival of and attack by the North Korean Army from the front (west) added to the confusion of conducting an unfamiliar maneuver over unfamiliar terrain. A chaotic situation resulted as men from different units intermingled and units attacked in several directions at once as some tried to hold their positions to allow others to leave under the pressure of the NKPA attack.

At 2:45 P.M. on July 25, 1950, Colonel Nist issued the following order to the 7th Cavalry Regiment:

1. We shall be prepared to move forward and do one of the following things:
   a. Take over from the 8th Cavalry on the right of the road.
   b. Take over from the 5th Cavalry on the left of the road.
   c. Straddle the road with the 5th and 8th Cavalry behind us.
2. I am going forward on a reconnaissance and the following are to be done:
   a. When the order is received, the regiment will move forward under the command of Lt. Col. Huff.
   b. The 2nd Battalion will lead.
   c. The 1st Battalion will move forward upon its arrival from Pohang-dong.
   d. The 2nd Battalion will motor, detruck, and transportation will return to pick up the 1st Battalion and move it forward.

e. Strip down to the bare essentials. No heavy transportation forward.

f. Necessary communications for rather compact set up.

g. Regimental CP within the perimeter of a battalion.

h. Staff to operate out of hip pocket.

i. Security platoon to be reinforced out of Headquarters and Headquarters Company and armed with M1s if possible.

j. Plenty of antipersonnel and antitank mines.

k. Bazookas—pull out enough 3.5 inch for 1st Battalion to get proportionate share.

l. All transportation not essential forward to be back in field bivouac.

3. Am now going up to CP of the 8th and possibly farther. May not be back in time if we move this afternoon but will send back Capt. Cochrane, S-2, with details for moving the regiment.

4. For your information: the field trains bivouac will probably move further back tomorrow.

5. Ambulatory jeeps, Medical Company, go forward.

NIST

Colonel, Comdg. 7th Cavalry[47]

The order for the 2nd Battalion 7th Cavalry to move out arrived late that afternoon. At 1850 that day, the battalion began to move forward on trucks to its blocking position.[48] As the 5th Cavalry was sliding backwards from Yongdong, several kilometers to the east, the men of the 2nd Battalion 7th Cavalry unloaded and were walking into their positions in a line that was intended to provide cover for the rest of the division. Notwithstanding the intent, that was not what happened.

LANDSLIDE

The situation was already fluid as the men of the 7th Cavalry moved west from their temporary positions as the division reserve in the vicinity of Hwanggan on the evening of July 25. Some of the men moved on foot, some in trucks; a few recall that their unit moved this short distance (roughly five miles) on open bed cars of a small train. No matter the method of movement, the battalion did not reach its positions until near sunset on the evening of July 25. Throughout this movement, the soldiers witnessed a steady stream of people moving backwards to the east from Yongdong. They were not just the retiring soldiers of their sister infantry regiments, the 5th and 8th Cavalries, but men from all sorts of units. There were soldiers from the field artillery, signal corps, and military police units, and elements of the division's aviation detachment—all of the associated support that accompanies a U.S. infantry division, all moving to the rear. When added to the steady stream of refugees moving away from the fighting, a significant flow of people greeted the 2nd Battalion 7th Cavalry as it slowly moved forward towards its position.

The main route from Taejon to Taegu makes some twists and turns in the mountains to accommodate the geography of the region. At this point, the valley from Yongdong to Hwanggan actually runs from the southwest to the northeast. The hills on both sides of the valley are tall and exceptionally steep, and running through the middle of the valley were the main road and a double set of railway tracks. Two different railroad tunnels are found in this short stretch of the valley, along with several small overpasses for the railroad and highway to cross some of the minor watercourses, little more than intermittent streams, that run through the area.

The 2nd Battalion 7th Cavalry occupied its first position along a finger of a ridge that stuck out into the valley from the northern valley wall, generally perpendicular to the direction of the road and the railroad that ran beside it. This location was several miles to the south and west of No Gun Ri and a few miles to the north and east of Yongdong. The companies deployed on line, apparently fairly conventionally. The weapons company, H Company, deployed in support of the three "line" rifle companies but focused its guns on the roadway and set its company headquarters by the road. F, E, and G companies deployed side by side on the hillside, tied in closely to each other. The positions of all three companies on the forward slope of the hill gave some soldiers the added advantage of a longer line of sight to their front. Given their already strained resources (riflemen were in especially short supply), the companies deployed in a fairly conventional layout. The battalion headquarters with its tactical operation center was at the center and slightly to the rear of the three line companies, on the very crest of the hill. This was the battalion's first tactical deployment in combat, and something for which it had never trained to do as a whole battalion. With only a vague understanding of the situation, even in the headquarters, and with most of the squads led by privates, it was a recipe for disaster.

Understanding what happened next means knowing the full story of Team Field, that element of tanks and infantrymen based upon F Company, 2nd Battalion 8th Cavalry, and commanded by Captain Terry Field, that had been cut off to the south of Yongdong earlier that morning.

This small force seems to have held its position to the southwest of Yongdong just a little too long. When it found itself cut off from using the route followed by the rest of the division up the highway to Hwanggan,

Team Field tried to move due east through some of the valleys containing tributary streams of the main watercourse. As the sunlight faded, so did the unit's land navigation ability. By this point the unit's troops had traveled several miles from their starting point, a position southwest of Yongdong, but they still had a long distance to go based upon their understanding of where the main body of their unit, the 8th Cavalry, was located. Earlier in the day, a light aircraft had dropped a message and some food to them. The message read:

> Proceed to place marked X. Members of your regiment will meet you there. Watch for antitank and antipersonnel mines along trails. About twenty to thirty members of your battalion are also lost in your vicinity and are on way out to meet at X. Be careful not to fire upon them; they have Koreans carrying wounded.[49]

Unfortunately, Team Field did not understand that the 8th Cavalry was no longer on the front lines and was now in reserve well behind friendly lines. If the map dropped to Team Field revealed an accurate depiction of the location of the team's battalion, it would have shown the battalion well beyond where the actual front lines were. At that point the front was the 2nd Battalion 7th Cavalry. The 8th Cavalry had been but was by that time several miles beyond that point. In a classic case of crossed signals and mis-communication, Team Field took a wrong turn up one of the side valleys and stopped at a dead end canyon. Although this cannot be stated with cer-tainty, it appears that the wandering elements of Team Field and the other lost elements of 2nd Battalion 8th Cavalry contained some of the unknown soldiers who inadvertently swept up at least some of the villagers to the southwest of No Gun Ri and sent them on their way towards the road-block recently established by the 2nd Battalion 7th Cavalry several miles forward but still southwest of No Gun Ri.

In their dead-ended valley to the south, the 219 men of Team Field were lost. They knew that the enemy was advancing from Yongdong towards them; they had seen NKPA troops in the city itself before they entered the hills. Now they were stuck in a closed valley, and the only route of escape seemed to lead back towards the enemy. They had with them several light tanks and a few trucks, but the prospects for keeping their vehicles seemed less and less likely. The order went out to destroy those vehicles, tanks included, that could not turn around in the narrow confines of the valley. At the same time, probably around 9:30 P.M., some of the infantry soldiers went out on a foot patrol led by Lieutenant Matta of the 8th Cavalry. They backtracked down the small valley, found the main valley, and in the darkness spotted a strong roadblock a little farther up that main valley. As the roadblock blocked the route to where they believed the rest of their regiment was laagered, the members of Team Field believed themselves caught between a rock and a hard place.[50] Almost certainly in hindsight, the roadblock they saw was not the North Koreans, but the men of the 2nd Battalion 7th Cavalry.

Meanwhile, just a little farther up the main valley leading to Hwang-gan, the 2nd Battalion 7th Cavalry settled into its blocking position. At least two groups of refugees approached the roadblock that afternoon and evening. The soldiers stopped some of them and held them in place to the front of the battalion. No shots were fired, and no force was used. It appears that one small group of refugees was even allowed to pass through the position earlier in the evening, though the evidence for this is sketchy.[51]

As a member of the ammunition and pioneer platoon, part of the headquarters company of the 2nd Battalion 7th Cavalry, Norman Matthias manned a position near the road with one of the heavy machine guns that was normally mounted on a turret ring in the cab of a truck. He recalls: "The next afternoon we got in trucks and they took us up—I think that we went about seven miles . . . I had my fifty [caliber] up on the ring in the cab of the truck. When we got off, I carried the tripod and Dick got the gun, but somebody forgot to get the damned pintel. [The pintel matches the gun to the tripod by fitting into a socket in the tripod.] So we got off the trucks and went over the railroad and up this finger off the right side. We were on the left end of the line, with the line companies off to our right. [Platoon sergeant] Hinkle tells me to dig in and cover the rail-road track and the road. We could hear artillery in the distance, but where we were at, it was real quiet; it was late afternoon. I tried to dig but it was pretty useless. About two feet down, I hit rock."[52]

Jim Kerns was part of H Company's headquarters element. His position was just above Matthias's. Recalls Kerns, "We moved out that evening and went all night. I guess we switched sidings a few times. Captain Chandler had given me a Rand-McNally map, I remember it was from 1933. It felt like we hiked about twelve to fifteen miles up a dirt road. [The actual distance was far less than this estimate.] We walked until maybe 4:30 P.M. When we stopped walking, my group went to the left of the road. The rest of the battalion, well, part was on the left and it seems like most was on the right of the road. I dug a two-man [fox] hole for me and Captain Chandler.

"I stopped digging at about sunset. Captain Chandler looked at me and kidded me by saying, 'You trying to desert?' because the hole was so deep. There were trees all around, they were like what I would call scrub pine. We were on the side of a hill, I would guess that it was maybe six hundred feet high, but we're only about sixty feet above the road where we are. The mortars were to our left, around the front side of the hill; the machine guns, they were down covering the road, and the 75s were to our right rear. The temperature was maybe eighty or ninety degrees. It was about thirty or forty minutes after dark when I heard a whistle and Corporal [Samuel] Jones says to me, 'Kerns, that's incoming. Get in your hole.' Then I heard it impact about 500 yards behind us.

"We didn't have our company radios at that time. I don't know where they were, but I know we didn't have any in the company because we had to use runners all night that night. We'd go down to the mortars or over to the 75s every hour or so, same with the machine guns. We were up all night doing that. We didn't have any contact with battalion that I know of, 'cause, like I said, we didn't have any radios yet."[53]

Battalion headquarters was experiencing a fair amount of chaos even before sunset. Establishing a battalion command post in the field took time and practice, but as the light faded, these were two ingredients the battalion did not have. Excess men from the command post provided local security for the headquarters, and Corporal James Crume was one of those men. His position in the headquarters was almost anachronistic; he was assigned to the message center to receive and pass on messages by telegraph. The twenty-one-year-old Texan joined the army just eighteen months before and had been with the battalion for just over a year when the war broke out. He recalls, "At that time, we had three people working in the message center. The radio section was completely different, all we did was handle the messages. There really wasn't a whole lot for us to do. It was a holdover organization from World War I, when everyone used telegraphs, and so the message center would get those in morse code and write it down in English and give it to the operations center. By our day, everything was by voice, and so we didn't really have a lot to do."[54]

Crume spent that first night in a foxhole forward of the command post with another signal soldier from the headquarters element. For him, the scene was uneventful.

Back in the headquarters main command area, however, radioman Johnny Theodore had a front-row seat to the confusion of the battalion staff and the associated elements that make up a battalion headquarters in the field. "I remember that we had a hill on the right . . . there were some trees up there on the right, and we climbed up the hill. Now this is strange because we were on the forward slope of the hill. The hill had one crest and then a shelf, and another false crest beyond that. I believe that our headquarters setup was in the middle of the battalion line. That is what I was told anyway, that there was a company to our right and left and front, and the roadblock was a couple of hundred yards downhill to our left front. I couldn't see the other units because of the trees. I could see a very short stretch of the road, probably at about the eleven o'clock direction if I was pointed straight up the valley. We set up one SCR-300, and that took a while, and we also set up the CW-694."[55]

SCR-300, which stands for Set, Complete, Radio, Model 300, was the standard tactical radio at the time. The SCR-300 operated, like all infantry ground tactical radios then and now, with frequency modulation (FM), not amplitude modulation (AM). The CW-694 was a device used for ciphering and deciphering encrypted messages.

Theodore continues, "I saw a group of civilians, maybe forty, through the gap in the trees just as the sun was going down. They were allowed through the roadblock. Then a little while later, I heard from behind us, over the hill, there was a sound like a burp gun. Then there was a second group of civilians, this one was bigger, coming towards us when this flat trajectory round, midsized, impacts somewhere between the civilians and our roadblock."[56]

Most likely, the presence of these refugees dressed in white alerted Lieutenant Matta from Team Field of the roadblock on the road ahead. Unfortunately, he did not press in close enough that night to determine whose roadblock it was.

The impetus for what took place next has been ascribed to a misinterpreted radio message received at the headquarters of the 2nd Battalion 7th Cavalry at some point during the night, probably around midnight, but possibly earlier. A report sent from regimental headquarters to division headquarters the next day indicates that the battalion executive officer, Major Omar Hitchner, received word of what he understood to be a breakthrough by the North Koreans to the north (right) of the battalion.

According to the regimental logs, at 0035 hours, a call came from 1st Cavalry Division headquarters, ordering the regiment's operations officer to come to the division headquarters. At 0120, Lieutenant Colonel Heyer, commander of the 2nd Battalion, contacted the 7th Cavalry regimental command post and informed it that a large number of refugees were to his front and that a vehicle, possibly a tank, passed through his position moments earlier. Ten minutes later, Lieutenant Colonel Witherspoon, the regimental S-3, informed the 2nd Battalion headquarters of a breakthrough on its right, and that it must pull back.[57] At the time, the 2nd Battalion had only just settled in and had not yet managed to make contact with any units on either flank. The unit on its right (north) that night was the 27th Infantry Regiment (nicknamed the "Wolfhounds"), of the 25th Infantry Division. The Wolfhounds were defending the western approach to Hwanggan across the road that entered the area from Chongsan. Although fighting was occurring in that area at that time, there was no breakthrough.[58]

Not knowing that, and only having the order from Major Wither- spoon at regimental headquarters to pull back, either Major Hitchner or Lieutenant Colonel Heyer then sent a warning order to the 2nd Battalion's companies about the breakthrough on their right flank. At this time, the battalion was defending towards the west above the valley that ran from Yongdong in the southwest to Hwanggan in the northeast. The word went out to the company command posts via field telephone lines that the com- munications platoon had installed just a short while earlier.[59]

At that instant, the four tanks that had been with Team Field and the men of F Company, 2nd Battalion, 8th Cavalry, burst on the scene. The Team Field tanks had separated from the infantry, deciding to go their own way earlier in the day, and along the way had picked up more strag- glers in the dark. These tanks and men believed they were trying to break through an "enemy" roadblock so they could rejoin their regiment farther down the road toward Hwanggan. Between 1:00 A.M. and 2:00 A.M. in the darkness of July 26, their four remaining tanks ran through the minor barriers that the 2nd Battalion 7th Cavalry had just built and continued down the road towards Hwanggan. Naturally, when fired upon, these tanks returned fire with every machine gun on board. Their passage was the proximate cause of the collapse of the 2nd Battalion 7th Cavalry that night.

Staring out into the dark, unable to make out anything but the white of some of the refugees and the threatening bulk of the tanks, the men of the 2nd Battalion cut loose with every weapon at their disposal on anything that even remotely resembled a target to their front. Coming towards the line through the darkness were some of the infantry who could not keep up with the fast-moving tanks. Faced with the fires of the 2nd Battalion, the infantry cut south across the paddies, which placed them generally across the front of the 2nd Battalion 7th Cavalry. Despite the sporadic fire into the darkness, no casualties can be confirmed as having occurred among the soldiers of either U.S. unit.

At almost the same time, a message was sent from the battalion head- quarters to the companies saying that the battalion would be pulling back due to the heavy pressure to its front and would establish a line of defense to the northeast that would be less exposed to an enemy envelopment. This order accelerated the cascade to the rear, towards No Gun Ri, a small village farther up the valley to the northeast, a few miles closer to Hwang- gan.

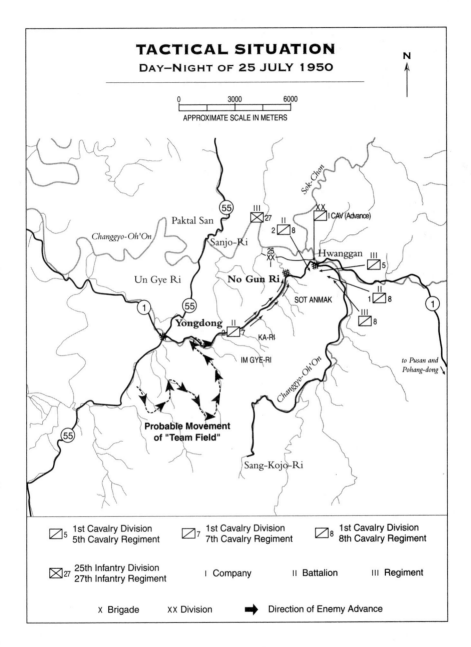

TACTICAL SITUATION
DAY–NIGHT OF 25 JULY 1950

N

APPROXIMATE SCALE IN METERS

| 0 | 3000 | 6000 |

Sok-Chon

Paktal San

Changgyo-Oh'On

Sanjo-Ri

No Gun Ri

I CAV (Advance)

Hwanggan

Un Gye Ri

SOT ANMAK

Yongdong

KA-RI

IM GYE-RI

Changgyo-Oh'On

to Pusan and
Pohang-dong

**Probable Movement
of "Team Field"**

Sang-Kojo-Ri

	1st Cavalry Division 5th Cavalry Regiment		1st Cavalry Division 7th Cavalry Regiment		1st Cavalry Division 8th Cavalry Regiment
	25th Infantry Division 27th Infantry Regiment	I Company	II Battalion	III Regiment	
X Brigade	XX Division	➡ Direction of Enemy Advance			

Soldiers can be jittery during their first night in combat and quick to fire at anything that moves in the darkness. When the tanks of the 71st Tank Company rushed through the battalion and large parts of the line opened up, often firing indiscriminately to its front, the battalion command group believed that a general engagement was occurring. The sounds of tank main guns, multiple machine guns, and rifle fire from its own men contributed to the din. The battalion surely believed that it was now under general attack by a combined arms force of the North Korean army. The sound of tanks and machine guns, coupled with company reports that these tanks were accelerating towards them, then passing by them in the darkness, led the battalion leaders to order the nighttime withdrawal to a position closer to Hwanggan to prevent encirclement.[60] If itchy trigger finger is a phenomenon of an individual soldier's panic, then such orders and reactions as those displayed in the 2nd Battalion 7th Cavalry command group that night are the officers' equivalent.

It was the final straw for the men of the 2nd Battalion 7th Cavalry.

CHAPTER 5

Washout

MIDNIGHT JULY 25 TO JULY 29, 1950

THE COLLAPSE OF THE 2ND BATTALION 7TH CAVALRY ON THE NIGHT OF July 25–26, 1950 was not instantaneous. The men of the 7th Cavalry largely made individual decisions. In action at night for the first time, separated into their individual positions without much leadership to help make sense of what they heard and dimly perceived through the darkness, the soldiers were forced to make sense of the sights and sounds of night combat by themselves. The men of the 7th Cavalry had too many stimuli coming in that would, unchecked, create fear.

Compounding the problem was a lack of leadership on the ground to hold the battalion in place. Though the battalion had a full complement of officers led by Lieutenant Colonel Herbert Heyer, few of the leaders had much more large-unit-night operations training than did their men. But even if all of the officers were combat-hardened veterans, there were barely any sergeants to make the link between the orders of officers and the actions of men. As a result, the unit disintegrated. Between midnight and about 2 A.M. on July 26, the 2nd Battalion 7th Cavalry went from being an organized, cohesive force operating under the command and the control of its officers to a scattered and random collection of men operating according to their own perceptions and fears—the classic example of the term "bug-out" that came into popular use in the opening days of the Korean War.

Obviously, exceptions to this general statement could be found, and some groups held together better than others.

Although they were not actually attacked by a North Korean force, the men of the 2nd Battalion 7th Cavalry believed that they were. Gunfire crossed the valley in two directions, tanks were loose on the valley floor and apparently firing wildly as well, and the whole experience took place in the darkness to men who had not slept much in the preceding two days.

Without the steadying influence of the noncommissioned officers who would normally be with them, the men took counsel of the fears that had been building since their movement forward from Pohang-dong to Hwanggan. These fears were fueled by the stories from the men of the 24th passing them on the way up to the line and were expressed in the tragic fratricidal loss of Lieutenant Plummer and the wounding of Private Sanderlin to panicked fire. They were fears of the unknown and the suspected. When faced with an overload of information, visual and audile, each man individually interpreted it as being extremely dangerous to his personal being. Without the backbone of their unit, the experienced sergeants who had been transferred to the 24th Infantry Division, the men of the 7th Cavalry Regiment operated under even more handicaps. Barely a single man in the ranks had any combat experience. Few battle veterans were there to help them separate the sounds of friendly weapons from enemy weapons, to distinguish the sound of an American tank from the sound of an enemy tank. At a minimum, experienced combat veterans might have counseled those around them to wait and see how the situation developed.

As the sounds of the tanks reverberated through the valley at 2:00 A.M. on July 26, isolated elements of the battalion fired their weapons into the dark. Although never mentioned in the postcombat reports or in the more current media reports, it is possible that at least some of the refugees already stopped in front of the battalion were caught in the fratricidal crossfire between Team Field and the 2nd Battalion 7th Cavalry Regiment that dark night. Numbers and accounts of this, however, are lost to history.

In E Company, the confusion of the night was thorough. Bazooka gunner Marvin Daniels was among those close to a recognizable source of authority when the chaos descended on the unit: "I could hear the radioman relaying a message to the commander. I could hear the radioman asking for confirmation of that command. It wasn't but a few minutes passed that we started taking heavy fire from all directions. If we'd a got the command earlier, we might've gotten out of there. And this lieutenant said, 'Let's get outta here' . . . then I was sliding down a hill, skidding all the way and finally I caught a sapling and stopped sliding. Me, my ammo bearer, and a couple of others. We ran all night, and we were being chased. We pulled back to this position overlooking the railroad trestle. I stayed with this lieutenant and sergeant. We were on somewhat of a rise, overlooking the railroad trestle and a bridge, and stragglers came in all day."[1]

Lieutenants John Potts and John Lippincott had a slightly better idea of the situation in F Company, but only slightly. Their positions as the second and third platoon leaders meant that they, of anyone, ought to have heard what was going on in the company shortly after the commander did. As it turned out, that was not the case. Lieutenant Lippincott remembers, "That night we had no opposition. I had not seen the company commander the whole time, 'cause we were moving into position. It was pitch black dark. We heard tanks starting up, but we couldn't see anything. We heard, and I saw personally, some vehicle with a tank cannon that moved down the tracks. That tank stopped; I heard Koreans speaking out there. Then, about thirty minutes later, a runner came to me and said that the unit on the right had been under intense attack. The order said withdraw down the hill to the road. It was a very sketchy order. As for the tank, I couldn't see it all the time, but there was something that silhouetted it; maybe it fired, I don't remember that though. Maybe it was sparks from the engine. It was something that gave me that view. Anyway, it just sat there. We came out as a platoon relatively intact down to that road. Then we moved down the road for the rest of the night."[2]

Lieutenant Potts's experience was not much different. He remembers that night this way: "The second battalion moved out and arrived at this little railhead place near Yongdong. We dismounted and moved out to a hill off to the right. The railroad tracks and the road were close together here. We moved out maybe 200 or 300 yards and then were directed up a hill to the right. I spread my platoon out. I was on the right of the company, and my platoon was tied in on the left. The company CP (command post) was something like 200 yards or so to our rear, to the side. I'm not sure though, because I never saw it. I am judging based upon the amount of time that it took the wireman to run the line there and come back. Anyway, during the night one of my men came up to my platoon CP and said that he heard voices and people moving out there. I tried to contact the company CP, but there was no answer. I sent a man down to check the line, make sure everyone was up and alert and had their ammo and such. At the same time, I sent a runner back, following the wire, to the company CP to pass the word. He came back in a little while saying that there was nobody there. At that point, I went down the right side of my line and the platoon sergeant went down the left to make sure everyone had all their gear, their packs on and such. I got another report from the right side of the line that they could hear even more voices out to the front, and I decided that if the whole North Korean army was out there and I was alone, I didn't want to be there. I gave the order, and we moved out. Along the way, we picked up some others, I think a section from weapons company (H Company), but I'm not sure if that's who they were. We walked down off that hill and across country. It was nearing dawn by the time we got close to that railroad drop point where we'd been the day before. Off to the left, we could see some people clustering, so we went down there to see who was there. Captain Chandler was out there on the road collecting people up and he was chewig everyone's ass. He got us all together. Then shortly after that, we moved out again, down the road. We marched for a while, maybe an hour before we stopped and set up again."[3]

At the battalion command post near the crest of the ridge, radioman Johnny Theodore had a front row seat to the chaos. He says, ". . . . we were on this knoll and somebody was setting up a tent for the command post on our left front. I remember seeing Lieutenant Lester in the area. That was unusual that he was up there, 'cause he usually liked to stay in the back . . . . I know that I didn't see Colonel Heyer up there at all, not the whole time. Then everything fell apart. Somebody yelled, 'Get the hell outta here!' and I saw everyone running all over. I know they left the tent. I grabbed the 300; I remember that especially because it was really light. I later noticed that it didn't have a battery in it, that's why it was so light. I didn't grab the antenna, just the radio. At this point, the sun was down. There was maybe five in my group. We went straight back, over the top of the hill and into the valley, and then curved around to the road after, maybe, 300 or 500 yards. By the time I got to the road, everyone on the road was walking to the rear."[4]

Larry Levine was also part of the battalion headquarters signal section. Levine was a corporal at the time with a prior hitch in the marines after the Second World War, but like the others, this was his first night at the front. Levine recalls that night this way: "My first concrete memory is that first night up on the hill. We had dug shallow foxholes. I couldn't raise anyone at regiment, and we never did achieve radio contact. But I remember that because that night the first hair-raising incident occurred. In total darkness, I hear a voice from somewhere ahead of me whispering, 'Hey Joe, where is everyone?' At that point I think I'm living a scene in one of those WWII movies where the Japanese soldier says that and the GI answers and ends up with a bayonet in his gut. There is no one in my outfit named Joe, so I don't answer. The next clear memory I have of that night is that we are ordered down from the hill. I don't know where the order came from or who told me, but we went down that hill. At the bottom of the hill is a railroad track, and we turn to our left and walk along the track bed. Shortly a tank comes down the track behind us and opens fire. When a tank fires, you hear the explosion a split second after the report. We scattered. I don't know what happened right after that."[5]

Apparently some elements of the battalion were still on the move when the tanks of Team Field arrived. Larry "Buddy" Wenzel was a private that summer. He served in both G and H Companies during the war, but that night he was among a group that was either late in arriving or was on patrol when the chaos descended upon the battalion. Says Wenzel, "We spent the night before outside some town, and then the next day we moved up. We walked alongside of some railroad tracks, and we went off to the right side of the road into like an open area while it was still daytime. It was kind of like a narrow road. We were still moving down the narrow road after the sun set. We came up on a wide ravine, and I heard someone in the platoon yell 'Tanks!' When I heard that, I turned around and hauled ass with the rest of them. Then I heard the tank, and it must have been just about a hundred yards behind us. I didn't hear any main guns to start with, but I heard a lot of machine guns. It sounded like there were two or three of them. I never did see him, but you could sure hear him, coming through the brush, and I'll tell you, that's a scary sound.

"I think there was maybe thirty or forty guys with me running from that tank. Everybody was scared that we were surrounded by the North Koreans. I was carrying some ammo, and we all took off running straight back the way we went up there. It was dark, and you could not make out the guys around you. We ran for quite a ways, but then we gave out of air, and we just stopped running and started walking. We were just following whoever was leading the pack. Sometime in the night, we stopped, I don't really know why, but somebody was in charge up there I guess. There were railroad tracks to the left of me; up that way was F Company. It went F Company, G Company, then H Company. It was a raised railroad track; on the left side of the track, there was a hill that sloped up."[6]

Like some of the others, Wenzel arrived at No Gun Ri tired and without his leaders.

Confusion and disintegration reigned nearly universally that night throughout the 2nd Battalion, with one major exception: Large parts of H Company, the heavy weapons company, did not fall apart. It maintained composure, in part because it was already next to or astride the road and therefore did not have to contend with a confusing nighttime cross-country movement without the benefit of maps and in part because this accident of deployment allowed the company's leaders to be very visible, or audible, to its soldiers. The leaders, therefore, acted like the psychological anchors they are supposed to be, allowing their men to spend most of their energy following orders and less energy on trying to figure out how to distance themselves from what they believed was a North Korean combined arms onslaught.

This was not the case across the entire line. In G Company, a lieutenant found that he was not all that he believed himself to be prior to deployment: "There was a West Point lieutenant with us. I remember him specifically because he was so short. He cracked up. I don't know how to explain that. I mean I don't understand why a guy like that would be in the infantry to begin with. Maybe they just couldn't tell that he wasn't cut out for the infantry. We were supposed to be following him, but the fact is he was unable to make any decisions. Hell, sometimes he couldn't even talk. He had no idea where he was, where he was going, or what he was going to do. Eventually the platoon sergeant took over, a guy that had been a private the month before. He had enough and finally just told him, 'Just follow me.' We were shot at that night. Who was shooting, I don't really know. Was it our people or the enemy or what? But we were shot at. We wandered, then lay down. The next morning, we woke up, and there was G Company right next to us. It was the strangest thing, 'cause we didn't know where we were. Once we got back, where did that lieutenant go? I don't know. He had been the platoon leader at the time. I never saw anybody fall apart like that before. I remember that he was slim, rather short; he didn't have a large build at all."[7]

Another soldier who appears to have been in that same cluster of G Company soldiers that night was mortarman Russell McKinley. He remembers that first day and the following night this way: "The next day we got on a train; I got on a flatbed. When we stopped, we got off on the right side of the train and started climbing a hill. We didn't dig the mortars in, but we dug in on the crest. Then, sometime after dark, I'm not sure when, we were told to move out. We started down the hill and it was dark, down one hill and up another that was really steep. Now this I remember specifically . . . we stopped to take a break, I remember because my calves were cramping up bad, I was stretching and about to rub them when CLANG . . . I kicked that [mortar] tube over and it went clanging down the hillside. After that, all hell broke loose below us, about a hundred yards, all sorts of shooting starts. I didn't actually see any tracers or anything, but the sound of it was like every gun in the valley was going off at once. We waited there for a second and then take off sideways across the face of the hill, down the same goat trail. After a while, an hour maybe, we stopped again to take a break. I think it was the whole company with us, but I don't really know. All I could see was the guy or two ahead of me and a few behind me, so what do I know?

Well, we were stopped there for a while, a long while, when somebody notices this and goes up forward to see what's happening. They go up the trail and find this guy asleep. He had been in the middle of the column, but now everyone in front of him is gone. Seems like the rest had moved out and because he was asleep, we lost contact. So then this lieutenant starts up; he takes over. I don't know what he was doing before. We moved along that trail for maybe another hour when we stopped again. The lieutenant was several men ahead of me . . . he was sobbing, sort of blubbering, and at that point somebody said, 'Sergeant so-and-so is going to take over.' Then that sergeant took us out of there.[8]

Another mortarman, John De Borde, also of G Company, remembered that night fairly clearly: "We had gone up a hill, and we took up positions, and the next thing I know Hank [company commander Captain Henry West] was moving us again. That's when we got split up, about a platoon-sized group. We were moving and then we were by ourselves. I don't know what the organizations were, but somewhere along there, other units got mixed up with us in there too. We got lost. I don't know why we moved out."[9]

Down on the road below, Norman Matthias still manned the .50-caliber gun of the ammunition and pioneer platoon. As night fell, Matthias had one of the least enviable positions—not only was he close to the road, but because of the ad hoc nature of his presence on the front lines, no well-established chain of command was watching for him. The ammunition and pioneer platoon is supposed to haul ammunition and work on field fortifications, but because of the heavy weapons it had, and the fact that the unit was so short-handed, Matthias found himself in a frontline position. From his perspective, the disintegration was an almost casual affair.

Matthias recalls, "Then this lieutenant came down to my hole and says, 'We'll be pulling back. Go down to the railroad track and wait for me down there.' Just Dick and I are in the hole, and we pick up the gun and started down. All we had to do was walk down the finger, and there we were. I don't know where the squad leader was, or the platoon leader or the platoon sergeant either. There was some officer there at the railroad—a lieutenant. I don't know who he was, but he saw our gun and said to us, 'I want you to set up here,' and pointed down the tracks. At this time, it seemed like everyone was coming off the hill and going on back down the tracks. About that time, a red flare goes up, and that's when I saw a bunch of civilians up ahead. Well, after that flare, you could see the civilians going off the road to the left; they did not cross the river or the bridge in front of me. Then I heard tanks. You could hear it clanking on the railroad tracks. I'll tell you, that is a scary sound, just clanking and clanking closer to you. I could see the silhouette . . . then it stopped, just short of the bridge but past where the civilians had gone to left. I dove off to the right side of the embankment when I saw that. Dick dove over too, and a guy named McNaulty was with us then too, I think.

"Then I saw the flash of the main gun. I saw red for a while after that, I don't think it was 200 yards away. I'm not sure what they were firing at, but it wasn't me. They started cutting loose with their machine guns then, sort of wild fire, all over the place. After a couple minutes, Wright [the assistant platoon sergeant] comes up, he comes walking right up the railroad tracks from behind and says, 'What the hell are you doing up here?! Everybody's pulled back.' So we picked up and started walking. After a while, I said to Dick, 'Screw this shit; we can't fire it anyway; and I tossed it [the gun barrel] over the embankment. Dick was still holding on to the receiver, and he went over the edge with it 'cause we hadn't broken it down. He starts crying, 'We can't leave the gun!'"[10]

At about that point, Matthias and his partner joined in with a larger group of soldiers from the battalion but personally unknown to them. They too were carrying disassembled machine-gun components. Together the group trudged down the road, without security or apparently anything on their minds beyond getting to the rear. According to Matthias, they continued up and over a slight rise, sharing the considerable weight of the .50-caliber machine gun among them until, out of sheer frustration, Matthias destroyed a part of the gun by smashing the rear of the assembly. Later, when he discovered that it was his own weapon he destroyed, he was furious with himself. Throughout the rest of the night he never saw a sergeant or an officer.

Soldiers and a few sergeants and lieutenants were out on their own, working their way backwards as individuals and small groups towards the last place they considered safe—the place where they had been dropped off, the village of No Gun Ri. In the confusion and terror of the night, many of the men did as soldiers throughout military history have done before them—they abandoned their equipment and even their weapons, anything that might be a hindrance to their flight.

From the testimony of the veterans fifty years later, it appears that in all of this chaos and confusion, there was one officer who managed to hold things together through the night and into the next morning, one officer around whom the new line formed—an officer originally commissioned into the medical service corps but now serving as the company commander of H Company, 2nd Battalion 7th Cavalry, Captain Melbourne Chandler.

Chandler was apparently one of the first, and for periods of time the only, officer down on the road. He quickly assembled most of his own men and led them back to the northeast, along the road that they had come down in the afternoon. Yet even Chandler was not wholly successful, as some elements of his company took council of their fears and joined the general rout to the rear. It was apparently at least partly his decision to stop in a spot where the valley narrowed and the road made a bend. Looking back in the direction his company had come from, he saw the valley stretching straight for almost a mile, giving clear fields of fire for the battalion should it set up there. Although no sign of pursuit in the predawn darkness of July 26, Chandler could certainly hear the sporadic gunfire still echoing through the hills as isolated elements of the scattered battalion confronted their own fears in the darkness. Chandler stopped his company and the stragglers who had attached themselves to his command and set them up astride the roadway and the railway that ran parallel.[11] The 2nd Battalion 7th Cavalry had, more or less, arrived at No Gun Ri.

CONSOLIDATION

When the sun came up on the morning of July 26, 1950, the battalion was, with the exception of most of H Company, scattered across the South Korean countryside. The battalion ceased to exist as a viable force over those several hours. When daylight came, hundreds of men were still wandering in the hills. The initial report from the 2nd Battalion 7th Cavalry that appeared in the 1st Cavalry Division G-2 log at 0714 that morning states that the entire battalion had eighty effectives, meaning that eighty soldiers were under the direct command and control of their officers at a known place on the ground.[12]

No accurate morning reports were filed that day as many of the men who would file them were themselves wandering among the hills or strung out on the road between Yongdong and No Gun Ri. Personnel strength reports were either ignored or skipped for the morning of July 26. At the same time, the battalion reported to regiment and division the loss of one light set (used to illuminate the inside of a command post tent), four .30-caliber light machine guns, four .30-caliber water-cooled heavy machine guns, three .50-caliber heavy machine guns, 119 M1 Garand rifles, and more.[13] For all intents and purposes, the 2nd Battalion existed in name only at that point. Recovery from the disintegration of the night before did not mean just getting all the men back; it also meant recovering the weapons and equipment abandoned during the night, establishing new positions, and reestablishing the chain of command.

Chandler started this process, ordering his direct-fire weapons such as the remaining machine guns, to locations where they could cover the valley floor. He sent his mortars to the rear and took charge of the men who started straggling down the road again once the sun came up. He assembled the soldiers of different companies to their own areas where they might sort themselves out with their own chains of command, if and when those leaders arrived. By midmorning, the battalion headquarters established itself on the reverse side of a hill overlooking the village of No Gun Ri, several miles to the northeast from where it had started the night before. The main line of the battalion, coalescing around the core of Chandler's company, spread across the valley floor and onto the slopes of the hills on either side. On the right side of the line, the railway passed through the defenses just past the spot where it passed over a small creek. Carrying the rail line over the creek was a sturdy concrete bridge, the bridge at No Gun Ri.

By late morning, enough men returned to the control of the battalion for recovery teams to start moving forward and collect the equipment dropped by the panicked soldiers during the night. Although impossible to pinpoint unit strength at any particular instant during the day, it appears that the number of men climbed slowly from the initial 300 gathered by Chandler as stragglers made their way down the road or over the hills. Again, Chandler appeared at the center of this activity.

Organizing men around those who appeared steadiest, Chandler set about recovering the lost equipment. Several of the trips made forward were escorted by men from his own, mostly fully armed, company. Chandler himself led a few of these patrols forward along the path of the rout.[14] This process continued all day, with ad hoc platoons of men walking forward to recover their weapons wherever they were abandoned. Fortunately for the battalion, most of the men found their way to the road at some point in the night, and so much of the equipment was easy to find. Over the course of the day, the battalion recovered the following material, not all of which had originally been reported as missing: nine light machine guns, two .50-caliber heavy machine guns, five SCR-300 tactical radios, four 536 [walkie-talkie] radios, one hundred twenty M1 rifles, twenty-six M1 carbines, seven Browning automatic rifles (BARs), and six 60-mm mortars.[15] In some ways, this recovery list was even more damning than the original report of the material lost. Not only was it more material (the mortars and BARs, for example, were not mentioned in the first message to higher headquarters), but that so much gear lay abandoned by the road paints a picture of complete and utter chaos.

By evening, the battalion was almost back in form, although more than one hundred men were still missing or unaccounted for by their sergeants and officers.[16] Most of the company commanders now had at least the rump elements of two or more platoons under their control, and the initial hodgepodge defensive line established by Chandler when he placed returning men wherever they were needed was beginning to resemble a standard battalion defense. Still, had the North Korean army attacked that day, the disaster might have extended far beyond the 7th Cavalry Regiment.

At Eighth U.S. Army, Korea (EUSAK) headquarters, the issue of refugees finally received serious attention. Staff officers and liaison officers from the South Korean national police and the ROK army worked out a plan to reduce the confusion caused by the passage and presence of so many civilians on the battlefield. At ten o'clock on the morning of July 26, a written order was issued by EUSAK headquarters in Taegu. The order dictated an orderly process for dealing with civilians through liaisons with the ROK army and the national police. The order stated, in part:

Part I
Effective immediately, the following procedures will be adhered to by all commands relative to the flow of refugees in battle areas and rear areas. No refugees will be permitted to cross battle lines at any time. Movement of all Koreans in groups will cease immediately. No areas will be evacuated by Koreans without a direct order from commanding general EUSAK or upon orders of division commanders. Each division will be assigned three national police liaison officers to assist in clearing any area of the civilian populace that will interfere with the successful accomplishment of his mission.

Part II
Procedure for clearing areas. Division commanders will inform national police officers of the area or sector to be evacuated, the route, and the time the area will be cleared. National police will immediately clear the area. Food, water, and comfort items for these refugees will be provided by the Vice Minister of Social Affairs through the national police. All refugees will move along their predetermined route to selected concentration areas from sun-up to sun-down. This will be a controlled movement under the direction and supervision of the national police and representatives from the office of Korean Welfare Affairs.

Part III
Movement of Koreans during hours of darkness. There will be absolutely no movement of Korean civilians, as individuals or groups in battle areas or rear areas, after the hours of darkness. Uniformed Korean police will rigidly enforce this directive.

Part IV
To accomplish this procedure, as outlined in this directive, leaflets will be prepared and dropped in all areas forward and rear of the battle line to effectively disseminate this information. National police will further disseminate this information to all Korean civilians by means of radio, messenger, and the press.[17]

It was probably an earlier discussion about this problem that the 8th Cavalry regimental liaison officer at 1st Cavalry Division headquarters garbled badly in his phone call to the regiment (page 83).

No corps-level command structure separated EUSAK from the 1st Cavalry Division, so the order passed quickly. Not long after its receipt of the order, the 1st Cavalry Division issued its own instructions. Based upon the orders from EUSAK, the 1st Cavalry Division's instructions were almost a verbatim retransmission.[18]

At the same time, however, all was not proceeding smoothly on the ground. The same South Korean liaison officers who were supposed to be screening and escorting the civilians through the lines found themselves continually stopped and challenged by nervous American troops wary of any Korean holding a gun, regardless of uniform. Over and over, these South Korean soldiers and national police were captured and interrogated. Time and again, they lost their weapons to Americans leery of the threat of infiltration. One South Korean counter intelligence corps (CIC) officer operating in the 1st Cavalry Division area, identified in a report only as Lieutenant Choi, made the extent of the problem very clear on the morning of July 26, 1950. The text of the report is telling.

> Lieutenant Choi therefore requested that his CIC agents be issued identification cards, written in English, and signed by a responsible person. As the situation now stands, according to Lt. Choi, his men are afraid to assist in the refugee program in the forward area because of their not having identification cards which the American soldiers can read.[19]

Choi's report makes it clear: On July 26, 1950, at least, no South Korean army liaison teams were up front with the most forward unit of the 1st Cavalry Division, the 7th Cavalry Regiment. Choi and his team of four were in the rear attempting to rectify a situation that had plagued the division for more than a week.

By this point, reports from line units talked about being attacked behind the lines by Koreans wearing American uniforms and armed with

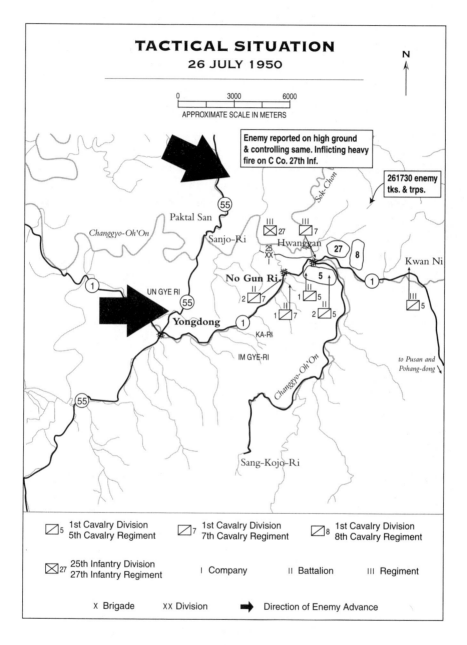

TACTICAL SITUATION
26 JULY 1950

N

0   3000   6000
APPROXIMATE SCALE IN METERS

Enemy reported on high ground & controlling same. Inflicting heavy fire on C Co. 27th Inf.

261730 enemy tks. & trps.

Paktal San

Changgyo-Oh'On

Sanjo-Ri

Hwanggan

Kwan Ni

No Gun Ri

UN GYE RI

Yongdong

KA-RI

IM GYE-RI

to Pusan and Pohang-dong

Changgyo-Oh'On

Sok-Chon

Sang-Kojo-Ri

	1st Cavalry Division 5th Cavalry Regiment		1st Cavalry Division 7th Cavalry Regiment		1st Cavalry Division 8th Cavalry Regiment
	25th Infantry Division 27th Infantry Regiment		I Company	II Battalion	III Regiment
	X Brigade	XX Division	➡ Direction of Enemy Advance		

American weapons. Although the front line was not aware of the problem of South Korean communists and guerilla combatants among the rest of the population, the problem was beginning to sink in at higher headquarters. One report gives a clear indication of the division's growing awareness of the guerilla problem in its rear areas.

A diary removed from a guerilla KIA near [unintelligible] indicated that there is an OP in our rear area which commands almost all our positions. An est. 20 men set an ambush along our MSR [main supply route] and during early morning hours attacked 3 vehicles using the road, inflicting 4 casualties. A KIA guerilla was reported carrying a Russian-manufactured pistol. The guerilla force is still at large in our area.[20]

An interrogation report of three civilians who led a group of four lost Americans back to friendly lines at around the same time painted the picture even more clearly. The "Headquarters, 1st Cavalry Division (Inf), Office of the ACofS, G-2, Interrogation of Civilians Report" of July 29 provided the following image of the scale of guerilla activities in the immediate area. Based upon observations of Sun Yong Pok (age thirty-three at the time), Yong Shig Yu (then twenty-three) and Whong Yong Pok (also twenty-three), the report in part says:

The above-mentioned individuals stated that guerillas were active in the area between Solchon (1077–1455) and Mupungjang (1083–1448). The guerilla was organized by the natives living around Mt. Chiru (1070–1370) and has an estimated strength of 30. The guerillas are equipped with M-1 rifles, Jap 38 rifles, Russian SMGs [submachine guns], but have no light or heavy MGs or mortars.[21]

At noon on July 26, 1st Battalion 7th Cavalry arrived by train at the Hwanggan railway station. Word of the collapse of the 2nd Battalion had spread quickly, and the 7th Cavalry regimental headquarters wasted no time in ordering the 1st Battalion to the front to support the 2nd Battalion. At this time, no friendly troops were near No Gun Ri either to the west or south. To the north, the 27th Infantry Regiment of the 25th Infantry Division, held its line in the valley that led into Hwanggan from the northwest. By sunset on July 26, 1950, as the 2nd Battalion was finally regaining control of all of its men and equipment, the 1st Battalion started to arrive and fill in positions on the left, to the south of the 2nd Battalion's positions astride the road.

As far as the official records are concerned, this is about all the information that can be fully and accurately supported with documentation. Moving beyond this point requires a fusion of human memory, supported by documents that would make little sense without oral history filling in the gaps, and a small measure of historical interpretation. What follows are the accounts of just a few of the men who were with the 2nd Battalion 7th Cavalry on July 26, 1950 at a place called No Gun Ri, South Korea.

THE NO GUN RI INCIDENT

Radioman John Theodore provides his memories of No Gun Ri: "We walked back, I guess, a max of three or four miles. It was more than an hour for sure. We didn't really set up; we just sort of stopped there next to the road. We waited for daylight to get organized because I didn't really know who I was with. I knew these guys were from my unit, but I didn't know what company or anything. Then the sun came up, and the radio truck came up from the rear.

"Sergeant Eldrige, he was the person that was in charge of the linesmen, he starts organizing us. Somebody gave us [the communications detachment] orders to go up this hill to the right front. Frank [Baylock, another soldier from the communications section] was back with the truck, and battalion headquarters was even further back. We went up this hill and set up the SCR-300. I really don't know who we were supposed to make commo for at that point. It may have been that we were supposed to be a relay station, because we'd left the large antenna all the way back at the other site. But we never got any commo for them, only messages for us.

"I had a beautiful view from that hill—the road was on my left if I looked up the valley, then there is like a wash, a dry riverbed with lots of sand wash or something like that, then the railroad tracks, with the overpass or something. Beyond that bridge, there is a pretty good-sized hill, probably the size of the one that I am on. I can't see the rifle companies; there's a lot of small vegetation around me that sort of cuts off my view. But I could hear them down by the road. We're setting in there and I see a jeep go down the road. There are two people in the jeep, and it's driving forward and something about it didn't look right 'cause there was one GI in there and another guy without a helmet. This was around noon or so. About twenty minutes later, I see the jeep come back. Then a little while later, I saw somewhere around fifty to seventy-five people coming down the valley in the low ground between the road and the railroad. They were about a mile away."[22]

From his elevated position, Theodore may have been one of the first to see the refugees coming down the road. History may never know exactly who these refugees were, where they were from, and where they went after this. It is entirely possible, probable even, that these refugees originated from Yongdong and two of the villages just slightly up the road, Im Ke Ri and Chu Gok Ri. Some elements of what the people from those villages say they experienced and what the veterans of the 7th Cavalry say happened match fairly well, if varying interpretations of some events are taken into account. Still, what exists is testimony, and little else, from both sides about the events that followed.

Remembers Johnny Theodore, "Now I did not hear a word on the battalion command net. There was nothing. On the other hand, I could have been on the wrong channel. I mean, I could hear and talk to my guys back in the battalion, but I never really heard any of the normal chatter that went on over a battalion net, so while I was on the channel that they told me to be on, that could have been the wrong channel. Frankly, I don't know what the hell I was doin' up there.

"Then a round of white phosphorus [an artillery or mortar shell] came way in front of that group. I guess it was supposed to stop them, and it worked—it stopped them momentarily but not for very long. They started coming again. Then thirteen or fourteen rounds came in on them, right into them, right in the center. I don't know if this was artillery or 4.2 mortars or what. I am guessing that they were around a thousand yards away when the white phosphorus came in, and when the high explosive came in, they would have been about six hundred or so yards away. Some idiots down there opened up with a machine gun too. I couldn't say if there was any small arms fire, 'cause I couldn't hear it, but that doesn't mean anything 'cause it could have been covered up by the machine guns.

"That stopped them. When the shells came in, a lot of them hit the ground, but some of them just stood there for a while. They stayed right there. I don't know how many were killed, or what happened. They were there until the night set. Sometime the next morning when I looked over that way, I saw a bunch of them under that railroad and maybe twenty-five bodies out where the shelling had hit them. I couldn't see more than maybe fifteen or twenty back under there. My angle was pretty good, but I couldn't see all the way through the tunnel."[23]

From his testimony, it appears that Larry Levine, also of the communications section, was on another part of the hill from Theodore, giving him a slightly different angle on the events that unfolded below him.

"That day at No Gun Ri was terribly hot. I remember that I couldn't understand how those people could just stand there in that heat. My position was behind a small knoll and it seems to me that it was 500 to 700 yards from the bridge. I'm judging that by what size I see in my mind's eye of the little girl. Again in my mind's eye, the terrain placed me slightly below the top of the bridge. I don't remember when the people arrived. I don't remember if they all came at once, or if the crowd grew. I can't really determine how many people were there—perhaps a hundred. I know that no one walked down to the crowd to talk to them. They never moved. It seemed so obvious to us that the reason they didn't move was because they couldn't. North Koreans among them would have killed them.

"I recall the thunk-thunk of two heavy mortars being fired. When the shells landed among the crowd and they started running about; [then] the machine guns and small arms began. It didn't last long, maybe a minute, but it was frenzied. It was like these guys had never shot at human beings before and now they had permission to shoot at anything that moved. Maybe two or three minutes after it began, this little girl started running across the top of the bridge. I could hear a nearby machine gun firing at her and I don't know how many others. And soldiers were yelling, 'Stop firing! Stop firing!' But she was hit. Maybe four or five GIs ran to the bridge and picked her up. I don't know what happened to her. That was the end of it."[24]

Levine was almost certainly mistaken in his assumption about North Korean infiltrators. Most likely, he had this belief in 1950, and time and the reading of histories of the war have reinforced it, but it appears that no North Koreans, infiltrators or otherwise, were among this batch of civilians. *Armed men, however, were among them.*

Back on the same hill with Larry Levine, James Crume found that he had no real mission. Normally Crume served in the battalion headquarters, which had just gone through a very drastic pruning the night before. Non-essential personnel found themselves shunted to other jobs. As a message-center soldier trained to receive and send messages in morse code over telegraphs that were no longer in use in the American army any more, Crume had no messages to pass. Thus it appears that he was sent off to provide local security for some of the radiomen farther up the hill. His position on the side of the hill gave him an angled view of the front of the battalion, and when the critical moment came, he recalls two other people on the hillside near him.

James Crume remembers, "The battalion was astraddle the road coming down from the north, and the battalion CP was on a relatively gentle slope on the back of that hill. At this time, I recall that I was about ten to fifteen yards from the battalion commander and the battalion S-3. It was just them up there; I don't really remember anyone else there at the time. I was just standing there carrying my rifle. It was a clear day. The first thing that I remember seeing was the individuals coming down the road. They were about 300 to 500 yards away at the time, the road sort of went obliquely to where I was standing. They were fairly well grouped together, about a hundred yards of them.

"The next thing I know the mortar rounds started going into them. There's a different sound between artillery and mortars, so that's how I knew it was mortars. If it had been artillery, the bursts would have been bigger. There was a burst of mortar rounds, and then it stopped, and they continued coming down the road, and more came in. Well, the refugees sort of dispersed out on the road, and then it stopped, and they got back up on the road, and then when they started coming again, more mortar rounds came in. I don't remember seeing any bodies. I was just about four or five feet lower on the hill than he [Lieutenant Colonel Heyer, the battalion commander] was and off to his left. As the mortars were coming in, I looked over my shoulder and looked at him, and I could see that he didn't agree with that at all. He had kind of a craggy face anyhow, and he was very slow in speaking, and it [his face] was drawn, and he was frowning.

"I don't remember seeing any sort of bridge at all, or any gunfire for that matter. I think that this sort of emotionally affected Colonel Heyer. Before that, he was taking care of business, but after that he just sort of seemed to sit there on the side of the hill."[25]

Buddy Wenzel's wide-angle view of the attack on the refugees was not as clear. Assigned to H Company at the time, he was positioned down and to the right side of the tracks facing southwest. His version of events is closer, more personal, and was echoed by several others. Although not all are repeated here, the recollections of many veterans are a variation of Wenzel's account.

Wenzel recalls: "We waited about an hour, and they started coming through down the tracks, on paths on both sides of the tracks. The tracks kinda made a turn to the right about five hundred yards away, maybe a thousand yards at the most. The front ones, there were like maybe fifteen or twenty of them, and they were getting thicker beyond that. Somebody said, "Fire over their heads for a warning." Our line went sort of diagonal, from where I was the line went diagonal forward to my left. So when I got out of my hole, with about thirty other guys, we all had M1s.

"Now we had one machine gun up on the railroad tracks, and another air-cooled machine gun on the right, sort of up above us to the right. Well, when we fired over their heads they panicked. I guess that maybe fifty of them ran down into that little flat area and then the rest of the way down into the valley, they were trying to get into the culvert. Well, that's when some of them started to run towards us. We were firing over them all this time."[26]

Despite the mild conflicts in testimony among the American sources, it appears probable that the mortars impacted first, or perhaps simultaneously with Wenzel's group's warning shots. Aside from Wenzel's group on the right (north) side of the tracks, several soldiers on the main line apparently took action on their own initiative when they saw the shells impacting among the civilians. Among them were men like machine-gunner Norman Tinkler who stated that from his position to the south of the trestle bridge, he fired one belt (approximately 250 rounds) from his .30-caliber machine gun towards the civilians. Tinkler is adamant that he did this on his own without orders or direction. Most likely, some, perhaps twenty or thirty, riflemen from the main line to the south of the railway also fired a few rounds towards the civilians at ranges from 100 to 500 yards. Things then went from bad to worse.

After the mortar shells and the initial gunfire shot over the heads of the group of seventy-five to a hundred South Korean peasants, South Korean local guerillas within the group returned the American fire.[27] At least one submachine gun and one Japanese rifle were fired from among the villagers in response to the Americans' firing. It was a fatal mistake. The Americans in the area—anywhere from 50 to 150 soldiers had a clear shot towards the refugees—returned fire in a lethal although brief fusillade. Some, however, remember the sequence slightly differently.

Buddy Wenzel recalls those seconds this way, "Somebody yelled, 'We're being fired at.' Then there was a bunch that started shooting into the refugees. And that's when, maybe five or six shells come in down there near the refugees in the culvert. The round made a sound like 'shrwirrr, shrwirrr, shrwirr . . .' and that's different than the sound that mortars make; they make like a 'ssshhhwwrrr' sound. So that's why I thought that it was a tank or something, a North Korean tank. This all happened in a minute, but it all came out when we panicked 'cause we thought we were getting shot at and I thought that was a tank shooting at us and just landing in the refugees.

"There was a lieutenant that was running down to that group I was with from the right towards the tracks. I saw this little girl that was sort of in front—she was maybe four or five years old—and she was coming down the track, and I shot towards her and she fell. Well this lieutenant ran out there and picked up this little girl. Why . . . why I did that I can't tell you. Her hair was cut real short. She was wearing a dress with like bloomers underneath. The bloomers were white, but the dress was like a drab color. That's why the lieutenant was yelling cease fire, and he was running. She was out there in front, by herself, and flailing her arms and throwing her arms down.

"Well, after the cease-fire, I stayed where I was, maybe ten or fifteen yards from the track, and maybe six or eight guys went down the tracks from the group that I was with, and a few that went down from on top of the tracks. The culvert was probably about a hundred yards ahead of me. One of the guys went down there and searched a few of the bodies. He went down there and searched and found a body with a burp gun and yelled, 'Here's the goddamned gun,' and he held it straight up and slammed it down on the tracks."[28]

Thirty to ninety seconds was all it took. Thirty to ninety seconds of intense fire and all that remained to the front were at least two dead guerillas and several wounded and killed civilians. The combined number of casualties, from both the mortar fire and the direct fire from the line of the 2nd Battalion 7th Cavalry, appears to have been between eight and thirty-five civilians, who were wounded or killed in the vicinity of the railroad overpass and culverts. These figures are, by necessity, an estimate. No forensic evidence exists that anyone at all died outside the village of No Gun Ri. No bones, no bodies, no mass or individual graves remain today or were photographed by South Koreans, North Koreans, or U.S. Air Force reconnaissance aircraft that took pictures of the area as part of a normal mission in the days that followed. If one fully accepts the South Korean witnesses' version of events, only some half a dozen people can be accounted for, physically, as only that many bodies were recovered.[29] This estimate of the casualties then is based in part upon the lack of evidence supporting any higher number. It is also based upon photographic evidence that does exist. The camera images taken by a reconnaissance flight a little more than one week later show no evidence of mass graves, individual graves, cremation, or any human remains.

There is no practical way for 400, 300, or even 100 bodies to simply disappear. Although entirely possible that all the people claimed by the South Korean litigants did die during the Korean War, no evidence exists that they did so in one mass heap of 400 at No Gun Ri, or anywhere near No Gun Ri.

Added to the eyewitness accounts of return fire from among the refugees is the material evidence. Wenzel and several other veterans noted that weapons were found among the refugees, even though South Korean witnesses and the Associated Press reporters make claims to the contrary. According to the AP story on this incident, "There were no guns among the refugees, the Korean survivors insisted. The record supports them: The regiment's war diary included no such report, even though any weapons captured or enemy killed would have been the first for the newly arrived 7th Cavalry."[30]

This is not true. There were guns, and these guns were collected, turned in to the company supply sergeant, and then passed through him to the battalion supply sergeant, finally working their way up to regiment.

Soldiers from one of the nearby platoons collected a Japanese rifle and the Russian submachine gun during a subsequent sweep through the refugees and sent the weapons up through the supply channels, thereby giving some of the only documentary evidence that South Korean communist guerillas were among the South Korean refugees.[31] These weapons were accounted for in the logistics reports at the time.

Further bolstering the account given by the soldiers is forensic evidence. Examinations of the site by the South Korean government fifty years later found not only American-made .30-caliber rounds and shell casings near the former American positions but also some of the Russian weapon's cartridges, a discovery that supports the American veterans who said they received fire.[32] As no fighting occurred at this particular site any time later in the war, it seems reasonable, given the eyewitness accounts of gunfire and later the discovery of the weapons themselves, which were turned in and duly recorded in the S-4 log of the 7th Cavalry as "one Russian submachine gun, one Japanese rifle," to believe that a guerilla's weapon fired from among the refugees left these cartridges on July 26, 1950.

The day ended uncomfortably. As late as sundown, more than a hundred American soldiers from the 2nd Battalion were still unaccounted for and wandering the hills.

For most of the civilians who remained in the area, primarily under the bridge in front of the 7th Cavalry's line, the night would have only brought more stark terror and confusion. Above them, to their front, and to their left and right, the Americans remained. With darkness, many of those who could slipped away, but for those who remained, the fear and chaos continued. A few were helped by American soldiers, not as part of a deliberate plan to help, but as the result of individual U.S. soldiers deciding that the civilians to their front were not a threat and that they needed help. Some received medical aid, even to the point of being evacuated by U.S. Army ambulance to an American medical treatment center to the rear. Some of the South Korean accounts and the American veteran accounts concur that some peasants were helped. For the next few days, periodic gunfire continued, and although not aimed at the civilians but at the North Koreans beyond them, they would not know that. From where they were, all they could see were guns and gunfire coming in their direction.

The next day, July 27, found the Americans still in their positions. For a third day, no concentrated attacks took place against the regiment, and the only major action occurred when USAF fighters strafed the headquarters of the 1st Battalion 7th Cavalry, destroying one truck and damaging a jeep and a trailer.[33] From their front, coming from the village of Sot Anmak, two NKPA T-34 tanks sent desultory harassing fire toward the 7th

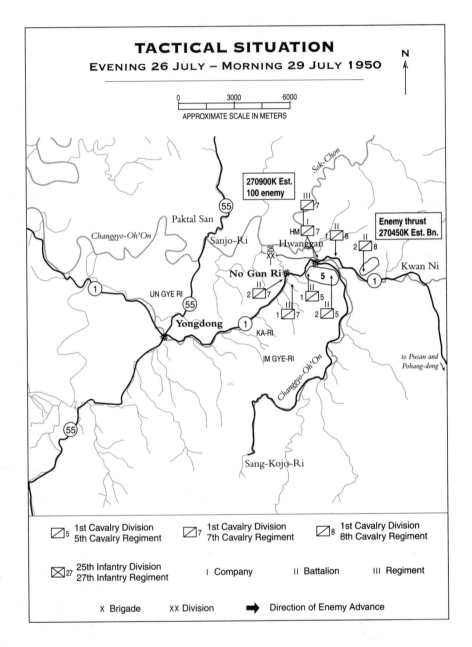

TACTICAL SITUATION
EVENING 26 JULY – MORNING 29 JULY 1950

N

0   3000   6000
APPROXIMATE SCALE IN METERS

270900K Est.
100 enemy

Enemy thrust
270450K Est. Bn.

Paktal San

Changgyo-Oh'On

Sanjo-Ri

Hwanggan

Kwan Ni

No Gun Ri

UN GYE RI

KA-RI

Yongdong

IM GYE-RI

to Pusan and
Pohang-dong

Sang-Kojo-Ri

	1st Cavalry Division 5th Cavalry Regiment		1st Cavalry Division 7th Cavalry Regiment		1st Cavalry Division 8th Cavalry Regiment
	25th Infantry Division 27th Infantry Regiment	I Company	II Battalion	III Regiment

X Brigade   XX Division   ➡ Direction of Enemy Advance

Cavalry positions near No Gun Ri. An airstrike later that day appears to
have been targeted against those tanks. The American troops remained at
No Gun Ri, offering little to no assistance for another day to the South
Korean villagers to their front. On July 29, the regiment pulled out and
established a new line to the south and east of Hwanggan.

WHAT HAPPENED AT NO GUN RI?

This question was the foundation of the research for this book. Every time I felt myself digressing in my historical inquiries, I attempted to return to that central issue. The accounts of the South Korean claimants as reported by the Associated Press and other national and international news agencies obviously played into my thought process, but in the end I determined that the most reliable methods to employ were those of traditional historical inquiry. In its reporting, the AP related the South Korean claims that 300 to 400 civilians died near No Gun Ri; 100 in an aerial attack and another 300 from direct fire in the vicinity of the culvert and railroad bridge just outside the village of No Gun Ri on July 26. Although I do not directly use the South Korean testimony on these events, I would like to address what I speculate might have happened to create the story line that continued to evolve between 1994 and the present.

Part of the problem in assessing this testimony is not being able to determine if any given South Korean witness was actually there or not. No accurate records exist of the inhabitants of the villages in question prior to the start of the Korean War. No accurate census records can be checked for any time from 1945 to 1950. While the American veterans can be verified against rosters, the same cannot be done for the South Korean sources. Furthermore, a claim for $400 million in reparations from the United States calls to question a significant incentive to modify testimony. There is absolutely no sure way to determine who was telling the truth about their own personal history and who was supplementing reality for their own gain.

The only written South Korean record was an account made by the head of one village who recorded all of the names of the people who had left and had not returned to the village after the South Korean forces returned. The report does not say what became of these people, whether they were dead, had resettled in the Pusan area, or had moved to another village. It only says who left and did not return. Did they meet their fate at No Gun Ri? Did they run afoul of the South Korean national police near Kumchon? Were they gunned down by ROK marines near Naksong-dong? Or did they just plant roots inside the Pusan perimeter and restart life there? Did they keep moving and eventually resettle on the east coast or the west coast or the plains to the northwest? Nobody knows. The only thing that the list provided was names of people who left and did not return, and so for a historian, it was an artifact but not proof.

Then there was the problem of memories. For starters, the inescapable fact that these people had been discussing these events among themselves for fifty years can not be overlooked.[34] That alone was an almost insurmountable barrier. After so many decades of not just periodic recitation but near constant repetition, the Koreans' stories developed from a group of individual memories into a collective tale with but one approved story-line. This is how folklore is created. With each succeeding retelling of the stories and a melding of the various accounts into a single narrative, many of the South Koreans apparently came to believe with all of their hearts that what they were saying was an account of the reality as it actually occurred.

The best and most obvious example of how their memories may not reflect the reality of events comes from their own accounts. In 1994, a South Korean social activist named Oh Yeon Ho wrote a feature essay for a South Korean magazine based upon an interview he did with a novelist who claimed that a massacre had occurred in the vicinity of No Gun Ri. The novelist, a former South Korean policeman named Chung Eun Yong, had written a novel that claimed that there was a massacre at No Gun Ri. The title of the novel was *Do You Know Our Agony?* Interviewed by Oh Yeon Ho, Yong stated that his novel was actually a factual account and that he had been forced to write it as a novel to get it published. Yong is one of the leading compensation claimants among the South Koreans.[35]

The activist then interviewed, with Yong's help, some of the people who Yong said were witnesses to a deliberate massacre of South Korean civilians by American soldiers. His article attracted more compensation claimants who said that they too had been shot at by American troops at No Gun Ri, and these tales were incorporated into the collective narrative. This was the very beginning of the No Gun Ri story that the Associated Press would later pick up on and further modify.

One witness, Chung Gu Shik, who turned fifteen that summer, relates what he experienced during an American inspection of the refugee group he was with: "All that the refugees had with them were blankets and rice. We thought inspecting this was not a big deal. But all of a sudden, a soldier with a communications radio on his back transmitted something to some-where and stopped the inspection and hurried away from us. We were all wondering why they were acting this way, when all of a sudden, we saw a fighter jet plane fly over us and drop a bomb. When I woke up from the blast, there was something hanging over my back. I reached back to see what it was; I found that it was a cut-off head of a boy. The railway was bent as if steel chopsticks were bent by a person and everything was in chaos. Dead people, dead cows were laid here and there. The bombing lasted for over twenty minutes. Later on, machine guns were also fired."[36]

It may well be that Shik believed that his statement was true. It may be that his statement represents an account of an event that occurred somewhere else or at some other time. But there is solid evidence to demon-strate that what he described did not happen anywhere near the village of No Gun Ri. At least, not in the way described by this witness. There were certainly air strikes in that part of Korea at that time, since we have records for at least two air missions that occurred within five to ten miles of the No Gun Ri underpass on the evening of July 26. But none of these air strikes were called in by troops with radios on the ground. We can be just as sure of that. Moreover, the aircraft could not inflict the sort of damage described by this witness. It just wasn't physically possible at that time.

When collecting his stories to write the novel *Do You Know Our Agony?*, Yong was unaware that an American reconnaissance plane flew the length of that valley just a few days *after* American troops were pushed out of the area. The plane took photographs of every foot of the railway from Hwanggan to Yongdong in the course of its mission, and those pho-tographs are available and were examined in the United States and South Korean Review Teams in their investigations conducted in 2001. In these photos, taken just days later, the railway is completely intact, not just near No Gun Ri itself, but for miles in each direction. While two spots near No Gun Ri show the distinctive pattern of dirt thrown up by machine gun fire, no accompanying bomb markings are noted.[37] No sections of the track are twisted "as if steel chopsticks were bent by a person."

The second element that causes problems for this version of events was the issue of the radio. Yong, Shik, and several other Koreans claiming to have been attacked by American troops, state or imply that *the soldiers used a handheld or backpack radio to call in an airstrike.* Again, technology, as well as common sense, plays a role here. American tactical radios like the SCR-300 and the walkie-talkie used by the 7th Cavalry infantrymen, transmit and receive using frequency modulation (FM). Airplanes—United States Air Force airplanes to be exact—use AM, or amplitude modulation. The two radio systems are incapable of communicating with one another. On top of that there are issues relating to the region of the electromagnetic spectrum used for each, all of which points to one conclusion. Only some-body equipped with the special radios that are normally used by USAF tac-tical air control parties (TACPs) can call in an airstrike from the ground.

None of the soldiers or officers of the 7th Cavalry could talk to aircraft overhead. Definitive proof that no United States Air Force TACPs were operating in the area or with the 7th Cavalry came on July 27, 1950 when the USAF strafed the 7th Cavalry itself. This attack destroyed one truck, one jeep, and one trailer and prompted the regimental commander to repeat his pleas to the 1st Cavalry Division headquarters for somebody who could talk to aircraft, specifically a TACP.[38] (Ironically, the after action report of the pilot who conducted the attack against the 7th Cavalry on the morning of July 27, 1950 was deliberately ignored by the AP team in their later book about the events. Instead they used the report of a second mission, flying in the early evening that reported firing at an "unidentified object." The implication was that this was evidence of a strafing against the refugees that day. They did this despite the fact that they had access to the records describing the presence of North Korean tanks at Sot Anmak that evening.[39] The tanks were the most probable target of the AP-cited airstrike, especially since at that point the civilians were just 100 yards from the American soldiers.

Finally, the practical matters of range and fuel must be addressed. Fully loaded with bombs, the only combat jet available, the F-80, had a range of only a hundred miles. If it carried no bombs, but drop tanks of fuel instead, this range increased to 225 miles. Since the aircraft were flying from Japan, these jets could not carry bombs and accomplish their mission.[40] However, these planes could, and did, carry limited numbers of aerial rockets, and it is entirely reasonable to conclude that in any aerial attack they would use these rockets. The explosions from these weapons may well be the foundation of some of the South Koreans' memories.

Downplayed significantly by the Associated Press was the fact that the South Koreans who claimed to have been at No Gun Ri have demanded monetary compensation from the outset. In the ordinary scheme of things, once money gets involved, especially the large sums demanded by the claimants, it is perfectly normal for anyone involved in trying to determine the facts behind an event to become just a little more skeptical.

At the time of this writing the South Koreans have asked for a total of $400 million, a fact that cannot be ignored when evaluating the South Koreans' testimony. Suggesting that money could not possibly be a motive for any of the claimants is naïve, even if bringing the point up is impolitic.

Much of the testimony from Koreans claiming to have been at No Gun Ri is also from people who have been sharing their accounts for years. The unanimity of the Koreans' testimony suggests that it is the product of years of group and individual discussions about events that happened when some of the claimants were children of six, seven, or ten years of age. Human memory is a tricky thing; not inviolate, it is susceptible to change over time.[41] Change in memories may be the product of outside influences, such as group discussions and individual interviews in which the interviewer, a person perceived to have expert knowledge of an event, may ask subtly leading questions. Over the years, the effects of these influences are changes to memories.[42] The end result is the same. While some of these people may believe what they are saying with all of their hearts and souls, there are just too many discrepancies between what they state took place and the mute testimony of the forensic evidence on the ground and the contradicting testimony of the veterans.

In hindsight, the Korean accounts appear to be a montage, a collection of the memories of several different events that took place at other times and other places, if they took place as described at all. The skillful pen of a bereaved Korean man who lost children in the war wove these disparate experiences together into the 1994 novel *Do You Know Our Agony?* The result was the story as it appeared in the national and international media in 1999. Verifiable sources whose presence at No Gun Ri can be proven relate a somewhat different version of events than those described by the South Korean accounts. A summary of these points of difference follows:

First: I believe that the accounts of the South Koreans are a collage of several different events that occurred at several different places over the course of a few days and that in writing his 1994 novel *Do You Know Our Agony?*, the South Korean author and former policeman under the Japanese Chung Eun Yong wove these various accounts together into a single narrative that seriously distorts the truth of what actually happened. I do believe sufficient evidence exists to support the contention that hundreds, if not thousands of Korean civilians, both North and South, were killed by American forces over the course of the two-year war. But not in one mass deliberate action. Rather, the killings occurred in dozens and possibly hundreds of the small misfortunes that make war so horrible. Based upon the materials available from that time, it appears that at least six American battalions found themselves in similar situations on at least nine different occasions, and those are only the ones that were recorded.

Second: I do not believe a massive execution-style massacre of 300, 200, or even "hundreds" of civilians by direct ground fire at the railroad overpass just outside No Gun Ri, South Korea, occurred as depicted in the media accounts of 1999 and 2000 and most recently in the book, *The Bridge at No Gun Ri, A Hidden Nightmare from the Korean War*, by the same AP team that reported the original story. Anytime civilians are caught in the path of war, it is tragic, yet the true extent of this tragedy at this spot must be examined. Understanding how mistakes may be made in combat is also important. In this case, not only were mistakes made (the initial call for fire from the mortars was perhaps the dumbest possible action that could have been taken), but two-way fire was exchanged, albeit on a lopsided basis, between some person or persons from among the Korean refugees and members of the 2nd Battalion 7th Cavalry.

Third: In their official claims for reparations, the South Koreans testified that they were attacked from the air by U.S. fighter planes that strafed and killed approximately a hundred civilians before they arrived at No Gun Ri.[43]

While several veterans saw fighter aircraft making attack runs well to their front, none that I interviewed witnessed just whom or what the aircraft were shooting at during that time.

Most veterans stated that the aircraft they saw on that day were three or four miles away, down the valley toward Yongdong. This occurred some distance away from the 7th Cavalry's lines at No Gun Ri, and some time before the events took place between the refugees and the soldiers at No Gun Ri. But, it is quite possible that elements of the South Korean testimony about aerial attacks are accurate. Independent evidence exists that the U.S. Air Force was strafing indiscriminately in this area at this time. Memorandums and memoirs make it clear that the war from the air was generally indiscriminate.[44] However, the fact is that there was no air strike called in by the 7th Cavalry to its immediate front, or anywhere for that matter, on July 25 or 26 or 27, 1950. It wasn't technically possible, and none of the veterans remembers an air strike so close to their own lines, as the South Korean version makes it seem like the air strike was just a few dozen yards from the underpass. It therefore appears likely that memories of the mortar rounds impacting, to which several American veterans testify, may have been the foundation for some of the South Koreans' recollections of an attack from the air. Based on a reasonable interpretation of these accounts and the actual ammunition expenditures from both the U.S. Air Force and the 7th Cavalry, most likely an aerial attack on civilians had occurred *farther up the valley,* possibly the day before, or possibly to people in a different group than that which eventually came under fire from ground troops near No Gun Ri. Memories of several attacks may have been fused, through careless research, with memories of being attacked by mortars near the bridge at No Gun Ri, thus creating a single narrative that does not match the facts.

Fourth: At this point, no evidence supports the figure of a hundred deaths, as the South Koreans and the Associated Press claim, from any air attack. The experience of others who suffered from American aerial attacks, unless large area weapons are used, shows that attacks from the air rarely produce that many casualties among people walking on the ground in the open. In photographs taken just days after the events of July 26, 1950, markings of disturbed earth on the road near where the civilians state they were strafed match similar markings identified as strafing patterns. Two such areas near No Gun Ri are only about fifty yards long, not long enough for a hundred casualties to have been taken from either, or both, of these passes.

One of the members of the blue-ribbon panel commissioned to oversee the U.S. Review Team's investigation into No Gun Ri was former congressman Paul N. "Pete" McCloskey. McCloskey, a marine who served in

Korea, had several bad personal experiences with the 7th Cavalry and was not shy about expressing his negative opinion of the 7th Cavalry and the army in general in his book *The Taking of Hill 600*. His book, however, provides an illustration of just how ineffective 1950-style air strikes against human-sized targets could be. One day in 1951, one of the companies of McClosky's battalion was attacked by a flight of four Marine Corps F-4U Corsairs. In multiple passes, the planes dropped 500-pound high-explosive bombs of napalm, fired 2.75-inch rockets, and made multiple strafing runs, yet not a single marine was injured. Nothing can more clearly demonstrate the relative ineffectiveness of 1950's airpower against individual human targets than this first-person account.[45]

The diminutive length of the ground marks in the photographic evidence of No Gun Ri also suggest one of three things. If done by aircraft, the aircraft conducting the strafing initiated its runs from an extremely low altitude, the target was itself small, or the aircraft conducted its strafing in an extremely steep dive. The first is unlikely as no ground fire was recorded in the area at the time (the air force is rather exacting in reporting that), and therefore extremely low-level flights to enhance survivability were not likely. The last suggestion is possible, but such a steep attack is inefficient and would suggest that the pilot would likely come around again for a second pass. With only two ground markings in the area, most likely this forensic evidence was left by a single pair of aircraft conducting a single pass. That leaves the second possibility that the target was fairly small as the most likely.

If aircraft guns left these marks, the pattern on the ground suggests a total firing time of between one and two seconds. If, as seems to be the case, the pilots could have fired longer but did not, then the target was most likely smaller than the area actually strafed. Assuming a few yards on each end, the U.S. Air Force was strafing two targets just a few dozen yards long. Given the width of the tracks, it is unlikely in the extreme that the 400 to 600 people claimed by South Korean witnesses were all within that area. Yet material evidence exists that strafing attacks occurred in this general area during the last week of July 1950, and so it is plausible that at least some South Koreans were wounded or killed by aerial attack along the route leading to No Gun Ri. Based upon the total lack of human remains in the same photographs or the existence of mass or even large graves, this number was most likely far lower than that claimed by the people interviewed by the media. A more accurate estimate, based upon the volume of fire and the angles of fire, would place the casualties from such an aerial attack at between ten and thirty-five, with perhaps up to one-third of that group being deaths. We do not really know with any degree of certainty if anyone was killed at all in these places at that time. What we do know is that multiple air missions were conducted into the vicinity of Yongdong as well as in the general vicinity of Hwanggon on July 26, 1950.[46] We know that Yongdong itself was attacked from the air during that same time frame, and almost certainly dozens if not hundreds of casualties resulted from that air strike. But within a few hundred yards of the bridge at No Gun Ri, no irrefutable evidence of aerial strafing can be found, only some vague memories from American veterans of a distant strafing and vivid accounts with wildly glaring inaccuracies from South Korean civilians.

In the end, most likely somewhere between eighteen and seventy civilians died from both ground and air attacks in the area of No Gun Ri sometime at the end of July 1950. Based on the military and historical analysis of the credible material evidence, and taking into consideration the chaotic nature of the veteran accounts, and the extreme exaggeration in the other accounts put forth as part of claims, I believe that the most accurate total of casualties at the No Gun Ri site itself is around twenty-five dead, with at least that many wounded. Among those deaths were at least two armed South Korean communist guerillas who made the very bad mistake of opening fire on American soldiers from within a crowd of civilians. The incident at No Gun Ri was, therefore, not the massacre of war crime proportions one might think it was after reading the Pulitzer Prize-winning news article.

PART TWO

The Story of the Story

CHAPTER 6

The Strange Tale of Edward Daily

It was a story no one wanted to hear: Early in the Korean War, villagers said, American soldiers machine-gunned hundreds of helpless civilians under a railroad bridge in the South Korean countryside.[1]

—Original Associated Press story,
September 30, 1999

Some research was just a subway ride away: 1950 magazines and obscure books on the Korean War at the New York Public Library. . . . All in all, Herschaft made more than fifty trips to public and university libraries. He checked U.S. and European newspapers from those days and consulted every available bibliography and index to periodical literature to confirm such a massacre was never reported.[2]

—AP Reporter Martha Mendoza,
January 2000, making the claim that their story
was brand new, just after the Associated Press submitted
No Gun Ri stories for the Pulitzer Prize

Fear of infiltrators led to the slaughter of hundreds of South Korean civilians, women as well as men, by some U.S. troops . . . .[3]

—Charles Grutzer,
Front page of *The New York Times*, September 30, 1950,
referring to actions in July 1950

133

*. . . a report has come that our riflemen have had to fire into
another party of refugees. From the command post an urgent and
remonstrating voice speaks over the wire into the hills, 'My God
John, it's gone too far when we are shooting women and children.'[4]*
                                    —John Osborne,
                        Life Magazine, August 21, 1950

*Memory is often less about the truth than about what we want it
to be.*

                                    —David Halberstam,
                                    The New York Times

"IT WAS A STORY
NO ONE WANTED TO HEAR . . . "

UNFORTUNATELY FOR TWO BASTIONS OF AMERICAN JOURNALISM, THIS
quote was not quite true. The story of No Gun Ri written by the Associated Press (AP) about the events surrounding the opening days of the
Korean War was a story that very many people wanted to hear. More than
that, it was a story that many people were willing to investigate. There is a
tad of irony in the process: The investigations by both the United States
government and the government of South Korea into No Gun Ri after the
AP stories were published contributed, at least in part, to the AP's receipt of
the most coveted prize for American journalism, the Pulitzer.[5] The only
problem for the Pulitzer team was not having the time or the resources to
check the veracity of the stories it received to be judged in the competition.
The panels of distinguished journalists who award the Pulitzer Prize make a
valid assumption that no news organization would print something about
which it had doubts. Submission of a story to the awards competition,
while not itself a verification, sends the message that someone believes the
piece to be one of the best works produced by that particular news agency
during the year. The panelists then assume that no problems exist with the
story, that all of the sources are solid, and that the reporting is verified.[6]

As a result, in April of 2000, the prize for investigative journalism went
to a team of reporters who failed to tell the Pulitzer committee, and the
American public, the problems with the credibility of its sources and who
inflated, perhaps unintentionally, the originality of its story.

In all fairness, making sense of the events near No Gun Ri in the summer of 1950 was not easy. Fifty years is a long time for memories to atro-
phy, or even to change. Unraveling those memories and weaving them back
into a cohesive whole could prove difficult even under the best of circumstances. Add the pressures of money, reputation, and the random wildcard

of people who are not quite what they seem to be, and the task is all the more challenging.[7]

On the other hand, after more than a year of what the AP team described as exhaustive archival research as well as interviews with survivors and veterans alike, how could they have missed so many basic facts and allowed themselves to be taken in by persons who were not actually there?

Even the contention that this was a new story might be questioned. Events similar to what the AP wrote about taking place near No Gun Ri were certainly reported back in 1950. However, the discovery of new American eyewitnesses made this new news. The greatest problem with this theory was that apparently the AP inadvertently created new witnesses in the process of finding and interviewing them.[8] Yet their central witnesses (from the American side) were not actually there. One may be inclined to give them the benefit of the doubt here: Despite the time the team apparently devoted to research, it appears that the reporters did not conduct sufficient research to discover the errors relating to their sources. The only other interpretation is that they deliberately published a news story to create an international sensation (and incident) knowingly relying upon the testimony of men whom they knew were unreliable as witnesses.

In either case, when other reporters and historians checked their sources and discovered the truth, the AP was called to task by other national media outlets as well as by historians.[9] The end result was another situation akin to the infamous Tailwind reporting scandal that rocked Cable News Network (CNN) and *Time* magazine.[10] In those cases, the media fell for stories that said more about what the reporters wanted to hear than they did about what actually happened. The only difference was that this time the Pulitzer Prize was involved as well.

The AP account of the events at No Gun Ri was published around three central issues: First, hundreds of South Korean civilians were massacred; second, this massacre took place under the orders of American officers; and third, the soldiers themselves verify that this information is true.[11] While an in-depth dissection of the original reporting appears in the next chapter, this chapter will focus on these three issues to understand how the reporters arrived at the positions they did. Nine veterans were cited in the original story, and six of them contributed in some way to the main thesis of the AP story. Three men—Edward Daily, Delos Flint, and Eugene Hesselman—were explicit in their indictments. The testimony of a fourth man, Louis Allen, was made to appear as though it supported the comments by Daily, Flint, and Hesselman. This chapter focuses on the first three men.

This analysis discounts, for the moment, the testimony of the South Koreans who have increased their claims to $400 million and were used as sources by the Associated Press without comment.[12] An evaluation of the reliability of witnesses who stood to become millionaires had their story been accepted as the basis for their reparations claims may be found in the afterword, "Sources and History." For now, let us concentrate on how this story hinged upon the testimony of three men who claimed to have been at No Gun Ri and either committed or witnessed these crimes.

In reality, none of these three men were actually at No Gun Ri during the events of July 26–29, 1950. Louis Allen was not there either. Their accounts of the incident to the Associated Press had credibility because they were supposed to have been at No Gun Ri and participated in the events they described to the AP. But this was not the truth.

The Associated Press used these accounts despite its knowledge of the problems with witness credibility. Although the reporting team knew the witnesses had significant problems with reliability before publishing the stories, it chose to rely upon the information provided by these men about themselves rather than the documentary evidence contained in the historical records that the reporters state they had seen and reviewed.

Why these veterans might have invented or exaggerated the story of a massacre at No Gun Ri and claimed to have been a part of it is also part of the story of the story. The Associated Press had documentary evidence that these three men, the main witnesses in the story, were fabricating information, yet the news service went ahead and submitted the story for journalism's highest award anyway.[13]

At the center of all of this was Edward Daily, a man who had been impersonating an officer for almost fifteen years.[14]

At about this time, I became part of the story. To provide the reader with all of the information relevant to this part of the second tragedy of No Gun Ri, I will use the first person in this chapter.

As mentioned in the introduction, my knowledge of Edward Daily was based upon more than just a review of the primary sources and the reports in newspapers. As a company commander in 2nd Battalion 7th Cavalry at Fort Hood for twenty-five months from 1994 to 1996, I became closely acquainted with Daily. I knew him as a battlefield-commissioned officer, a man who had earned the Distinguished Service Cross, in short a proven battlefield leader. He was the 7th Cavalry's most famous veteran of the Korean War, the author of two books on the history of the regiment and mentioned in several others. He was also the perfect guest on the days that he visited our battalion.

As the company commander with the most interest in history at that time, I was regularly assigned as his escort officer on the days he visited the unit, and I personally sponsored him into the active-duty Garryowen Association (the social body of the serving officers of the battalion) and lobbied the battalion commander to present him with a battalion coin (a social ritual in many units) at one of these events. We continued to talk regularly about the history of the 7th Cavalry during my years in graduate school and on the history faculty of the United States Military Academy.

Ironically, the material I received from Daily—names and phone numbers of people contacted by the Associated Press who were not on the regimental association roster, as well as several long letters about the events from his perspective—ultimately led to the unraveling of his account. We were friends until my research into this event revealed the troubled truth about Daily's personal history.

In the original AP story, Daily was one of only two men—the other being his friend Eugene Hesselman—who claimed that an order to fire on the refugees came from an officer of the battalion.[15] Although Daily's and Hesselman's claims differed in the officers they accused, the two men both agreed that a deliberate order was issued to fire at the civilians. Hesselman said that he clearly heard his company commander, Captain Chandler, shout out the order to shoot the civilians. Yet Hesselman also stated that he clearly remembered Daily's presence as well, stating over and over to one reporter that he knew Ed Daily was there, even after Daily admitted that the documentary evidence proved that he had not been there.[16]

Daily's claims were even more troubling. It was reported and repeated in newspapers, magazines, and television interviews seen around the world that he was a machine gunner in the 2nd Battalion of the 7th Cavalry and that he received the order to shoot from a runner who was conveying the orders of the battalion executive officer, Major Omar Hitchner.[17]

Because his comments in the original story were the most poignant to come from a veteran, Daily received, by his estimate, more than a hundred phone calls after the original story broke.[18] This is understandable, given the quote that the Associated Press used in its story from Daily:

> 'On summer nights when the breeze is blowing, I can still hear their cries, the little kids screaming,' said Daily, of Clarksville, Tenn., who went on to earn a battlefield commission in Korea.[19]

This quote alone guaranteed additional media attention, because this was an American war hero admitting to a war crime. In later interviews other media outlets described Daily as not just a plain-vanilla dogface G.I. but rather a hero to the nth degree. According to various sources, including Daily himself, he was wounded three times, the winner of the nation's second highest award for valor, the Distinguished Service Cross, and a man who earned a commission the hard way, on the battlefield.[20] On top of all that, he told reporters, as he had been telling fellow veterans for years, that he was one of the men captured along the Naktong River line a few weeks later, who then managed to escape and rejoin friendly forces a few weeks later.

In the days and weeks following the first publication of the story, Ed Daily became the most quoted, most visible, and most repentant of the soldiers from the original AP story.[21] He became the face of the soldiers at No Gun Ri for the American and international audiences following the story.[22] His face was on the front pages of newspapers around the country. He gave dozens upon dozens of interviews to other reporters in the wake of the AP's sensational massacre story.

The apogee of Ed Daily's fame came when the NBC news show *Dateline* flew him to South Korea to meet the claimants and, it was hoped, apologize for the horrible things that he had done to them fifty years earlier.

NEWS, HISTORY, AND TOM BROKAW

It was a dramatic moment seen around the world. The decorated American hero, Ed Daily, meets the people he said he turned his machine gun against under the orders of his officers. Despite the fact that the producers and reporters from NBC never apparently checked his credentials, verified his military service, or investigated the story in any significant way themselves, reporter Tom Brokaw was there for all the action. He asked Daily the hard questions.

> *DATELINE Announcer: "In the chaos of war, an act so horrific it would remain a secret for half a century."*
> *Daily: "Just shoot them all."*
> *Brokaw, NBC: "You heard that order?"*
> *Daily: "Yes, sir."*
> *Brokaw, NBC: "Kill them all?"*
> *Daily: "Yes, sir."*

In the next minute, Brokaw repeats most of Daily's self-constructed mythology.

> *Brokaw, NBC: "The GIs moved on. Leaving behind, Daily estimates, 150 to 200 dead, no survivors. Two weeks later, Daily was wounded and captured by the enemy. He escaped, he went back to the front, and somewhere that horrible afternoon at No Gun Ri became another day, another horrible memory among many."*

A few seconds later, Brokaw makes Daily a tragic figure.

> *Brokaw, NBC: "The war took its toll. Daily divorced and lost touch with his family. He says he couldn't sleep or eat. By 1986, he was desperate and turned to the Veterans Administration for help. Doctors diagnosed him with post-traumatic stress disorder and put him on antidepressant medications, drugs he still takes."*

The visual images at this point are of Daily walking in the sunlight, a VA sign, an American flag; Daily at his house in Kentucky; and Daily singing in church. The show aired just after Christmas in 1999.[23] From all appearances, NBC did not conduct any original research in their news reporting of the events at No Gun Ri. In fact, it appears NBC did little more than repeat the accusations made by the AP.

Incredibly, Brokaw was later invited to speak to the Kennedy School of Government at Harvard University on the proliferation of news outlets and how this might be decreasing the quality of journalism. In what must be one of the most ironic speeches ever given, Brokaw outlined for the Harvard audience what he called the "Brokaw Theorem." This concept consists of the following elements: First, the newness and importance of the news must be determined; next, the truth of the story must be established beyond a doubt; then, the story must be presented in a way that both encompasses the context and engages the audience.[24] As he accomplished only the last part of this theorem in his reporting on No Gun Ri, one wonders if Brokaw had simply assumed all of this was taken care of by the AP.

In several interviews, Ed Daily claimed that on July 26, 1950 he was a corporal, a machine gunner with H Company of the 2nd Battalion 7th Cavalry. He said that as the sun went down that evening, he received the order to open fire on the milling refugees to his front. This order was brought to him by a messenger from the company headquarters, straight from the executive officer of the battalion, Major Hitchner.[25] Although he said that he questioned the man who brought him the order, he claims that the man, a soldier named Skaggs, told him that a senior officer of the battalion had issued the order, and so he followed that command. When I first read this account, something about it did not make sense. In viewing it from the perspective of an infantry captain, I noticed pieces of the puzzle sticking out at odd angles. Although I had known Daily for years and had no good reason at the time to doubt him, several things still seemed questionable about this account, the first thing being the nature of that order.

The military is a hierarchical organization. When orders are issued, they follow a chain of command. At the battalion level, an explicit order from higher headquarters, especially a potentially explosive order such as this one, is not passed from a major to a junior enlisted man for execution.

Except in the most dire circumstances, communications, especially orders, do not skip echelons. Any order from the battalion headquarters would first go to the company commander, who would pass that order to the platoon leaders. The platoon leaders would then pass the order to the squad leaders, who would issue commands to the soldiers to put the order into effect. Edward Daily's version, in which an order was passed directly from the second highest-ranking officer in the battalion to a private who communicated it to another private, made absolutely no sense to me as a professional soldier, let alone as an historian. But I was ready to acknowledge that strange things happen in combat, especially in a unit that had just disintegrated only a few hours earlier, and so I thought I should go straight to the source. I called Ed Daily.

As I noted in the introduction, at the time the AP story of No Gun Ri appeared, Ed Daily was the author of two books of 7th Cavalry history, *From Custer to MacArthur* and *Skirmish: Red, White, and Blue* (both self-published), and the past president of both the 7th Cavalry Association and the Korean War Veterans Chapter of the 7th Cavalry Association. He was also involved with the board of directors of the 1st Cavalry Division Association. Besides being a very engaged veteran, Daily was a man with whom I had a personal relationship. I thought that some time with him on the phone, several hours as it turned out, would help me make sense of these events. They only added to the confusion.

As I talked with Daily, the mystery deepened. Not only did his version of how he got the orders "straight from Major Hitchner" not jibe with the chain of command, but his account of where his machine gun was placed also confused me.[26]

Since the first widespread use of the water-cooled heavy machine gun in the First World War, not much has changed doctrinally about where these high-casualty-producing weapons are placed. Because machine guns represent a major portion of an infantry unit's firepower, officers take special care in placing them. They are not haphazardly scattered along the line, or even evenly distributed; instead they are individually emplaced by the officers with the advice of their noncommissioned officers. The lieutenants and the company commander will personally approve the location of each of these crucial weapons to ensure that they are placed in the most effective positions to engage the enemy with what the army calls grazing fire.

Bullets do not travel in straight lines. Simple Newtonian physics dictates that reality. Grazing fire is defined as fire that will hit the targets at about waist height. Units place their machine guns where they will have a broad flat expanse to their front, so that their fire will graze across several hundred square yards of ground to the front. This way, the enemy cannot approach or attack your position without coming under a high volume of

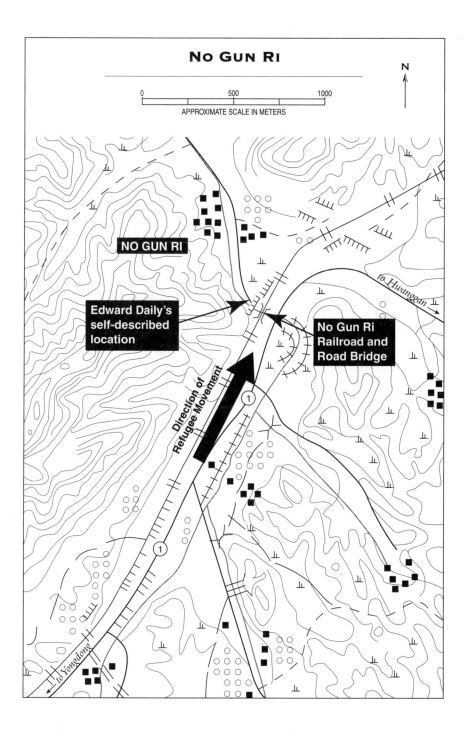

NO GUN RI

0   500   1000

APPROXIMATE SCALE IN METERS

N

NO GUN RI

Edward Daily's self-described location

No Gun Ri Railroad and Road Bridge

to Hwanggan

Direction of Refugee Movement

to Yongdong

fire. It was this way at the Somme. It was this way in Korea. It is this way today. Yet that was not where Daily was describing his gun was that day.

In his version, his machine gun was on the north side of the railroad bridge and the railroad embankment.[27] He said that he was off to the side far enough so that he could see the far side of the underside of the bridge. He described being able to see about halfway through the underpass and being down low enough from the level of the ground to point his weapon at people down below.

Ordinarily his position as described might not make a difference, but the topographic map of the area shows some things that did not make sense. Moreover, thanks to the wonder of modern technology, I was also able to go on the Internet and look at a 360-degree panoramic and variable point of view video of the site, thanks to the Associated Press new Web site, *The Wire*. So although I had not physically walked the ground, I was able to see the area very clearly and virtually walk around the area. What I saw on the map and in the video was that the north side of the bridge abutted a hillside and the northern wall of the valley. Because of the raised railway embankment, Daily's gun would have been placed not where it would achieve long-range fires or maximum grazing fire across a broad frontage, but as he described it, in a pinched area between the embankment and the hillsides. That emplacement made absolutely no tactical sense. I knew already that H Company had come through the night of July 25–26 fairly well intact.[28] So it made no sense to me why, if H Company had been there as a group since the early morning, an infantry officer would deliberately place one of his most valuable guns in a spot of low ground or behind a hill away from the direction from which he expected the enemy to advance.

As we talked about his version of the events, a few things became glaringly obvious: Daily was recounting to me something he had said many times before. Down to the smallest detail, I was hearing the words that I could read simultaneously in the newspaper in front of me. He was, in effect, recounting to me from his own internal script, one he had obviously repeated many times and which he had difficulty deviating from when asked. When I asked him about such things as the placement of his machine gun, he became vague and then almost immediately changed the conversation to another topic. Over and over, we went in this cycle throughout the first conversation and in several follow-up phone calls in November and December of 1999. All the while, I believed I was hearing the absolute truth, just one colored by repetition so that some details stood out in Daily's memory better than others. I chalked it up to the hazards of conducting oral history.[29]

I made my first trip to the National Archives in the middle of November. While there, I photocopied everything I possibly could. After scanning thousands of pages I selected and photocopied hundreds of them so that I might mentally digest them later. If I had any doubts that something might prove useful in the future, I paid the money and made a copy.

At this point, I was still unsure about what had happened at No Gun Ri. The troubling discrepancies in Daily's account were just one part of the puzzle. Not just Ed Daily's account did not make sense; other statements that the veterans made when I interviewed them seemed out of place. For example, at that point in my research, many of the veterans I interviewed had told me the story of the tanks attacking on their first night in combat. Yet in the written sources I read, both contemporary newspaper stories from reporters just a few miles away and history books that dealt with that period of time and that area, there was no mention of any tank attack, behind the men of the 2nd Battalion 7th Cavalry. Were they making up stories about an attack by tanks on the night of July 25–26? If not, where did these attacking tanks go after they broke through the battalion?

I was confused and uncertain at that point in my research. I had adopted and discarded half a dozen hypotheses about the events surrounding No Gun Ri, and I still could not make sense of the evidence I was collecting.

By December of 1999, I reached a point where I felt I had conducted enough interviews with other veterans of the regiment and read enough of the primary source documents to believe that I had some grasp of what had gone on in those opening days of the 7th Cavalry's action in Korea. I read secondary sources of varying quality as well, dissecting each for problems in their sources or interpretations. At that point, I decided that it was time to start looking at the oral history sources, even my personal friend Ed Daily, with a critical eye as well.

This might not have happened were it not for a coincidence: I had just finished reading a book by a Vietnam veteran named B. G. Burkett. His book, *Stolen Valor*, was scrupulously documented and presented new insights into the phenomena of fake Vietnam veterans.[30] I was so impressed by the depth of his research and his amazing revelations that I wrote a review of the book for publication and called the author. Burkett had exposed these false combat veterans by using the Freedom of Information Act (FOIA) to gain summaries of the military records of veterans. I had just finished writing my review of this book when the AP story of No Gun Ri splashed across the headlines. This led me to file a FOIA request on the men mentioned by name in the stories. By December, several of my requests for information had already come back either confirming the men's presence in the unit or unable to confirm it based upon available records. I assumed that the reason I had not gotten a response back on Ed Daily was because of a problem with the records.

In 1973 there was a fire at the National Military Personnel Records Center in Saint Louis that destroyed the personal records of large segments of our veteran population from the Second World War up to the Vietnam War. Some of the men's records I requested had been lost in that fire, and the FOIA requests on them came back annotated as such.

I assumed, from the delay, that Daily's records must have been among the millions of records destroyed so I thought that I might as well look into other sources while I waited for that report.

What many people do not know is that while individual records were burned in that fire, none of the unit records were destroyed. They survived because most unit records are stored at the National Archives in College Park, Maryland, where I had already collected much of what was available about the 7th Cavalry in Korea. This is the army after all; it is not for nothing that we do everything in triplicate. One copy of every document relating to an individual goes in that person's records, while the other copies stay with the unit. Almost anyone's military record may be reconstructed by the simple matter of looking by unit for the duplicate information originally contained in the serviceman's personal records. And I already had those records sitting on my kitchen floor.

Apparently, Daily had not thought about the triplicate nature of army records when he began researching the 7th Cavalry for the first of the books that he published on the unit. Around that time, in the early to mid 1980s, he began reconstructing his personal history. In his books about the 7th Cavalry, Edward Daily became a hero.

In the front of each book, underneath a picture of Daily himself, is his autobiography. These quasi-autobiographical books were what Daily provided to the Associated Press when it first contacted him about No Gun Ri.[31] But the Associated Press also had the same records I had months before it went to press with its original story. According to the AP's own stories, and the archivists at the National Archives who saw the reporters there, the AP had combed through the very same material that I had photocopied but not yet read by that December. The fact that the AP had conducted exhaustive research into the archival material of the period was a large part of its claim to credibility.[32]

According to the autobiography Daily supplied to the AP, he was a machine gunner in H Company of the 7th Cavalry in July 1950. In the book, he goes on to explain that during the chaos of the withdrawal between July 26 and July 30 he was promoted to sergeant. Daily claimed that on August 10, 1950 he became one of the youngest officers in the U.S. Army by virtue of a battlefield commission to temporary lieutenant in the 7th Cavalry. On August 12, just two days after his commissioning, during a major engagement along the Naktong River defensive line, Daily claimed that he was captured by the North Koreans. After a little more than three weeks as a prisoner of the North Koreans, he said, he escaped and made his way to and across the Naktong River and back into friendly lines. For his heroic actions in the defense and his subsequent escape, Daily claimed he was awarded the Distinguished Service Cross, an award just below the Medal of Honor. A short time later, he said, he rejoined his unit and fought through the rest of the regiment's fights in Korea, subsequently earning three Purple Heart medals for wounds suffered in combat and another promotion, this one to first lieutenant.[33] This was the same basic biography that Daily gave to Tom Brokaw, and Tom Brokaw gave to the world on NBC's *Dateline* television program. My omission was that until now I had also not looked closely at this self-reported biography.[34]

For years, the self-published biographical information in the front of his books was the basis for my understanding of Edward Daily. It formed the foundation of my admiration for him, even though the part about the temporary promotion to second lieutenant had struck me as curious even back in 1994 when I first read it because the Army has no such category as temporary second lieutenant. In 1999, reading the information skeptically for the first time, I knew better. It was a simple matter to verify names on the rosters of the officers of the entire regiment. A few moments later, I was solidly confronted with a contradiction; Ed Daily was not listed on the rosters of the 7th Cavalry as an officer in H Company in August 1950. Moreover, his Distinguished Service Cross was nowhere to be found among the many special orders and general orders listed in the 1st Cavalry Division G-1 logs or the 7th Cavalry Regiment S-1 logs. On top of all of that, the regimental diary and S-3 (Operations) logs did not mention him anywhere, ever—not in July, not in August, not in September.[35]

Battlefield commissions are rare, the rarest of all commissions, in fact, which is why they are considered a strong validation of a combat soldier's competence as a warrior. Ed Daily's claim to be one of these men should have been extremely easy to verify.

In the opening days of the Korean War in 1950, the 1st Cavalry Division and the 7th Cavalry Regiment were certainly in search of leadership. The situation was so desperate that the division was given the almost unprecedented authority to distribute battlefield commissions, a power normally reserved for a higher echelon. The 7th Cavalry did, in fact, grant four battlefield commissions to senior sergeants, men with years of service already before the war started. Portions of the records for all four men are neatly located in the 7th Cavalry Regiment's combat log now stored in the National Archives in College Park, Maryland. The records are clear—only a few select men are promoted; Ed Daily was not one of them. One man who was promoted—a man who had accepted Ed Daily as a peer for years—was Robert Gray.

Gray's real story was almost as fantastic as Daily's imagined one. As mentioned in chapter two, Gray originally enlisted in the army in 1945. In the scarecrow years between World War II and the Korean War, leaders, especially noncommissioned officers, were tough to keep in uniform. Gray was a career soldier from the first. By 1950, he was already a platoon sergeant. In March 1951, he was commissioned from the ranks. An experienced and battle-proven leader, he stayed in the army for a full career, retiring as a major after more than twenty years' service with experience in Korea and in Vietnam, where he fought as a special forces officer. When I interviewed him in October and November, Gray was one of Daily's strongest supporters. But when I called him again and asked him specific questions about his memories of Daily in Korea, he faltered.

It all came down to a very simple question: "Do you personally remember a time when you saw Ed Daily while you were in Korea?" When asked this directly, Gary apparently realized that many of his memories of Daily were actually based upon stories told to him by Daily himself. They were framed by Daily as accounts of events that they mutually witnessed. It had never occurred to Gray to examine his memories and separate out his own from those memories placed there by Edward Daily.[36]

Despite the fact that Gray might not remember Daily from Japan or the opening months of Korea, I still had doubts.[37] I could not say for sure that Ed Daily was not in the unit as he said he was. Until this point, all I had was a theory, an increasingly strong theory, but it was based upon the absence of recorded evidence. Despite what would have been an incredible coincidence for all of the eighteen different records that should have mentioned Daily to accidentally miss making any reference to him, I did not have strong enough material to make an assertion of fact. I did not have the presence of any evidence, and arguably Gray might just never have met Daily in Japan or the beginnings of the Korean War even if Daily had been there.[38] Then the momentum of the project took over and provided me with my break.

Just after the AP story appeared, I made a mass mail query to the veteran members of the 7th Cavalry Association who had been in the 2nd Battalion in the summer of 1950. This let many of the veterans know what I was doing. At the same time, I kept the honorary colonel of the regiment, Lieutenant General (Retired) Harold Moore, informed of the status of my research as it progressed. His interactions also included another somewhat smaller group—active and retired generals who previously served in the 7th Cavalry. The roster of these men is long and distinguished, but one man in particular proved crucial to me, a retired major general named William Webb.

In January of 2000, General Webb called me out of the blue and he was mad. In no uncertain terms, he informed me that my then-working thesis about the events of July 1950 was totally wrong. Once we got past that initial outburst and settled down into an interview, things got interesting. Webb had been raised in Texas and attended Texas A&M University before choosing a military career and competing for and getting a slot at the United States Military Academy at West Point in 1944. He was graduated in 1947, the last of the three-year classes. (West Point's normal four-year program was shortened for a period because of the army's desperate need for officers in WWII.) After attending the General Ground Combat Course at Fort Riley and the Armor Officer Basic Course at Fort Knox, he was assigned in the summer of 1948 to E Company in the 2nd Battalion 7th Cavalry Regiment in downtown Tokyo. In January 1950, First Lieutenant Webb became the battalion adjutant. He was still in that position when the unit went to war and all through the time that Daily stated he had been promoted to sergeant, had been discharged for commissioning, had received his alleged temporary commission—the whole collective period when he was becoming a hero of the 7th Cavalry and winning the nation's second highest award for valor—through all of that time, the officer who was directly responsible for creating, maintaining, filing, and recording all of that information was First Lieutenant Webb.[39] In addition, Webb had later served as the company commander of F Company. If any man alive should have known Ed Daily, it would have been William Webb.

Webb had absolutely no memories of Ed Daily from Korea.[40]

Here was the one man who would have had to have known Ed Daily in Korea and he was telling me point blank that he never saw the man there.

It was a strange moment. As a historian, as a man who had invested so much time into trying to figure out the truth behind the original stories of No Gun Ri that were repeated over and over in the newspapers and television, to finally have this sort of proof that I was right was satisfying. At the same time, I started regretting what I had done. I began to regret the research and reading and searching that finally resulted in this moment when I was, as far as I knew, the only man other than Daily who knew the truth. (I was wrong, of course. By that point, the Department of the Army Inspector General's team, acting as the U.S. Review Team, must have known as well, but I was not aware of that at the time.) In any event, now that I knew for sure that Daily had been lying to me all these years, it made me wonder: Why? Why would somebody go to the lengths that he had to create a false personal history?

Burkett exposed a lot of fake veterans in *Stolen Valor*, but he had not spilled much ink trying to explain why people might do something like this. Subsequent research uncovered fake veterans reaching all the way back to the American Civil War. I had read personal accounts of actual veterans confronting fake veterans in the 1880s, but I was still, and to a degree still am, mystified by the phenomenon. As far as I know, no name even exists for this sort of behavior. Perhaps "military Munchausen syndrome" might be appropriate.[41]

Lying a little on your resume and puffing up your high school football exploits are one thing. Creating an entirely false history, impersonating a commissioned officer, and awarding yourself the Distinguished Service Cross is beyond the pale. Was it attention that Daily craved? Was it the kudos and applause he received from serving officers when he visited active-duty units? Was it the access to generals, such as the division commander of the 1st Cavalry Division, then-Major General Eric Shinseki, that Daily had as a president of the 7th Cavalry Regimental Association that made him do this? All of these were possible motives, yet creating a fake biography, doctoring documents, and then living that false biography seems extreme. It was, and is, something that does not make sense.

At this point, I still did not have the official version of Daily's service from the National Military Personnel Records Center. Assuming my request for information got lost, I mailed another. A month later, I mailed a third. At this point, I knew where Daily had not been, but I still did not know where he had been. Besides, records can be wrong, even the triple redundancy of the records that I had on hand. To close the loop, I needed to figure out where he had been all this time.

Ed Daily provided me that information himself in one of the books he wrote. In *Skirmish: Red, White and Blue*, two photographs of Edward Daily are found purporting to show him in the 7th Cavalry. I looked closely at both photos and thought that in these might rest the answers to my questions. In the end, I was right, but in the beginning, I was 180 degrees off. I fell into the trap of hubris—I thought I knew something and acted upon it, and I was wrong. By now, it was late February 2000.

One of the photos shows Ed Daily standing alone against a nondescript wall with the caption, "2nd Lt. Edward Daily, 1st Platoon Leader, Co. H, 2nd Battalion, 7th Cavalry."[42] As no additional features were in the photo, I discarded that picture as useless for my purposes and moved on to the second photo. That was my mistake.

The second photo shows Ed Daily with three other soldiers hamming for the camera, arms around each other, and grinning. The caption gave the names of the other soldiers, which I cross-referenced against the roster of the 7th Cavalry Association. Although two of the men were dead, the third was alive. I called him and heard his version of who Ed Daily was. Unfortunately, either his memory was faulty or he was confusing Daily's picture with somebody else because this veteran told me Daily had been in L Company, a part of the 3rd Battalion 7th Cavalry, a unit that did not exist until late August 1950.[43] To my mind, that answered a lot, and I believed that I had the full story: Daily was a veteran of the 7th Calvary, L Company, not H Company. He had created the personal history of his service in H Company in order to be a part of the history of the retreat and defense of the Naktong River line. I still thought he had been a lieutenant, but perhaps not a battle-field-commissioned one. This was my working hypothesis at that time.

Looking back as I write this, I see that I desperately wanted Ed Daily to be at least some of what he said he was. I wanted him to keep being the man I had known for so long. I needed his story to be true because I was starting to feel guilty about the truth. I thought that at this point the only decent thing to do would be to call Daily with the information I had and ask him, point blank, what was going on.

I called him with my information. I told him all about his absence in the various and disparate records and about the memory of his fellow veteran from L Company. Daily seemed confused and somewhat put out by my questions, and continually said, "Well, Bob, I just don't know what to say. I know where I was and what I did, and I can't explain what you're saying here."[44]

It was naïve to think that when I asked him, based upon our years-long relationship and the weight of what I had uncovered, Daily would come clean and tell the truth about having actually served as a lieutenant in L Company, that he would confess that he was not in H Company and that he had made that part up. Then we could both go on with trying to figure out what really happened. It would have been painful for him, embarrassing, yes, but I assumed that when people are given the chance to get the great weight of a big lie off their chests, they would take that opportunity.

I was wrong. I was wrong in more ways than one actually, but at the time I only knew that my assumption about people generally wanting to tell the truth when confronted with evidence was wrong. Stymied at getting the truth from Ed Daily himself, I decided to call the man whom I thought might help me unravel this mystery directly, the author of *Stolen Valor*, B. G. Burkett.

That phone call was an education. Burkett is a fascinating man, a Vietnam veteran who by his own admission never did anything even remotely heroic while stationed as a logistics officer in Vietnam. In the decades after his military service, he became a successful businessman. When contacted to help raise money for the Texas Vietnam Veterans' Memorial, he discovered that many people had a false impression about the nature of Vietnam veterans. Burkett then made it his mission to uncover why.

The answer turned out to be easier to find than the general impression was to the reverse. Most people based their negative stereotypes of Vietnam veterans as prone to drug abuse, homelessness, crime, and bouts with post-traumatic stress disorder (PTSD) upon images in the media. Burkett found that inevitably at Vietnam veterans' functions the media would bypass the majority of the men, most of them well-dressed and successful veterans, and focus on the one or two whom the reporters considered "real veterans." Unshaven, unkempt, and wearing the bedraggled remnants of uniforms, these "real veterans" would invariably be the ones who appeared in the paper, telling their horrific tales of PTSD and drug abuse caused, of course, by The Nam.[45]

Annoyed, Burkett did the media's job for them and researched the background of these men.[46] The news stories gave him all the information he needed. He filed a simple FOIA request on each veteran that was interviewed. When information came back that the aggrieved Vietnam veteran of the reporter's stories was actually a truck driver in Kansas during his twenty-four months in the army, Burkett sent this information to the reporters. The responses he received from the media were almost uniformly negative. Moreover, almost none of them published retractions. Among the numerous stories of fake combat veterans described in Burkett's book was that of Darrow "Duke" Tully, the publisher of the *Phoenix Gazette* and the *Arizona Republic,* who had concocted a heroic but false military record of combat in Korea and Vietnam and former U.S. Representative Wesley Cooley of Oregon who was actually convicted in 1997 of lying on official documents and creating his own false records of combat service in Korea. Burkett's favorite tale was when his research helped to send convicted murderer Joseph Yandle back to prison in 1998. Yandle had managed to get his life sentence commuted in 1995 by convincing television reporters that his actions were the result of the vicious combat he experienced in Vietnam that resulted in what his supporters characterized as post-traumatic stress disorder, the same syndrome Daily claimed. Like Daily, Yandle appeared on television and was portrayed as a victim of the system and the horrors of war. And like Daily, Yandle was also a fake. He had not served in Vietnam, but had been a clerk in Japan. Eventually Burkett had enough material for a book, and thus *Stolen Valor* was born.[47]

Burkett reminded me of something from his book. Most of the fakes he uncovered were easy to expose. Their records existed. Many had done nothing to build up a reputation other than talk about their time in The

Nam. Among them were actors and judges, local politicians, and men who made a living by speaking about their trauma. A few others, however, combined both oral stories with a web of written history. These were somewhat more difficult to uncover. Surprisingly enough, right there in *Stolen Valor* was an account of another past president of the 7th Cavalry Association, another man with whom I had talked on the phone. Although he was actually a legitimate combat veteran of the 7th Cavalry, he had apparently felt that this was not enough and so had contrived to give himself additional awards for valor which he then parlayed into what others claimed made him the most decorated Vietnam veteran in New York state.[48] Moreover, Burkett informed me, that this man was not the only fake Vietnam veteran of the 7th Cavalry to gain national prominence. There was another that Burkett never included in his book out of personal respect for a senior military leader.

This man, too, had at one point been the president of both the 7th Cavalry Association and the 1st Cavalry Division Association. (Amazingly, Daily actually thanks this man for his help in the acknowledgements to his book, *From Custer to MacArthur: The History of the 7th Cavalry 1866–1945*. It is unknown if Daily knew that this man was also a fake.) Burkett's point to me was that the 7th Cavalry, perhaps due to its heritage, seemed to attract fakes like flies.[49] At that point I remembered yet another fake 7th Cavalryman who appeared in the media in the 1930s in relation to the Massacre at Wounded Knee. That "veteran" had conveniently appeared on the site of the massacre just as a reporter was walking the ground during the time when the Battle of Pine Ridge was becoming known as the Massacre at Wounded Knee.[50] The veteran had guided the reporter across the killing fields, describing the disposition of each troop of cavalry and his own role in the fight. The guilt-stricken veteran even went so far as to demonstrate where the Gatling guns had been positioned, right next to his own location. The reporter dutifully reported the entire event as portrayed by the soldier. Unfortunately for that reporter, a moment of historical research reveals that no Gatling gun was present at Wounded Knee, nor were most of the things he had written even marginally accurate. The reporter had been taken in by a fake 7th Cavalry veteran who confessed to a massacre that he neither saw nor participated in. It was a pure case of advocacy journalism, although in the case of Wounded Knee, at least the event itself had occurred.[51] I was beginning to see a trend.[52]

Burkett explained it to me very carefully. The most difficult fakes to uncover tended to develop their stories slowly. They would attend veterans' reunions for the organization quietly for some time, taking in stories. They might even do significant research, reading all of the secondary sources that talk about the unit in combat. Finally, they begin to tell stories themselves, but not stories they made up from scratch. They were the stories of other veterans and claimed by the false veteran as his own. As each yearly reunion occurred, they might even tell a man his own story from a slightly different perspective, as though they had both witnessed the same obscure event. The real veteran can do little but agree with the storyteller since in his mind, the storyteller must have been there, for who else would know about this obscure event? After seven or ten or fifteen years with reunions and phone calls and letters, a memory implanted by the fake is as real as his own memories.

Edward Daily was also a salesman. As with many successful salesmen, he knew how to read a customer. Good salesmen learn how to read body language and how to decipher unspoken desires from the tone of a person's voice, and they slowly change their sales pitch until it matches that of the buyer's desires. Daily used this skill on the reporters from the Associated Press. When later asked why he had talked to the AP, Daily told Charles Hanley of the AP that "he felt compassion for the Korean survivors who were seeking the truth in the face of Pentagon denials that the No Gun Ri killings could have occurred. 'I was sympathetic with those people and what they had gone through over their many years of suffering and pain,' he told a reporter. 'I thought it would be appropriate to talk to you about No Gun Ri.'"[53] In other words, by his own admission, Daily knew at the *beginning* of the interview what the South Koreans were claiming took place. He was sympathetic. When the AP told him the South Koreans' story of the events, Daily simply inserted himself into the story—again. But that does not explain the other veterans' memories of Daily on the battle-field or some of the other contradictory accounts that they remembered.

The simple fact is that human memory is not the same as computer memory. Data stored in a human memory is not fresh and ready to be called upon in its original form at any later point in life. Most studies on human memory break it down into three stages: acquisition, retention, and retrieval. Variations in each stage are normal, and clinical studies demonstrate that at any point after a memory is acquired, it may be modified, unconsciously, through outside stimuli. Moreover, when confronted with an authority on a subject, many people will say something that the authority wants to hear, whether consciously or unconsciously.[54] Thus, a memory formed ten, twenty, or forty-five years earlier may be modified by someone who presents himself as what sociologists call a referent authority, that is, they appear to know more about the event than does the person who was actually there. It is therefore easy to influence fifty-year-old memories. To avoid doing this, one must never ask leading questions. Unlike interviewing eyewitnesses in the present, memories of the distant past must be assumed to be incomplete and not fully accurate from the beginning. Deferred interviews, such as those of veterans from distant wars, should begin without any assumptions, even about the man's unit. The oral history interviewer should let the veteran talk and then try to put the pieces together.

Even when interviewing in the present, good journalists shun a technique that essentially says: "We understand this is the situation . . . can you please confirm what we are telling you about your own actions so that we can report that you told us this and use it as a quote?" That is not a sound method for getting to the truth in an historical investigation, if the truth is really being sought.

Evidence that this was the process followed by the Associated Press came from a member of the team's own lips. In a sympathetic interview with Internet media reporter Sean Elder of *Salon.com*, Martha Mendoza explained how the No Gun Ri story slowly evolved. Elder reports:

> Their accounts mirrored what the Korean survivors had told them—so much so that the veterans would correct their imprecise questions to more perfectly match the Korean testimony. "I'd say it was at a tunnel and they'd say, 'Ma'am, we didn't do this at a tunnel, we did it at a culvert underneath a railroad, it was M shaped.'" They would take the maps the survivors had drawn from memory and redraw them, placing the troops and weapons differently. "I sat down with a veteran and said, 'Here's where they said the machine guns were,' and he looked at the map and said, 'No, no,' and put an X somewhere else on the map and said, '*Here's* where my machine gun was. And I was on it with these two other guys; they're dead now.'"[55]

Here, the Associated Press described the exact process of creating false memories. But later reporters discovered that Daily's link to the veterans who supplied the No Gun Ri story was even stronger than that. Daily was part and parcel of the memories of many of the veterans quoted by the AP. The reasons why are clear and are exactly as outlined by Burkett in his book about the syndrome of fake Vietnam veterans. According to Burkett, many, if not most, of those claiming to suffer from PTSD brought on by horrific combat they supposedly experienced in Vietnam are actually fakes. His published research exposes hundreds of them, and he is still working on hundreds more. When I learned that Daily suffered from PTSD brought on by his memories of No Gun Ri, one more piece of the puzzle snapped into place.

I later learned that Daily received roughly $2,300 a month tax free in disability from the Veterans Administration for his PTSD brought on by the horrors he witnessed in combat in the opening days of the Korean War.[56] Just as Burkett described, Daily also attempted to bring others into this circle, among them one of the AP's other star sources, James Kerns. *The New York Times* reported it this way:

> Mr. Daily went on the road to help other veterans who suffer from post-traumatic stress syndrome. In the fall of 1998, James Kerns, 70, a former sergeant in Piedmont, S.C., said Mr. Daily invited him to a workshop in Columbia, where Mr. Daily opened the session by talking about the affliction. At the time, Mr. Kerns said, he had not yet been contacted by The Associated Press, but its reporters had begun asking others, including Mr. Daily, about No Gun Ri. While at the workshop, Mr. Kerns said, Mr. Daily asked him about the massacre.[57]

The fact is that just after Daily was contacted by the AP, he started talking to as many men as he thought might be relevant about the "Massacre at No Gun Ri."[58]

Burkett reminded me of something else that I knew but had never connected as a historical source. The army takes attendance every single morning, and those records are saved although not kept in the same part of the building as the individuals' files. These records can be used by archivists or very, very dedicated individuals to precisely reconstruct the service and movements of every single person who was ever in the army during time of war. There is nothing ambiguous about them. They are not an inexact science as the AP would later try to claim. They are specific snapshots at the company level taken once each day for every unit in the army. Moreover, those records had not been burned in the 1973 fire. They are called morning reports, and I requested copies of them. While I was waiting, I considered the issue of the awards.

Daily claimed in his book *Skirmish: Red White and Blue* that during the Korean War he was awarded the Distinguished Service Cross by the 1st Cavalry Division. He also claimed that he earned the Silver Star, a Bronze Star, and three Purple Hearts. Yet none of these awards were reflected in the 1st Cavalry personnel records. Divisions do not issue the Distinguished Service Cross, but they do write up recommendations for such awards. No such recommendation existed in the archives. So how did Daily get those awards of which he sent me photocopies? How did Ed Daily become the hero that I had known? The question bothered me and would continue to bother me until another reporter dug up the truth some months later.[59]

Just a day after I called Daily to ask him about the record, I got a call from Associated Press reporter Charles Hanley. He was calling at Ed Daily's request. When I last talked to Daily, I told him of the stories I had read in the English-language version of *Ibon Chouson* (a South Korean newspaper) that mentioned the North Korean version of the events and I told him my understanding that reporters in South Korea were now working on that thesis. After telling him about the total lack of records verifying that he was ever in the 2nd Battalion 7th Cavalry in July, August, and September of 1950, I asked him to tell me what the answer to this mystery might be. Ed stonewalled, then apparently called Charles Hanley, and asked him to contact me.

In a polite conversation lasting more than an hour, Hanley and I discussed our competing views of the sources and the events, and I told him everything that I had found and where he could find it too. Hanley was convinced that Ed Daily's record was valid as portrayed in the Associated Press stories, but he also revealed that the AP too had had doubts about Daily. The evidence that Hanley suggested "proved" Daily was there stunned me. Here was a reporter from an internationally known news source telling me that, despite the mounds of documents that said Daily's tale was not true, he preferred to rely upon the dubious materials provided to him by the man suspected of being a fake. Nothing could have more clearly illustrated to me that the AP in general, and Hanley in particular, wanted to believe Daily no matter what. If he were not important to the story, then why keep a source who had such blatantly obvious problems of credibility? The next day my E-mail mail box contained several letters from Hanley.

> From: Charles J. Hanley [mail to: E-mail address deleted for privacy]
> Sent: Sunday, March 26, 2000 2:28 P.M.
> To: Robert L. Bateman [E-mail address deleted for privacy]
> Subject: 'Evidence'
>
> Bob:
> Good hearing from you yesterday. If you have a chance to turn up the 7th Cav communications log in your files, I'd sure be interested in hearing about it from you. Meantime, after hanging up yesterday, and knowing I hadn't conveyed to you anywhere near a com-

plete idea of the items Ed Daily's dug up from closets etc., I found I'd noted a couple of other things in my notes and I've remembered one or two others:

- An old letter from the Pentagon to Daily's mother, dated in late August 1950, saying he was MIA. (I don't believe there was a unit designation attached to his name; I'd remember that.)
- A faded letter from Daily to his mother, dated and postmarked in September 1950. Writing from a Taegu hospital, he tells her he was a prisoner but is no longer, he's fine, and says something admiring about "my company commander, Capt. Chandler," who visited with him at some point along the way.
- A discharge document (it was not the DD 214 familiar to me). It identifies him as a first lieutenant. It must list his latest assignment (at Aberdeen); I'm sure it didn't list previous assignments (and neither does my DD 214, which has space only for "last duty assignment.")
- An old, folded-up yellow scarf (a symbol of the 7th Cav, no?) that he said was given to the battalion officers by Col. Harris. I could see writing on it, apparently noting "Kunu-ri," "Unsan-ni" etc.
- A faded newspaper obit of Col. Wadsworth, his later Co. H commander. It's from 1978. I may have mentioned to you that he also has the 1st Cav Assn. newsletter from '77 in which he asks, "Where is Melbourne Chandler? Please contact me."

You raised the question of personal snapshots. I've learned from other vets that they all lost their personal possessions left behind in Tokyo in 1950. I asked Daily what was in his lost foot locker and he said, among other things, "all my photos," meaning, of course, his Japan photos. Those are just some random items that come to mind. There was more, but I stopped paying rapt attention. By the way, re the discharge, my DD-214 form was developed in 1966, according to the small print at the bottom. I guess there was another type and number before that. And mine, as I said, does not list my undeserved but duly awarded Bronze Star. I guess I'd better stop boasting of my "heroism" and just keep quiet.

Cheers,
Charlie Hanley

I wrote Hanley, once again reiterating the basis for my belief that Ed Daily was not whom he claimed to be. I suggested that he read Burkett's book and re-examine the files that he had from the archives. I told him about my FOIA request for Edward Daily's records, and how I was still waiting, now almost six months, to hear something back from the National Military Personnel Records Center. At this point, I had no idea that Hanley and his team were being considered for the Pulitzer Prize.

I thought that our interaction was just one man looking for the truth talking to another man who was seeking the same. I was trying to explain the process of history, the need to reevaluate sources as new evidence appeared, and the relative value of some sources over others provided by the person whose veracity was in doubt. I told him of the pitfalls of oral history, how it was not the same as interviewing people about recent events. I told him about the phenomena of created memories. I did not make much headway as the next day, I received the following E-mail.

From: Charles J. Hanley [mail to: E-mail address deleted for privacy]
Sent: Monday, March 27, 2000 11:11 A.M.
To: Robert L. Bateman, CPT
Cc: Charles Hanley
Subject: Re: 'Evidence'

Bob:
Thanks for your very thoughtful E-mail. I appreciate your sharing this troubling business with me. I understand completely your need to question and probe. We felt a similar need when we first heard about the discrepancies. But I then, first, turned back to our more than 100 interviews with 84 men of the 2nd Battalion and saw enough Daily connections and overall context—i.e., the common sense of it all—to begin to feel comfortable again. Then when Ed told me on the phone about the driver's license and other things, I felt more comfortable. When I saw them myself, that was it. The H Co. driver's license alone is unassailable—old, worn-at-the-corners dark blue cardboard, with appropriately faded typescript, signature, rubber stamp of the provost marshal. All the rest is convincing, too; as I said, I stopped paying rapt attention because of the overkill. Obviously, it would be a superhuman hoax—by a man who never knew he'd be challenged in this way—to have constructed such a personal history. You've got to understand, also,

that I am intimately familiar with the way Daily's No Gun Ri account very slowly emerged over a series of interviews, first by telephone, then in person. And how it fit together—in intricate, he-had-to-be-there detail—with the independent accounts of other vets, and of the Koreans. I've also spoken at length with his therapist; I know the history of his nightmares re July 1950. I simply have absorbed so much that when I hear that someone says Daily was in Co. L, I say, "Show me." Anyway, I don't believe anyone in our copy is all he has ever said he was, and our interviews, obviously, are rife with bullshit and deceptions. In the journalism, as I said, we sought the least common denominator—a large-scale killing, 2nd of the 7th Cav, some dispute over "gunfire out." On the ammunition expenditure: No, I don't believe we saw S-4 logs. Remember, though, that Daily and others have flip-flopped on elapsed time, duration of heavy firing etc. I'm sure somewhere, probably to us at one point, he taled about a five-minute barrage. But then he also talks about pot-shotting at people emerging, etc. As for killing 300, it's pretty clear to me that the BARs were firing, and an unknown number of riflemen. And we don't really know how many .30-cal MGs were firing. Tinkler was way down the line somewhere deciding to get in his own licks with his MG. By the way, the book will not attempt to be the definitive story of what happened at No Gun Ri. Instead, it will be a human story, about the people whose lives intersected there. So, I don't imagine the Pentagon will waste its time trying to besmirch us by noting that we overlooked a bonafide report of a "woman with a radio" 10 miles away, or whatever. Again, let me stress I totally respect and understand what you see as your duty on Daily. And we'd very much appreciate your sharing any smoking gun with us. It's great to make contact with you finally. I'll keep things low-profile. But it's nice to have a knowledgable professional to vent with. If you're ever down this way (I'm working at home these days, in Midtown), let me know. We can have a little lunch and you can tell me about Custer.

Cheers,
Charlie[60]

I really did not know what to make of these letters. I could almost understand how Ed Daily would continue to insist that he had been a commissioned officer, a recipient of the Distinguished Service Cross, and everything else. After all, he had been playing that role for so many years that I was almost convinced that he now believed his own stories to be true. But this was a reporter, a journalist with a major news agency. I assumed that he would agree with me about the evidence. I assumed too much.

I was surprised that when I spelled out for him everything about the records—all the information about Daily that should have been in dozens of different places but wasn't, all of the discrepancies in Daily's accounts— he would see that the weight of the evidence was overwhelming. Hanley's E-mails told me otherwise.

Then, in the first week of April 2000, the FOIA request I had filed on Ed Daily finally came in from the National Military Personnel Records Center. On just one sheet of paper, a summary was given of Ed Daily's military service based upon the reconstruction of his records from a variety of sources, but mostly from the morning reports. The summary included his initial assignment, subsequent assignments, the records of his ribbons and awards, and his discharge information, all of which had been painfully reconstructed through an exhaustive process involving hundreds if not thousands of documents. This secondary source was unequivocal.

Edward Daily was a mechanic.

The single sheet was pretty clear about this. Ed Daily served in the 27th Ordnance Maintenance Battalion from his 18 March 1949 assignment to the division in Japan through the spring of 1951. At that point, March 15,1951, he transferred to the 2nd Battalion 7th Cavalry where he was a sergeant in H Company for fifty-four days. On May 9, 1951, he was sent home from Korea for undisclosed reasons. At that point, Daily would not have had sufficient time in a combat unit to be among the very first men rotated home, nor had he been wounded as there is no record of a Purple Heart. He was discharged in 1952 as a sergeant. He was never commissioned; he was never captured and escaped from the North Koreans; he was never awarded the Purple Heart or the Silver Star or the Distinguished Service Cross; he never changed his military occupation specialty either. Perhaps it was for this reason that he did not earn, or at least was not awarded, the Combat Infantryman's Badge that he wore.[61]

For fifteen years, he had been impersonating an officer. For all those years, Daily had duped me, as well as dozens of other active-duty officers and NCOs, from the division commanders of the 1st Cavalry Division between 1992 to 1996 right down to the battalion sergeants major of the 1st and 2nd Battalions of the 7th Cavalry. He was not the decorated, battlefield-commissioned, heroic cavalryman we all thought he was. Sure, by this point, I expected some sort of confirmation that he was not all that he had claimed, but this level of deception was incredible. Backed up with the records of numerous morning reports, it was solid evidence. Moreover, the first photograph of Daily that I discarded in haste (page 148) contains additional evidence. The uniform he was wearing was a mechanic's coverall. The only thing more stunning about this revelation was something I learned later.

The Associated Press team received this information about Daily on December 7, 1999, weeks before Daily appeared on NBC with Tom Brokaw, four months before I did, several months before Mr. Hanley's March 2000 E-mail letters to me, and almost a month before submitting its application to the Pulitzer committee.[62] If I had known at that time that Mr. Hanley actually had the information I was still waiting for, I might not have spent the time that I did trying to help him understand what I was uncovering about Daily. To this day, I do not understand why Hanley kept this information to himself in December 1999 and allowed other journalists to use Daily as the centerpiece for their stories.

I told the honorary colonel of the 7th Cavalry, General Moore, as well as my friends who had been following my research, about the results from the FOIA. These men quickly did their own independent research on this material because just days after I received that report, the Associated Press won the Pulitzer Prize for its account of a massacre allegedly committed by American troops at No Gun Ri. The AP team was awarded the prize based on its in-depth research and the fact that a low-level U.S. government lawyer in South Korea ignorantly denied the fact that the 1st Cavalry Division was even in the area.

Soon after that, the research done by reporters Joseph Galloway and Edward Offley paid off. I had known these men for years and had been asking them questions about how reporters work in my quest to understand how the Associated Press got the story wrong, even as I was warning them of the problems with Ed Daily's records. In the process, I told these colleagues about all that Burkett had passed to me; the specific mechanics of morning reports and how to file FOIA requests for relevant documents. Although Galloway and Offley probably knew more about this process of investigation than I did, I told them about the G-1 and S-1 records so that they could go to the archives and see for themselves the sources that covered this period. These reporters did all of that and more. They not only went to the archives, they interviewed the archivists. Now that they had a solid reason to, they called and interviewed veterans as well. They looked at the archival material for themselves. Galloway and Offley filed FOIA requests and, with the wondrous persuasion that reporters have, had their requests answered almost immediately. (Mine almost always took months to get a reply.) In short, they went far beyond the point that my limited resources had carried me. The ultimate result was a series of stories in *U.S. News and World Report* and *Stripes.com*, exposing not only Ed Daily, but two of the six other witnesses in the AP story as being factually challenged.

Because I had been talking to veterans about their interaction with Ed Daily, the Department of the Army Inspector General (DAIG) investigators thought I was contaminating their sources before they had the chance to complete their own investigation. They were right. By talking to veterans of my regiment, I may have been modifying the veterans' memories of Ed Daily's duplicity. The DAIG wanted to collect testimony from each veteran before he learned that Daily was a fake. Advised of this, I stopped my own research for several months while I worked on understanding the primary and secondary documentary sources I had collected. It was therefore another reporter, this one from *The New York Times*, who ended up doing the research to make sense of who Edward Daily really was and how he fit in to the Associated Press story.[63]

Ed Daily went through a bad time when his marriage broke up in the mid-1980s, around the same time that he started to attend many more veterans' organization functions and became very active in the 1st Cavalry Division Association. At one reunion, he told others that he was going to write a book on the 7th Cavalry, and that if they would send him their stories, he would include them in the book. During the research for this book, Daily must have learned about the status of his records at the National Military Personnel Records Center because at around that time he submitted his own paperwork—fairly amateur forgeries apparently based upon things he had seen in the records at the National Archives—to the army in an effort to "finally get issued" the awards that he had won in combat but which had never been issued to him.[64]

At the time, the Army Reserve Command handled such requests, apparently without checking the records too closely. As a result of Daily's doctored documents, the Army Reserve Command unwittingly issued him a replacement Distinguished Service Cross. Apparently nobody in the Reserve Command then responsible for such requests even realized that despite the paperwork that Daily submitted with his claim, lower-level units such as divisions are not authorized to award the Distinguished Service Cross. The award added depth to his subterfuge and an apparent layer of respectability to his claims.[65] If the army had looked closely at Daily's request at the time, it might also have noted other discrepancies. Daily's claimed Silver Star was issued on a day that the 1st Cavalry Division's records indicate that no awards were given, and the sequence number (used by the army to track its official orders) is one that was never used. Then of course, he was at that time a clerk in a maintenance battalion, so this is not surprising. In all, it appears that most of Daily's records were fakes.

Daily was only one of several other veterans cited by the AP in its story who had modified the truth, or perhaps their memories. Another of the veterans who claimed to have witnessed the incident at No Gun Ri, Delos Flint, was also not there.

DELOS FLINT

Delos K. Flint, who at least was in the unit that he claimed to have been in, could not possibly have been at No Gun Ri on July 26, 1950 as he had been shot and evacuated the day or night before. Flint appears in the regimental records and the morning reports of both his company of the 7th Cavalry and the medical battalion as a casualty on July 25, 1950. He was a casualty of the disintegration that night, well before the alleged incidents of No Gun Ri.

Once again, those morning reports came in handy. Every servicemember knows about the morning report. Each duty day, during the formation of the unit, usually at the company level, the sergeants count heads to make sure everyone can be accounted for. If any men or women are absent from the ranks, the platoon sergeant will report them to the first sergeant. The first sergeant fills out a daily written report of this information, noting the soldiers absent from the ranks and any changes in the company since the morning report of the previous day. Wounds are not recorded in this log unless the serviceman was evacuated because of them. The log simply indicates presence or absence.

When a unit is in garrison, this report is a quick and simple part of daily routine. In the field or in combat, while still routine, the log requires a little more effort. All the men of the company cannot be called out of their fighting positions to one central location for an administrative formation to count heads.

In combat, these reports are still generated in the morning, usually around the time of the breakfast meal. Under normal circumstances, the platoon sergeants count heads one by one in their individual positions or, more likely, rely upon their squad leaders to submit reports of their own. Then, when a detachment of soldiers is sent back to the company first sergeant to get the morning meal, a copy of this report—jotted on a piece of cardboard or a scrap of paper—is carried to the first sergeant who compiles the report on the official army document and submits it to the battalion personnel (S-1) office. If, for any reason a unit cannot or does not submit a morning report on a particular day, it does so the next day and notes any men from the previous day who had been "off the books" as of the date of the morning report on which they should have been accounted. This process may be extended. For example, if a man was missing on one day (let's call that day X), but his absence was not known to the company until three days later (X+3 for our purposes), his name would appear on the next morning report (the morning report of the fourth day: X+4). Although the missing soldier is on the morning report for X+4, the entry would note that he was off the company roster as of the morning report of the day after his actual disappearance (X+1).

Morning reports list people by exception. Rather than listing everyone in the unit every morning, the report lists only the changes in the company status. Only those soldiers who have arrived or departed in some way during the past twenty-four hours since the last report are listed by name. The reports are saved by the army and stored by the government on microfilm at the National Personnel Records Center in St. Louis, Missouri. The morning reports for the various companies of the 7th Cavalry never showed Ed Daily as captured, wounded, returning, or anything in H Company until 1951. The reports did show that he was in the 27th Ordnance Maintenance Company. When reports of the problems with the Associated Press sources first appeared a week after winning the Pulitzer Prize, the reports of the period around July 24–29 became part of the news service's defense of its crumbling story. Perhaps more tellingly, statements given by the Associated Press in May 2000 highlight its lack of understanding about military records in general and morning reports specifically. Comments made at that time make one thing very clear: the Associated Press did not know how to read the reports it had.

In a statement released by the Associated Press just after an exposé published in *U.S. News and World Report*, AP Executive Editor Jonathan Wolman said the following in reference to Delos K. Flint:

> In the AP story, Flint remembers being caught with other soldiers in the strafing and piling into a culvert with refugees. Then, "somebody, maybe our guys, was shooting in at us," he said. He and his comrades eventually slipped out. *U.S. News* contends a regimental war diary entry indicates Flint was transferred out of No Gun Ri on July 25—a day before the shootings. But a reading of that war diary says that he was wounded, but it does not say that he was evacuated. In addition, the more reliable company morning report for July 27, reporting on his wounds, shows he was still with the unit on July 26. The war diaries were generally compiled from scattered sources, days or weeks later, at the rear; the morning report was written each day at the front.[66]

If this comment does not reflect that the reporters and editors of the Associated Press did not understand what they were looking at, then it is a case of a major news agency deliberately misleading the public to protect its own reputation.

The original AP story only casually mentions the disintegration of the battalion on the night of July 25–26. One sentence is devoted to the events that are covered in chapter five of this book. The veterans whom the AP talked to say the reporters knew about the disintegration of that night. It was a conscious decision on the part of the reporters and editors not to include this information in their story.

The AP, therefore, tried to make it appear that Flint was actually at No Gun Ri since he was not on the morning report of the twenty-sixth. Soldiers who were wounded and evacuated anytime after the morning report of July 25 would have shown up on the next day's morning report. But think about the actual status of the 2nd Battalion 7th Cavalry as the sun came up that morning. On the morning of July 26, with the units of 2nd Battalion 7th Cavalry still scattered across the Korean countryside, only limited and incomplete reports were ever sent in that day. (H Company, the only unit to make it through the night fairly intact, did submit a report stating that all but two soldiers, who were listed as wounded in action and evacuated, were present that morning, but this too was almost certainly an incomplete report.[67]) A full report for most of the companies of the battalion was not submitted until the unit reassembled. Since more than a hundred men were still unaccounted for as late as 2100 hours on July 26, a complete report could not be submitted that day. Thus, men wounded on July 25, including Delos Flint, did not appear on the more accurate morning report until July 27. If you know what you are reading, the morning report for July 27 clearly states that the morning reports from the morning of July 26 were not accurate at all, as they did not reflect the actual status of the unit.

The morning report for F Company, 7th Cav (Inf) at Rockin-Ri Korea APO 201, for the morning of July 27, 1950 has the following entries:

Bowie, Phom	RA 6951842 Sfc
	Dy to KIA Rockin-Ri off 26 July 1950
Flint Delos K	RA 6250045 Pvt
	Dy to 15th Med Clr Bn WIA Rockin-Ri off 26 Jul 50
Collins William T.	RA 13307764 Pfc
	Dy to abs ok 15th Med Clr Bn LD yes off 26 Jul 50
Alicea Robert	RA 12322305 Pfc
Maddox Jesse J.	RA 39711770 Sfc

> Above 2 EM dy to abs ok 15th Med Clr Bn LD yes
> off 26 Jul 50
> Culver Charles L RA 16323801 Pfc
> Dy to MIA Yongdong off 26 Jul 50[68]

Translated into plain English, this report says that SFC Bowie was killed sometime between the morning report of July 25, 1950 and the morning report of July 26, 1950. It further notes that Collins, Alicea, and Maddox went from being present for duty ("Dy") to absent ("abs") by their transfer to the 15th Medical Clearance Battalion and that their evacuation, while not as a result of wounds (there is no "WIA" annotation), was considered "in the line of duty"("LD yes") for the purposes of determining their legal status. Private First class Charles Culver became missing in action (MIA) sometime between the morning of the twenty-fifth and the morning of the twenty-sixth. From reading the regimental diary, written with the aid of the radio logs from the battalions, I learned that Culver actually disappeared on the twenty-fifth. By using both sources, I also learned that Bowie was killed on the night of July 25–26, probably during the chaotic withdrawal that night. Now what of the entry for Flint?

According to that morning report filed on the morning of July 27, 1950, Delos Flint, a soldier in the regular army (RA) with the identification number of 6250045 and the rank of private, is off the roster for this company of the 2nd Battalion 7th Cavalry as of the morning report of the twenty-sixth. The Associated Press, either through ignorance or intent, attempted to portray this document otherwise. The AP tried to convince the public that since the morning report was filed on July 27, Flint was present through the events of the evening of July 26. Moreover, the AP knew about the problems with its source Delos Flint long before going to press the first time with the No Gun Ri story.

This claim that the morning report was more accurate and therefore a more reliable source than the regimental diary was repeated over and over by the Associated Press to defend its sources and story in May 2000. Knowing what both documents, the regimental diary and the morning reports, said, the AP thought that the morning report could be used to validate Flint's presence. Amazingly, this information on Flint was not discovered during the AP's subsequent fact checking in December of 1999 but had been known long before the AP ever printed the first story. In a May 12, 2000 report, the AP responded to the media accounts about the problems with Flint's records with a recitation of its same line. In the quote below, the AP tried to discredit the regimental war diary because it was written after the fact, not as a running journal contemporaneously:

The *Stripes.com* report, citing a regimental document, asserted that Delos K. Flint, an ex-GI eyewitness quoted by the AP, was wounded and evacuated July 25, the day before the shooting started. But a company morning report obtained by the AP in June 1998 says he was wounded the next day, July 26.[69]

In other words, the AP had this information about Delos Flint in the summer of 1998, almost a year before citing him as one of its sources in the original story. That story made it appear as though Flint was present on the afternoon and evening of July 26, 1950. If read correctly, the morning report does not show him wounded on the twenty-sixth, but notes him as off the rolls at the time that the morning report for July 26 should have been submitted. If he had been wounded on the twenty-sixth, there would be no caveat date on the morning report of the twenty-seventh. The report would just list his name. Had that been the case, standard operating procedure would have informed the reader of that report that he was wounded between the morning report of the twenty-sixth and that of the twenty-seventh if that were the case. The AP states that it had this documentary evidence, yet either it did not have the knowledge to correctly interpret a basic morning report, or it wanted to deliberately mislead the American public by using a source that it knew had not been there.

EUGENE HESSELMAN

Eugene Hesselman's story is somewhat more convoluted, and for good reason. Hesselman also claims that he was on the front lines on the evening of July 26, 1950 and that he witnessed and participated in what he described as a massacre. That would have been tough to do, however, since Hesselman was shot in the foot either on the night of the twenty-fifth or on the morning of the twenty-sixth and had already been evacuated.[70]

Hesselman was in close contact with Daily through the period when the AP was investigating and reporting on its version of the events at No Gun Ri. Most likely, Hesselman's version of events was what he received from Daily, since he himself was not present at No Gun Ri. His story then was a version Daily developed in response to the way that the AP conducted its interviews and Daily's own need to maintain his charade as a decorated battlefield-commissioned officer. Daily had already convinced Hesselman that Daily was a soldier in H Company of the 7th Cavalry and was later commissioned as an officer. He had also made Hesselman think that he had seen Daily at a certain place and a time where he was not, and could not have been. When confronted with the fact that Daily was not at No Gun Ri, and that in fact he was not even in the unit, Hesselman could do little but repeat over and over, "I know that Daily was there. I know that. I know that."[71]

Again, this is either a classic demonstration of the power of implanted memories or prime evidence that if Hesselman's memory is so faulty as to believe that Ed Daily was there, then it is unreliable for anything else that he might have discussed with Daily, including their mutual testimony to the Associated Press.

These three men—Ed Daily, Delos Flint, and Eugene Hesselman—formed the core of the Associated Press's Pulitzer Prize-winning story.

Archivists at the National Military Personnel Records Center were greatly annoyed about the tenor of the original AP story, as well as the spin that the AP subsequently put on the quality of its own research. One archivist flatly likened the situation to the now infamous Tailwind story in which a veteran of dubious credentials spun a story that made international headlines (much as No Gun Ri did). These archivists claim that they were explicit with reporter Charles Hanley and his research assistant Randy Herschaft, showing both of them Daily's reconstructed records as well as the morning reports and explaining how these worked. They detailed for the reporters exactly how materials gathered from a dozen different locations could be used to reconstruct a serviceman's real records when the records the serviceman submitted were considered forgeries. When the story came out with Edward Daily on center stage, the archivists from the National Military Personnel Records Center were furious that a man whom they considered a fake had now received national recognition.[72]

Edward Daily was at the center of the circle. It was his contacts, and his subsequent implanting of memories in the minds of some of the veterans of the 2nd Battalion 7th Cavalry that directly led to the quotes that the Associated Press used. The Associated Press knew about the problems with all three of these veterans' accounts, at least as far back as the summer of 1998, yet chose to ignore both the expert advice of the archivists and the documentary evidence that it culled from the archives. The AP published its story, with Edward Daily, Eugene Hesselman, and Delos Flint at the core, without so much as a sidebar or comment about the problems with the credibility of these sources. It never informed their fellow journalists—Michael Dobbs of *The Washington Post* or NBC's Tom Brokaw—about the very real problems with Ed Daily's record even though, since Daily kept in touch with the AP team after the initial publication of the story, the AP probably knew about both major stories featuring Daily before they ever appeared in print or on the screen.[73] The AP did all of this because to do otherwise might impinge upon the quality of its reporting or damage its reputation.

LOUIS ALLEN

The story of Louis Allen is simple and straightforward. In March 1950, he re-enlisted in the U.S. Army, and as part of the incentive program to get him to do that, he was granted ninety days of leave in the United States. Getting back to the states was via troopship in those days, and your leave did not start until you were stateside. According to the AP version of events, Allen witnessed no return fire from the refugees. In the AP story, he is quoted as saying, "I don't remember shooting coming out." But this is understandable, since Allen was in the United States at the time. Recalls Allen, "After my leave, I returned to Camp Stoneman. That was in the beginning of June, but then I was sent to Governors Island to pick up and be an escort for a prisoner. By the time I got back from that, the Korean War had already broken out. I got on a troopship on the East Coast to go to Japan, but it went to Seattle first. When we got there, there were some others like me in the same situation; we were sent to McChord Air Force Base, Washington and they flew us over to Japan. We in-processed back at Drake, and from there, I went and rejoined the 7th Cavalry in Korea. I spent about two weeks as part of the regimental security platoon, guarding the head-quarters, before I went down to F Company. We were on the Naktong River line at that point."[74]

The 7th Cavalry did not reach the Naktong River until August 1950.

In recent months, the Associated Press has been very careful to make sure it states that its story "clearly reflected" the ambiguities of the various sources and their stories. It says this, but what might an in-depth analysis of its reporting reveal about its true message? The next chapter takes an in-depth look at the Associated Press's reporting in its award-winning No Gun Ri story.

CHAPTER 7

Making (Up) History

*In the summer of 1950, in the first weeks of the Korean War,
U.S. military forces opened fire on a group of South Korean civilian refugees at a place called No Gun Ri, killing hundreds of
men, women, and children. What happened next was equally
shocking: Nothing. Apparently no one in the U.S. military
reported the killings. No one investigated them. As the years
passed, historians remained unaware of what had happened . . . .[1]*
—AP Reporter Martha Mendoza,
January 2000

*According to a [N]KPA detachment that got to Yongdong on July
20 and spoke to ten eyewitnesses, American troops herded some
two thousand civilians from two villages in Yongdong County into
the mountains in this guerilla-infested county and then when Taejon fell, slaughtered them . . . .[2]*
—Historian Bruce Cumings
The Origins of the Korean War

Civilian Deaths in Korea Aren't News
—Title of editorial from
Korean War historian Stanley Weintraub,
The Wall Street Journal, June 5, 2000

IN THE END, A LARGE PART OF THIS TALE COMES DOWN TO THE DIFFERENCE
between history and muckraking.[3] As any careful researcher would learn,
the calamity of civilians caught by American fires, either intentional or accidental, was neither unknown to historians nor unreported at the time that it
occurred. Stories and first-person accounts of such tragedies of the war in
South Korea appeared during the opening days of the conflict in *Life* magazine and on the front page of *The New York Times*. Historians later used
these accounts, as well as the combat reports of U.S. and South Korean

units, to reconstruct the history of those chaotic opening days of the war. What they created was a viable description of some units performing well and others disintegrating in panic. Even the official U. S. Army history of this period—*South to the Naktong, North to the Yalu* by Roy Appleman— acknowledged that some civilians were killed by U.S. troops and that, among other things, the 2nd Battalion of the 7th Cavalry had disintegrated on its first night near the front lines.

In looking at this official history, Mendoza and the rest of the AP team apparently overestimated their research skills and ability to reconstruct military historical events.[4] Not surprising since from the days of the Vietnam War, the tendency in the media has been to examine the military with a high level of skepticism and, in some cases, to view and describe it with positive disdain.[5] At the same time, as the number of reporters with direct experience in the military has declined, so too has the professional ability of the media to describe military events. While *The New York Times, The L.A. Times, Time* magazine, *Newsweek*, the *Miami Herald*, the *San Francisco Chronicle*, and the *Boston Globe* all have theater, film, and restaurant critics, none of them has a full-time military affairs correspondent.[6] Reporter Fred Reed made it plain when he said, "I know that I can easily sell articles criticizing the military, but a piece praising anything the services do is nearly impossible to peddle. In conversations, magazine editors almost without exception are hostile and contemptuous of the military."[7] This editorial environment exists at many of the media organizations that subscribe to the Associated Press news services.[8] This antimilitary editorial environment is a large part of the second tragedy of No Gun Ri.

Understanding how the media got this story so wrong—not just the Associated Press but the other media that accepted the story at face value and jumped on the bandwagon following the AP story—requires some understanding of the history of military-media relations. Throughout American history, reporting on the military was always something of a catch-as-catch-can situation. It is the history of a relationship that was rocky in the best of times and, for the past thirty years, has been blatantly adversarial in some of the most celebrated cases.

A FREE PRESS

Freedom in the United States stands upon a tradition of a free and open press. The Founding Fathers who established the concept of a free and open press as a precondition for liberty, took pains to embed it deep in the foundations of our nation. Freedom of the press is one of the central tenets of the Constitution of the United States. Over time, the realities of military necessity, social trends, and communications technology have slowly acted to separate the interests of the two greatest defenders of our nation—the military and the press. Taken in the abstract, one could claim that while the military defends our liberty, the media defends our freedoms. Unfortunately, these two do not always work side-by-side.

From the beginning of the nation, journalists have filed reports from the battlefields of America's armies and navies. As early as the Revolutionary War, men wrote and published accounts of the events that they witnessed for the benefit of readers elsewhere. During the Revolution, however, newspaper articles did not compromise military secrecy because simply put, news traveled too slowly. Although certain battles, such as the ones around Boston in 1775, were known in all the major population centers within a week or two of the clash, word of most events did not travel as quickly. News of battles and troop movements, such as those in the hinterlands of North and South Carolina and, at such places as Kings Mountain and Guilford Courthouse, might not appear in print for more than a month after the event no matter how militarily important. Word traveled only at the speed of a man on horseback, and the roads of the new nation were not the superhighways of today.

From the standpoint of a historian examining the media, another factor missing in that early coverage was a commitment to honest and unbiased reporting. News as we know it today was only a secondary consideration in early papers. Reporters and editors spilled almost as much ink, and in some cases far more, on diatribes about various issues than on the facts themselves. Reporting just the facts was something yet to be invented. In both political and social issues, each and every item in the paper was generally colored by the writer's or editor's interpretation or bias. In some ways, the origins of the American media help explain its later development because from the very beginning, members of the media saw their primary role not as informers, but as people who advocate change.[9]

By the time of the Mexican War (1846–1848), some of this had started to change. Newspapers were now employing reporters on a full-time basis, and their reports were more than matched in volume by the somewhat informal reports of the participants. While the media was on its way to becoming a profession, it was not yet there. Still, accuracy in reporting was becoming increasingly important, and unlike during the Revolutionary War (and to a lesser degree the War of 1812), editors were not applying as much of a slant to their stories. Extreme editorial slants tended to be limited to news of a political nature. During the Revolutionary War, newspapers acted as much as explicit political tools as providers of the news, and readers read them with this understanding. By 1848, in a major shift that would have interesting implications twelve years later, newspapers were expected to provide information in addition to polemics. This does not mean that newspapers were not biased, only that they were beginning to work on presenting the facts in addition to the stories. During this period, the Associated Press appeared.

The AP was born in 1848 as a cooperative venture by six New York City newspapers trying to reduce the high costs of sending long news stories over the telegraph.[10] With the fighting front of the Mexican war so far away, reporters were hard-pressed to file timely stories in this national news event. Reporters covering the action in Texas and south of the Texas-Mexico border could, at least, send their reports overland to the nearest American telegraph station, but the individual papers at home balked at paying for the costs of sending all of that text. Moreover, because of the collaborative nature of the reporters themselves, the material that each paper received was not significantly different than that of others. Thus, the news co-op was founded to defray the expenses. During the Mexican War, many papers disapproved of the president's actions, but their disapproval of political decisions did not transfer to biased reporting of the actions of the American soldiers fighting in Mexico. Instead, the newspapers began to separate their reporting slightly from their editorializing.

The election of Abraham Lincoln in 1860 and the subsequent attack on Fort Sumter in the harbor of Charleston, South Carolina, ignited the worst war in American history. When President Lincoln called for 75,000 volunteers in early 1861 to suppress the rebellion, he inadvertently sent seven more states into the arms of the Confederacy. That first call for volunteers was more than met by enthusiastic young men in the Union, and when the Confederacy made calls of its own for volunteers, the flood of men who responded exceeded the initial estimated requirements by as much as a third. As these men swelled the ranks in the North and the South, they created instant news interest in all things military among those who stayed at home. The soldier-reporter provided the answer to this demand for military news.

Soldiers doubling as reporters were certainly not a new phenomena during the American Civil War. More than eighty years earlier, some soldiers had written to their favorite editors during the Revolutionary War. Soldier-reporters had also appeared in the ranks—during the Mexican War—not many, but they were there. Starting in 1861, however, what had been a rare occurrence became the norm.

Historian James McPherson suggests that the armies of the Civil War may well have been the most literate armies ever fielded.[11] In an era when reading was the sole form of entertainment readily available to the majority of the population, the ability to read was no longer a luxury, it had become a necessity. Beyond the major cities, hundreds of small towns had daily or at least weekly papers, and editors around the nation had to fill these local papers with news of local interest.

Military participation and increasing literacy combined in the Civil War, so that when the young men of this war set out from their homes, many had agreements with the editors of their local papers to write back and report on their units. It was bottom-up and egalitarian reporting of a type generally unknown today.

In addition to this reporting from the front lines, plain and unvarnished, by the men who were there, and another trend in military reporting during the Civil War was the appearance of professional reporters on the battlefield, or at least in the area of where battles occurred.

With the rise in importance of the news media in the first half of the Nineteenth century reporting became a full-time occupation. By the time of the Civil War, reporters had not only become somewhat professionalized, they flourished. Such newspapers as *The New York Times*, the *Herald*, and the *Tribune* sent correspondents out with all of the major Union field armies.[12] Two crucial differences set these men apart from the soldier-reporters: what they reported and how quickly they reported it to the reading public.

From the military professional's point of view, the first problem with the professional reporter was that the news they reported could be read in a major newspaper within a day of the event. At a time when armies generally moved at three to five miles per hour, and even cavalry corps could only average about seven miles an hour, the speed of information now greatly exceeded that of the armies. The invention of the telegraph was the event that changed the equation. While the stories sent by the soldiers homeward may have been more accurate and more telling (providing the writer did not stray too far from the events that he actually witnessed), they were sent by regular mail. That method created a built-in delay that made the soldier-reporter's information out-of-date by the time of publication. Professional reporters working for major newspapers could, and did, use the wires of the telegraph. Their articles about the campaign plans or the defensive works of the armies could actually have an effect on military operations in real-time.[13] Some concerned military leaders used this as an excuse to place severe restrictions on the press in their areas of operations.[14]

Union Major General William T. Sherman was perhaps one of the most direct war leaders in his dislike, even hatred, of the media. Given the unsubstantiated allegations of insanity that some politically inclined reporters made, his attitude may be considered understandable. The journalist were far from subtle in their insinuations, as evidenced by December 11, 1861 article in the *Cincinnati Commercial*:

> Gen. William T. Sherman, late commander of the Department of the Cumberland, is insane. It appears that he was at the time while commanding in Kentucky, stark mad . . . . The harsh criticisms that have been lavished on this gentlemen, provoked by his strange conduct, will now give way to feelings of deepest sympathy for him in his great calamity.[15]

Although this sort of unfounded personal attack wounded Sherman, his true anger was reserved for the reporters who sent out information for publication that affected current military operations. Sherman wrote in a letter to a personal friend:

> As I have more leisure than usual now, I will illustrate by examples fresh in the memory of all, why I regard newspaper correspondents as spies and why as a servant of an enlightened government I feel bound in honor and in common honesty to shape my official conduct accordingly. A spy is one who furnishes an enemy with knowledge useful to him and dangerous to us. One who bears into a fortress or camp a baleful influence that encourages sedition or weakens us . . . . I know that the northern papers reach the enemy regularly and promptly and I know that all the vigilance of our army cannot prevent it and I know that by this means the enemy can defeat us to the end of time . . . I say in giving intelligence to the enemy, in sowing discord and discontent in an army, these men fulfill all the conditions of spies. Shall we succumb, or shall we meet and overcome the evil?"[16]

Sherman, while certainly one of the most extreme of the Union commanders to express his displeasure with the press, was by no means alone. Other Union generals, including McClellan, Burnsides, Meade, and Grant, also had more than their share of troubles with the media on some of the same issues.

The other problem that military professionals had with professional reporters involved several defects that very few reporters worked hard to overcome. The first was a lack of tradition in seeking the whole truth, or even in some cases any form of the truth. At the time, no schools offered degrees in journalism. It was a trade to be learned on the job, and for most reporters, this meant that they learned at the foot of their editors. Unfortunately, editors were men who were often so desperate for sensational news that they were willing to overlook issues such as accuracy.[17] One of the most famous examples of this trend in military reporting, was when the editor of the *Chicago Times* told one of his reporters covering the actions of General Ulysses S. Grant's army, "I want news, and if there is no news, I want rumors!"[18]

Along similar lines, a professional newsman following the Battle of Shiloh reported, "The decisive blow was given by General Grant, who headed a charge of six regiments in person . . . on the enemy's center with such force that they broke and ran."[19] In that case, mere sensationalism and a case of pure fiction were pawned off as an eyewitness account. Grant never led any such attack. Although there was a victory for Union forces, the reporter invented the how, who, and where to make his story a "good read." In fact, the reporter was miles away at the time and neither witnessed the action nor interviewed Grant. He created his report using only the sketchiest of accounts from staff officers who themselves may not have seen the events they were passing on. He was, in short, reporting rumors as factual news. Similar reports, because they sold papers, became more and more common as the war progressed. This trend led to the slandering of Union Major General U.S. Grant as reporters suggested that he was drunk at various times during the war and even in battle.[20]

The Spanish-American War in 1898 represented the apogee of this trend toward a casual treatment of the truth and led to the heightening of the second defect of the contemporary professional reporter. The maturation of this type of journalism made Joseph Pulitzer so rich that he could personally found the Columbia School of Journalism and fund the prizes for American journalism that are named after him. Journalism in this era focused less on the accuracy of the events recorded and more on the sensationalism of the idea. Named after a cartoon character that ran in one of Pulitzer's papers, the Yellow Kid, this period is known to most Americans as the era of Yellow Journalism.

Similarly, the media war between the newspapers of William Randolph Hearst and Joseph Pulitzer made both of them rich. Each story collected and filed by their reporters became more and more sensational. The objective was not only mercenary—to increase readership and thereby profits, but also one-upmanship in the competition between the two men and their papers. This trend reached a crescendo with the Cuban insurrection against Spain and the subsequent Spanish-American War.[21]

By the First World War, the ability of the media to compromise military planning (and thereby endanger lives) had become so serious that for the first time the U.S. Army instituted widespread and systematic censor-ship of military news stories. In its efforts to control the flow of informa-tion that might cost lives, the army clamped down and declared everything even remotely associated with current operations sensitive. Ironically, it was none other than Douglas MacArthur who in 1916 first recommended this course of action.[22] What later emerged was something of a compromise between the military and the media. The Committee on Public Informa-tion, better known as the Creel Commission, would help the Wilson administration mobilize public support for U.S. involvement in World War I.[23] The compromise was a broad-brushed attempt to ensure that all news published in the United States was favorable to the Allied cause. In practice that meant draconian censorship, control of reporters accompanying the American armies in France, and deliberate manipulation of the news at home. But from the public's point of view, the Wilson administration's cen-sorship policies were an acceptable cost to bear in the short term for domestic support during wartime.

The Creel Commission arrangement, which worked reasonably well in WWI, was a temporary and perhaps arbitrarily extreme measure. A similar, though larger, structure emerged during the next total war, but this could only happen with the cooperation of the press, a cooperation created by editors attuned to the attitudes of the general public. One can hardly imag-ine today the interaction of members of any western military force with the modern western media such as that remembered by Sergeant Philip Bailey just after his aircrew returned from a particularly disastrous bombing mis-sion over Germany. Describing the newspaper reporters at his airfield upon the return of his battered squadron, Bailey recalled the reporters' reactions this way: "They watched and waited so considerately whilst the lads were coming in but, as the time went on, they too became aware that there were some losses. I shall never ever forget the faces of two of them—both mid-dle aged—when it was quietly put to them that six crews were unac-counted for, forty-two men out of the 119 they had watched set off. The notebooks and cameras were put away and their owners quietly left, obvi-ously not wishing to intrude on our feelings."[24]

With the general approval of the nation, Presidents Lincoln, Wilson, and Roosevelt all suspended the freedom of the press to some degree. Politically risky, censorship was considered necessary by these national leaders in order to win their wars. Getting that public approval, however, could only really come with the total mobilization of the public that such wars as the Civil War and the two world wars entailed. Lesser conflicts could not be used to justify infringing on the First Amendment and the idea of a free press.

The system started wobbling in Korea and finally derailed in Vietnam.[25] Over the next few decades, the general level of journalistic interest in the military would steadily drop to such low levels that when the Persian Gulf crisis first broke, most news agencies were without qualified people available to cover the story.[26] Scrambling to fill the gap, the industry overcompensated. During the Vietnam War, some sixty to seventy reporters covered the Tet Offensive of 1968. Depending upon the source, between 1,400 and 1,600 reporters and news media crews were in the Gulf at the beginning of the air war.[27]

Moreover, the general decrease in the military experience of reporters throughout the United States affected not only the quality of reporting on military affairs, but the methods and topics that reporters focused upon. As fewer and fewer reporters had direct contact with the military, they became increasingly less comfortable in reporting on the central missions of the military and instead focused on social issues and their applications within the military. The trend was so pronounced that one study of major newspapers' military reporting between 1995 and 1999 revealed 1,550 articles on women in the military, another 432 on gays in the military, and a grand total of 64 articles on military preparedness.[28]

On the other hand, journalism as a whole advanced considerably in the first five decades of the twentieth century. For a variety of reasons, a professional ethic dedicated to accuracy and disinterested honesty in reporting developed. Wartime reporting also developed along the same lines. A culture flourished among combat correspondents whereby a reporter commenting on the infantry ought to be there with the infantry. The near-legendary World War II reporter Ernie Pyle epitomized this trend. Pyle's frontline reporting from infantry units captured the flavor of life in the war for the average combatant.

On the other hand, this period also carried with it a classic example of how the ability to write could convey an inordinate amount of illegitimate authority, especially to a historian. The mere act of writing and publishing a book was, and arguably still is, considered by many people as evidence of legitimacy. Books are the currency of historians. If the historian is also a part of that book, then his or her story becomes interlaced with the events recorded between the covers of that text. Beginning in World War II one self-taught historian took great advantage of that perception.

What follows is a classic case study of how one man, by mixing his own story with those of people around him, can create a history about himself and convince others of his legitimacy. This example ties together all four elements that concern us—the military, the media, historians, and liars.

S. L. A. MARSHALL AND THE
FALSE AUTHORITY SYNDROME

*History should consist of the artistic grouping of subordinate
details around a central idea . . . some facts are not really worth
the evident trouble of searching them out.*[29]
                                        —Alfred Thayer Mahan

*His arguments were consonantly effective, so that he had the
unusual experience for a historian of seeing his message not merely
accepted in his own lifetime but translated into practice.*[30]
                                        —John Keegan
                                        (on Marshall)

Samuel Lyman Atwood Marshall, better known as "SLAM" Marshall, was
a soldier-turned-reporter-turned-historian-turned military commentator
during the middle part of the twentieth century. He illustrates, in a single
neat package, how one man's self-vetted autobiography, through constant
repetition and publication, can gain credence for the life he created as
opposed to the one that he actually lived. In Marshall's case, he accumu-
lated enough credence for himself that many accepted his ideas. As a result,
he actually played a part in affecting a change in the way that the United
States Army organized and trained for combat.

   Although not widely known outside the military except by those with
a strong interest in military history, several of Marshall's books are still generally considered military "classics." His two most famous works, *Men
Against Fire* and *The Soldier's Load and the Mobility of the Nation*, are actually
more works of military theory. *Men Against Fire* was recently selected as one
of the recommended works for professional development by the chief of
staff of the United States Army. *The Soldier's Load* is on the United States
Marine Corp commandant's professional reading list. Marshall's works of
pure military history—*Blitzkrieg* (1940), *Armies on Wheels* (1941), *The River
and the Gauntlet* (1953), *Battles in the Monsoon* (1967), and *Bringing Up the
Rear* (posthumous autobiography, 1979), among others—are of varying
quality but several of them still sell fairly well because of Marshall's reputation. Ironically, it was probably a reputation he did not deserve.

   S. L. A. Marshall disliked what he perceived as the awkward nature of
his given name.[31] Born in Catskill, New York, in 1900, he was raised as the
only son of a bricklayer. Marshall grew up all over the country as his father
moved along following the needs of the building industry.[32] Marshall

enlisted in the army in 1917 and was a lieutenant when he was discharged in 1919. After World War I, he became a newspaper reporter.

Marshall specialized in sports reporting and, in particular, in the sub-genre of sports feature writing. His bread and butter was the human-interest story. Creating American heroes from sports figures has never been difficult, but there are ways to make the task easier. Americans love the underdog; they thrive on the story of the common man displaying uncommon attributes, stories that touch upon the egalitarian philosophy of America in general. During his years as a sports feature writer, Marshall honed the skills of writing tight and efficient prose and creating heroes and villains as well as any novelist. He would later transfer these skills to his reporting of "history" when the Second World War broke out.

Marshall couldn't find the drama needed for his writing style at headquarters in the rear. What happens there at best resembles the stories found on a factory floor or in a soap opera. On the other hand, stories such as those he was used to reporting, with the added fuel of danger, could readily be found in ground combat units. This realization pushed Marshall in the direction of the tactical engagement, where Marshall wrote history in the purely journalistic style of the sports feature writer of the 1930s. The consummate storyteller, he created narrative nonfiction accounts of events that took place on the front lines. During the course of that, he began to insert himself into some of the stories, a process we will see in action in the next chapter of his life.[33]

Just as with one of the alleged main witnesses to No Gun Ri—Edward Daily—Marshall wanted to be accepted by combat veterans. To gain credibility with the military leaders and soldiers of the Second World War, Marshall wove a legend about himself and his own accomplishments in the First World War. According to his autobiography, Marshall was commissioned as the youngest lieutenant in the American Expeditionary Force and served in the Soissons, St. Mihiel, and Meuse-Argonne campaigns, the three major combat engagements of the United States Army in the First World War. He claimed that he ended the war as an infantry lieutenant, on 11 November 1918, in a foxhole not far from Stenay, the point of a farthest advance of the American Expeditionary Force.[34]

The facts, however, appear to be otherwise. According to author and combat veteran Harold Leinbaugh, Marshall was actually a private in an engineer unit, although he eventually made the rank of sergeant before the end of World War I. Throughout the period of America's participation in the war Marshall's unit, the 315th Engineers, built roads and camps well behind the lines. In other words, Marshall's self-reported combat record was fiction.[35]

Yet Marshall was never discovered as a fake combat veteran while he was alive, in part because he so skillfully mixed historical fact with absolute fiction to create a plausible history for himself.

At the end of the First World War, the army demobilized from 4.27 million men down to 225,000. Men were released from service almost the second they reached the United States. Yet America still needed officers to command the forces that remained in France and on occupation duty along the Rhine River in Germany. As a result, some volunteers were given the chance to attend a brief in-country commissioning program. This was how Marshall got his commission. It was only after the war that Marshall attended the American Expeditionary Forces' Officer Candidate School in France.[36] Despite the heroic past he created for himself, Marshall was never an infantryman in combat, never fought in direct ground combat against the Germans in World War I in any capacity, and did not lead soldiers in combat in any of the campaigns as he claimed. Why he made up stories about his personal history seems obvious: he craved validation. Marshall died in 1977, but in the written records he left behind, one can still see how he used this false combat record, buttressed by the books he wrote, to create an air of authority.

As Marshall published more and more books of military history, he gained additional credence within military circles. His published version of events as they appeared in his books was accepted as fact by many soldiers and officers of the army and marine corps.[37] In fact, some army and marine training doctrines changed in the post-WWII period, at least partially as a result of Marshall's suggestions.[38] Yet this was not enough for Marshall. The evidence of his own writing makes it clear—he felt the need to be a part of the story, not just to tell the story.

In three of the most obvious examples of this, Marshall very clearly inserts himself into the history of an event after the fact. The first, mentioned in a footnote earlier, occurred when Marshall made the claim that he was the origin for the famous response "Nuts," given by the American commander in response to the German commander's suggestion to surrender during the siege of Bastogne, Belgium, in December 1944.

In the second example, Marshall claims that he personally witnessed one of the last bayonet attacks in American history, that of Captain Lew Millett's company of the 27th Infantry Regiment in Korea. But in his account, Marshall was tripped up by some of the other details he had added to the history. Marshall embellished his account slightly when he asserts that immediately after that attack he met a young noncommissioned officer named David Hackworth who had participated in the assault and earned a battlefield commission as a result.[39] The problem was that Hackworth was not in Korea at the time, and he was never in Captain Lew Millett's company at all.[40] In the third example of Marshall inserting himself into the historical record, he again interacts with Hackworth, this time in Vietnam. In the 1967 version of an encounter recorded in Marshall's book *Battles in the Monsoon*, he explains how he arrived the day after a minor skirmish took place near the command post of Hackworth, now a battalion commander. By the time he published his autobiography, Marshall claimed that he was actually there during the Viet Cong assault.[41] Hackworth contradicts this and states that the original 1967 account was closer to the facts.[42] Once again, in an effort to appear to be something that he was not, Marshall inserted himself into the history of an event.

We see now how this sort of thing can spin out of control. With the famous example of S. L. A. Marshall in mind, we can now turn our attention back to the story of No Gun Ri. Understanding the story of the story is not easy. It is a tale wrapped up in misdirection, lies, and self-delusion, and it represents the second tragedy of No Gun Ri. We have seen how one man who masters the material of history may portray himself as something far larger than he actually was, even on a national scale. We have seen how, through the power of the pen, one man might appropriate the experiences of others and either make them his own or twist them to his own purposes. All of this makes it slightly easier to understand how somebody might perpetrate this same fraud on a smaller scale. It makes it possible to comprehend how it was that Charles Hanley and the rest of the AP team were taken in by Edward Daily and his tall tales. On the other hand, nobody ever wrote a story based on Marshall's lies. Nobody used his personal story as the basis for an investigation. It was not until historians started digging into Marshall's stories that the truth came out. The AP team was supposed to be doing just that, investigating.

Making sense of the twisted threads in the No Gun Ri story is a complex process that stretches throughout this book. But at the heart of it all was one man who tied a lot of the threads together into one neat package. A package that the Associated Press did not unwrap.

ANALYSIS OF THE
ASSOCIATED PRESS STORY

In the No Gun Ri story, a team of journalists attempted to sell what should have been a history as new "news." The AP denied that it had a "thesis" or that it argued any one specific point in favor of other assertions. According to a senior editor at the Associated Press, all sides of the story of No Gun Ri were represented and the AP itself did not claim that anything happened; it only reported that others made conflicting claims.[43] This, however, was not the case.

One of the lead reporters of the AP story, Martha Mendoza, made this clear with comments she made just twelve weeks after the original story appeared. In an article published in a professional news reporters' journal, just as the Pulitzer Prize committee convened to evaluate the submissions that year Mendoza wrote, "In the summer of 1950, in the first weeks of the Korean War, U.S. military forces opened fire on a group of South Korean civilian refugees at a place called No Gun Ri, killing hundreds of men, women, and children."[44] It is hard to label this statement as anything but an assertion of fact.

This statement from an Associated Press reporter, a member of the team that would later win the Pulitzer Prize, makes it clear that the AP did, in fact, believe one side and not the other. It did not believe that only a few people, perhaps as few as a dozen, were killed at No Gun Ri. It did not believe that the fire from the American soldiers might have been directed at South Korean guerillas within the group of refugees, guerillas who were shooting towards the soldiers. Its position was that what happened at No Gun Ri was a clear case of civilians fired upon without provocation, reason, or mercy, resulting in hundreds dead. If, as executive editors from the AP maintained, the AP did not adhere to one thesis or interpretation of the events, Mendoza could not have made that statement. This one sentence contains several of the central elements of the Associated Press thesis that a deliberate attack by the U.S. Army resulted in the massacre of hundreds of civilians.

The sentence led off her article in the *Investigative Reporters and Editors Journal*, a professional journal with a very narrow subscriber base. To hammer home the depth of her team's reporting, however, required the creation of a villain, preferably a bureaucratic one. A civilian lawyer employed by the United States in Korea conveniently provided additional ammunition. This lawyer had no training in military history, no knowledge of the history of the Korean War, and no qualifications to make a statement on the events of the Korean War. Yet because she was "official," she could be painted as part of a monolithic U.S. government cover-up against the South Korean citizens making their claim.[45]

Mendoza wrote: "In its official response to the claim, the U.S. Armed Forces Claims Service had said there was no evidence the U.S. 1st Cavalry Division—blamed by the survivors for the killings—was even in the No Gun Ri area at the time."[46]

Before discussing the way that the Associated Press reporters portrayed their story to the audience of *Investigative Reporters and Editors Journal* and spun their story to the Pulitzer Prize Committee, perhaps we should start with the original AP story about No Gun Ri. When it appeared in late September 1999, the Associated Press story of No Gun Ri read like this:

"THE BRIDGE AT NO GUN RI" [47]

It was a story no one wanted to hear: Early in the Korean War, villagers said, American soldiers machine-gunned hundreds of helpless civilians, under a railroad bridge in the South Korean countryside.

When the families spoke out, seeking redress, they met only rejection and denial, from the U.S. military and their own government in Seoul. Now a dozen ex-GIs have spoken, too, and support their story with haunting memories from a "forgotten" war.

These American veterans of the Korean War say that in late July 1950, in the conflict's first desperate weeks, U.S. troops—young, green and scared—killed a large number of South Korean refugees, many of them women and children, trapped beneath a bridge at a place called No Gun Ri.

In interviews with The Associated Press, ex-GIs speak of 100, 200 or simply hundreds dead. The Koreans, whose claim for compensation was rejected last year, say 300 were shot to death at the bridge and 100 died in a preceding air attack.

American soldiers, in their third day at the warfront, feared North Korean infiltrators among the fleeing South Korean peasants, veterans said. "It was assumed there were enemy in these people," ex-rifleman Herman Patterson of Greer, South Carolina, told The AP.

American commanders had ordered units retreating through South Korea to shoot civilians as a defense against disguised enemy soldiers, according to once-classified documents found by the AP in months of researching U.S. military archives and interviewing veterans across the United States.

Six veterans of the 1st Cavalry Division said they fired on the refugee throng at the South Korean hamlet of No Gun Ri, and six others said they witnessed the mass killing. More said they knew or heard about it.

"We just annihilated them," said ex-machine gunner Norman Tinkler of Glasco, Kan.

After five decades, none gave a complete, detailed account. But ex-GIs agreed on such elements as time and place, and on the preponderance of women, children and old men among the victims. They also disagreed: Some said they were fired on from beneath the bridge, but others said they don't remember hostile fire. One said they later found a few disguised North Korean soldiers among the dead. But others disputed this.

Some soldiers refused to shoot what one described as "civilians just trying to hide."

The 30 Korean claimants—survivors and victims' relatives—said it was an unprovoked, three-day carnage. "The American soldiers played with our lives like boys playing with flies," said Chun Choon-ja, a 12-year-old girl at the time.

Armed with new evidence that U.S. GIs had confirmed much of their account, the Korean claimants called for a U.S. investigation into the killings.

"We hope the U.S. government will meet our demands and console the wandering souls of those who died an unfair death," the claimants said in a statement.

In the end, the Koreans have said in a series of petitions, some 300 refugees lay dead under the bridge's twin arches. About 100 others were killed in a preceding attack by U.S. Air Force planes, they say.

That would make No Gun Ri one of only two known cases of large-scale killings of noncombatants by U.S. ground troops in this century's major wars, military law experts note. The other was Vietnam's My Lai massacre, in 1968, in which more than 500 Vietnamese may have died.

From the start of the 1950–53 conflict, North Korean atrocities were widely reported. But the story of No Gun Ri has re-mained undisclosed for a half-century, despite sketchy news reports in 1950 implying U.S. troops may have fired on refugees.

No Gun Ri's dead were not alone. Veterans told the AP of two smaller but similar refugee killings in July and August 1950. They also told of refusing orders to fire on civilians in other cases.

Hundreds more South Koreans were killed on August 3, 1950, when retreating U.S. commanders blew up two bridges as refugees streamed across, according to ex-GIs, Korean eyewitnesses and declassified documents.

The Americans wanted to deny the crossings to the enemy, reported massing more than 15 miles away. But the general overseeing one bridge-blowing, the 1st Cavalry Division commander, had sought to stop the refugee flow as well. He told a correspondent he was sure most refugees were North Korean guerrillas.

For decades in U.S.-allied South Korea, the No Gun Ri claimants were discouraged from speaking out. After they filed for compensation in 1997, their claim was rejected by the South Korean government on a technicality.

The U.S. military has said repeatedly it found no basis for the allegations. On Wednesday, just after the AP report was released,

Pentagon spokesman P.J. Crowley said, "We just have no information in historical files to lend any clarity to what might have happened in July 1950."

AP research also found no official army account of the events.

Defense Secretary William Cohen said on Thursday that the claims could be examined if there were new evidence.

"I am not aware of any evidence that would support or substantiate those claims. But to the degree that any substantive information is forthcoming, we certainly would look at it," he told a press conference in Jakarta, Indonesia.

Speaking at a press conference in Washington later Thursday, Army Secretary Louis Caldera promised a "complete and thorough review" of the allegations.

The South Korean government said it will investigate whether the survivors' claims are true or not.

"With keen attention, we'll try to verify the truth of all related things concerning the case," Foreign Ministry spokesman Chang Chul-kyun said. "Any further action will be decided after those efforts are finished."

Some elements of the No Gun Ri episode are unclear: What chain of officers gave open-fire orders? Did GIs see gunfire from the refugees or their own ricochets? How many soldiers refused to fire? How high in the ranks did knowledge of the events extend?

The Korean conflict, which ended in stalemate, began on June 25, 1950, when the communist North invaded and sent the South Korean army and a small U.S. force reeling southward toward the peninsula's tip.

American units who rushed from Japan to stop the North Koreans were poorly equipped and ill-trained. The 1st Cavalry went in with little understanding of Korea. Half its sergeants had been transferred to other divisions. Teen-aged riflemen and young officers with no combat experience were thrust overnight into a hellish war, told to expect guerilla fighting and be wary of the tens of thousands of South Korean civilians pouring south with retreating Americans.

The untested 7th Cavalry Regiment, part of the 1st Cavalry Division, reached the front July 24. Within a day many of its 2nd Battalion infantrymen were scattering in panic, tossing away weapons, at word of an enemy breakthrough nearby.

Records show that on the third day, July 26, the battalion's 660 men were regrouped and dug in at No Gun Ri, a hamlet 100 miles southeast of Seoul, South Korea's capital. Word was circulating that northern soldiers disguised in white peasant garb might try to penetrate U.S. lines via refugee groups.

The refugees who approached the 2nd Battalion's lines on July 26 were South Koreans ordered out of two nearby villages by American soldiers, who warned them the North Koreans were coming, Korean claimants told the AP.

Declassified records show that 1st Cavalry Division soldiers did move through that village area the previous three days.

As the refugees neared No Gun Ri, leading ox carts, some with children on their backs, American soldiers ordered them off the southbound dirt road and onto a parallel railroad track, the South Koreans said. Ex-sergeant George Preece remembered the way was being cleared for U.S. Army vehicles.

What then happened under the concrete bridge cannot be reconstructed in full detail five decades later. Some ex-GIs poured out chilling memories of the scene, but others offered only fragments, or abruptly ended their interviews. Over the three days, no one saw everything: Koreans were cowering under fire, and Americans were dug into positions over hundreds of yards of hilly terrain.

But old soldiers in their late 60s or 70s identified the No Gun Ri bridge from photographs, re-membered the approximate dates, and corroborated the core of the Koreans' account: that American troops kept the refugees pinned under the bridge in late July 1950, and killed almost all of them.

"It was just wholesale slaughter," Patterson said.

Both Koreans and several ex-GIs said the killing began when American planes suddenly swooped in and strafed an area where the white-clad refugees were resting.

Bodies fell everywhere, and terrified parents dragged children into a narrow culvert beneath the tracks, the Koreans told the AP.

Declassified U.S. Air Force mission reports from mid-1950 show that pilots sometimes attacked "people in white," apparently because of suspicions North Korean soldiers were disguised among them. The report for one mission of four F-80 jets, for example, said the airborne controller "said to fire on people in white clothes. Were about 50 in group."

Forward controllers in light planes directed pilots to such unplanned targets in midflight. The Korean claimants say a light plane circled their area immediately before the strafing.

But ex-GIs said the strafing may have been a mistake. A company commander had called for an airstrike, but against enemy artillery miles up the road, they said.

Veteran Delos Flint remembers being caught with other soldiers in the strafing and piling into a culvert with refugees. Then "somebody, maybe our guys, was shooting in at us," he said. He and his comrades eventually slipped out.

Retired Col. Robert M. Carroll, then a 25-year-old first lieutenant, remembers battalion riflemen opening fire on the refugees from their foxholes.

"This is right after we get orders that nobody comes through, civilian, military, nobody," said Carroll, of Lansdowne, Va.

That morning, the U.S. 8th Army had radioed orders throughout the Korean front that began, "No repeat no refugees will be permitted to cross battle lines at any time," according to declassified documents located at the National Archives in Washington.

Two days earlier, 1st Cavalry Division headquarters issued a more explicit order: "No refugees to cross the front line. Fire everyone trying to cross lines. Use discretion in case of women and children."

In the neighboring 25th Infantry Division, the commander, Maj. Gen. William B. Kean, told his troops that since South Koreans were to have been evacuated from the battle zone, "all civilians seen in this area are to be considered as enemy and action taken accordingly." His staff relayed this as "considered as unfriendly and shot."

Military experts in the law of war told the AP they had never heard of such blanket "kill" orders in the U.S. military.

"An order to fire on civilians is patently an illegal order," said retired Col. Scott Silliman of Duke University, an Air Force lawyer for 25 years.

Carroll said he "wasn't convinced this was enemy," and he got the rifle companies to cease firing on the refugees. The lieutenant then shepherded a boy to safety under a double-arched concrete railroad bridge nearby, where shaken and wounded Koreans were gathered. He said he saw no threat.

"There weren't any North Koreans in there the first day, I'll tell you that. It was mainly women and kids and old men," recalled Carroll, who said he then left the area and knows nothing about what followed.

The Americans directed the refugees into the bridge underpasses—each 80 feet long, 23 feet wide, 30 feet high—and after dark opened fire on them from nearby machine-gun positions, the Koreans said.

Veterans said Capt. Melbourne C. Chandler, after speaking with superior officers by radio, had ordered machine gunners from his heavy-weapons company to set up near the tunnel mouths and open fire.

"Chandler said, 'The hell with all those people. Let's get rid of all of them,' " said Eugene Hesselman of Fort Mitchell, Ky. " . . . We didn't know if they were North or South Koreans . . . . We were there only a couple of days and we didn't know them from a load of coal."

Ex-GIs believe the order was cleared at battalion headquarters, a half-mile to the rear, or at a higher level. Chandler and other key officers are now dead, but the AP was able to locate the colonel who commanded the battalion, Herbert B. Heyer, 88.

Heyer, of Sandy Springs, Ga., denied knowing anything about the shootings and said, "I know I didn't give such an order." Veterans said the colonel apparently was leaving battalion operations to subordinates at the time.

The bursts of gunfire killed those near the tunnel entrances first, the Korean claimants said.

"People pulled dead bodies around them for protection," said Chung Koo-ho, 61. "Mothers wrapped their children with blankets and hugged them with their backs toward the entrances

. . . . My mother died on the second day of shooting."

Recalled machine gunner Edward L. Daily: "Some may have been trying to crawl deeper for protection. When you see something like that and you're frightened, you start to claw."

During three nights under fire, some trapped refugees managed to slip away, but others were shot as they tried to escape or crawled out to find clean water to drink, the Koreans said.

Veterans disagreed on whether gunfire came from the underpasses.

Some, like ex-sergeant James T. Kerns of Piedmont, S.C., said the Americans were answering fire from among the refugees. Hesselman said, "Every now and then you'd hear a shot, like a rifle shot." But others recalled only heavy barrages of American firepower, not hostile fire. "I don't remember shooting coming out," said ex-rifleman Louis Allen of Bristol, Tenn.

The Koreans said the Americans may have been seeing their own comrades' fire, ricocheting through from the tunnels' opposite ends. That's possible, said Preece.

"It could actually have happened, that they were seeing our own fire . . . . We were scared to death," said Preece, a career soldier who later fought in Vietnam.

On July 28, the 7th Cavalry was told to prepare to pull back again early the next morning. The final barrage still echoes in the memories of old soldiers.

"On summer nights when the breeze is blowing, I can still hear their cries, the little kids screaming," said Daily, of Clarksville, Tenn., who went on to earn a battlefield commission in Korea.

Sounds of slaughter haunt Park Hee-sook's memory, too.

"I can still hear the moans of women dying in a pool of blood," said Park, then a girl of 16. "Children cried and clung to their dead mothers."

Not everyone fired, veterans said.

"Some of us did and some of us didn't," said Flint, of Clio, Mich., the soldier who had been briefly caught in the culvert with the refugees." . . . I wouldn't fire at anybody in the tunnel like that. It was civilians just trying to hide."

Kerns, a machine gunner, said he fired over the refugees' heads. "I would not fire into a bunch of women."

Once the fury subsided, Kerns said, he, Preece and another GI found at least seven dead North Korean soldiers in the underpasses, wearing uniforms under peasant white.

But Preece, of Dunville, Ky., said he doesn't remember making

such a search or even hearing that North Koreans were found. None of the other veterans, when asked, remembered seeing North Koreans.

Kerns also said weapons were recovered. Hesselman said someone later displayed a submachine gun. Preece recalled only "hearsay" about weapons.

All 24 South Korean survivors interviewed individually by the AP said they remembered no North Koreans or gunfire directed at the Americans.

Secret U.S. military intelligence reports from those days, since declassified, place the North Korean front line four miles from No Gun Ri on July 26, when the refugees entered the underpasses.

Early on July 29, the 7th Cavalry pulled back. North Korean troops who moved in found "about 400 bodies of old and young people and children," the North Korean newspaper Cho Sun In Min Bo reported three weeks later.

Some ex-GIs today estimate 100 or fewer were killed. But those close to the bridge, from Chandler's H Company, generally put the total at about 200. "A lot" also were killed in the strafing, they say.

The North Koreans buried some dead in unknown locations and surviving relatives buried others, the villagers said. Because families then scattered across South Korea, the claimants said, they have the names of only 120 dead, primarily their own relatives.

The war, in all, claimed an estimated 1 million South Korean civilian casualties—killed, wounded or missing. Almost 37,000 Americans died.

At 1st Cavalry headquarters, division commander Maj. Gen. Hobart R. Gay was told South Korean refugees were killed by North Korean troops in a crossfire at No Gun Ri, the division information officer recalled. "I think that's what he believed," said Harold D. Steward, an ex-colonel from San Diego.

Relevant unit documents say nothing about a crossfire, about North Korean soldiers killed under a bridge, or anything else about No Gun Ri.

One battalion lieutenant located by the AP said he was in the area but knew nothing about the killing of civilians. "I have honestly never, ever heard of this from either my soldiers or superiors or my friends," said John C. Lippincott of Stone Mountain, Ga. He said he could have missed it because "we were extremely spread out."

The villagers say they tried to file a compensation claim with a U.S. claims office in Seoul in 1960, but were told they missed a deadline. Later, they say, Korean police warned one man, survivor Yang Hae-chan, to keep quiet about the 1950 events. But as authoritarian South Korea liberalized in the 1990s, they revived their case and sent petitions to Washington. None was acknowledged, they say.

In August 1997, a claim signed by 30 petitioners was filed with South Korea's Government Compensation Committee. Having researched histories, they pointed a finger at the 1st Cavalry.

In response, the U.S. Armed Forces Claims Service said there was "no evidence . . . to show that the U.S. 1st Cavalry Division was in the area." A lower-level South Korean compensation committee said people were killed at No Gun Ri but it had no proof of U.S. involvement. In April 1998, the national panel rejected the case, saying a five-year statute of limitations expired long ago.

The AP subsequently reconstructed unit movements from map coordinates in declassified war records. They showed that four 1st Cavalry Division battalions were in the area at the time of the alleged incident.

Months of tracing veterans— some 130 interviews by telephone and in person—then pinpointed the companies involved. The AP also pored through hundreds of boxes of once-secret documents at the National Archives and other repositories to find pieces of the story.

The laws and customs of war condemn indiscriminate killing of civilians, even if a few enemy soldiers are among a large number of noncombatants killed, military experts note. The Korean War record shows Army courts-martial only for individual murders of Koreans, nothing on a large scale.

As for civil liability, the U.S. government is largely protected by U.S. law against foreign claims related to "combatant activities." The Korean claimants say the killings were not combat-related—the enemy was miles away.

"We want the truth, justice and due respect for our human rights," they wrote in a 1997 petition to President Clinton.

One ex-GI objects that "a bunch of lawyers" can't run a war.

"War is not just," said Norman Tinkler. "There's things that goes on that we can't comprehend, but it has to be done. And it's the individual that has to make the decision."

But others who were there said No Gun Ri didn't have to happen. The refugees could have been screened up on the road or checked out under the bridge, Kerns and Hesselman said.

"The command looked at it as getting rid of the problem in the easiest way. That was to shoot them in a group," said Daily. Today, he said, "we all share a guilt feeling, something that remains with everyone."

The late Col. Gilmon A. Huff, who took over the 2nd Battalion from Heyer three days after the pullback from No Gun Ri, was interviewed before his death earlier this year and said he knew nothing of what happened at the bridge.

But he "heard" about refugee killings and told his men it was wrong, Huff said at his Abbeville, S.C., home.

"You can't kill people just for being there," he told the AP.

The bridge at No Gun Ri still stands today. For 49 years its concrete was deeply scarred by bullets—until railroad workers this month patched over the holes.

The Associated Press story, released simultaneously to the news wire subscribers and on the AP's Web site, "The Wire," started off with a bombshell. In the structure and formatting of the story, as well as in the material used, the AP deliberately created a work designed to elicit powerful emotions from readers and create a sense of outrage.

Journalism professors take great care to continually remind their students to obey the three guiding principles of the profession: accuracy, accuracy, and accuracy. They are also concerned that the reporting be fair. The previous chapter evaluated the story on the basis of accuracy. Evaluating the AP's assertion that its story had no thesis and was balanced in its presentation of the conflicting accounts requires an additional more stringent set of criteria. To see if balanced and fair reporting was achieved, examine the AP story using two other criteria, sequence and content.

Balance is the objective in any story to which there are two sides. Sequence refers to the order that information and especially dramatic personal quotes appear in the story, while content refers to the substance of that information. On all three counts, the AP's story advocated not only a specific thesis, despite the news service's later protests to the contrary, but its authors crossed the line from objective reporters to social and political advocates for the South Korean claimants.[48]

This is not to suggest that the AP editors and reporters were hamhanded in their dealings with the evidence they had collected. On the contrary, the very first lines of the story sought to convince the reader but not to bludgeon him or her. In their text, the reporters very carefully and deliberately avoided inflammatory language such as the words "massacre" and "slaughter" and instead used a more subtle form of indictment.[49]

It was a story no one wanted to hear: Early in the Korean War, villagers said, American soldiers machine-gunned hundreds of helpless civilians, under a railroad bridge in the South Korean countryside.[50]

This was the lead sentence of the AP report. It establishes two elements designed to attract the reader's attention: the killing of innocent civilians and the denial of it. In journalistic parlance, this is referred to as the "lead." Reporters and editors often spend a disproportionate amount of time during the actual writing of a story attempting to craft the best lead possible. This one sentence, according to journalism professors, is the most important sentence in the story.

In the lead to a good straight news story, the reporter hopes to quickly establish the who, what, when, where and why, which the remainder of the story will support. Theoretically, the lead in straight news does not advance a thesis, but in practice it often does because at the same time it must grab the reader's attention. The lead is therefore one of the best indicators to understand what the writers and editors believe are the central ideas or theme of the story. In this lead, the AP established the who, "American soldiers" and "helpless civilians," the what, "machine-gunned," and the when and where, "early in the Korean War" and "in the South Korean countryside." These central elements therefore form the main theme of the AP story that the writers intend to support with the rest of the material provided. Yet at this point, they have not addressed the issue of "why."

The structure of a story involves a lot of wrangling and discussion between reporters and editors. Apparently in the AP's reporting of the No Gun Ri story, there was even more than usual.[51] Although they deliberately strove for the appearance of impartial reporting by avoiding such obvious red-flag words as "massacre" and "war crime," the story maintains the tone of scandal. Reporters and editors attempt to grab the reader's attention in the first twenty seconds of reading. This philosophy was the foundation for deciding to follow the lead sentence with an emotionally grabbing sentence:

> When the families spoke out, seeking redress, they met only rejection and denial, from the U.S. military and their own government in Seoul. Now a dozen ex-GIs have spoken, too, and support their story with haunting memories from a "forgotten" war.[52]

The Associated Press's style of using just one or two sentences as separate paragraphs breaks the story into something that might be considered bite-sized chunks. This stylistic issue has some minor advantages when reporting current events and some major disadvantages when attempting to write history. The minor advantage is that the writer who masters this style can quickly place small portions of information from many different sources before the reader in a very short amount of space. This format also makes it very simple for the hundreds of editors from the more than 130 different media outlets that subscribe to the AP to edit out what they do not need or cannot use. The major disadvantage to this format is the attendant lack of context surrounding the information the writer is providing. The reader cannot tell from the context of the quote from the limited words provided, and must rely wholly upon the reporter and his editor.

At the same time, this style reveals in stark contrast what those at the AP feel is the second critical element of the story, the "denial." This is also an important point in understanding how the story developed. As noted earlier, since the Vietnam War, a generally adversarial environment has existed between the military and the media. Not necessarily the fault of one side or the other, it could be demonstrated that this adversarial relationship is usually a good thing for the nation. In the foundations of that relationship, however, we may find the reason that the story of No Gun Ri appeared the way that it did.

Generally speaking, the culture of the media, and investigative journalism in particular, attracts people interested in social change. People who become investigative reporters often state that they do so because they wanted to fight for the underdog and help the downtrodden get justice from a sometimes uncaring system, whether a local government, the courts, or in this case the federal governments of two different nations. This field also attracts people generally distrustful of centralized authority or hierarchical organizations or societies. People in this line of work are predisposed to seeing an enemy in every direction, just as the military is sometimes accused of. This is understandable. When a person confronts enough graft, corruption, corporate greed, or military intransigence over the course of a career, he or she begins to see every situation suspiciously. Reporters in any free society are the guardians of the people's rights, especially civil rights, and this is the foundation of the First Amendment.

Those who choose the military as a profession might also, and without conflict, argue that they, too, are the guardians of the people's rights. Through the blood and sweat that they are willing to shed on foreign fields at the behest of the civilian authorities of the nation, most military professionals see themselves as the champions of the people's rights. At the same time, this profession, by its very nature, is hierarchical, and as a result, tends to attract a certain type of personality, one more inclined towards a belief in the system and in the inherent good of the people within the organization. To those drawn to this institution, criticism from outside is almost akin to criticism of the nation, something which runs directly counter to their personal credo.

The inevitable result is that the two institutions that most directly protect the freedoms of the nation—one from threats from the inside and one against threats from the outside—are inclined to distrust each other. Both sides also have developed plenty of personal ammunition to support this sentiment. The reporter can point to the lies, half-truths, and misunderstandings that characterized military relations with the press in Vietnam. Events like the slap-on-the-wrist sentence for the war crimes committed by

Lieutenant Calley and his platoon at My Lai 4, the $400 hammers of the U.S. Air Force, and the inevitable secrecy that surrounds many military operations provide evidence for the reporter's contentions. The military side can find a fair amount of material from the media that contributes to their distrust as well. The misleading reporting on army procurement of the Bradley fighting vehicle in the 1980s, the false accusations of the use of nerve gas in the *Time/CNN* Tailwind story, and television news reports from Baghdad during Desert Storm (complete with video) giving prominence to an Iraqi story that allied fighter-bombers had hit a baby milk factory contribute to this sentiment. The result is distrust on both sides. All of this fed, consciously or unconsciously, into the investigation into No Gun Ri conducted by the Associated Press.

In the case of No Gun Ri, the denial (and obviously an implied cover-up) by the U.S. military and the government of South Korea made this story attractive to the Associated Press. This denial then becomes the hook presented in the second paragraph of the story. For the AP, rejection and denial of the South Korean claims were the key elements that would impel the reader to continue reading.

Supporting the Korean claimants, the AP story states are "a dozen ex-GIs." This part of the story contains a truth (several soldiers and a former officer had told the AP that civilians were killed at No Gun Ri, and at least one had used the word "massacre") and an omission (dozens upon dozens of soldiers interviewed by the AP did not recall the events claimed by the villagers).

In fact, the AP reporters admitted later that they had gone through more than thirty-four interviews before they found a single person who supported their thesis.[53] After that, from more interviews, some 130 in all according to the story, they culled a few who supported the thesis put forward by the Korean claimants.[54] This crucial omission—that apparently the majority of those contacted denied that the event happened or denied knowledge of any such event—is never addressed in the story. Instead one has to puzzle it out. Of 130 interviewees, the AP claims that six of these witnessed or participated in the event; that leaves 124 veterans, or at least 78 if reporter Charles Hanley's numbers are taken into account, who did not or were not quote worthy.[55] Yet the story is structured to create in the reader a certainty that the event happened. The implication is left unstated: Six "witnesses" trump 124 because obviously those 124 must be hiding something. The possibility that the overwhelming majority of the interviews could represent a version of events closer to the truth and that some of the six identified by the AP might be misrepresented or fakes is not raised. My later interviews with veterans suggest that the AP reporters discounted any veteran's testimony that conflicted with the accounts of the South Koreans.[56]

Only after these six soldier-witnesses are paraded through the story is the reader introduced to even a single voice who says anything to the contrary about the situation. Instead of a random selection of the individuals used to present the countering opinion, it appears that they were selected specifically (either consciously or unconsciously) not to present a balanced opinion, but to add to the notion that there was a cover-up.

Finally, the phrasing of the second sentence in the second paragraph of the story, "Now a dozen ex-GIs support their story . . ." is misleading. As the AP was later forced to admit, there were not actually "a dozen," as it tried to contend. *Only two of the ex-GIs fully supported their story in all regards.* The South Korean claimants' story was that U.S. soldiers stopped them, frisked them, used a radio to call in an airstrike that killed approximately a hundred, and then turned machine guns against the survivors over a period of three days. This lethal use of force as the direct result of orders given by officers becomes one of the central questions of the AP story. Only two men in the AP story fully substantiate that contention, Edward Daily and Eugene Hesselman, with some support from Delos Flint. Within the AP text, another two soldiers had something to suggest for the story, and several had memories that could be used, out of context, and be made to appear to support the AP storyline of a deliberate massacre of between 100 and 400 civilians.

By the third paragraph (or line) of the story, the tone of the denial is established, and the AP immediately rushes to provide supporting evidence. At this point, only the opinions of the veterans who will be quoted as supporting the thesis of the story are mentioned. The cardinal rule of journalism—balance in a disputed story—is cast aside in favor of hyperbole.

> These American veterans of the Korean War say that in late July 1950, in the conflict's first desperate weeks, U.S. troops—young, green and scared—killed a large number of South Korean refugees, many of them women and children, trapped beneath a bridge at a place called No Gun Ri.
>
> In interviews with The Associated Press, ex-GIs speak of 100, 200 or simply hundreds dead. The Koreans, whose claim for compensation was rejected last year, say 300 were shot to death at the bridge and 100 died in a preceding air attack.[57]

Now the shocking numbers appear, just four "paragraphs" into the story. "Hundreds," ranging from 100 to as many as 400, were killed. This is news with a capital 'N', it is massive, it is the stuff of Pulitzer Prizes. At this point, the Associated Press reporters have still somehow failed to mention that the majority of soldiers or officers who were also there, some within a few yards of the spot where the events supposedly occurred, specifically stated that there were fewer casualties, or denied any knowledge that any such large-scale mass killing happened. Although the AP casually mentions that the survivors were calling for compensation, it fails to note that the value of this compensation was $170 million at that time (later raised to $400 million). To hammer home the generalizations made in the earlier sentences, the AP now moves to the "why" that did not appear in the lead.

> American soldiers, in their third day at the warfront, feared North Korean infiltrators among the fleeing South Korean peasants, veterans said. "It was assumed there were enemy in these people," ex-rifleman Herman Patterson of Greer, S.C., told The AP.[58]

Now the question arises, what specifically was Herman Patterson talking about? Was he referring generally to the great flood of refugees, estimated in the tens of thousands, who passed through the lines of his unit and others in the first weeks of the war, or was he talking specifically about the refugees who the AP suggests were machine-gunned by the soldiers at a specific time and place? More specifically, why was his quote decided upon as the first in the story? Might it be to raise the specter of a red herring? Later comments by reporters from the AP suggest that this was the case.[59] At this point, Patterson's is the only voice the reader of the story has heard. From an interview that lasted several hours, Patterson garnered just nine words. Roughly five seconds of spoken English. This raises the issue of context, an issue that becomes important in the next line of their special report.

> American commanders had ordered units retreating through South Korea to shoot civilians as a defense against disguised enemy soldiers, according to once-classified documents found by the AP in months of researching U.S. military archives and interviewing veterans across the United States.[60]

On the surface, as was covered in the preceding portion of this book, this is a true statement, albeit a half statement. At the division level, prior to

No Gun Ri, a minor staff officer passed word over the telephone to a different regiment to "shoot civilians" as a defense against North Korean soldiers disguised as civilians. There was a similar order in another division. It is in what the AP does not mention that the true nature of its reporting comes out: no mention is made that this so-called "order" came via a phone call, not a broadcast order. That is, only one unit got this message, and it was not sent out over the radio by somebody in authority. Instead, the AP implied that it was an order from the division, not a message from a liaison officer of that same unit. It did not mention that the officer was a major, and that majors from a regiment do not issue orders to their colonel who is in command of the regiment, even if they are liaison officers to higher headquarters. It did not mention in its initial report that the only order from a general officer that was even vaguely related to the message portrayed in the story was a general in an entirely different division, the 25th Infantry Division, a unit that was not at No Gun Ri and had nothing at all to do with anything that was going on in that area. The AP did not mention that the 7th Cavalry never got the so-called order because at the time the major called his regiment with the order, the 7th Cavalry was still moving in trains and trucks from Pohang-dong. It did not mention that the order the major conveyed was a garbled version of a more complete, written refugee-control order, which the 7th Cavalry did receive later. None of this information appeared in the AP story, even though the Associated Press saw all of these documents at the National Archives and this information was relevant. These documents were exactly the same records ominously referred to as being "once classified" in the AP's story. The AP had all of this information but chose to present only the information that fit its thesis, however misleading that information might have been. Subsequently, the AP team has uncovered no less than nineteen separate orders relating to the shooting of civilians by U.S. forces in Korea from August 1950 all the way to the end of the war. None of these orders, however, was relevant to the 7th Cavalry Regiment at No Gun Ri in late July 1950.

The truth, supported by historical evidence, is that some civilians were stopped on the road south of No Gun Ri by the 2nd Battalion 7th Cavalry. Division orders stated that refugees were to be screened by South Korean police, who were not yet on hand in sufficient numbers to screen the flow of civilians. In an effort to stop the civilians, somebody, probably a company-grade officer, ordered a salvo of mortars to be fired in the refugees' path. These rounds were intended to land between the refugees and the front line of U.S. troops to stop the refugees from coming closer to the American troops. Tragically, probably due to the delay between the call for fire and the mortar unit's ability to aim and shoot, the initial rounds landed among the refugees instead of in front of them. At the same time, approximately thirty soldiers armed with small arms who were also moved forward of the line had started firing over the civilians' heads.

At the time, the refugee column of between fifty to a hundred was roughly two hundred to three hundred yards away from the American positions, but only one hundred yards from the most advanced Americans. The refugees scattered and took cover. Then at least two South Korean guerillas, probably residents of one of the nearby villages, returned fire against the U.S. positions and the soldiers lowered their muzzles in response. A general fusillade followed for anywhere from thirty to ninety seconds during which somewhere between a dozen to slightly more than two dozen South Korean refugees were killed. After their officers ordered a cease-fire, some soldiers from the battalion went forward and, while searching the area, found one Russian-made submachine gun and one Japanese-made rifle among the refugees. These were turned in to their company, which later turned them in to the battalion supply office, the S-4.

To illustrate the fallacies and deliberate misleading nature of the "shoot them" phrasing by the AP, one has to look back to the first chapter of this book where the organizational structure of the army was explained.

First, in all situations and in all contexts, colonels outrank majors. That is the simple part of the "order" that went out on July 24, 1950.[61]

Second, despite the general public impression (further played upon by the AP later in its story), the military is not all-knowing. The members of one division in the 1950 army generally had little idea what was going on in another division while both were in combat. Soldiers of the 1st Cavalry Division did not have any idea what the commanding general of the neighboring 25th Infantry Division was saying to his troops.

Ordinarily the mistakes in the AP story might be ascribed to a simple lack of knowledge on the part of the AP reporters. That is not quite true, however, in the case of the lead reporter, Charles Hanley, who states that he is a veteran of the Vietnam War who earned a Bronze Star Medal while in the army. One does not serve in the armed forces without at least gaining some knowledge about how the armed forces operate.[62]

To continue with our analysis of the story, in the next paragraph, the rhetoric of the AP piece falls apart when the first of the internal inconsistencies that run throughout the story is presented:

> Six veterans of the 1st Cavalry Division said they fired on the refugee throng at the South Korean hamlet of No Gun Ri, and six others said they witnessed the mass killing. More said they knew or heard about it.[63]

In the second paragraph of the story, the reporters explicitly stated, "Now a dozen ex-GIs have spoken, too, and support their story . . . . "They do not say "dozens and more." They do not say "more than a dozen." They do not say "dozens support the story" directly or indirectly. This, despite the apparent nit-picking nature of the observation, is an important point. Of all the hundreds of men present, it appears that the overwhelming majority did not say that anything significant occurred at No Gun Ri. The issue, remember, is the deliberate killing of hundreds of human beings. This is not an issue of mere impropriety, but a charge of mass murder. With the weight of that sort of accusation implicit in its reporting, how could the AP rest with only six witnesses from a regiment of (then) 600 men, who could testify that they took part in mass killings? Especially when they knew beforehand that there were questions about the reliability of at least half of those witnesses in one way or another, or, in Hanley's words in his E-mail to the author cited in the last chapter, "rife with bullshit."

In light of the evidence that the reporters had strong reasons to doubt the veracity of the people they selected from among those who said they either "knew or heard about" the incident at No Gun Ri why did they not choose some of those other veterans to use as sources?[64] The AP is vague here, stating in its story that "more" knew or heard about it. If a group exists beyond those who eventually appeared in the story, why would any reporter rely upon those sources who are the least likely to be telling the truth—sources such as Daily and Flint—even if unable to prove that they are not telling the truth at the time the story goes to press? Why use those sources if others effectively state the same thing? Occam's razor suggests that the simplist answer is usually right. The simple answer would be that most men interviewed knew nothing of 200-400 civilians killed at No Gun Ri.

Four paragraphs later, in the eleventh paragraph of the story, the next directly attributable comment appears, this time from one of the "victims." This quote was used to play upon the general perceptions of nonmilitary readers about the military.

> The 30 Korean claimants—survivors and victims' relatives—said it was an unprovoked, three-day carnage. "The American soldiers played with our lives like boys playing with flies," said Chun Choon-ja, a 12-year-old girl at the time.[65]

With that line, the emotional floodgates are opened. Most readers of this story would be horrified by the image of a frightened twelve-year-old girl trapped by merciless soldiers who "played with our lives" as boys are wont to do with insects. Yet here again, the selection and placement of this quote are deliberately contrived to evoke emotion, not establish the journalistic qualities that reporters theoretically strive for: balance, through the medium of sequence.

Sequence is not an inconsequential issue when analyzing a media report, especially one sent out by the Associated Press. To understand why this is so requires an understanding of how news articles are written. In Journalism 101 courses on campuses across the United States, students are taught that news is reported in descending order of importance. Just as an inordinate amount of the writer's and editor's time is devoted to the construction of an attention-grabbing lead, so too is attention paid to teaching reporters not to bury important elements in the story. More specifically in any news story, the importance of the facts (at least as perceived by the reporter) is presented in rank order. There is a very good journalistic reason for this: Editors cut from the bottom.

A central problem facing editors is, and has been for a long time, space. Newspapers generally do not, for economic reasons, decide, "Gee, we really have a lot of good stories today. Let's make the 'A' section thirty-two pages instead of the normal twelve." As a result, over the last 140 years, a journalistic standard has emerged that reporters should structure their stories so that the least important or less relevant elements of their story appear last. In fact, the whole story should be written with the expectation that editors will cut from the bottom upwards. In the main, editors do not deviate from this methodology.

At this point in the AP story, the reader is now primed, on the basis of two quotes, to make a call for justice.

> Armed with new evidence that U.S. GIs had confirmed much of their account, the Korean claimants called for a U.S. investigation into the killings.
>
> We hope the U.S. government will meet our demands and console the wandering souls of those who died an unfair death, the claimants said in a statement.[66]

In this and the succeeding paragraph the AP reporters make it appear that these claimants have only the interest of their dearly departed loved ones at heart. They are not vengeful; they only seek acknowledgement of the grievous loss they have suffered, and perhaps some statement of atonement. The AP reporters, however, neglected to relay one fact that most reporters of compensation claims actions would have included in the very first sentences—that these claimants stood to make a profit if their claims were accepted as presented. In reporting the claim for reparations made by those who stepped forward, the AP quoted its lead South Korean source as wanting to "console the wandering souls." In this case, consolation amounts to $400 million.

Two sentences later, the AP reminds any reader that this would be the largest massacre committed by U.S. troops other than the massacre at My Lai during the Vietnam War, also a Pulitzer Prize-winning story.

In the twentieth-eighth paragraph of the story, the AP finally raises some questions, but these questions are predicated upon assumptions that the AP had already tried to pass off as facts. It seeks the appearance of objective questioning, but the questions themselves tell a story:

> Some elements of the No Gun Ri episode are unclear: What chain of officers gave open-fire orders? Did GIs see gunfire from the refugees or their own ricochets? How many soldiers refused to fire? How high in the ranks did knowledge of the events extend?[67]

Obviously, asking "what chain of officers" assumes that an order was passed to the troops from somewhere. In this, the AP is attempting to transfer implicit criminality from the "frightened and confused soldiers" to those higher in the military order, who ordered this massacre. The journalistic competence of the AP editors is brought to task with the next question of whether GIs saw gunfire from the refugees or their own ricochets. Rather than getting orders from on high this question suggests that individual soldiers responded to a direct threat, or the legitimate perception of a direct threat. This question and the next asking how many soldiers refused to fire are obvious gestures to the pride of the soldiers who provided the 130 interviews, all but twelve of whom presumably denied any knowledge of the incident or denied that such an event occurred.

The paragraph represents another disingenuous attempt at misdirection by the reporters and editors of the story; these sentences are an attempt to cover themselves with a cloak of respectability as critical reporters. By asking these questions, they are trying to portray the idea that their reporting is open to other interpretations. These three sentences, which may only be asked if the South Korean claimants' version and the supporting testimony of Edward Daily and Eugene Hesselman are assumed to be wholly correct, focus on the issue of orders from officers and do not consider any other possibility. Orders could only come from officers if indeed there was a massacre of hundreds in the first place. In later testimony, the AP attempted to reinforce that theme: "Our copy reflects the many ambiguities in events that occurred so long ago. We just said that point-blank in the first place. There's little doubt that something terrible happened there. That was the point of the story. This underscores the care and attention we were giving it."[68] But from this point, the AP's story devolves to actual errors of fact.

> The untested 7th Cavalry Regiment, part of the 1st Cavalry Division, reached the front July 24.[69]

The Associated Press claimed that this was a story "more than a year in the making."[70] Some accounts place the reporting time at up to eighteen months.[71] Only later would reporter Charles Hanley publicly state that the story actually only took a few months of reporting and writing—about ninety days as it turns out—and the rest of the time was spent in editorial wrangling with his editors.[72] Officially, the AP stated that its team cross-checked and double-checked every single fact, yet the reporters missed, or deliberately ignored, all of the archival sources that pointed to Daily as a fraud, to Flint as a misguided and physically ill man with a failing memory, and to Hesselman as another questionable source. Thus far in its story the AP presents little more than a litany of "he said, she agreed" statements. Now, however, comes a verifiable fact: The 7th Cavalry reached the front on July 24, 1950. In reality, on that day, the headquarters and the 2nd Battalion of the 7th Cavalry were south of Hwanggan, twelve miles from the front as one of the AP's own sources inadvertently points out later. Hwanggan was the division rear area, the realm of the logistics and service support units that fill the many support needs of a combat division. The soldiers of the 2nd Battalion 7th Cavalry and the rest of the regiment were not at the front on July 24, 1950. They may have been in the 1st Cavalry Division area of operations, but they were not, by any stretch of the imagination, at what the army calls the "main line of resistance."

Lest one assume that this was an innocent mistake made by militarily unknowledgeable civilian reporters, the reader might remember that the lead reporter, Charles Hanley, is a veteran.[73] It doesn't take a general to know the difference between the front and the rear, especially when that distance can be measured in tens of kilometers.

A few paragraphs later, we get the next direct quote from a veteran, once again Herman Patterson:

> "It was just wholesale slaughter," Patterson said.[74]

Remember those journalistic ethics? They were developed from the guiding principles of balance through sequence, content, and accuracy. At this point in the AP story—the thirty-eighth paragraph of a ninety-nine paragraph story—the reader has yet to see a mention of any possible alternative other than a massacre of up to 400 civilians by Americans who appear to be acting under orders. The misrepresentation and imbalance of the AP reporting gets worse once it is discovered that in those five words Herman Patterson was referring, not to events at No Gun Ri, but to a battle that occurred several days later when the 2nd Battalion 7th Cavalry was overrun by the North Korean Peoples Army.[75]

The AP's choice of sources and attributions demonstrates how desperate it was when it published its story. If the AP had, as claimed, a dozen sources who could verify the events or recall with clarity circumstances resembling what the South Korean claimants were suggesting, why then is the very next source that the AP uses the one man it should have known with certainty was nowhere near No Gun Ri?

Delos Flint was a soldier in F Company, 2nd Battalion 7th Cavalry. Unfortunately, as the records clearly show, Flint was also one of the three men wounded and evacuated, killed, or missing from his company either during or slightly after the disintegration of the company on the night of July 25–26, just before the events at No Gun Ri.[76] Yet despite the facts that this information is clear in the records and that Flint's major source of information about the regiment and the events leading up to his wounding was Edward Daily, the Associated Press team went ahead and used his account. Given the nature of Flint's relationship with Daily, it seems quite possible that Flint's memories were influenced or placed there by the ubiquitous Daily.[77] But even as it stands, Flint does not recall anything resembling a massacre like the AP and the South Koreans described.

What Flint is passing on is a curious mixture of items, but taken in all, they don't represent a massacre. Flint is quoted as saying that he took cover when some U.S. Air Force fighters swooped low on a strafing run against himself and other U.S. soldiers. The only culverts in the area are well forward of the U.S. lines on July 26, nearer where the unit had been on July 25, 1950. Flint is talking about U.S. soldiers being strafed by the U.S. Air Force. He then refers to unknown fire, presumably small-arms fire, again directed towards the American soldiers in the culvet but, significantly, he does not state that even a single soldier or refugee was wounded by the strafing. He says that the culvert where he took shelter from the fighters had refugees within it, and that is all. Yet from the way that his quote is placed in the story, a reader might think that the civilians had been the target of the strafing, and that this was the airstrike the South Koreans alleged began the massacre of the refugees.[78]

The next veteran witness who appears in the story is one of the platoon leaders, lieutenant Robert Carroll. According to the AP story, Carroll "remembers battalion riflemen opening fire on the refugees from their foxholes."[79] He was quoted as saying that he did not believe that the refugees were a threat and that he ordered a cease-fire. He then moved a young boy to safety, apparently at the railroad overpass, where other refugees were gathered, before he left the area.

Again, Carroll's testimony, like Flint's, is construed to make it appear that this was the beginning of the deliberate three-day-long massacre alleged by the South Koreans. Yet again, these veterans' descriptions did not include a single word about any Koreans actually being hit by fire (though it appears that some were). Carroll's testimony almost certainly referred to the late morning or middle of the afternoon of July 26, 1950. He is talking about the thirty to ninety seconds of gunfire described in chapter six. Throughout that day, as described in earlier chapters of this book, the men of the scattered battalion were making their way in ones, twos, fives, and tens to the rear, hoping to find their lines again. At the same time, the slowly building second line, made in fits and starts as more and more men dribbled in over the course of the day, was filled with nervous men who had been shaken by the events of the night before and were expecting at any moment to see North Korean T-34s and infantry coming down the valley. Even so, small patrols of men were sent forward to search for and begin collecting the ammunition, weapons, and equipment that soldiers in the grip of panic had dropped the night before. More than a few of these patrols, returning to the lines of the 2nd Battalion 7th Cavalry, were taken under fire by their own unit. Casualty records for the night of July 25–26 indicated that five men were evacuated due to dehydration (heat sickness) brought on by the stress of the flight and the lack of water, while Sergeant First Class Pham Bowie of F Company was killed and five others were wounded by gunfire and evacuated.[80] Yet we know there were no NKPA troops in the area. The answer is obvious; there was much nervous lead flying over the course of that night—enough to kill one wound five.

The AP then provides more specifics about the orders that were issued to other divisions, notably the 25th Infantry Division, and to the 8th Cavalry Regiment by a staff officer in the 1st Cavalry Division before the 7th Cavalry arrived in the division area of operations on July 25, 1950. Only after all of this does the first veteran directly quoted make an assertion that the battalion deliberately shot South Korean villagers and did so, moreover, at the direction of one of its officers. The AP went to great lengths to make the stretch from orders issued to one division miles away (the 25th Infantry Division) to actions taken days later by companies in a regiment in an entirely different division. In doing so, it was relying on the general public's lack of knowledge about the military.

> Veterans said Capt. Melbourne C. Chandler, after speaking with superior officers by radio, had ordered machine-gunners from his heavy-weapons company to set up near the tunnel mouths and open fire.
>
> "Chandler said, 'The hell with all those people. Let's get rid of all of them,'" said Eugene Hesselman of Fort Mitchell, Ky. . . . "We didn't know if they were North or South Koreans. . . . We were there only a couple of days and we didn't know them from a load of coal."[81]

Although Hesselman is the only one quoted, the AP gives the impression that a body of veterans support this assertion that Chandler gave those orders, instead of the only two who were quoted—Eugene Hesselman and Edward Daily. Again, because the AP knew of the problems with both of these sources, why did it rely upon these two men alone to "prove" that this was not just a case of unfortunate civilians being caught in the line of fire between combat forces, but a deliberate act of murder committed under the orders of superior officers? The most likely answer is that these were the only sources who told the AP what it wanted to hear.[82] These were not 'heroic veterans finally telling the truth,' these were men willing to tell reporters what they wanted to hear, for their own reasons.[83]

Only at this point—fifty-eight paragraphs into the story and just ahead of the account of Ed Daily—did the Associated Press offer even a slight possibility that what occurred at No Gun Ri may not have happened in quite the way the AP had portrayed it thus far. Yet the way that they do this is actually set up as an indictment. With the first fifty-seven paragraphs of the story supporting the contentions of the South Koreans, despite the many unpublished interviews with individuals who disagree with the AP's thesis as presented, the AP had skewed its balance of the story: At this point, the AP was no longer investigating but rather trying to "prove" something that it already believed. This statement is supported by the manner in which the reporters terminated an interview if the veteran did not agree with their thesis.

To try to bring balance to the story, the AP chose the one man who might possibly have something to hide if all of this were true. Not until the fifty-eighth paragraph (thus indicating that the AP itself did not consider this as important as all that went before) was the reader introduced to a counterbalancing opinion through the only witness alive most likely to be considered guilty by a reader, the former battalion commander of the 2nd Battalion 7th Cavalry, Lieutenant Colonel Herbert Heyer.

After problems with the AP's sources appeared in the national news media in May 2000, the AP tried to make a point that the placement of elements within the story indicated the relevant importance of that information to the story. In this, the AP inadvertently confirmed that sequence is a measure of importance. At the same time, what it unwittingly admitted is that it did not even attempt to reach any balance in its reporting because it placed the counterbalancing witness statements so far down in the story. Balanced reporting would have given a higher position to the reports and accounts of the eighty-four members of the battalion who disagreed. It would at least acknowledge there were many others who denied such an event happened or stated that they never heard of such an event. In a statement in defense of the AP story, Jonathan Wolman, an Associated Press executive editor, clearly indicated that the importance of a figure is directly related to its position in the story. In reference to Edward Daily, whom the AP was attempting to disassociate itself from at the time, Wolman made much of the fact that Daily was not mentioned in the story until the fifty-sixth paragraph, and that he was therefore not central to their story.

Wolman also neglected to mention that Daily had put the AP reporters in touch with many of the sources that the AP actually went to press with, or that Daily was in contact with many of the sources immediately after he was first contacted by the AP team. The AP never mentioned that after contacting Edward Daily, he started talking to Korean War veterans of the regiment, asking them if they remembered No Gun Ri and at the same time probably planting memories in some of their minds.

From this point onward, the AP story revolves around Edward Daily and the men whom he contacted for the Associated Press. The only source outside the veterans' and South Koreans' testimony from this point forward is, amazingly, supporting documentation from the North Korean communist propaganda organ, the *Cho Sun In Min Bo*. No comment is made about the veracity or reliability of this source in the story. In the rest of the story, Daily gets quoted again and again. In the remaining few lines of the story, the five quotes are from Daily, Flint, or Hesselman. Daily garnered an additional four paragraphs and a photograph in the sidebar story that accompanied the main story. Framed by a replica of the company guidon of H Company, 2nd Battalion 7th Cavalry, Daily appeared thoughtful and dignified.[84] In the entire story, there was just one more quote from a veteran who stated that he did not see anything, and this came with a qualifier that the unit was extremely spread out. That quote, from former Lieutenant John Lippincott appeared this way, just fifteen lines from the end of the story:

> One battalion lieutenant located by the AP said he was in the area but knew nothing about the killing of civilians. "I have honestly never, ever heard of this from either my soldiers or superiors or my friends," said John C. Lippincott of Stone Mountain, Ga. He said he could have missed it because "we were extremely spread out."[85]

Somehow the AP failed to mention that Lippincott was a platoon leader in the very same company as one of its primary sources who claimed to be in the very thick of things, Delos K. Flint. Instead Lippincott's comment stood without noting the connection for the reader and thus possibly casting doubt upon one of the AP's star witnesses. The AP also deliberately avoided using a quote from another former lieutenant who was in the battalion command post at the time, presumably because his testimony would have been damaging to its thesis.[86]

In the end, after reading this analysis of the AP's story, the reader must determine for himself or herself if the Associated Press lived up to the journalistic standard of balance through either the sequence of its information or the content of that information in reporting the events at No Gun Ri.

THE MAKING OF A PULITZER PRIZE

The Pulitzer Prize for investigative reporting is awarded for a distinguished example of investigative reporting by an individual or team, presented as a single article or series.

Awarded to Sang-Hun Choe, Charles J. Hanley and Martha Mendoza of the Associated Press for revealing, with extensive documentation, the decades-old secret of how American soldiers early in the Korean War killed hundreds of Korean civilians in a massacre at the No Gun Ri Bridge.

—Text of the 2000 Pulitzer Prize

From the very first day that the explosive Associated Press version of the events at No Gun Ri appeared, it was evident that this was a story with the potential to win the Pulitzer Prize. The story had all the necessary elements—a shocking event of international proportions, the implication of a massive government cover-up exposed through the dutiful attention of the members of the fourth estate, and the drama of the testimony provided by the soldiers in the story. More than that, the story gained immediate credibility when President William Clinton directed the secretary of defense to conduct an investigation into the matter. To some closely involved with the Pulitzer Prize, this attention by the Pentagon was evidence of the quality of the reporting.[87]

The AP team decided to do what it could to add legs to the story (that is, to prolong the time that the story was in the public eye). Its follow-up stories, representing additional material spun out of the same original research conducted for the base story, appeared regularly on the AP wire services for the next two months. In January, the Associated Press submitted its version of No Gun Ri for the Pulitzer Prize in the category of investigative journalism. Perhaps by coincidence, that same month, the January-February issue of the *Investigative Reporters and Editors* (IRE) *Journal* published an article by Martha Mendoza titled, "Digging Into History—AP Investigates U.S. Actions During the Korean War."

In her article, Mendoza described how the AP team went about investigating the story of the events at No Gun Ri. She worked hard to make it appear that the incident the AP was reporting was not just history, but current news based upon the "fact" that credible new sources, primarily Edward Daily, Delos Flint, and Eugene Hessleman, substantiated the claims of the South Koreans. Her claim was that nothing like this had ever been reported, even at the time. Therefore, rather than a new look at an old and lightly-reported original report, this was a totally new story. Just as with the dramatic opening line in the original AP story, Mendoza refers to the reporting on No Gun Ri as "the story that nobody wanted to hear." In one interview she gave just after their story came out Ms. Mendoza went so far as to openly state, "We knew from the beginning that the U.S. Army had lied," but even more outrageously, she made the claim that solely through her team's investigative work was it determined that army units had been in the area at that time.[88] How did Mendoza and the AP researcher Randy Herschaft miss the following that appeared in the official U.S. Army-published history, *South to the Naktong, North to the Yalu*, written by Roy Appleman:

> During the battle for Yongdong the 7th Cavalry Regiment headquarters and the 2d Battalion arrived from P'ohang-dong and took up a position west of Kumch'on. Reports reached them the night of July 25–26 of enemy gains in the 27th Infantry sector northward, which increased the uneasiness of the untested staff and

troops. After midnight there came a report that the enemy had achieved a breakthrough. Somehow, the constant pressure under which the 27th Infantry fought its delaying action on the Poun road had become magnified and exaggerated. The 7th Cavalry Regiment headquarters immediately decided to arouse all personnel and withdraw. During the withdrawal the 2d Battalion, an untried unit, scattered in panic. That evening 119 of its men were still missing.

In this frantic departure from its position on July 26, the 2d Battalion left behind a switchboard, an emergency lighting unit, and weapons of all types. After daylight truck drivers and platoon sergeants returned to the scene and recovered 14 machine guns, 9 radios, 120 M1 rifles, 26 carbines, 7 BARs, and 6 60-mm mortars.

While this untoward incident was taking place in their rear, other elements of the 1st Cavalry Division held their defensive positions east of Yongdong. The 7th Regiment of the N.K. 3d Division, meanwhile, started southwest from Yongdong on the Muju road in a sweeping flank movement through Chirye against Kumch'on, twenty air miles eastward. That night, elements of the enemy division in Yongdong attacked the 1st Cavalry troops east of the town. Four enemy tanks and an infantry force started this action by driving several hundred refugees ahead of them through American mine fields."[89]

Appleman certainly got several of the aspects of this fight muddled, but that does not imply that he was lying. Appleman's book was the official, published, and readily available United States Army account of the fighting in this area. He got the right units in the right locations, albeit inexactly. "West of Kumch'on" does not precisely locate the 2nd Battalion 7th Cavalry in its first position, nor does "defensive positions east of Yongdong" specifically place elements of the 1st Cavalry Division in No Gun Ri, but it does locate them within a few miles. For a book that covers the actions of whole divisions over the course of six months of fighting, that was not bad. It certainly represents considerable labor on the part of Appleman to reconstruct the movement of units across the battlefield.

The AP's statements about the depth of its research imply that it took the time to read the army's official account of the fighting and examine the detailed maps that accompanied the book. In interviews with several magazines and journals just after the AP story came out, but before the Pulitzer or other awards came to the team, Mendoza portrayed the research the AP team conducted as such:

One thing we did, that the army has not done, was to reconstruct unit movement. When we were at the National Archives we were trying to figure out where [the soldiers] were. At the National Archives they have 1950 maps, so we pulled the maps and found their numbers corresponded to these maps and they were telling us where troops were. We covered the walls of our office with these maps and spent weeks putting them up. It took us weeks and weeks to confirm which exact units had been at the same place that these villagers said they were. And these villagers in Korea, working with Mr. Choe, were also drawing maps for him of where they thought [the soldiers] were. And it is an oversimplification to say that we looked at the maps, because it took weeks putting these stickers on these maps.[90]

In another interview with Mendoza, a similar story line appears:

In fact, the Pentagon had denied that U.S. forces were in the area at the time the massacre occurred—a contention that Mendoza set out to verify or disprove during the course of her research for the story.

"That took quite a lot of work, a lot of digging and filing of Freedom of Information Acts," Mendoza says. "And for me, putting stickers on 1950 vintage army maps for three weeks to plot coordinates of where certain troops were on certain days."[91]

And in her own article in the *IRE Journal* she put it this way:

The walls of our small Special Assignment Team office were soon covered with big maps dotted with little stickers, each map representing one day in late July 1950, as I tracked the movements of American units.

We still didn't know whether the South Korean survivors were telling the truth. But more than ever we realized the U.S. military had it wrong when it said the 1st Cavalry Division was not near No Gun Ri.[92]

Assuming that the AP team took the time to read the official U.S. Army history available at the New York City Public Library, its contention that the U.S. Army claimed not to be in the area east of Yongdong and west of Kumch'on seems incredible.

Still, according to Mendoza's version of history, "What happened at No Gun Ri is shocking and the historians wrote their accounts with these stories untold."[93] Curiously she seems to have overlooked several of the prominent historians who could have easily been tracked down through a phone call or two to the history department of any major university. Even stranger is the fact that the one historian who is interviewed by the AP and appears on the AP news wire Web site, "The Wire," is Bruce Cumings, whose 1990 book, *Origins of the Korean War, Volume II, The Roaring of the Cataract,* even has a chapter subheading titled, "American Atrocities." In that chapter, he excerpts from two 1950 front-page or headline news articles about potential massacres in South Korea.

In the early fall of 1950 *The New York Times* reported on the front page that unconfirmed reports cited that soldiers of the 1st Cavalry had killed South Korean civilians in the early days of the war at an unidentified location. This story appeared to be confirmed with an off-handed comment to the effect of "yea, they were pretty ill-disciplined" made by an unidentified staff officer at a higher echelon, who was not present at the event.[94] The origin of this story was almost certainly not solid investigative reporting by the journalist, but the translated copy of a North Korean propaganda newspaper then being circulated through the 1st Cavalry and Eighth Army headquarters.[95]

The question then is: if information is already in a respected academic history book available around the world for a decade, how can it be "news" in 1999 and how could Mendoza claim that "historians wrote with these stories untold?"

Perhaps more graphically, and tragically in fact, was another 1950 article that appeared in *Life* magazine. Since *Life* was known as a photo journal and not a bastion of hard-hitting investigative journalism, its reporters and photographers had to be close to the front to get the images that would sell back in the United States. So it was that one reporter, John Osborne, was with a regimental command post at some point in the opening weeks of the war. Osborne's article, published in the August 21, 1950 edition of *Life* magazine and probably based on events around Waegwan or Taegu during the second week of August, brought the nature of the war home to the American readers of *Life* in a decidedly unpleasant manner:

> And there is savagery by proxy, the savagery of the South Korean police and (in some sectors) South Korean marines upon whom we rely for contact with the population and for ferreting out hidden enemies. I am not presuming to issue righteous indictments—or to ignore the even greater savagery of the North Korean army. I am

simply stating the elementary facts of war in Korea. The South Korean police and South Korean marines whom I observed in front line areas are brutal. They murder to save themselves the trouble of escorting prisoners to the rear; they murder civilians simply to get them out of the way or to avoid the trouble of searching and cross-examining them. And they extort information—information our forces need and require of the South Korean interrogators—by means so brutal that they cannot be described. Too often they murder prisoners of war and civilians before they have had a chance to give any information they may have . . . .[96]

But as critical as he was of the South Korean police and marines for their war crimes, Osborne was sympathetic, perhaps too sympathetic, to the conflict of conscience that trapped the Americans. On the one hand, the Americans knew that they had to rely on the South Korean military and police to provide information and screen the thousands of refugees. On the other hand, these brutal methods were still not enough to stem the tide of refugees, or even to make it manageable, as the North Koreans began to abandon their moderate infiltration techniques as time went on in favor of another tactic—using the refugees as human shields for their own frontal assaults. In the same article, Osborne relates a scene he personally witnessed:

It is midnight and all around the hills are astir. Here a sharp burst of small arms fire, there the flashing life and death of an American shell searching out the enemy who we know are gathering within 5,000 yards of this command post. One of the field telephones rings, an officer of the staff picks it up, listens a moment and says, "Oh, Christ, there's a column of refugees, three or four hundred of them, coming right down on B company." A major in the command tent says to the regimental commander, "Don't let them through." And of course the major is right. Time and again, at position after position, this silent approach of whitened figures has covered enemy attacks and, before our men had become hardened to the necessities of the Korean War, had often and fatally delayed and confused their own fire. Finally the colonel says, in a voice wracked with wretchedness, "All right, don't let them through. But try to talk to them, try to tell them to go back."

"Yea," says one of the little staff group, "but what if they don't go back?"

"Well then," the colonel says, as though dragging himself towards some pit, "then fire over their heads."

"Okay," an officer says, "we fire over their heads. Then what?"

The colonel seems to brace himself in the semidarkness of the blacked out tent.

"Well then, fire into them if you have to. If you have to, I said."

An officer speaks into the telephone, and the order goes across the wire into the dark hills.

It is afternoon. From one of our most advanced posts, a foxhole or two far out in the hills among the constantly infiltrating enemy, a report has come that our riflemen have had to fire into another party of refugees who march at them, against shouted warnings and wavings. From the command post an urgent and remonstrating voice speaks over the wire into the hills, "My God, John, it's gone too far when we are shooting children." There is some reply from the hills, unheard by all save the officer on the telephone, and at the end the officer says, "Watch it, John, watch it! But don't take any chances."[97]

Therein lies another tragedy of No Gun Ri.

Unless Osborne was writing fiction, and there is no reason to believe that he made up that command post scene, then an event similar to the one described in the AP story actually did take place and unarmed South Korean civilians were fired upon by American soldiers without direct provocation. The real tragedy was that the Associated Press did not discover or uncover the facts of that event; instead it focused on an account with decidedly weaker roots. In other words, it reported the wrong story.

The only thing that can be asserted as a fact was that the command post described by Osborne was not the 7th Cavalry.[98]

Historian Bruce Cumings made note of this article, although he used it selectively in his own writing.[99] Yet Mendoza claimed that the AP article was extensively researched to ensure that nobody else had ever reported any event like this and the AP story was written because historians did not know about civilian deaths in Korea. Her assertion gives the definite impression that the AP scooped Cumings, one of the most noted Korean War historians working in the field today. In hindsight, the AP report was neither new nor news, and only by boosting its claims to originality could the AP team make a case for the importance of its foray in history. Both before and after their actual awarding of the Pulitzer Prize for investigative journalism, the members of the AP team inflated the depth of the research they claimed to have done for the story. This is fairly amazing, given what we know about how they went to print quoting three men who were not there. Yet the AP team felt its documentation was ironclad, affirming over and over that its sources were solid. According to an interview that Mendoza gave in October 1999, the research that resulted in the AP's use of such sources as Edward Daily, Eugene Hesselman, and Delos Flint was exhaustive. She said:

> Well, we have been sort of working solely on it for four or five months. And then we began the editing process. We went through many, many rewrites. Maybe more than 20. We knew we had to have every little bit of this right. We could not have even one tiny detail questionable because it was going to come back and haunt us.[100]

An ironic statement in light of the material that the Associated Press had on hand to document Daily's military biography prior to publishing its story.

Despite the six, or dozen, or two dozen sources who the AP said confirmed its story, the AP apparently felt that the background to the story as it stood was not strong enough. Accordingly, it then went a step further in modifying the accounts of how well documented and supported its story had been. This was done in May of 2000 during the defense of its original story.

This time, in an official release by the news organization itself, the AP stuck with the original number of veterans as being just "twelve." Although only a half a dozen were construed as supporting the AP's thesis in the original published account, in May 2000 the AP stated that its basic story quoted "a dozen U.S. veterans" who substantiated that a "large number" of civilians were shot to death under the bridge at No Gun Ri.[101] This is another case of a curious mutation in numbers.

By this point, in late May 2000, without doubt, the AP reporters had transitioned from objective reporters to strong advocates of the South Korean version of events, no longer willing to entertain the possibility that some of their South Korean sources might not be all that they claimed they were, or that these sources might have been influenced by the possibility of millions of dollars in reparation money. In another *The New York Times* article following the controversy over the AP's sources, AP reporter Charles Hanley was portrayed and quoted this way:

> But Mr. Hanley bristles at the idea that their quest for reparations casts doubt on their memories. "Frankly," he said, "it is analogous to questioning the right of Holocaust victims to seek some token of reparation."[102]

It appears that this was a play to strike an emotional chord by equating what happened at No Gun Ri with the slaughter of six million Jews by Adolf Hitler's Nazi regime during World War II. At the same time, the overall number of sources that the AP reporters claimed to contact in its investigation also climbed. In an interview granted to her alma mater not long after she won the Pulitzer, Mendoza bumped up once again the number of total interviews the AP conducted in researching the story.

In the original AP story, the number of interviews was quoted at 130. In Hanley's E-mails, this number was refined by identifying that one hundred of these interviews were with eighty-four different men of the 2nd Battalion 7th Cavalry. That implies that the remaining thirty interviews were with others—perhaps veterans of other battalions and headquarters units, or modern historians. Mendoza took the inflation of the number of sources interviewed for the story to a new level in an interview at Northern Arizona University, where she was receiving an award for her journalism. Nicole Loftus reported the following in *Flagstaff Life:*

> What Mendoza uncovered after a year and a half of interviewing more than 220 sources, researching archives, confronting Pentagon officials, and mapping troop movement was the horror story of what happened to hundreds of unsuspecting South Koreans under a bridge in late July 50 years ago.[103]

The same article contains the amazing revelation, unmentioned by the AP prior to this, that a host of general officers were interviewed for the story. The reporter at Northern Arizona University, unless she misquoted Mendoza (and Mendoza did not publish or request a correction of this number), passed on the news that more than twenty-four former general officers were among Mendoza's sources.[104] So at this point in April 2000, some 220 interviews with two-dozen retired general officers among them went into the original 1999 story. A remarkable feat, since of the officers from the 7th Cavalry during that period who were still alive in 1997, no more than a handful of those former lieutenants and captains ever made the rank of brigadier general, and none of those men were quoted in the AP story. Indeed, if twenty-four general officers were among Mendoza's sources, why did not a single one of them appear in the AP story?

If, however, the more widely cited and quasi-official number of 130 interviews originally provided by the AP is used along with Hanley's account that 100 of these interviews were with members of the 2nd Battalion 7th Cavalry, then the remaining 30 interviews (130-100 = 30), the overwhelming mass, 24 out of 30, came from retired generals. Since the AP included an interview with historian Bruce Cumings on its Web site, and further research reveals that at least two interviews were with former officers in the 545th Military Police Company of the 1st Cavalry Division, the number of 30 is further reduced to 27 men, of whom 24 were retired generals, unless Mendoza was inflating her numbers or was misquoted by the reporters. Giving Mendoza the benefit of the doubt and assuming that the reporter did misquote her by equating "officer" with "general," interesting questions still remain.

Only three officers appeared in the story: one (Carroll) had his quote taken out of context, and the other two (Lippincott and Heyer) denied that such an event as described by the South Koreans ever took place. So what of the other twenty-one officers? At this time, the Associated Press has refused to release the names of those twenty-one officers despite repeated requests.[105] Regardless of the number of sources, how did the AP find the sources who supported its thesis if so many denied or made statements contrary to the claims of the South Korean witnesses. How did the AP come to find all of these veterans who confessed to their part in an atrocity?

In a follow-up story on Edward Daily after problems with the AP's central witnesses were revealed in May 2000, *The New York Times* gave this version of the AP's investigation as related by Charles Hanley:

> Charles J. Hanley, a reporter who worked on the Associated Press project and staunchly defends it, said that as many as twenty veterans confirmed some or all of Mr. Daily's account, and that the reporting team found sources outside Mr. Daily's sphere of contacts. Mr. Hanley acknowledged that Mr. Daily was a valuable source for the AP, supplying ex-soldiers' telephone numbers early in the inquiry.[106]

Hanley's increased count to twenty from the original dozen veterans who confirmed the claims of a massacre was actually a step down from his partner, Martha Mendoza. In her article in the *IRE Journal*, she claimed that more than twenty-four veterans supported the basic contention of the AP story. Mendoza said, "We had pinned down the core story. We eventually had more than two dozen veterans acknowledging that it had happened, and about half of those were strong sources, discussing it in detail on the record."[107]

That first claim, by Hanley, is important because it demonstrated how, despite the AP's claims that Daily was not central to its story, he was, in fact, central to the AP's access to the people it used in creating its story. He was the "in" with many of the veterans quoted and, in fact, had been in contact with those veterans about their testimony to the AP himself. In other words, it appears that Daily contacted and talked in depth with all of the AP's sources either before the AP did or at about the same time.

The Associated Press's claim that it contacted people outside of Daily's sphere of influence would only be relevant if those sources were used in the story. If the AP in its reporting of the story of No Gun Ri contacted anyone beyond Daily's sphere of influence, it did not use that man in its report. Perhaps more importantly, if Edward Daily was the first man who the news service contacted who told the AP what it wanted to hear, then, given Daily's many opportunities to plant memories in other veterans' minds, a lot of things might fall into place.

In December 1999, Daily sent me a list, complete with the names, home addresses, and phone numbers, of all of the men actually quoted in the AP story. Moreover, he also sent to me a handwritten note, stating that several of these men were not part of the 7th Cavalry Veterans' Association but were men whom he himself had come in contact with and passed on to the AP. I confirmed that these men were not on any of the regiment's veterans rosters that I had. While it is possible that Daily was not telling the truth and was attempting to garner credit for the research done by the AP, the fact remains that either he gave the AP the names and telephone numbers or the AP shared its list of sources with Daily. In either event, this demonstrated that Daily was central to the AP's story through his interaction with every single witness cited by the AP.[108]

In his written note and in a subsequent phone conversation, Daily explicitly told me who he thought had the best memories of the events and who might be most willing to work with me in my own research. He then went a step further and sent a letter to the 1st Cavalry Division Association and the 7th Cavalry Regiment Association, asking them to make a general notice that all veterans in the association lend me whatever assistance they could.[109]

In late October 1999, the magazine *City on a Hill* published the first version of how the Associated Press found the first American veteran to confirm the South Koreans' story. In this interview with Martha Mendoza, the story of the story came out this way: "Very often their response came right to this instance. We figured out which exact company. We probably did 35 interviews before one guy told me about this incident, and those 35 interviews were long."[110]

Two months later, in the *Investigative Reporters and Editors Journal* article, Mendoza included a little more detail: "Finally, on our 34th interview, I found a man who said he witnessed what happened at No Gun Ri. His detail was convincing. But it wasn't until 15 interviews later that we hit another."[111]

But in April 2000, just after the AP won the Pulitzer Prize, that all-important first source was described like this in *Flagstaff Life*: "On Mendoza's 34th call to a former general, she got her first informant. The first thing he said was, 'We had to shoot them all.'"[112] As noted earlier, that *Flagstaff Life* reporter might have confused the term officer with general.

In the summer of 2000, another version of this story appeared in *University of California Santa Cruz Review*, this time closing the loop: "After three dozen dead-end interviews, one veteran told Mendoza he had been at the No Gun Ri railroad trestle. 'He was providing the exact same details that these South Koreans had provided about the incident. Except his perspective was that he was sitting behind the machine gun firing at them,' Mendoza says."[113]

Finally, in their 2001 book about the incident, the AP reporters repeat this tale once again, but this time the thirty-fourth interviewee who gave them their first crucial break was a former sergeant.[114]

Thirty-four, thirty-five, or thirty-six interviews into their investigation, the Associated Press reporters finally found the only man who might make their story for them. In this whole convoluted story, only one man claimed to be both a machine gunner at No Gun Ri, a former sergeant, and a former officer. Only one man might politely listen to the AP's version of events and echo it back one tantalizing detail at a time. Only one man had the personal connections to give the AP rosters of the 7th Cavalry and contacts that might support its thesis. Only one man might then contact other Korean War veterans of the 7th Cavalry and propagate this story among susceptible veterans.

Based on the evidence of their own words, the Associated Press reporters inadvertently made it clear that the man they found on their thirty-fourth interview was Edward L. Daily. The AP would not return my phone calls on this question.

AFTERWORD

Official records are indispensable for fixing dates and time of major events and troop movements. But anyone familiar with the way the records of combat units during battle are made up will know that they seldom tell the essential facts of what happened, and how, and why. They are often the products of indifferent clerks transcribing, at places remote from the scene of action, a minimum of messages for something—anything—that will satisfy the official requirement for a report. Those who know the most about an action or an event seldom take the time to tell, or write, about it. They are too tired, or too nearly dead, or they are dead.

In the early months of the Korean War there was little time for the military organizations committed there to keep adequate records of what they did, even had there been the desire to do so. Always they were stopping only briefly, fighting hazardous rear-guard actions, and then on the run again. No one had time to write down what had happened and why, even if he knew. And no one in the various headquarters had the time or the energy or the will to search out those who survived each action and from them learn firsthand of the event. Everyone was too much concerned with survival.

—Roy G. Appleman,
South to the Naktong, North to the Yalu.

APPLEMAN HIT THE NAIL ON THE HEAD, AS WELL HE MIGHT, SINCE HE WAS the primary author of the United States Army's official history of the opening phases of the Korean War. In my research through various archives and the personal papers of men ranging from privates to colonels to General of the Army Douglas MacArthur, I repeatedly ran into traces of evidence that Appleman was there before me. His single volume is one of the best works of traditional military history on the subject. Although his book was tightly defined in scope, Appleman clearly tried very hard to leave no stone unturned. Yet obviously some things had to be left out, or were not quite researched completely back when Appleman was writing in the early 1960s. Moreover, in some ways, he was inclined to believe some sources more than others.[1] These missing pieces are valid considering Appleman was just one man working on a comprehensive history of an event as huge as the first six months of the Korean War.

But Appleman understood from the very beginning that his was a generalist work that future generations would rely on as the starting point for their own research. Therefore, he tried hard to get at least something of everything in there.

Appleman's account of the events between the fall of Yongdong and the fall of Hwanggan in the last week of July is brief, only two pages. Yet in those few paragraphs, he at least demonstrated that he had dug up some of the best sources available and tried to make sense of them. He describes in passing the disintegration of the 2nd Battalion 7th Cavalry on the night of July 25–26 and even goes so far as to mention the most likely causes for this. He brings up the issues of guerillas in the area and the almost random nature of strafing by USAF aircraft any time their missions brought them close to the front lines. All of this appears in Appleman's version of the events. But obviously with months of war to cover, he could not dwell on this one small unit on this one small patch of ground for hundreds of pages as this book has done. So he left off his account with a moderate amount of supplemental information garnered from interviews he conducted after the war with officers, including Major General Hobart Gay, the division commander.

In this book, I tried to move beyond that level by digging deeper than Appleman could, and trying to make sense out of records left by one group of men who became "too much concerned with survival" during one very specific period of time. That is the job of a historian, to make sense out of a host of disparate sources, weave them together into a substantiated cohesive whole, and interpret them for the reader. A large part of this digging, quite naturally, involves knowing what to make of those sources. This afterword deals with those sources.

The biggest division in historical sources falls between what are categorized as primary and secondary sources. Both have their own unique advantages and disadvantages, both may be useful in different circumstances, and both come with unique hazards and pitfalls. The measure of a work of history is the quality of these sources.

A secondary source is one created by a nonparticipant. Most non-autobiographical histories are based on secondary sources. Most newspaper reports and magazine articles are also. This book is a secondary source.

A primary source is something created by a participant or a witness. General William Dean's book about his own experiences in Korea is a primary source. Letters written home by soldiers on the front lines and collected by wives or sweethearts or parents are primary sources. Operations orders created by participants are primary sources, as are most contemporary documents. Some newpaper or magazine articles, if the reporter was on the scene, are primary sources. A photo can be a primary source.

It seems simple enough, yet there is far more to sources than separating them into primary and secondary. It would seem obvious that any work based mainly on primary sources would be superior to anything done using mostly secondary sources, as long as the primary sources were not biased and the author understood what sources were available, used all of the relevant materials, and understood the context in which those documents (or for that matter, memories) were created. This is not always the case, and in some of the reporting about the events at No Gun Ri, modern-day journalists demonstrated the fact that their degrees were not in history.

The starting point then must be in an evaluation of the secondary source literature available about the Korean War. This book relied upon a fairly wide range of works of history, especially military history. These books spanned the types of military history mentioned earlier in the book: regimental, patriotic, popular, and academic. All found their way into my understanding of the general sequence of events. I evaluated each of these books against each other as well as against my knowledge of the available primary sources that went into each book, the potential biases of the authors, and even the social context within which the book was written. For example, an academic historian known to have written other books extolling the virtues of Marxism and writing his book on an East coast campus known for liberal activism might well write a very different book than an academic historian known for supporting a realist theory of international relations and writing his book from a fairly conservative Midwestern university. They may both be brilliant men, they may even both examine all of the same sources, but the material they create will probably look somewhat different. A seventy-year old veteran of the war, trying to write a comprehensive narrative of its battles, some of which he participated in, will create something different than the twenty-eight-year-old hobbiest-author whose lifelong interest in the war became his first book. How do you learn all of this background information about an author? Research.

Academic historians are the easiest to learn about. They are generally a prolific lot, and through the body of work that they previously created, one can gain a sense of their general directions and interests. Moreover, they often include a roadmap about their inclinations and influences right in the acknowledgements, for those who understand whom they are thanking. Perhaps their mentor was a known social activist, or a business historian, or a labor historian, or an army general. If they were, and the scholar is fairly young, most likely at least a nod in that direction is right up front in the "thank you" section. The acknowledgments also provide a clear indication of how authors used the sources they accessed. Did they thank the archivists? If not, but they cite archival material, then they may have just skimmed over the material in that repository, perhaps in favor of some other source. Do they thank academic peers, and if so, what are the areas of expertise of those peers? Do they acknowledge a grant of research money? Most grants come without significant strings attached, but at the same time grants are provided for research in some specified field or even on one very narrow topic in a specified field. All of this goes into the analysis of an academic historian's work.

Unaffiliated authors, sometimes veterans or just particularly interested hobbyists, are more difficult to track down. Their works rarely contain footnotes that can be checked for accuracy, which makes it tough to reference them or examine their sources. This type of author is also more inclined to rely upon material of dubious quality because they often do not have any training in the skepticism that comes with time spent learning how history is created. They may also have written their book with a specific purpose in mind, either to make a profit or to make a point, neither of which fully supports the idea of getting to the truth. All of these things must be taken into account when looking at a secondary source. Once this is done, it is time to move on and deal with the real meat of military history, the primary source material.

Once again, the sources must be evaluated, this time, however, looking at the historian's background information, his general knowledge about the history of the period, and the elements relating to his source. This is really what being a historian is all about. For example, anyone can find an old letter in an attic and determine that this is a letter from a Union soldier named Boylan during the American Civil War written to his sweetheart back home in New York. From internal clues, the reader may determine that it was written in early December of 1862 while the soldier was at someplace called Aquia, and that the soldier seems upset about some group called the Fenians and an officer named Meagher. A journalist reading this might take the letter and conclude that there was discontent in the Union army and write a story on that basis. The journalist may check the archives and confirm that the soldier was in the army, and that his unit was at a place called Aquia Landing, which was a supply base for the Union army at that time in the American Civil War. The headline might read, "Soldier's Letters Reveal Discontent in Union Army."

A historian finding that letter, and the others it is wrapped with, will start leaping for joy. The historian immediately makes the connection that this soldier is in the renowned Irish Brigade of the Union army, a unit made up of Irish immigrants. He knows that because Meagher is a well-known name among military historians. The historian already knows that just a few days after the letter was written that soldier almost certainly marched with the rest of his unit into a horrific hail of confederate musketry and cannon fire just a few miles away at Fredericksburg, Virginia, in one of the bloodiest and most futile attacks of the war. From the letter, the historian gathers new information that fits into the broader mosaic of his knowledge of that period. For example, he might recognize a potential mood of dissatisfaction within that much-storied unit just prior to its most heroic moment, but he would not extend that to the whole Union army. For the historian, who already knows what the accepted version of this information is from years of reading secondary sources, this letter raises new and different questions.

The historian is the ultimate skeptic. He wants to know who was this woman the soldier was writing to. Who were her parents? Were they politically active? After some additional research, he may discover that the family had loomed large in Irish-American politics of the period. So now the historian might ask, "Was the soldier possibly writing this letter in an effort to plant seeds of distrust for the brigade's leaders among the growing political powers of the Irish-American community in New York?" By that point in 1862, postwar political credibility would rely heavily upon military reputations earned during the "War to Save the Union." If so, might the letter have been written for the soldier's personal gain? That raises the question (which the historian is obligated to track down) of what happened to this soldier later? Eventually, the historian publishes an article in a revered historical journal suggesting the possibility that deliberate political maneuvering occurred within the Irish Brigade just prior to its climactic battle, and that the command structure that emerged from the ashes of that fight was the result not only of physical casualties, but political ones back in New York City. This somewhat different lead would certainly never be a headline in a modern paper.

As much as possible, I tried to apply this second method to the sources in this book. So that you can evaluate how well I did or did not succeed in doing this, I am providing you information on these sources here.

WAR DIARIES

The first and most controversial source I dealt with in researching this book straddled the line between primary and secondary. That is the various war diary entries of the 1st Cavalry Division and the 5th, 7th, and 8th Cavalry Regiments. These accounts of the units' actions during wartime are stored at the National Archives repository in College Park, Maryland. They are simple narratives of the events that took place in each unit. The problem comes in the way that these diaries were created after the fact. As diaries, narrative was added to them as events occurred. Most recordings seem to have been authored in the range of days to several weeks after a recordable event occurred.

Since no author is listed on the document, there is no way to confirm what the writer used to put together these reports and what external influences might have been acting on the author at the time. This is where my own experience as an officer helped me understand what I was seeing. These documents were, to my eyes, a typical after-action report of the type usually assigned to junior officers in the S-3 or G-3 sections of the headquarters, but possibly to the regimental adjutant, the S-1 officer. Through the misspellings, the typos, and the overblown language, I could see the hand of a young captain, probably somewhere between twenty-four and twenty-six, trying his best to record what the materials at hand told him. But what materials did he have?

Most obviously, these unknown authors had access to a primary source that I repeatedly wished I had during this research: the radio traffic records, also known as tactical operation center (TOC) logs, of the battalion and regimental headquarters. In every command post in the field, as far down as the battalion (but not to the company level), a written record is kept of everything that is heard or transmitted over the radios. This is not a verbatim record, but rather a series of handwritten notes created at that instant in time in a running journal.[2] Usually the people who do this initial writing are the enlisted soldiers manning the radios of the headquarters, perhaps supplemented by comments provided by one of the staff officers on duty at the time. Because the army at that time created these war diaries, it did not keep a large volume of paperwork that the logs of the individual battalions make up. This paperwork was preserved for a while, at least a few months by my estimation, and used to create the diaries, but after that, these records were discarded.

These journals contained all sorts of information, from the radio message sent by the S-4 as he was searching in the dark for one of the rifle companies to deliver water for the night to the orders received from higher headquarters to the reports of casualties submitted as they occurred by the companies. All of this information appears in the TOC log and was the basis for much of what became the regimental journals and war diaries.

The officers who compiled the war diaries were also probably working at a point in time relatively close to the events they recorded. In some units, war diary entries took place on a daily basis; in others, it was a weekly event. Although I have no direct evidence that entries were recorded daily for the 7th Cavalry in July 1950, it makes sense in light of some of the information recorded. Remember that contingency operations order that Colonel Nist wrote on July 24 where he protested the division order requiring him to create a provisional company from his newly arrived regimental advance party? That order was entered, verbatim, into the regimental diary. The obvious question is why. It was never put into effect, and so it was just an OPLAN, not an OPORD. (An operation plan not an operation order.) It had no bearing on the tactical disposition of the regiment and was overcome by events (the arrival of the 2nd Battalion) almost as soon as it had been written. So why was it added to the diary?

I believe this order was added at Colonel Nist's personal direction. Material related to Colonel Nist suggests that while he may very well have been a decent fellow, he was more accustomed to the workings of higher level staffs than he was to commanding infantrymen. Written memorandums for record are the hallmark of staff officers. They are written to record their understanding of events or decisions, should it ever become necessary. The fact that he wrote it in the first place says a lot about Nist; that he had it added to his regimental war diary says even more. No doubt, he did this deliberately since the document is annotated, "From the colonel's personal notes." The only logical reason for its inclusion in the historical record would be Nist's demand that it be recorded. Since Nist was relieved of command just weeks later and transferred to higher headquarters, this portion of the regimental diary was probably not written months or years later as some journalists have contended. It was probably written days, or at most a week or two, after the events, while Nist was still in command.

The possibility is therefore introduced that if something deliberate and untoward occurred during those days at the end of July and Nist was in command at the time the diary was written, Nist may well have excised any portions that he believed might reflect poorly upon him. This is where cross-checking with other regimental diaries, as well as some more specific primary sources, comes into play. On the other hand, the evidence of Nist's personal interaction with the creation of the war diary and his insistence in including such items as his protest of irregular orders suggests even more strongly that Nist never received an order to shoot all civilians, since he most certainly would protected himself with a written memorandum or copy of the order in his regimental TOC log and the war diary.

MORNING REPORTS

The next primary source that arrived on center stage prior to the publication of this book is something known as a morning report. This attendance report was crucial in demonstrating why three of the men who claimed that a deliberate massacre occurred at No Gun Ri were not actually there, and again illustrates the lack of care (or understanding) evidenced by the Associated Press in its reporting. The chapter about Edward Daily, Delos Flint, and Eugene Hesselman already covers most of the explanation about how a morning report is made. It is a simple document that only requires professional knowledge to correctly interpret.

After these documentary sources, the personal interviews I conducted or the transcripts of interviews conducted by others went into my evaluation of what actually happened at No Gu Ri. The obvious disparity between the accounts of the South Korean claimants and the American veterans provides a ready-made fault line here.

VETERANS' ACCOUNTS

The process of interviewing a veteran about memories that are almost half a century old is fraught with the potential for abuse. Misleading or directing questions might lead the veteran to say what the interviewer wants to hear. Asking too few questions, on the other hand, allows the veteran to fall back into a memory developed over the five decades since his initial impressions. As discovered in the chapter relating to Edward Daily, human memory is not a solid storage device but something flexible and amenable to change and modification from outside sources. Because I recognized this from the outset, I thought long and hard about exactly how to conduct my interviews of veterans.

Memories are tricky. They can be triggered by a whole host of things. Different sounds, colors, and most interestingly smells can bring back very clear memories that the person had not consciously thought of in a long time. The easiest way to convey this concept is to ask the reader to think about the smell of paste. For many people, just stopping and thinking about that smell will immediately bring forth a whole host of memories associated with kindergarten, an experience they had possibly decades earlier. I tried to use this phenomenon to my advantage to get past the barriers of created memories that some veterans had of their time in Korea.

When I started my interviews, the veterans often wanted to say such things as, "then we were ordered . . . " or "then they told us . . . " They would then try to tell me something about the bigger picture of the events that surrounded their experiences. This tendency stemmed from two sources. The first was general frustration from decades of trying to explain to nonveterans what went on in Korea. Confronted with family and friends who did not know the basics of military organization or combat operations, these veterans simplified their stories further and further until they had a pat routine down that could succinctly explain the broader outlines of the days of the war as they experienced them. The end result was that their own memories changed in the interim, becoming more broad until in some cases they barely had any personal memories remaining. The second influence was the veteran's own reading about "his" war. This too modified memories. To help make sense of and understand what had been going on in the big picture when they were junior enlisted soldiers and officers, many of the veterans later read books about the war. The result was that they developed a bigger picture than their own memories could originally provide. These factors, combined with the retelling to nonveterans or veterans from other units or wars, served as the first barrier I had to get past in my interviews.

My method to accomplish this was simple: I started very, very small and well out of range from my ultimate objective of questions about the events around No Gun Ri. In many cases, when I introduced myself and explained my intent, the veterans were ready to start with their account of events between July 26–30, 1950. But I wanted to get them used to specifics, so we started earlier with such questions as, "Where were you born? What was your family like? What was it like during the Depression? What was it like being a teenager during World War II? Did your father fight in World War II? Brothers or uncles?" Questions like these were designed to help the veteran get past the barrier of artificially modified memories and get used to speaking in the first person. Then we would move to questions about why they enlisted, what their basic training was like, and what "snapshots of memories" of life in occupied Japan they recalled. The process usually took between one and two hours before we could move on to the opening days of the Korean War. By that point, many of the veterans were used to my interrupting them when they said such things as, "and then we saw" or "and then they told us" and asking them to examine their memories and see if they could recall specifics. I would ask, "What did the man's voice who told you that sound like? Was it deep or high pitched? Where were you when that person said that thing? Were you standing? Sitting? Lying down?" Through questions like this, I would try to get to their personal memories and separate these from the modified third-person memories they had developed over the years.

By the time that the interviews moved on to Korea, the veterans were usually fairly comfortable with my constant challenging and took no offense. They realized that I was not attacking them personally. During my questioning of such nonthreatening issues as life during the Second World War, they discovered that many of the things they had tried to tell me were not things they specifically remembered, but things they had read or been told or had been telling themselves for so long that they forgot the original event that created their memory narrative. With these thoughts about human memory in mind, we would move forward and begin to talk about Korea.

The hours thus devoted to getting to their own memories, rather than the "memories" they had created over the course of years of reading, telling stories, and attending reunions, paid the largest dividends and formed the foundations for this book. Still, some things the veterans told me made little sense for months and months after I recorded their interviews. The best example of this was the story of the tanks.

Just about every veteran I talked to remembered being attacked by North Korean tanks that first night. Before I had seen the combat reports from that night at the National Archives, I mentally chalked this story up to one of "collective memory modification," but I recorded their accounts as they told them to me. I knew from the secondary sources that I had already seen that no T-34s were rampaging behind the 7th Cavalry that night, so I naively assumed that their memories were in some way off. Perhaps over the years, I thought, some stories had become crossed. I knew that the 7th faced tanks a few days later, and perhaps over the years of reunions, somebody's account of that action had been crossed with the memories of the first night. Still, the details that many had about that event did not match the normal profile I had come to expect when uncovering modified memories.

When I later read Lieutenant Colonel Heyer's radio message sent through regimental headquarters to division headquarters, that a section of tanks had just blasted through the battalion's position, I thought I knew the source for the memories, but I was not convinced of its validity. Only during the cross-referencing that I did as the manuscript to this book emerged did I finally make the connection between the unit I have called Team Field and the experiences of the men of 2nd Battalion 7th Cavalry on the night of July 25–26, 1950. This was how many aspects of the story emerged and were subsequently validated.

At the same time, many of the men demonstrated false memories based upon their interaction with Edward Daily. In initial interviews, several remembered Daily in the opening days of the war. Others, however, were adamant that they could not recall him at all prior to their first reunions when he introduced himself. In hindsight, these initial interviews with veterans who suspected Daily was a fraud but had absolutely no evidence first set me to wondering about his role, not only in the 7th Cavalry, but in the creation of the Associated Press's story of No Gun Ri.

Certainly Daily's position, as the president of both the 7th Cavalry Regiment Association and member of the board of directors of the 1st Cavalry Division Association lent him credibility in all those years of reunions.

The fact that he knew more about the history of the 7th Cavalry than any-body else made it appear that he was there. Nobody suspected that his memory was actually based upon his research into such books as Chandler's obscure self-published work *Of Garryowen in Glory* and the archival records at the National Archives. His seeming ability to recall details that many of the veterans had seen during events that were not covered in any of the broader histories of the war gave his memories that extra degree of credibil-ity. Thus, he insinuated himself into so many other veterans' memories that he appeared legitimate to the Associated Press. As Associated Press reporter Charles Hanley put it, "It would be a superhuman hoax—by a man who never knew he'd be challenged in this way—to have constructed such a per-sonal history." What Hanley failed to realize and refused to accept until con-fronted by outside media sources was that this sort of research and memory implantation is actually common among fake combat veterans.

THE SOUTH KOREAN ACCOUNTS

I determined fairly early in my research that analyzing the accounts of the South Koreans as individuals was almost a lost cause. Too many barriers, including those of language, records, and the foibles of fifty-year-old mem-ories, existed for me to make any credible analysis of the South Koreans' accounts in the way that I had with the American veterans of the 7th Cav-alry Regiment.

I determined the first blockage—language—was insurmountable in the time I had available to write this book. I do not speak or read the Korean language, and therefore would have to rely upon others to accurately trans-late and transcribe any materials coming from South Korean sources. This ignorance also extended to my knowledge of South Korean culture. Although during the course of my research I have developed some under-standing of the history and culture of that nation and used some translated sources, I am by no means an expert. The same elements about me that made it possible for me to understand the American soldiers (common her-itage, profession, and similar education) stood in the way of my compre-hension of the South Koreans.

At the same time, I recognized that if the yearly reunions of the 7th Cavalry Association, Korean War Veterans chapter, which have occurred since the mid-1980s, could cause a fusion of some veterans' memories, the South Koreans, many from the same villages, were doubly liable to this con-tamination of their memories. There was also the request for extraordinarily large reparations made by those who claimed to be survivors or relatives of victims. One cannot overlook the fact that the potential for becoming a millionaire may influence the accuracy of a person's memory.

PHOTOGRAPHS, FORENSICS, AND NUMBERS

Finally, the forensic evidence as a source for this book must be considered. Some of this evidence was touched upon in the main body of the text. This was an area that I myself could not investigate, as I did not personally have the resources to look into this and I am not trained in forensics. Since the Republic of Korea Review Team and the United States Review Team both applied resources to this investigation, however, they answered many of the questions dealing with the detritus of battle. In other words, what physical evidence remained that could prove something similar to the South Korean claim of a massacre of 300 to 400 people occurred.

Eun Yong Chung, the former novelist turned representative for the South Korean version of events, clearly stated the South Koreans' position in his original letter to President Clinton. In this claim, he stated that an estimated 100 people were killed in the air attack and 300 more were killed by direct fire under the railroad bridge at No Gun Ri. The question that I had almost immediately upon starting this project was, "Where are the bodies?"

Four hundred human remains do not travel far. In most of the massacres that I have researched, such as those of Fort William Henry, New York (1757), Wounded Knee (at the Pine Ridge reservation, 1890), Malmedy, Belgium (1944), and My Lai, South Vietnam (1968), the victims are buried in a mass grave, or in some cases their remains are recovered and returned to their families after a large logistic effort. The reconnaissance flight that flew over the area on August 6 and found no sections of railway "bent as if steel chopsticks were bent by a person," as one South Korean witness stated, also failed to find any evidence of a mass grave anywhere in the area. Again, the photographic experts of the United States do not have to be taken at their word. The photos are readily available to anyone who cares to examine them personally at the National Archives or by downloading the images off the Internet from the DAIG report. The flight also captured an image of the overpass from a slight angle, which gave some view under the overpass, roughly eighteen feet inward. Again, not a body is in sight.

Arguably those bodies might have either been recovered by that point, or lain underneath the overpass out of sight, but that was not the South Koreans' testimony when they first talked about this story. They referred to many people being killed as they tried to leave the underpass, yet again, no bodies appear in the photographic record. Some accounts (including the North Korean version) state that the North Koreans buried the victims in a mass grave right there at the site. Nobody has found this grave because it does not exist, not in contemporary photographs and not in present day investigations.

This suggests that the number of casualties is grossly inflated by the claimants, either due to their sincere belief that 400 died, or for other reasons. If there was not one mass grave, then 400 or even 100 individual graves would have shown up clearly in the photographs that were taken with a high enough resolution that individual fighting positions in the area showed up, as well as the dirt marks kicked up where strafing occurred.

Then there was the issue of bullets. Discounting the difficulty in deciding which chips in a cement wall came from the impact of bullets and which ones were the result of the natural spalling of ice over the course of sixty winters, bullet casings and fragments should exist. In fact, if the South Korean version of events had taken place, 5,000 to 10,000 bullet marks should be found on the walls. The Browning water-cooled machine gun has a high rate of fire, and this is not an unreasonable number of bullets given the South Korean version. According to the South Korean claimants' testimony, at least two of these machine guns fired directly into the tunnel for several hours in addition to the dozens of rifles fired by American soldiers. This fire allegedly continued sporadically over the course of three more days of supposedly deliberate slaughter. Unfortunately, one of the walls of the underpass—the one most likely to be hit by incoming fire based upon the location of the American troops in the area—was covered in cement in what South Korean railroad officials called routine maintenance just a few weeks before the AP story came out. On the off side of the underpass, the South Korean investigative team categorized 316 marks as bullet impacts.[3] This number seemed too low by several orders of magnitude to support the South Korean civilian claims. If the South Korean version were true, even the off side of the underpass should have had thousands of bullet marks. But other bullet evidence came to light at the same time.

In early January 2001, the AP reported that the investigation had also discovered Russian-made cartridges near the trestle, cartridges of the type used by South Korean guerillas as well as the North Koreans.[4] Adding the eyewitness testimony of American veterans who say gun fire came from among the refugees, to testimony that at least one soldier found a Russian submachine gun among the refugees, to the documentary evidence that one Russian submachine gun was turned in to supply channels soon after this, to the evidence that Russian-made bullet casings were found near the underpass, and one can reasonably draw the conclusions that I have in this book, that there were communist guerilla infiltrators among the refugees. If there are other conclusions to be drawn from this evidence, I do not know what they could be.

True, limited fighting occurred in this area when U.S. forces swept back through, counterattacking out of the Pusan perimeter in the fall of

1950. It cannot, therefore, be determined exactly when these Russian-made cartridges were discharged, but that would open the door to the possibility that the bullet marks under the bridge (from which twenty-nine American bullet fragments were removed) were created at that same time.

After evaluating all of this information, I concluded that the most likely scenario was that which I presented in chapter six.

United States No Gun Ri Review January 2001

EXECUTIVE SUMMARY★

INTRODUCTION

Following the release of the Associated Press story concerning the matter on September 29, 1999, the United States (U.S.) and the Republic of Korea (ROK) initiated independent, but cooperative, reviews of the incident at No Gun Ri. This story brought to the forefront the earlier efforts of Korean citizens to secure an official inquiry into their claims surrounding certain events that occurred in the vicinity of No Gun Ri, including the firing upon Korean refugees at the double railroad overpass and an air strike on the railroad track.

Over the last year, the U.S. Review Team has conducted an exhaustive factual review by examining over a million documents from the National Archives, conducting interviews with approximately 200 American witnesses, and analyzing the interview transcripts and oral statements of approximately 75 Korean witnesses. The U.S. Review Team also closely examined press reports, aerial imagery, and other forensic examination results. This U.S. Report reflects the U.S. Review Team's factual findings based upon all the evidence available on the incident.

Unfortunately, the passage of 50 years greatly reduces the possibility that we will ever know all of the facts surrounding this particular event. A large number of factors, including but not limited to trauma, age, and the media,

---

★This is the complete Executive Summary of the U.S. Government's report of its investigation of the incident at No Gun Ri.

influenced the recollection of Korean and U.S. witnesses. By comparing and contrasting all of these available information sources, the U.S. Review Team has developed a clearer picture of the events that occurred in the vicinity of No Gun Ri in July 1950. The findings of the U.S. Review Team have been organized into several key issues, which describe the Team's conclusions regarding what occurred at No Gun Ri based upon all the information available half a century later.

I. Background—The Korean Account

The Korean villagers stated that on July 25, 1950, U.S. soldiers evacuated approximately 500 to 600 villagers from their homes in Im Gae Ri and Joo Gok Ri. The villagers said the U.S. soldiers escorted them towards the south. Later that evening, the American soldiers led the villagers near a riverbank at Ha Ga Ri and ordered them to stay there that night. During the night, the villagers witnessed a long parade of U.S. troops and vehicles moving towards Pusan.

On the morning of July 26, 1950, the villagers continued south along the Seoul-Pusan road. According to their statements, when the villagers reached the vicinity of No Gun Ri, U.S. soldiers stopped them at a road-block and ordered the group onto the railroad tracks, where the soldiers searched them and their personal belongings. The Koreans state that, although the soldiers found no prohibited items (such as weapons or other military contraband), the soldiers ordered an air attack upon the villagers via radio communications with U.S. aircraft. Shortly afterwards, planes flew over and dropped bombs and fired machine guns, killing approximately 100 villagers on the railroad tracks. Those villagers who survived sought protection in a small culvert underneath the railroad tracks. The U.S. soldiers drove the villagers out of the culvert and into the larger double tunnels nearby (this report subsequently refers to these tunnels as the "double rail-road overpass"). The Koreans state that the U.S. soldiers then fired into both ends of the tunnels over a period of four days (July 26–29, 1950), resulting in approximately 300 additional deaths.

II. Department of Defense Review Directives

On September 30, 1999, the Secretary of Defense directed the Secretary of the Army to lead a review to determine "the full scope of the facts sur-rounding these [No Gun Ri] press reports." On October 25, 1999, the Secretary of the Army directed The Inspector General to conduct a thor-ough review of the allegations, pursue every reasonable lead to determine the facts, and then prepare and submit a report of the findings with regard to the allegations.

The Office of the Secretary of Defense established a Steering Group chaired by the Under Secretary of Defense (Personnel and Readiness) to oversee the conduct of the review. In addition, the Secretary of Defense invited eight distinguished Americans, who are not affiliated with the Department of Defense, to advise on the conduct of the review based upon their expertise in academia, journalism, the Korean War, and U.S.–ROK relations.

III. Department of the Army Inspector General Review Effort

The Inspector General developed a four-phase concept plan: Preparation; Research and Interviews; Review and Analysis; and Production of the Final Report. The Inspector General then formed the No Gun Ri Review Team (U.S. Review Team) into a Research Team and an Interview Team. The research effort, led by an Army historian, began in October 1999. The Research Team consisted of Department of the Army military and civilian members augmented by a United States Air Force research team, an imagery analyst, a Korean linguist, and professional research assistants from the U.S. Army Corps of Engineers. The researchers examined over one million pages of text from the National Archives and other repositories and approximately 45,000 containers of United States Air Force reconnaissance film.

The interview process started on December 29, 1999, after the Interview Team located former soldiers assigned to the major combat units that passed through the Yongdong–Hwanggan area in mid- to late July 1950. The Interview Team and Air Force researchers culled through over 7,375 names to locate and interview approximately 200 U.S. veterans. While every effort was made to make this a comprehensive sample, the U.S. Review Team had no power to compel a witness to grant an interview and no authority to issue subpoenas or to grant immunity. In fact, eleven veterans contacted by the U.S. Review Team declined to be interviewed. The U.S. Review Team did review, however, the published accounts of some witnesses who declined to be interviewed by the Team.

IV. U.S. and ROK Cooperation

The Department of the Army and the Department of Defense worked in close cooperation with the representatives of the government of the Republic of Korea who were conducting a parallel review of the allegations. Members from the U.S. Review Team, the Republic of Korea Investigation Team (ROK Review Team), and government officials from both countries met on approximately a dozen occasions in both the United States and Korea, to include the Secretary of the Army's meetings with President Kim Dae-Jung and Minister of National Defense Cho Song-Tae in January 2000. The U.S. Review Team provided the ROK Review Team with copies of all relevant documents and other information discovered in the course of the review in support of the ROK's parallel investigation. On two occasions, the U.S. Review Team supported working visits by a ROK Review Team researcher to the National Archives in College Park, Maryland. The U.S. Review Team provided full access to, and funded the reproduction costs of, any materials already gathered by the U.S. researchers. No information was withheld.

V. Organization of the U.S. Report

The U.S. Review Team conducted this review and prepared this report fully aware of the political, military, and emotional significance of the allegations. This report is not intended as a point-by-point response to the media and Korean accounts. The report presents an independent assessment of the facts derived directly from an exhaustive review of primary and secondary sources, the statements of U.S. veterans and Koreans, ballistic and pathology forensics, and imagery analysis.

The report consists of an Executive Summary, five chapters, and five appendices. Chapter 1 (Introduction) outlines the purpose, background, and overall organization and conduct of the review. Chapter 2 (Background and History) describes the ground events unfolding on the Korean Peninsula in July 1950. Chapter 3 (Combat Operations—July 1950) examines the state of U.S. intelligence and U.S. ground forces in July 1950 and provides a day-by-day account of the tactical operations of the 1st Cavalry Division in the vicinity of No Gun Ri during the last week of July 1950. This chapter also includes research on U.S. and allied air operations in the Yongdong-Hwanggan area for the same time period. Several photographs from 1950 are inserted between Chapters 2 and 3. Chapter 4 (Analysis of Interview Data) provides the analysis of interviews of American and Korean witnesses. The review of witness statements identifies areas of consensus between statements and outlines possible sequences of events. Finally, Chapter 5 (Key Issue Analysis and Findings) synthesizes the analysis of documentary research and witness interviews into a thorough, fact-based set of findings.

The appendices supplement the material in the main body of the report.

Appendix A (Research Methodology) documents in detail the methodology used in the research of the historical records. Appendix B (Forensic Evidence) provides an analysis of the forensic evidence associated with the No Gun Ri site. This appendix discusses the sources of Korean casualty estimates, analysis of the ballistic evidence collected by Korean authorities, and an analysis of the USAF reconnaissance film taken over the No Gun Ri area on August 6, 1950. Appendix C (Imagery Analysis) contains the analysis of the August 6, 1950, USAF reconnaissance photograph performed by the National Imagery and Mapping Agency (NIMA). This appendix includes the NIMA response to the ROK Investigation Team's questions concerning this analysis. Appendix D (Joint Cooperation) discusses the actions taken to ensure a cooperative and coordinated effort between the ROK and U.S. Review Teams, including joint meetings and the exchange of documents and other information. Appendix E (Supporting Documents) contains explanatory charts and maps.

VI. Findings
Given the challenge of ascertaining facts a half century after their occurrence, the U.S. Review Team made findings when possible, identified possibilities, and noted when the evidence was not sufficient to identify a possibility or reach a finding about what may have occurred at No Gun Ri in July 1950 based upon an analysis of available information. A summary of its factual findings has been organized into several key issues. These issues were identified and developed in coordination with the Office of the Secretary of Defense Steering Group, U.S. outside experts, and counterparts from the Republic of Korea.

A. Key Issue 1: Condition of U.S. Forces in July 1950
Background. U.S. soldiers were young, under-trained, under-equipped, and unprepared for the fight they would wage against the North Korean People's Army (NKPA). The soldiers of the Army of Occupation in Japan functioned primarily as a constabulary in a conquered land and not as combat-ready warfighters.

Their lack of combat preparedness was a direct result of deficiencies in training, equipment, structure, personnel strength, and leadership. Proper training areas were not available to conduct more than small-unit training. Classes for critical specialties such as maintenance and communications were also inadequate. Most of their equipment, including ammunition, was of World War II vintage, and had been poorly stored and maintained. The three infantry regiments in the 1st Cavalry Division had only two of the three battalions normally assigned. Likewise, each regiment lacked its authorized tank company, and the division artillery battalions contained only two of the normal three firing batteries. In response to a requirement to bring the 24th Infantry Division up to strength prior to that division's departure for Korea, the 1st Cavalry Division transferred nearly 800 men, most of them from the top four senior non-commissioned officer grades, to the 24th. This loss of non-commissioned officers with whom the soldiers had trained weakened the cohesion of the division and significantly reduced the number of leaders with combat experience at the small-unit level.

Finding. Based on the documentary evidence, as well as the statements by U.S. veterans, the U.S. Review Team concluded that most American units and soldiers were not adequately prepared for the combat conditions that they confronted in Korea in June and July 1950. No experience or training equipped them to deal with an aggressive enemy that employed both conventional and guerilla warfare tactics or with a large refugee population, which the enemy was known to have infiltrated. Shortages of experienced non-commissioned officers, along with inadequate equipment and doctrine, made it difficult for individuals or units to adapt to these conditions.

B. Key Issue 2: U.S. and ROK Refugee Control Policies

Background. The U.S. troops were completely unprepared for the stark reality of dealing with the numerous, uncontrolled refugees who clogged the roads and complicated the battlefield to an unexpected degree. Early on in the war, U.S. forces encountered the NKPA practice of infiltrating soldiers dressed as civilians among large refugee concentrations. Once behind American lines, these infiltrated soldiers would then conduct guerilla-style combat operations against American rear-area units and activities.

In late July 1950, the ROK government and the Eighth U.S. Army Headquarters issued refugee control policies to protect the U.S. and ROK forces from NKPA infiltration and attacks from the rear. Additionally, these policies were aimed at reducing the adverse impact of large refugee concentrations on main supply routes, which stymied the U.S. and UN troops' ability to rush ammunition forward and evacuate casualties to the rear. These U.S. and ROK refugee policies depended heavily upon the constant presence of, and coordination with, the ROK National Police to handle the uncontrolled refugee population.

Despite comments attributed to Major General Gay, the 1st Cavalry Division Commander, that he would not employ the Korean National Police in his division's area of operations, his refugee policy directive of July 23, 1950, made the National Police responsible for handling refugees. The movement of civilians and refugees in the 1st Cavalry Division area was restricted to specific hours and for specific purposes by a limited number of people, and the National Police were responsible for enforcing the policy.

On July 26, 1950, the Eighth U.S. Army Korea (EUSAK), in coordination with the ROK government, established and disseminated a plan to control refugee movement which:

— precluded movement of refugees across battle lines at all times, prohibited evacuation of villages without general officer approval, and established a National Police responsibility,

— prescribed procedures for Korean National Police to clear desired areas and routes,

— strictly precluded Korean civilian movement during the hours of darkness, and

— established requirements for disseminating the policy.

The Eighth Army's policy was intended to deny the NKPA their widely used infiltration tactic while also safeguarding civilians by prohibiting refugees from crossing <u>battle lines</u> (battle lines are the areas where there is contact with the enemy or contact is about to occur). The policy did not state that refugees could not cross <u>friendly lines</u> and contains instructions for the handling of refugees in friendly areas (friendly lines are the forward troop positions not in contact with the enemy). The policy emphasized the Korean government's responsibility for the control and screening of refugees to provide for their welfare. Nothing in this policy was intended to put refugees at risk.

Most veterans from the 7th Cavalry Regiment interviewed by the U.S. Review Team were enlisted men during the Korean War and did not receive copies of policies from higher headquarters. In general, most U.S. veterans remembered warnings that there were North Korean infiltrators among the refugees. The veterans who remembered more specific details about refugee control remembered specific actions to be taken; for example, keep refugees off the roads, do not let refugees pass, or search refugees and let them pass.

Finding. From its study of the refugee control policies in effect during the last week of July 1950, the U.S. Review Team found that the Eighth U.S. Army published, in coordination with the ROK government, refugee control policies that reflected two predominant concerns: (1) protecting U.S. and ROK troops from the danger of NKPA soldiers infiltrating U.S.–ROK lines; and (2) precluding uncontrolled refugee movements from impeding flows of supplies and troops. The published 1st Cavalry Division refugee control policy dated July 23, 1950, reflected the same two concerns. The task of keeping innocent civilians out of harm's way was left entirely to ROK authorities. By implication, these policies also protected refugees by attempting to ensure they were not in harm's way.

C. Key Issue 3: Tactical Situation July 22–29, 1950

Background. The 1st Cavalry Division relieved the 24th Infantry Division northwest of Yongdong on July 22, 1950. The 7th Cavalry Regiment of the 1st Cavalry Division arrived in Pohangdong, Korea, on July 22, 1950, and the 2nd Battalion, 7th Cavalry Regiment, moved forward to the Yongdong area. With friendly forces outnumbered by the NKPA, the Eighth Army developed a strategy to withdraw behind the last defensible terrain feature, the Naktong River. As events developed, the 1st Cavalry Division withdrew from Yongdong through a series of delaying actions in accordance with the Eighth Army strategy and to avoid a threatened envelopment. On the evening of July 25, 1950, the 7th Cavalry Regiment was supporting the 5th Cavalry Regiment in positions east of Yongdong.

Sometime during the night of July 25, the 7th Cavalry received a report that a breakthrough had occurred in the sector to the 7th Cavalry Regiment's north.

Finding. The U.S. Review Team found that, in the early morning hours of July 26, 1950, the 2nd Battalion of the 7th Cavalry Regiment, without specific orders but believing they were being enveloped, conducted a disorganized and undisciplined withdrawal from a position east of Yongdong to the vicinity of No Gun Ri. They spent the remaining hours of July 26 until late into that night recovering abandoned personnel and equipment from the area where the air strike and machine-gun firing on Korean refugees is alleged to have occurred. On July 26, 1950, at 9:30 at night, 119 men were still unaccounted for. It will probably never be possible to reconstruct the activities of the scattered soldiers of the 2nd Battalion.

The U.S. Review Team determined that the 1st Battalion, 7th Cavalry Regiment, arrived in the vicinity of No Gun Ri in the afternoon of July 26, 1950. They relieved the 2nd Battalion, 5th Cavalry Regiment, and established their position east of the 2nd Battalion, 7th Cavalry Regiment.

The U.S. Review Team found that there was repeated contact reported between the 7th Cavalry and enemy forces in the vicinity of No Gun Ri on July 27 and July 28. The records indicate by this time that the 7th Cavalry had been told that there were no friendly forces to the west and south of No Gun Ri (i.e. back toward Yongdong). The 2nd Battalion, 7th Cavalry, reported an enemy column on the railroad tracks on July 27, which they fired upon. On July 29, the battalion withdrew as the NKPA advanced.

The U.S. Review Team concluded that based on the available evidence, the 7th Cavalry Regiment was under attack, as they believed, between July 27 and July 29, 1950, when in position near No Gun Ri.

D. Key Issue 4: Assembly and Movement of Villagers

Background. The U.S. and ROK policy in July 1950 stated generally that Korean civilians should not evacuate their villages. The U.S. Review Team could not determine the reasons why the refugees gathered in Im Gae Ri, but this gathering of refugees was probably not the result of any U.S. action. Some witnesses stated that the Americans told them that they were being moved for their safety. Some U.S. veterans remember escorting refugees from villages, but these veterans cannot remember the villages' names or the dates the evacuations occurred. Therefore, the U.S. Review Team cannot rule out the possibility that U.S. soldiers told the villagers at Im Gae Ri to evacuate the village.

While the U.S. Review Team cannot rule out the possibility that the villagers were moved, there was no sound military reason for soldiers to travel approximately three miles off their designated movement route to the village of Im Gae Ri during a hasty withdrawal for the purpose of encouraging an additional 400 refugees onto the already crowded roads and further aggravating the congested conditions. It is also unlikely that the soldiers would have performed this evacuation given the widespread knowledge and fear of North Korean infiltrators believed to be present in refugee concentrations.

Some 7th Cavalry Regiment veterans recalled displacing South Koreans from unknown villages on unknown dates. The U.S. Review Team found that the 7th Cavalry Regiment was not in the vicinity of Im Gae Ri on July 25 based upon official records of the Regiment's positions. Some veterans of the 5th Cavalry Regiment indicated that they evacuated or escorted Korean civilians from unknown villages in late July and early August 1950. A patrol from the 5th Cavalry Regiment may have told the villagers who had assembled at Im Gae Ri to leave.

Finding. The U.S. Review Team could not determine the reasons why the refugees gathered in Im Gae Ri, but the U.S. Review Team concluded that this gathering of refugees was probably not the result of U.S. action. Based on some of the available evidence, the U.S. Review Team cannot rule out the possibility that U.S. soldiers told the villagers at Im Gae Ri to evacuate the village, but the soldiers who did so were not from the 7th Cavalry Regiment.

E. Key Issue 5: Air Strikes in the Vicinity of No Gun Ri

Background. Korean witnesses describe an air strike/strafing around noon on July 26, 1950 on the railroad tracks. The Korean witnesses describe the effects of machine gun fire and explosions.

The U.S. Review Team could not locate any records to substantiate the occurrence of an air strike/strafing incident in the vicinity of No Gun Ri around noon on July 26, 1950. While there are mission reports for July 26, 1950, that could not be located, the missions can be accounted for through other reports. The only documented USAF air strike in the immediate vicinity of the Hwanggan area occurred southwest of No Gun Ri on July 27. This air strike was a friendly fire incident in which a F-80 accidentally strafed the 1st Battalion, 7th Cavalry Regiment's command post at 7:15 in the morning. The strafing destroyed two U.S. trucks but claimed no lives.

The friendly strike on the 1st Battalion, 7th Cavalry Regiment, caused the 7th Cavalry Regimental Commander to request immediately that he be assigned a Tactical Air Control Party in order to control aircraft in his area and thereby preclude further friendly-fire incidents. Only a Tactical Air Control Party (TACP) with a jeep-mounted AN/VRC-1 radio could talk to the Air Force elements, including the strike aircraft. There was only one TACP operating in support of the 1st Cavalry Division during this period of time. This TACP was not located in the vicinity of No Gun Ri during the period of July 26 to July 29, 1950. Ordinary soldiers could not communicate on their radios with aircraft. Although it was possible for the Army to request an air strike from the Air Force, the process was cumbersome and took considerable time because the request had to be processed through Army and Air Force channels.

No U.S. Air Force veteran that the U.S. Review Team interviewed participated in, or had any knowledge of anyone participating in, the strafing of civilians in the vicinity of No Gun Ri in late July 1950. U.S. Air Force interviewees vividly recalled stern verbal policies implemented to prevent the attack of non–combatants.

The Navy discovered no evidence of naval aircraft operating in the vicinity of No Gun Ri on July 26 or 27. However, on July 28, Navy aircraft from the USS Valley Forge were directed into the area and attacked a railroad tunnel occupied by enemy troops and other targets forward of the 7th Cavalry in the direction of Yongdong with bombs and machine guns.

The Defense Intelligence Agency found 8th Tactical Reconnaissance Squadron photographs of the No Gun Ri area dated August 6 and September 19, 1950. The Air Force Team showed these photographs to four retired photo interpreters of national reputation, all of whom agree that the photographs show no signs of bombing or strafing on the railroad tracks. A NIMA photo interpreter maintains that some patterns near the tracks approximately 350 yards from the double railroad overpass show "an imagery signature of probable strafing" but no bomb damage. The location of the probable strafing is in the same relative location identified by the Korean witnesses as that location where they were strafed.

Finding. An exhaustive search of U.S. Air Force and U.S. Navy records and interviews with U.S. pilots did not identify an air strike in the No Gun Ri area on July 26, 1950. The number of Korean witness statements describing the strafing and the photograph interpretation by NIMA does not permit the U.S. Review Team to exclude the possibility that U.S. or allied aircraft might have hit civilian refugees in the vicinity of No Gun Ri during an air strike/strafing on July 26, 1950. On July 27, 1950, an air strike did in fact occur on the 1st Battalion, 7th Cavalry's position near No Gun Ri that both the Air Force and Army recorded in official documents. On July 28, there was also an air strike on NKPA forces near 1st Battalion, 7th Cavalry Regiment. Assuming Korean civilians were near the positions of these strikes, they could have been injured.

The U.S. Review Team concluded that strafing may have occurred near No Gun Ri in the last week of July 1950 and could have injured or killed Korean civilians but that any such air strikes were not deliberate attacks on Korean civilians. The U.S. Review Team concluded that any air strikes/strafing occurring on July 26 took place under the same conditions as the air strikes/strafing on July 27, specifically an accidental air strike/strafing caused by the misidentification of targets and not a pre-planned strike.

An accidental air strike/strafing could have happened due to several factors: target misidentification, lack of reliable communications, absence of a Tactical Air Control Party in the 7th Regiment, and the fluid nature of the battlefield. It was not a pre-planned strike on civilian refugees.

F. Key Issue 6: Ground Fire in the Vicinity of No Gun Ri

Background. Some U.S. and Korean witness statements indicate that U.S. ground forces fired toward refugees in the vicinity of No Gun Ri during the period July 26–29, 1950, as discussed below. According to the Korean description of the events on July 26, 1950, refugees were strafed or bombed on the railroad tracks. Some fled the area or hid in ditches and others went into the double railroad overpass tunnel where they were fired upon from different locations for a period of up to four days, with the heaviest fire occurring on July 26 (which was the first day they report spending in the double railroad overpass).

In interviews, some U.S. veterans stated they saw or heard firing of various types including machine-gun, mortar, artillery, and rifle fire, near unidentified individuals in civilian clothing outside the tunnels/bridges in the vicinity of No Gun Ri. Only a few veterans interviewed by the U.S.

Review Team stated they fired toward civilians in the vicinity of No Gun Ri. Two veterans fired over the heads of or into the ground in front to keep the civilians pinned down or to prevent them from moving. Several other veterans stated they either received hostile fire from, or saw hostile fire coming from, the civilian positions in the double railroad overpass and elsewhere. They also stated that they returned fire, or observed fire being returned, on the civilian positions as a response to the hostile fire they received or observed. Some veterans also remember intermittent NKPA and U.S. artillery and mortar fires.

Official records indicate that the NKPA attacked the 7th Cavalry on July 27 and 28, and the 7th Cavalry employed every means at its disposal to defend itself, including the use of small-arms fire, mortars, and artillery.

Finding. Although the U.S. Review Team cannot determine what happened near No Gun Ri with certainty, it is clear, based upon all available evidence, that an unknown number of Korean civilians were killed or injured by the effects of small-arms fire, artillery and mortar fire, and strafing that preceded or coincided with the NKPA's advance and the withdrawal of U.S. forces in the vicinity of No Gun Ri during the last week of July 1950. These Korean deaths and injuries occurred at different locations in the vicinity of No Gun Ri and were not concentrated exclusively at the double railroad overpass.

Some U.S. veterans describe fire that lasted for a few to 60 minutes. Some Korean witnesses describe fire day and night on the tunnel for as long as four days.

Because Korean estimates of the length of time they spent in the tunnel are so inconsistent, the U.S. Review Team drew no conclusion about the amount of time they spent in the tunnel.

The firing was a result of hostile fire seen or received from civilian positions or fire directed over their heads or near them to control their movement. The deaths and injuries of civilians, wherever they occurred, were an unfortunate tragedy inherent to war and not a deliberate killing.

G. Key Issue 7: Issuance of Orders to Fire on Refugees

Background. To determine if soldiers or pilots were issued orders to attack and fire on refugees in the vicinity of No Gun Ri, the Review Team reviewed documents and conducted interviews with Army and Air Force veterans. Based upon the available evidence, which included the statements of veterans, documents, and the absence of documents, the U.S. Review Team concluded that U.S. commanders did not issue oral or written orders to fire on refugees in the vicinity of No Gun Ri between July 25 and 29, 1950.

Pilots were not ordered to attack and kill civilian refugees in the vicinity of No Gun Ri. Air strikes in the vicinity of No Gun Ri on July 26 were either the result of a misidentification of a target or an accident as discussed above. No USAF veteran that the U.S. Review Team interviewed participated in, or had any knowledge of anyone participating in, the strafing of civilians in the vicinity of No Gun Ri in late July 1950.

U.S. Air Force interviewees vividly recalled stern verbal policies implemented to prevent the attack of non-combatants. In interviews, pilots stated that they sought out targets such as tanks, trucks, moving troops, and groups of men in uniform. Pilots fired when they were told a target was hostile and fired back when fired upon.

The U.S. Review Team found two documents that refer to an unknown Army request to the Air Force and the Navy to strafe civilian or refugee columns. The first reference is in a memorandum by COL T. C. Rogers, Fifth Air Force ADVON (Korea), dated 25 July 1950. The second reference is a Naval Activity Summary for the same date from the Aircraft Carrier *Valley Forge*. The U.S. Review Team could not find any originating request from the Army that prompted these two references. The Rogers' memorandum actually recommends that civilians not be attacked unless they are definitely known to be North Korean soldiers or have committed hostile acts. The Navy document stated that the first pass over personnel would be a non-firing run to identify if civilians were present. If the target was determined to be hostile, a firing run would follow.

Soldiers were not ordered to attack and kill civilian refugees in the vicinity of No Gun Ri. The veterans interviewed said that deadly force was not authorized against civilian refugees who posed no threat to the unit, and they were not given orders to shoot and kill civilian refugees in the vicinity of No Gun Ri. However, the U.S. Review Team found that soldiers who were in the vicinity of No Gun Ri were given an order to stop civilians and not to let them pass their position. Some soldiers did believe if civilian refugees did not stop, they could use deadly force to prevent them from passing.

Several other veterans stated they observed firing at the civilians in response to perceived hostile fire from the positions near the double railroad overpass and elsewhere. Based on veterans' interviews, the U.S. Review Team found that soldiers believed that they could take action in self-defense against civilians; that is, if they were fired upon or if they saw actions that indicated hostile intent. Some veterans said they observed firing in the direction of the double railroad overpass in response to fire from that location. Return fire in this case would have been an action in self-defense, and no orders were required. Two veterans fired over the heads of civilians, or into the ground in front to keep the civilians pinned down or prevent them from moving. The U.S. soldiers were repeatedly warned that North Korean soldiers wore civilian clothing over their uniforms in order to infiltrate U.S. positions. The U.S. soldiers were also told that North Korean soldiers would hide within refugee columns.

In interviews with the U.S. Review Team, several veterans stated that they assumed there was an order to fire on civilians because artillery and mortar fires were used that may have hit civilians. These veterans had no information to support their assertions. When interviewed, the veterans said they did not know who gave the order, they did not hear the order, they did not know when the order was given, and they personally did not receive the order. Former officers of the 2nd Battalion, 7th Cavalry Regiment, that the U.S. Review Team interviewed remain adamant that the battalion commander issued no order to fire on refugees at any time.

There are references that appear to authorize firing on Korean civilians in Army records. The first reference was an abbreviated message that appeared in an 8th Cavalry Regiment message log dated 10:00 A.M. on July 24, 1950, that stated: "No refugees to cross the frontline. Fire everyone trying to cross the lines. Use discretion in case of women and children." The U.S. Review Team found no similar entry in the records of the 1st Cavalry Division, its other two regiments (the 5th and 7th Cavalry Regiments), or in the records of units subordinate to the 8th Cavalry Regiment. The U.S. Review Team found no evidence that the 8th Cavalry message was transmitted to the 5th or 7th Cavalry Regiments or any other subordinate element of the division. In interviews, U.S. veterans in the vicinity of No Gun Ri do not recall instructions to fire on civilian refugees. The 7th Cavalry Regiment was the unit in the vicinity of No Gun Ri on July 26. By July 26, 1950, the last elements of the 8th Cavalry Regiment were withdrawing from the vicinity of No Gun Ri to the division rear near Hwanggan.

The refugee control policy set by the 1st Cavalry Division Commander in his order of July 23, 1950, titled "Control of Refugee Movement" makes no mention of the use of force by soldiers. It stated: "Municipal authorities, local police and the National Police will enforce this directive." The U.S. Review Team concluded that the 8th Cavalry Regiment log entry did not constitute a 1st Cavalry Division order to fire upon Korean civilians at No Gun Ri.

The second reference was a 25th Infantry Division commander's memorandum to commanders issued on July 27, 1950. On July 25, 1950, the 25th ID Activities Report stated: "Refugees and Korean Civilians were ordered out of the combat zone in order to eliminate possible serious traffic problems and to aid in blocking the infiltration of North Korean Forces through the lines. These instructions were passed to the civilians through the Korean Police." The July 27, 1950, memo to commanders reads: "Korean police have been directed to remove all civilians from the area between the blue lines shown on the attached overlay and report the evacuation has been accomplished. All civilians seen in this area are to be considered as enemy and action taken accordingly." The area "between the blue lines" was in front of the 25th Infantry Division's main line of defense, an area about to be occupied by the enemy. Two things are clear: actions had been taken in conjunction with the Korean National Police to clear the civilians out of the danger area, and those actions were intended to ensure that noncombatants would not find themselves in harm's way when the advancing NKPA subsequently made contact along the Division's front. After the area was cleared, anyone caught in civilian clothes and suspected of being an enemy agent was to be turned over to the Counter-Intelligence Corps immediately and not to the Korean Police.

There is nothing to suggest any summary measures were considered against refugees or people dressed like refugees. The 25th Infantry Division was not located in the vicinity of No Gun Ri during the last week of July 1950.

Finding. Based upon the available evidence, and despite some conflicting statements and misunderstandings, the U.S. Review Team concluded that U.S. commanders did not issue oral or written orders to shoot and kill Korean civilians during the last week of July 1950 in the vicinity of No Gun Ri.

A veteran stated that soldiers could have misunderstood the order not to let refugees pass or to stop refugees. Some veterans did believe that if a civilian would not stop, they could use deadly force to prevent civilians from passing.

Some veterans stated that there was an order to shoot civilians at No Gun Ri but had no information to support their assertions. These soldiers did not know who gave the order, did not hear the order, did not know when the order was given, and personally did not receive the order. As a result, the U.S. Review Team concluded that these veterans assumed that an order was given because artillery and mortars were fired. The U.S. Review Team also considered media statements quoting veterans who claimed that an order to shoot Korean civilians was given at No Gun Ri. The U.S. Review Team was unable to confirm these reports because the witnesses either were not at No Gun Ri at the time or refused to speak to the U.S. Army.

Although the U.S. Review Team found four references (entry in the 8th Cavalry Regiment message log, 25th Infantry Division Commander's order, Colonel Rogers' memorandum, and an extract from the U.S. Navy's Aircraft Carrier *Valley Forge* Activity Summary) discussing actions against civilians, it did not find evidence of an order given to soldiers by a U.S. commander, orally or in writing, to kill Korean civilians in the vicinity of No Gun Ri in the last week of July 1950.

H. Key Issue 8: Number of Korean Deaths and Injuries

Background. After taking the statements of U.S. veterans and securing the professional evaluation of the August 6, 1950, aerial reconnaissance photograph by the National Imagery and Mapping Agency and the Armed Forces Institute of Pathology, the U.S. Review Team asked the ROK Review Team to provide information on the number of casualties. The U.S. Review Team's research revealed no official records of refugee deaths or injuries in the vicinity of No Gun Ri between July 26 and July 29, 1950.

The initial Associated Press articles reported hundreds of people killed. Korean witness estimates range between 60–100 dead in the double tunnel and 50–150 dead or injured from strafing/bombing. Several U.S. veterans describe a lower number of dead or injured civilians. The soldiers did not check the areas where civilians came under fire to determine whether there were dead bodies, and some estimates appear to be guesswork or to be based on recollections not related to No Gun Ri.

At three different meetings, ROK officials reported an unverified number of 248 casualties, which they stated was provided to them by the Yongdong County Office. But the ROK Review Team acknowledges that the estimated figure of 248 is not considered factual and will have to be substantiated by an additional investigation at some future date by the ROK government.

Finding. Based on the available evidence, the U.S. Review Team is unable to determine the number of Korean civilians who were killed or injured in the vicinity of No Gun Ri. During their investigation, the ROK Review Team reported that the Korean survivors' organization claimed an unverified number of 248 South Korean civilians killed, injured, or missing in the vicinity of No Gun Ri between July 25 and 29, 1950. This report was recorded by the Yongdong County Office. The ROK Steering Group, at a ROK–U.S. Steering Group meeting on December 6–7, 2000, in Seoul, ROK, reiterated the claim of 248 casualties.

The actual number of Korean casualties cannot be derived from the U.S. veteran statements and Korean witness statements. The U.S. Team believes that number to be lower than the Korean claim. An aerial reconnaissance photograph of the No Gun Ri area taken on August 6, 1950, shows no indication of human remains or mass graves in the vicinity of the

No Gun Ri double railroad overpass. Korean burial customs, farming in the area, lack of reliable information, wartime disruptions of the country-side, and the passage of time preclude an accurate determination of the numbers involved.

CONCLUSION

During late July 1950, Korean civilians were caught between withdrawing U.S. forces and attacking enemy forces. As a result of U.S. actions during the Korean War in the last week of July 1950, Korean civilians were killed and injured in the vicinity of No Gun Ri. The U.S. Review Team did not find that the Korean deaths and injuries occurred exactly as described in the Korean account. To appraise these events, it is necessary to recall the circumstances of the period. U.S. forces on occupation duty in Japan, mostly without training for, or experience in, combat were suddenly ordered to join ROK forces in defending against a determined assault by well-armed and well-trained NKPA forces employing both conventional and guerilla warfare tactics. The U.S. troops had to give up position after position. In the week beginning July 25, 1950, the 1st Cavalry Division, withdrawing from Yongdong toward the Naktong River, passed through the vicinity of No Gun Ri. Earlier, roads and trails in South Korea had been choked with civilians fleeing south. Disguised NKPA soldiers had mingled with these refugees. U.S. and ROK commanders had published a policy designed to limit the threat from NKPA infiltrators, to protect U.S. forces from attacks from the rear, and to prevent civilians from interfering with the flow of supplies and troops. The ROK National Police were sup-posed to control and strictly limit the movements of innocent refugees.

In these circumstances, especially given the fact that many of the U.S. soldiers lacked combat-experienced officers and non-commissioned offi-cers, some soldiers may have fired out of fear in response to a perceived enemy threat without considering the possibility that they might be firing on Korean civilians.

Neither the documentary evidence nor the U.S. veterans' statements reviewed by the U.S. Review Team support a hypothesis of deliberate killing of Korean civilians.

What befell civilians in the vicinity of No Gun Ri in late July 1950 was a tragic and deeply regrettable accompaniment to a war forced upon unprepared U.S. and ROK forces.

NOTES

INTRODUCTION

1. Leading the charge was an editorial in *The Wall Street Journal* titled, "Civilians' Deaths in Korea Aren't News" by Stanley Weintraub. *The Washington Post* reporter Michael Dobbs, who had himself been fooled by one of the fake veterans, suggested that the AP be allowed to keep its Pulitzer Prize. However, Dobbs noted that the whole controversy illustrated the dangers of journalists dabbling in history in his essay "War and Remembrance," *The Washington Post*, (Sunday, May 21, 2000), pg. B01. In a rare occurrence of the two competing Washington papers agreeing on anything, Diana West of *The Washington Times* lambasted the Associated Press for its sloppy journalism in "The Fog of Reporting," *The Washington Times*, (Thursday, June 2, 2000).

2. Ronald Spector, "Military History and the Academic World," *A Guide to the Study and Use of Military History*, (Washington, D.C.: Center for Military History, 1988), pg. 432.

3. Thomas Greiss, "A Perspective on Military History," *A Guide to the Study and Use of Military History*, (Washington, D. C.: Center for Military History, 1988), pg. 27.

4. Ibid. Greiss suggested his own categories as well: operational, administrative and technical, and the military and society.

5. Although the insights Shay derives from his work with the Veterans Administration may be valid, the evidence he used may well be tainted. In the groundbreaking work *Stolen Valor*, authors B. G. Burkett and Glenna Whitley expose many of the so-called "veterans" of Shay's study as potential frauds.

6. For a more detailed treatment on the division of types of military history, see Allan R. Millett, "American Military History: Clio and Mars as 'Pards'," in David A. Charters, Marc Milner, and J. Brent Wilson, ed., *Military History and the Military Profession*, (Westport, CT: Praeger, 1992). Millett has written extensively on the state of the art of military history since the 1970s. See also "American Military History: Over the Top" in Herbert J. Bass, ed., *The State of American History*, (Chicago: Quadrangle, 1970), pgs. 157–182, and his 1975 International Commission for Military History conference paper, "American Military History: Struggling Through the Wire." Millet suggests that there are five distinct types of military history: antiquarian, patriotic, humanistic, military-utilitarian, and civilian-utilitarian. The reader should be aware of all of these types to critically evaluate the history presented here.

PART I: THE HISTORY
Chapter 1: War Clouds Gathering

1. Some historians such as Russell Weigley argue that even in the Second World War the United States had been conditioned by a tradition of total war dating back to the strategic legacy of the American Civil War. Weigley makes this clearest in his book *The American Way of War* in which he argues that it was the heritage of General U. S. Grant that guided American strategic and operational decision making, and not the more protracted experiences of the U.S. Army upon the frontiers of the American West. Thus, while a lesson of military history in the forty-odd years of warfare against Native Americans (1850–1890, in my opinion) was available to study, the United States did not make use of these experiences.

2. Allan R. Millett and Peter Maslowski, *For the Common Defense*, (New York, NY: The Free Press, 1984), pg. 507.

3. Harry S. Truman, speech, March 12, 1947. The full transcript of this and many other presidential speeches can be found at Texas A&M's Web site run by the Center for Presidential Studies and Department of Speech Communications. The university archives many key presidential addresses and analyzes the rhetoric as well. See *http://www.tamu.edu/scom/pres/speeches/hstaid.html.*

4. The unstated caveat to this concept obviously lay in the definition of "free peoples." For the purposes of most U.S. foreign policy for the rest of the Cold War, "free peoples" might more accurately be described as "any government demonstrably not communist." This too was a concession to the facts of *realpolitik* American style.

5. Dean Rusk, *As I Saw It*, by Dean Rusk as told to Richard Rusk, Daniel S. Papp, ed. (New York: W. W. Norton and Company, 1990), pg. 124. Rusk continued, "SWINK accepted it without too much haggling, and surprisingly, so did the Soviets. I had thought they might insist on a line farther south in view of our respective military positions. No one present at our meeting, including two young American colonels, was aware that at the turn of the century the Russians and Japanese had discussed spheres of influence in Korea, divided along the thirty-eighth parallel. Had we known that, we almost surely would have chosen another line of demarcation." The lessons of history, specifically military and diplomatic history, were lost once again on the civilian leaders of the United States.

6. Sergei N. Goncharov, John W. Lewis, Xue Litai, *Uncertain Partners: Stalin, Mao, and the Korean War*, (Stanford, CA: Stanford University Press, 1993), pgs.131–132.

7. Raymond Pearson, *The Rise and Fall of the Soviet Empire*, (New York: St. Martin's Press, 1998), pg. 91.

8. Among those who graduated or got commissions at about the same time as Nist are several well known to those with even a passing knowledge of American military history. One of Nist's year-group peers (although not a classmate), William Dean, commanded the 44th Infantry Division in WWII. In 1950, Dean was commanding the 24th Infantry Division and would win the Medal of Honor for his defense of Taejon. Others such as Maxwell Taylor (USMA '22 and commander of the 101st Airborne in WWII) would go on to even higher positions. See *Register of Graduates and Former Cadets, United States Military Academy*, 1995. (Hereafter *USMA Register*.) See also *The Howitzer, 1923* (this is the privately published yearbook of the United States Military Academy) and *General Cullum's Biographical Register of the Officers and Graduates of the U.S. Military Academy at West Point*, Supplemental Volume VII, William H. Donaldson, ed. (Chicago, IL: The Lakeside Press, 1930), pg. 1773.

9. Nist's thoughts appeared in the diplomat H. Merrell Benninghoff's report to the State Department, September 15, 1950, in *Foreign Relations of the United States* (Hereafter *FRUS*) (1945), Vol. 6, pgs. 1049–1053, as quoted in Bruce Cumings, *Korea's Place in the Sun, A Modern History*, (New York, NY: Norton, 1997), pg. 193. Emphasis mine.

10. Charles J. Hanley, Sang-Hun Choe, and Martha Mendoza, *The Bridge at No Gun Ri, A Hidden Nightmare from the Korean War*, (New York, NY: Henry Holt, 2001), pg. 43.

11. John J. Muccio, "Memorandum of Conversation," February 25, 1949 in *FRUS* (1949), Vol. 7, pgs. 958–959.

12. Bruce Cumings, *The Origins of the Korean War, Volume II, The Roaring of the Cataract, 1947–1950*, (Princeton, NJ: Princeton University Press, 1990), pg. 190. Although written primarily between 1977 and 1987 before significant access to the archives of the Soviet Union, Cumings remains a magnificent source for insights into the origins of the war.

13. Cumings, *Korea's Place in the Sun*, pg. 243.

14. See Charles J. Hanley, Sang-Hun Choe, and Martha Mendoza, *The Bridge at No Gun Ri, A Hidden Nightmare from the Korean War*, pg. 54, for Eun-Yong's participation as a

police lieutenant in the suppression of the Cheju Island rebellion. See Cumings, *Korea's Place in the Sun*, pgs. 220–221, for an account of the suppression of the rebellion by the Rhee government. Cumings notes that the Cheju governor told U.S. intelligence that the actual number killed by the national police and army was closer to 60,000, not "just" 30,000.

15. Walter Sullivan, "U.S. Movies Shown in Korean Wilds," *The New York Times*, (Sunday, March 19, 1950), pg. 30. See also *New York Times*, August 2, 1950.
16. Cumings, *Korea's Place in the Sun*, pg. 246. Cumings quotes and relies extensively on American reporter Walter Sullivan of *The New York Times* in describing the nature of the guerilla war in the South.
17. Charles J. Hanley, Sang-Hun Choe, and Martha Mendoza, *The Bridge at No Gun Ri, A Hidden Nightmare from the Korean War*, pgs. 54–55.
18. Cumings, *Origins of the Korean War, Vol. II*, pg. 246. In most of his works on Korea, Cumings advocates the idea that the history of Korea for the past fifty years has not been one of two nation-states at war, but one of a civil war within a single nation. At the time of this writing, Cumings is one of only two academically trained historians who have been quoted as substantiating the reports of the Associated Press and accepting its central contention that the events at No Gun Ri were the result of deliberate orders on the part of the United States. (These claims about Cumings position were made in a May 2000 press release by the AP in response to questions about the accuracy of its reporting. See The Associated Press, "A statement by Jonathan Wolman, Associated Press executive editor, regarding questions raised by *U.S. News & World Report* about the news service's investigation into the shootings of civilians at No Gun Ri during the Korean War," May 15, 2000.)
19. Walter Sullivan, "South Korea Fails in Guerilla Drive," *The New York Times*, March 15, 1950, pg. 18.
20. John J. Muccio, "Letter to Secretary of State," April 9, 1949, in *FRUS* (1949), Vol. 7, pgs. 983–984.
21. Muccio, "Letter to Secretary of State," October 13, 1949, in *FRUS* (1949), Vol. 7, pgs. 1086–1087.
22. See Department of the Army Inspector General, *No Gun Ri Review*, January 2001. This report is currently available on-line at *http://www.army.mil/nogunri/*. Printed manuscript in author's possession, and the executive summary is at the appendix to this book. The DAIG does not mention anywhere within the 300+ page report that a South Korean guerilla war existed prior to the conventional start of the Korean War, let alone the fact that the epicenter for some of this activity was the region around No Gun Ri.
23. Cumings, *The Origins of the Korean War, Vol. II*, pgs. 269–270. Cumings cites from the Korean Military Advisory Group weekly reports contained in National Archives, RG 335, Secretary of the Army file, box 78; CIA "Communist Capabilities in South Korea," ORE 32–48, February 21, 1949. In addition to that, he claims that North Korean sources corroborate this information.
24. Pearson, *The Rise and Fall of the Soviet Empire*, pg. 150. See also Stanley Weintraub, *MacArthur's War: Korea and the Undoing of an American Hero*, (New York, NY: The Free Press, 2000), or any of a dozen of the most recent works on the Korean War that tap into the now (somewhat) accessible archival resources of the former Soviet Union. The evolution of the history of the causes of the Korean War is itself a fascinating story. The generally accepted thesis for the beginning of the war taught prior to the fall of the Soviet Union was that Kim Il Sung acted independently and without the consent of Soviet Russia when he launched his invasion. How else to explain the fact that the Soviets were not in the United Nations (UN), having walked out in protest just a day before, on the crucial day when the Security Council voted for UN intervention. The opening of the former Soviet archives disabused the world of that notion, and it is

now known that not only was Stalin aware of Kim's actions and plans, but he supported them fully. He just did not expect American intervention. In a way, Stalin too was surprised.

25. The best known of those advocating this opinion was T. R. Ferenbach, a retired army officer whose 1963 book *This Kind of War* became (and remains) a military favorite, most likely because it ascribes blame everywhere but upon the leadership of the army itself.

26. Fred Ottoboni, *Korea Between the Wars, A Soldier's Story*, (Sparks, NV: Vincente Books, 1997), pgs. 127–264. Ottoboni describes some U.S. forces in Korea as being at starvation's edge and relates some episodes of actual mutiny among freezing and starving U.S. troops stationed near Kunsan in 1947. The amazing degree of outright neglect, to the point of rebellion, of some U.S. troops in Korea is in stark contrast to the life that other U.S. soldiers were living in Japan.

27. MacArthur's Far East command had the lion's share of the available combat soldiers stationed outside the United States. Of the ten divisions of the active army at the time, four were in Japan. Collectively, roughly 118,000 men were stationed around the Pacific Rim at the beginning of the Korean War, a time when the entire active-duty strength of the army dipped below 500,000 from its wartime high of more than eight million.

28. James F. Schnabel, *Policy and Direction: The First Year*, (Washington, D.C.: Center of Military History, United States Army, 1992), pg. 45.

29. "Crisis in Asia—An Examination of U.S. Policy," *Department of State Bulletin*. Vol. XXII. No. 551. (Washington, D.C.: Government Publishing Office, 23 January 1950), pg. 116.

30. "Statement by Secretary Acheson," *Department of State Bulletin*. Vol. XXII. No. 571. (Washington, D.C.: Government Publishing Office, 1950), pg. 944. This speech was made before the Senate Foreign Relations Committee and Senate Armed Services Committee on June 2, 1950.

31. The United States did not provide South Korea with anything more than small arms and rudimentary training for its military. Tanks, heavy artillery, aircraft, and other basic elements of a modern industrial-style military were not provided. U.S. military and diplomatic messages are clear on the reasons why—the well-justified fear that if Rhee were given these weapons, he would initiate his own attack and attempt reunification at the earliest possible moment.

32. Geoffrey Blainey, *The Causes of War*, (New York: The Free Press, 1977), pg. 159.

Chapter 2: In the Land of the Rising Sun

1. For the full text of these theories of motivation, see John Lynn, *The Bayonets of the Republic: Motivation and Tactics in the Army of Revolutionary France, 1791–94*, (Boulder, CO: Westview Press, 1996), pgs. 26–36. Although Lynn's subject matter is Napoleonic (or more accurately pre-Napoleonic), his comments and theories on motivation appear valid across all Western societies of the past three hundred years.

2. Allan R. Millett and Peter Maslowski, *For the Common Defense, A Military History of the United States of America*, (New York, NY: The Free Press, 1984), pg. 504.

3. Francis Baylock, interview with author, November 1999.

4. The military use of phonetic supplements to the alphabet often confuses those unfamiliar with the military. There is a very simple reason why the military adopted the use of a phonetic alphabet: radio communications. When talking and listening through a handset, or even on speakers, the reception of voice transmission is not always clear. "B" might sound like "C" or "E" when coming over a static-filled radio net while the listener himself may be under fire. To reduce the confusion, each letter was therefore given a word association. "E Company" became "Easy Company," while "G Company" was "George Company" and F Company "Fox."

5. Marvin Daniel, interview with author, November 1999.

6. John De Borde, interview with author, November 1999.

7. Leonard "Buddy" Wenzel, interview with author, February 2001.

8. Department of the Army, "Table of Organization and Equipment No. 7-11N, Infantry Regiment, 21 April 1948," (Washington, D.C.: Department of the Army, 1948). See also T/O&E 7-11N, dated 20 December 1949, and T/O&E No. 7-15N, "Infantry Battalion," dated 15 November 1950. A T/O&E is a comprehensive list of all the equipment and personnel a certain type of unit is supposed to have on-hand to accomplish the missions that the unit was designed to complete. Most of the material cited in this book regarding authorized (as opposed to actual) weapons, equipment, and organizational structure of the army stems from these base documents. For simplicity's sake, these will collectively be referred to hereafter as "T/O&E, 1950."

9. Robert L. Bateman, "Without Malice, Without Sympathy: Civilian Antipathy for the Military, 1607–2000." *Army* 49, No.1 (January 1999), pgs. 36–47.

10. For a more complete explanation of this military heritage and the history of the United States armed forces in general, see Allan R. Millet and Peter Maslowski, *For the Common Defense*, (New York: The Free Press, 1984). For a detailed look at the formation of a somewhat larger and more professional force around the turn of the century, see Graham Cosmos, *An Army for Empire, The United States Army in the Spanish-American War*, (Columbia, MO: University of Missouri Press, 1971).

11. Russell Weigley, *History of the United States Army*, (New York: Macmillan, 1967). Weigley is perhaps the best known advocate of the thesis that the army was, for all intents and purposes, a police force upon the frontier for the majority of the nineteenth century. As many modern pundits are rediscovering, it is fairly easy for a military force to either serve as a police force or serve as a combat force. Executing both missions is practically impossible.

12. The M-1 Garand, although invented for the First World War, took more than twenty years for the army to finally adopt. It was arguably one of the best rifles ever mass-produced. Rugged, accurate, and semiautomatic, this was the rifle that won the Second World War. See also the personal papers of Major General George Lynch, Chief Of Infantry, Center for Military History, Carlisle Barracks, Pennsylvania. Lynch was instrumental in bringing the M1 into full production and fielding it across the United States Army. The Browning automatic rifle (BAR) was also a product of the First World War. Although it too missed introduction in time to see action in that war, it was quickly accepted by the army soon afterwards. Despite the weight of the weapon, it served a valuable purpose for the infantry squad. The suppressive power of the BAR could help an infantry squad gain fire superiority over an equally sized force. With a twenty-round magazine and a high rate of fire, the BAR was worth its weight.

13. Describing the .30-caliber (light) MG as "light" is something of a misnomer. The weapon itself was fairly heavy, yet in comparison to the water-cooled version of the same weapon it was light. This was also the smallest caliber of machine gun in the U.S. inventory. Each weapon would normally have a full complement of three, a machine-gunner, an assistant, and an ammo bearer. None of the MG teams of the 7th Cavalry were at full strength in 1950, let alone before that point. This was the primary direct fire weapon of the company. The air-cooled version of the weapon could not sustain its maximum rate of fire for more than a few minutes without burning out the barrel of the gun. The sustained rate of fire was considerably lower, around 300 to 500 rounds per minute depending upon the skill of the gunner.

14. *Field Manual 7-40, Infantry Regiment*, (Fort Benning, GA: The Infantry Center and School, 1950). In this context, "volume" refers to the number of rounds of ammunition fired.

15. Although the TO&E called for recoilless rifles at the company level, most units in 1950 in the Far East command trained these antitank teams as bazookamen. The

bazooka, a creation of the Second World War, was designed to provide the average infantryman with a weapon that could at least disable if not destroy an enemy armored vehicle. The weapon consists of a tube and a missile. Unguided, the bazooka round depends upon the shape of the explosive charge in the warhead to penetrate enemy armor. It was found that a convex-shaped charge would concentrate its explosive power upon a single point. The intense heat at this point converted the metal of the armor to plasma, in effect melting its way through to the vulnerable interior. The heat (and therefore the thickness of armor that could be penetrated) was a function of the size of the charge. The original bazooka was insufficient for this reason against the sloped armor of the Soviet-supplied North Korean T-34 tanks.

Mortars were another story entirely. Technically speaking, mortars are indirect fire weapons that use extremely high-angle fire. In the First World War, the reality of the trenches forced the creation of a smaller caliber weapon that could fill the gap between the massive (but to some degree uncontrollable by the front line troops) shells of the artillery and mere hand grenades. From this genesis came the infantry mortar. Man-portable, the whole "system" consisted of a tube, a base plate to mount the tube, and a tripod and sight to steady and aim the weapon. Properly and expertly employed, this weapon can fill in the "dead space" of low ground where direct rifle and machine-gun fire cannot reach.

16. De Borde, November 1999.
17. R. C. Gray, interview with author, various dates, November 1999 to April 2000.
18. The 75mm recoilless rifle might be thought of as a bazooka writ large. An open-ended tube firing a rocket-propelled round, it is mounted on a tripod and is therefore steadier. The 81-mm mortar and .30-caliber heavy machine gun are variants of the weapons already discussed in a smaller caliber. The larger size of the 81mm mortar allows for increased range and lethality. The .30-caliber HMG used the same ammunition, but the barrel was water cooled. This added a lot of weight to the system but also allowed for sustained fire at near the maximum rate of the weapon. Again there appears some discrepancy between the authorized organization according to the tables of 1946 and the actual organization of the battalions of the 7th Cavalry in the summer of 1950. The TO&E only authorized two platoons—the mortars and the 75mm recoilless rifles.
19. The term "fire support" refers to all weapons and munitions fired by supporting units including the howitzers of the field artillery or the bombs of airplanes flying in "close support" of the unit. As the coordinator of all of these assets, the H Company commander in combat would be located at the battalion headquarters.
20. William Hoffman, interview with author, March 2001.
21. Unfamiliarity with military organization is what led to some of the wildly inaccurate initial reporting of the events at No Gun Ri. The separation between the military and the media resulted in reporters referring to 2nd Battalion 7th Cavalry Regiment as "the second unit of the 1st Cavalry Division" and at a lower level to "F Company, 1st Cavalry Division." This unfamiliarity with military subject matter is potentially dangerous. As national leaders turn to reporting through international news organs for information, there is an increased potential for massive miscommunication when naïve reporters blandly assign random identities to military units. In at least one case in recent history, this worked to the advantage of the United States. Reporters covering the initial deployment of U.S. troops to Saudi Arabia incorrectly reported that the "82nd Airborne" (a division of more than 16,000) was already on the ground in Saudi. The reality was only one battalion (roughly 700 men) was there at that point. It took more than a week for most of the rest of the division to arrive. Reporters therefore, unwittingly through their own ignorance of military organizations, conveyed to Saddam Hussein a false picture. Luckily for the United States and her allies, this media error worked to their advantage.
22. Melvin C. Chandler, *Of Garryowen in Glory*, (Self-published, 1960).

23. Contrary to popular belief, George Armstrong Custer was not the first commander of the 7th Cavalry. That officer, however, did not regularly move with the unit or command in the field. As a practical matter, Custer was the commander for much of the first ten years of the regiment's history.

24. A short nonacademic account of the history of the term and song "Garryowen" may be found at one of the several 7th Cavalry websites. The best is *http://www.naples.net/presents/7thcav/*. The short version is that the word is actually a compound of two words, which mean "Owen's Garden." This was a popular area for social activities outside the limits of the Irish city of Limerick. British soldiers stationed there in the seventeenth and eighteenth centuries apparently spent a fair amount of time in the town. In English, the Gallic name of the town becomes "Garry-Owen" and is phonetically reduced to a single word. By the time of Wellington's peninsular campaign against the French in Spain, several versions of drinking and marching songs making reference to "Garryowen" were popular with the soldiers of Wellington's Irish regiments. The massive Irish emigration to the United States starting in the 1840s provided the manpower to fill several Irish regiments in both the North and the South during the American Civil War. It was probably during this time that Custer first heard the tune around campfires during his service with the Army of the Potomac. The exact route that the song took into the regiment is not clear, but it is likely brought into the regiment in its present form by one of Custer's favorite officers, Captain Myles Keough. Keough was something of an adventurer, born in Ireland as the son of a British army officer stationed in Limerick. It was likely that he was the final source for Custer to adopt the song as the "regimental air" soon after the founding of the regiment. It is now the official song of not only the 7th Cavalry but the 1st Cavalry Division as well, and the rollicking tune is easily recognizable from a host of Western movies. When the regimental crest was developed, with a sword point sticking upwards, bisecting the word Garryowen into what appears to be two words, Garry and Owen, many came to believe that this was the name of a person of some historical importance.

25. MTO&E, Infantry Division, 1950.

26. See John W. Dower, *Embracing Defeat, Japan in the Wake of World War II*, (New York, NY: W. W. Norton and Co., 1999), pgs. 65–86, 121–154, and 346–442.

27. Although there has not been a serious discussion of the disbanding of the army in the past 180 years, the constitutional basis for a standing army is rather weak. In fact, the specific language in the U.S. Constitution states that Congress shall have the power to "raise" an army. This stands in contrast to the navy, which the Congress shall "maintain." From this historical foundation, we see that the army, such as it is, exists solely at the pleasure of Congress from year to year.

28. T. R. Fehrenbach, *This Kind of War; A Study in Unpreparedness*, (New York: Macmillan, 1963). See also Reports of Sec War, 1946–1950 inclusive, (Washington, D.C.: Government Publishing Office, 1947–1951).

29. MTO&E, 1950.

30. Chandler, *Of Garryowen in Glory*, pg. 229.

31. Don Donnelly, interview with author, November 1999.

32. H. Norman Matthias, interview with author, July 2000. See also Dower, *Embracing Defeat*, pgs. 121–154.

33. Interview with veteran, 2/7 Cavalry, November 1999.

34. Donnelly, November 1999.

35. Donnelly, July 2000.

36. William West, interview with author, March 2001.

37. Gray, November 1999.

38. West, March 2001.

39. For example, see author interviews with De Borde, Baylock, and Donald Donnelly.

40. As noted earlier, the unit status report, known throughout the army as the "USR," came about after the rough days of the beginning of the Korean War. Faced with the reality that the army's condition at the beginning of the Korean War could at least be partially blamed on Congress's ignorance, Congress directed that a system of reporting be developed upon which it could base informed decisions on the condition of the army. The result was a report from the battalion level that we collected and collated and may be subjectively upgraded or downgraded depending upon the military commander's own assessment of his unit's readiness.

41. John Lippincott, interview with author, November 1999.

42. John Potts, interview with author, November 1999.

43. John De Borde, interview with author, December 1999.

44. Marvin Daniel, interview with author, November 1999.

45. Gray, January 2000.

46. Alan Brister, interview with author, March 2001.

47. William West, March 2001. As an interesting historical sidebar, it was at this same postgame celebration that another member of West's winning team was selected to be a different general's aide. Lieutenant Alexander Haig was also called soon after the game and party to be the junior aide to a general he had met during the festivities, Major General Edward M. Almond, then MacArthur's chief of staff and also a football fan.

48. Although not all inclusive, for a good overview of the idea, see Sam C. Sarkesian, ed., *Combat Effectiveness: Cohesion, Stress, and the Volunteer Military*, (Beverly Hills, CA: Sage Publications, 1980), or William D. Henderson, *Cohesion, The Human Element in Combat: Leadership and Societal Influence in the Armies of the Soviet Union, the United States, North Vietnam, and Israel*, (Washington, D.C.: National Defense University Press, 1985).

49. Lippincott, June 2000.

Chapter 3: A Distant Thunder

1. John J. Muccio, "Letter to Secretary of State," June 25, 1950, in *Foreign Relations of the United States (FRUS)* (1950), Vol. 7, pgs. 125–126.

2. Bruce Cumings, *Korea's Place in the Sun, A Modern History*, (New York, NY: W. W. Norton and Company, 1997), pg. 253.

3. Although Cumings attempts to downplay, to some degree, the role of the Soviet Union in North Korea, other historians have discovered that although North Korea was not a true "satellite" state of USSR as it was perceived to be by the U.S. government at the time, neither was it exactly a free society. See Cumings, *Korea's Place in the Sun, A Modern History*, (New York, NY: W. W. Norton and Company, 1997), pg. 231.

4. Kim Chum-kon, *The Korean War, 1950–53*, (Seoul, Korea: Kwangmyong Publishing Co, 1973), pgs. 182–183. Chum-kon's numbers are derived from the South Korean official history of the war created under the auspices of the South Korean government between 1967 and 1977.

5. "Letter, Chief of the United States Military Advisory Group to the Republic of Korea (KMAG, Brigadier General W. L. Roberts) to the ambassador in Korea (Muccio), January 7, 1950," *FRUS*, 1950, Volume VII, pgs. 16–18. Roberts conveyed to Muccio at that time that there were an estimated forty YAK-3s then in the North Korean arsenal. He requested forty F-51s (the USAF redesignation of the P-51 Mustang of WWII fame) for the South Korean armed forces at that time. The South Koreans themselves had only requested twenty-five fighters, in addition to six long-range reconnaissance and nine transport aircraft. (See *FRUS*, 1950, Vol. VII, pg. 46.)

6. *FRUS*, 1950, Vol. VII, pgs. 44–47.

7. These numbers are an estimate. For obvious reasons, various sources cite different assessed strength levels for the North Koreans at the outset of the war. The ROK government both before and after the war tended to exaggerate the size of the NPKA. Before the war, this was probably for the purpose of gaining additional American arms support due to the size of the threat facing them. After the war, the matter of "face" comes in to play when trying to explain the precipitous retreat of the ROK army in the first weeks of the war. Yet despite this, it appears likely that its estimates were closer to the mark than were the Americans. In May 1950, the American ambassador to Korea reported both the ROK estimates as well as his own assessment of the strength of the NKPA. The ROK estimate of North Korean strength on May 11, 1950 was overall strength of 300,000-plus; the NKPA alone at 118,000; a tank brigade of 10,000; and naval forces of 15,000. North Korean armor was believed to be 155 medium tanks, 18 small tanks, and 30 armored cars. In contrast, and accompanying the statement of the ROK defense minister that released the above figures, the U.S. chargé (Drumright) estimated the North Koreans at one-third the size. The official estimate wired back to Washington was for a North Korean military of "103,000 including 'People's Army,' Korean Volunteer Army returnees from Manchuria, border constabulary, air division, armored formation and navy . . . . Only armored formation in North Korea is of brigade size and composed of estimated sixty-five tanks, heaviest of which is Soviet model T-34." Drumright made it clear in the next paragraph his opinion of the ROK estimates: "If Embassy estimates accurate, it follows Korean figures are exaggerated—probably deliberately so. Purpose of exaggeration undoubtedly is to convince friendly powers, especially U.S., of disparity of strength between North and South forces and thus to enlist for additional military aid." (See *FRUS*, May 11, 1950, Volume VII, pgs. 83–85.) One version of the "official" ROK army estimated prewar tank strength of the NKPA at 120 T-34s in the 105th Tank Brigade and an overall total of 242 tanks. (See again Kim Chum-kon, *The Korean War, 1950–53*, pgs. 182–183.)

8. There can be no better illustration of the problems involved in using, or even citing, North Korean news releases than the first of the announcements at the outset of hostilities. Below is the full text of the first radio broadcast about the war to come from Pyongyang radio on the morning of June 25, 1950. (*FRUS*, 1950, Vol. VII, pg. 132.)

Official Announcement made by the Home Affairs Bureau of the People's Republic of Korea. The so-called "defense army" of the South Korean puppet regime started a surprise invasion of the north along the whole of the front of the 38th parallel line at dawn on the 25th. The enemy, who started the surprise operation, invaded the territory north of the 38th parallel one to two kilometers at three points west of Haeju, Kumchon, and Chorwon. The Home Affairs Bureau of the People's Republic of Korea has issued an order to the security army of the People's Republic to repulse the enemy. At this moment, our security army is putting up stiff counter-operations against the enemy. The People's Army succeeded in repulsing the enemy force which penetrated into the north at Yangyang. In this connection, the People's Republic of Korea wishes to remind the South Korean puppet regime of the fact that, unless the puppets immediately suspend their adventurous military actions, the People's Republic will be obliged to resort to decisive countermeasures. At the same time the People's Republic entrusted the Home Affairs Bureau to call the attention of the South Korean puppet regime to the fact that the whole responsibility for the grave consequences arising from their reckless venture would squarely rest on the shoulders of the South Korean puppet regime.

9. Highlighting the failure of American intelligence in Korea was a June 19 assessment of the North Korean regime by the Central Intelligence Agency (CIA). (Report contained in *FRUS*, 1950, Vol. VII, pgs. 109–121.) The CIA estimated North Korean strength in the "People's Army" at "66,000 organized into at least three infantry divi-

sions and an independent brigade." This evaluation also claimed only sixty-five T-34s in the hands of the North Koreans. In part due to this and the KMAG reports, Ambassador Muccio cabled Secretary of State Dean Acheson that the ROK army was actually "superior" to the NKPA due to "superiority of training, leadership, morale, marksmanship, and better small-arms equipment, especially M-1s." He did take time to qualify that this only referred to the army and not the air forces. He then went on to claim that North Korean forces, solely due to their airpower and the lack of the same in the south, were superior overall. (See cable from Muccio to Acheson, June 14, 1950, *FRUS*, 1950, Vol. VII, pg. 105.)

10. Some question exists about the time and intent of the initiation of hostilities. Conflicting evidence suggests that fighting started on the Ongjin peninsula with a limited attack by the 17th Infantry Regiment (ROK). It remains for the opening of North Korean archives to determine if this was used as a spur-of-the-moment excuse by North Korea to initiate a preplanned assault on the South or merely a coincidence that there was a ROK limited attack (designed to capture one town and one hill) within hours of the general NKPA attack all along the border.

11. Major Walter Greenwood as quoted in Keyes Beech, *Tokyo and Points East*, (New York, NY: Doubleday, 1954), pgs. 111–112.

12. Ibid., 113.

13. Roy Appleman, *South to the Naktong, North to the Yalu*, (Washington, D.C.: Center for Military History, 1961), pg. 43.

14. Marguerite Higgins, *War in Korea, The Report of a Woman Combat Correspondent*, (New York, NY: Doubleday, 1951), pg. 26.

15. Alexander Haig, interview with author, March 2001. Haig was the aide to Major General Almond, the chief of staff to MacArthur. Haig later went on to command at every echelon of the army, ending as the commanding general of NATO forces and eventually becoming secretary of state under Ronald Reagan. See also Alexander M. Haig, *Inner Circles, How America Changed the World, A Memoir*, (New York, NY: Warner Books, 1992), pgs. 19–20.

16. Marvin C. Daniel, interview with author, November 1999. Daniel was a private in the 4th Squad (Weapons), 1st Platoon, E Company, 2nd Battalion 7th Cavalry. His primary weapon was the 2.36-inch bazooka.

17. Don Donnelly, interview with author, November 1999.

18. Johnny Theodore, interview with author July 2000.

19. James Kerns, interview with author, July 2000.

20. Russell McKinley, interview with author, July 2000.

21. H. Norman Matthias, interview with author, July 2000.

22. Appleman, *South to the Naktong, North to the Yalu*, pgs. 44–45, 48.

23. The best accounts for the defensive fight of Task Force Smith are in Appleman's *South to the Naktong, North to the Yalu* and the essay by Roy G. Flint in the compilation book, *America's First Battles*, Charles E. Heller and William A Stofft, ed. (Lawrence, KS: University Press of Kansas, 1986), pgs. 266–299. Both works, written by academically trained officers, rely extensively on primary source archival material and extensive interviews with veterans of the action. Most other secondary sources depend upon the groundwork laid down by these two historians.

24. Ibid., 61.

25. Smith's task force actually spent several days moving to different positions, digging in, and preparing defense. At one point (July 3), the TF divided down to the company level to defend the northern approaches to the towns of Pyongtaek and Ansong, which were (in 1950) about ten miles south of Osan and almost ten miles apart.

26. No. 77 Squadron was based at Iwakuni Air Base at the southern end of the Japanese island of Honshu at the beginning of the war, and therefore was the only F-51 RAAF squadron anywhere near Korea at the time. See Robert F. Futrell, *The United States Air*

Force in Korea, 1950–1953, (Washington, D.C.: Office of Air Force History, Second Edition, 1983), pg. 4. Accounts of the attack as by RAAF aircraft as witnessed by soldiers of TF Smith are recorded in Appleman, *South to the Naktong, North to the Yalu*, pg. 64, as well as the 24th Infantry Division War Diary located in the U.S. National Archives.

27. Futrell, *The United States Air Force in Korea, 1950–1953*, pg. 29.

28. Ibid., 58.

29. To their credit, the USAF leaders recognized this lack of plane range as a problem after the beginning of the war and set out to find a solution. The result was a locally produced hybrid wing-tip external fuel tank that could hold 265 gallons and thereby provide roughly an extra hour of flight time. See Futrell, pgs. 59–62.

30. Arguably the F-84 could have accomplished this mission, but conditions in Japan prohibited its use due to runway restrictions. Runways were not long enough to handle this type of aircraft in the areas of Japan that would have allowed the aircraft to fly missions over Korea.

31. For a terrific analysis of USAF operations in the Korean War, see Conrad C. Crane, *American Airpower Strategy in Korea, 1950–1953*, (Lawrence, KS: University Press of Kansas, 2000).

32. Futrell, *The United States Air Force in Korea, 1950–1953*, pg. 33.

33. At the time of the strafing described by American witnesses north of Osan and in Suwon, on July 3, the actual front line was still just some six miles south of the Han River and at least twelve miles north of Suwon. For an accurate description of this phase of the tactical fighting, see *The Korean War*, Vol. One, created under the auspices of the Korean Institute of Military History, (1997 revision, English translation edition published by University of Nebraska Press, 2000), pgs. 278–294. This translation of the original "official" South Korean history of the Korean War, the *Hanguk Chonchaengsa*, (which was never published in English after its original publication in South Korea between 1967 and 1977), gives a very readable translation compiled by a team of nine historians who were not only fluent in the two languages involved, but in that third very difficult language, "militareese."

34. Appleman, *South to the Naktong, North to the Yalu*, pg. 64.

35. 1st Cavalry War Diary, entries for June 25–July 1, 1950, RG 338, Box 25.

36. The term peacetime strength refers to the previously cited reduction of each infantry regiment to two battalions rather than three and fewer artillery and tanks. On June 25, the 1st Cavalry did not even have all the men needed to fill these understrength-by-design formations, let alone the wartime-authorized formations of three battalions per regiment, three full battalions of artillery, and one full tank battalion instead of the single tank company actually on hand.

37. Even before the order to provide NCOs came down, the 7th Cavalry Regiment was woefully short of qualified enlisted leadership. A snapshot of F Company from the time around Christmas 1949 demonstrated this in no uncertain terms. Of the twelve authorized rifle squad leader positions that call for an E-6, only five had an NCO of any kind, and all five of these were not sergeants but corporals (E-4). In the entire company, there were only four master sergeants, three sergeants first class, and five sergeants (E-5). Most squads were "led" by privates first class. (Christmas dinner menu and company roster, 1949, F Company, 7th Cavalry, courtesy of Al Clair.)

38. Matthias, July 2000.

39. McKinley, July 2000.

40. Donnelly, November 1999.

41. Al Clair, letter to author, November 15, 1999.

42. De Borde, November 1999.

43. Gray, October 1999.

44. Donnelly, August 2000.

45. Gray, November, 1999.
46. McKinley, July 2000.
47. 1st Cavalry War Diary, entry for July 18, 1950, RG 338, Box 25.
48. Theodore, July 2000.
49. Matthias, July 2000.
50. Al Clair, letter to author, November 15, 1999.
51. 1st Cavalry War Diary, entry for July 22, 1950, RG 338, Box 25.

Chapter 4: Erosion

1. The most extreme examples of this behavior were starkly reported by that original group of reporters who landed at Kimpo on the second day of the war, especially the reporting of Margaurite Higgins of *The New York Herald-Post* and Keyes Beech. Although Higgins's wartime news reports were fairly stark, Beech's postwar book is the most damning towards the behavior of the men of the 24th during the fighting in Taejon. See Keyes Beech, *Tokyo and Points East*, (New York, NY: Doubleday, 1954), pgs. 144–149.
2. William F. Dean, as told to William L Worden, *General Dean's Story*, (New York, NY: The Viking Press, 1954), pp. 32–39. Dean won the Congressional Medal of Honor for his actions in these opening days. In his own account of this period, both the actions of his division and his own behavior are somewhat skewed. While it appears that Dean is scrupulously honest about his own actions, including his own pitfalls, his account of the actions of his division stand at variance with the accounts from other members of the division, the archival records of the division, and the reports of civilian media present on the battlefield at the time. In short, he is too nice (in retrospect) when speaking of his former subordinates, taking most blame upon himself. As a good leader and good commander, Dean's personal ethics demanded that he could not blame the troops for the loss of Taejon, and could only obliquely refer to some of the less-than-stellar actions of his subordinate units.
3. Uzal Ent, *Fighting on the Brink: The Defense of the Pusan Perimeter*, (Paducah, KY: Turner Publishing Company, 1996), pg. 58. While the front-line infantry had this perception, the division commander, Major General Hobart Gay, was certainly aware of the planned Naktong line. That line was first put forward by the G3 of Lieutenant General Walton Walker (Commander, 8th United States Army, Korea [EUSAK]), Colonel Allan McClean, after an aerial reconnaissance on July 12, the day before Walker officially assumed command of EUSAK.
4. Regimental Diaries, 5th and 8th Cavalry Regiments. See also 1st Cavalry Division G-2 logs from period just prior to deployment. RG 338, Box 25. While the 5th and 8th Cavalry have their own files, duplicates of their regimental war diaries are also included as annexes within the 1st Cavalry Division report in that box.
5. The concept of mutual support is a complex one. In its simplest form, it might be thought of as the distance over which one unit might focus violence against an enemy attacking the unit next to it. At a minimum, it is the maximum distance over which one unit might reinforce another. This is obviously subject to several variables, including the types of weapons available, the terrain the units are operating on, and the type of enemy attacking. Thus, two infantry divisions, side by side, can obviously support each other quickly. They might even be separated by a few miles, as long as one division can send troops to the aid of the other before any enemy attack might break through and do greater damage. The distance apart might be dictated by the road network behind the lines. If there is only a single dirt track between the two, which would constrict the passage of the thousands of reinforcing soldiers and therefore slow them down, the two divisions must be closer to be mutually supporting. If, however,

there are two parallel superhighways running between and behind the two divisions, they might be spread farther apart since lateral movement could be done enmasse on trucks instead of on foot. If all of this takes place in mountains, the distance of separation must decrease to practically zero in the absence of the ideal of connecting superhighways in the rear.

6. Army manuals recommend the creation of a tactical reserve at all echelons, for the purpose of exploiting a penetration of the enemy line or blocking a penetration of American lines but not for rear area security.

7. Edwin P. Hoyt, *The Pusan Perimeter, Korea 1950*, (New York, NY: Stein and Day, 1984), pg. 101. Hoyt claims that Major General Gay did not select the positions for the 5th and 8th Cavalry, but that these were directed by Lieutenant General Walton Walker's 8th Army headquarters. "At Yongdong, however, General Gay learned that he was not a free agent. An officer of the operations section of the 8th Army indicated that he must place one battalion of his troops northwest of Yongdong and another battalion southeast. These battalions would have no contact. Thus they could easily be surrounded and cut off. The general said that he would not do this unless General Walker's headquarters confirmed the demand. So troops of the 8th Cavalry were placed in that fashion. The 5th Cavalry Regiment was placed east of Yongdong to protect the town."

8. *FM 100-5 Operations*, (Washington, D.C.: GPO, 1993), pgs. 7–12. This definition is adapted from the official definition. The 1941 edition of the same manual (*Field Service Regulation 1941*) did not address the topic, nor did the 1946 edition of *FM 100-5 Operations*. The concept, however, was known.

9. American reluctance to don enemy uniforms or doff their own to pass as a civilian stems from the fact that it is a violation of the laws of land warfare. A soldier dressed in civilian clothes attempting to pass through the lines of the enemy has lost the status of "soldier" and the protections attached to that role. Instead of being taken prisoner and held as a POW, he can (and usually is) considered a spy and may be tried and executed as such. See Geneva Conventions, 1949. To gain the protections under the conventions, a fighter must meet four criteria: 1) be commanded by a person responsible for his subordinates; 2) wear a distinctive sign or article of clothing visible at a distance in order to indicate that he is a combatant and potential target who may lawfully be attacked by opposing forces; 3) carry his weapon openly to indicate his combatant status and to distinguish fighters from the civilian population; and 4) observe the laws of war.

   See Jon Lee Anderson, "Guerillas" in *Crimes of War, What the Public Should Know*, Roy Gutman and David Rieff, ed., (New York, NY: W. W. Norton, 1999), pgs. 159–161.

10. Tens of thousands is only an estimate. For the obvious reason that nobody was systematically counting, no reliable figures can state with authority exactly how many refugees were on the roads.

11. Although not exactly replicating combat, the training maneuvers conducted by the United States Army at the National Training Center at Fort Irwin, California, and the Joint Readiness Training Center at Fort Polk, Louisiana, consistently confirm the observation that in more than eighty percent of the tactical engagements practiced at these centers since 1980, the side that gained the upper hand in the reconnaissance fight won the subsequent battle.

12. 1st Cavalry Division War Diary, July 1950, RG 338, Box 42. See also G2 logs for the same period. One of the major problems with this report is that no accompanying report of interrogation of the prisoner is available. This may mean one of several things: 1) The report may have actually originated with South Korean Army units and was "appropriated" accidentally during verbal retransmission as having occurred to an American unit. 2) The event did happen in an American unit, presumably in the 24th Infantry Division, and the records were lost during the calamitous retreat from Taejon.

3) The event occurred in an American unit but because the woman was a civilian at best and a spy at worst, she was immediately turned over to the South Korean National Police who almost certainly executed her soon thereafter. (Speedy executions were a common complaint of the American intelligence community and something that many civilian reporters noted and reported on during this period.) The issue is further clouded because an entry in the 1st Cavalry Division radio traffic log seems to reference an event similar to this taking place near the 77th Field Artillery, which was then just outside Yongdong.

13. At this point, fifty years after the event, many if not most of the soldiers interviewed for this book recall something about that particular report. Given the widespread repetition of this account in histories of the war, however, it is impossible to determine if the veterans are actually remembering hearing it through official or unofficial channels during the war or if they heard or read about it at some point after the war and subsequently incorporated it into their own memories.

14. A version of that particular account was repeated by several veterans of 2nd Battalion 7th Cavalry to the author. Unfortunately, as with many combat stories, the dates and times of this account do not match with the actual record of the regiment. As we will see later, there are often gaps in the official combat diary of the infantry regiments but rarely errors in the raw material of the daily casualty reports. In the case of this story, all of the soldiers who refer to the incident indicate that it occurred on either July 23 or 24, 1950. The casualties for those days, however, are accounted for by other substantiated causes. The next chapter will delve into this more.

15. This is especially true of the 2nd Battalion 7th Cavalry stationed at McKnight Barracks in downtown Tokyo. In addition to the many parades the battalion participated in due to its convenient proximity to MacArthur's headquarters, one of its full-time missions, performed on a rotating basis by nearly all of the companies, was guard duty at the Imperial Palace of the Japanese emperor.

16. Kim Chum-kon, *The Korean War*, (Seoul, South Korea: Kwangmyong Publishing Co., 1973), pgs. 206–210.

17. Ent, *Fighting on the Brink*, pg. 58.

18. Stanley Weintraub, *MacArthur's War, Korea and the Undoing of an American Hero*, (New York, NY: The Free Press, 2000), pgs. 106–130.

19. 1st Cavalry War Diary, July 1950, RG 338, Box 42. See also the War Diary of the 8th Cavalry.

20. Combat Log, 5th Cavalry, RG 338, Box 23, S2/3 Journals.

21. De Borde, November 1999.

22. Theodore, July 2000.

23. Matthias, July 2000.

24. Regimental log, 8th Cavalry. See also 1st Cavalry War Diary, RG 338, Box 25.

25. General Orders #82, Headquarters 1st Cavalry Division, 2 September 1950, found in RG 338, Box 41, G1 records of the 1st Cavalry Division.

26. G2 Journal, 1st Cavalry Division (Inf), RG 338, Box 25.

27. 1st Cavalry Division War Diary, July 1950, RG 338, Box 25. See also Box 27 (8th Cavalry records) for prisoner interrogation reports. At this point, it cannot be determined from the combat journals or any of the interviews if the attacking forces were North Korean People's Army troops or South Korean communists. Historian Bruce Cumings identified Yongdong as one of the most rebellious of the small cities of South Korea. It was specifically mentioned repeatedly in dispatches from the KMAG advisors and observers that accompanied South Korean army forces during the suppression campaigns of 1949 and into 1950. This raises the very real possibility that at least some of the enemy troops attacking U.S. forces around Yongdong originated from within the city itself. Since their attacks were successful, none of the attackers were taken prisoner, a moot point since there were no prisoner interrogations by the G2 of 1st Cav anywhere in those first chaotic days inside the city (division headquarters was twelve

miles to the rear). Thus there is no definitive English language record of the identity of the attackers.

28. Harold Levine, "Hell Country: Of Mud, Muck, and Human Excrement . . ." *Newsweek*, (August 7, 1950), pgs. 20–21.

29. General Orders #82, Headquarters 1st Cavalry Division, 2 September 1950, found in RG 338, Box 41, G1 records of the 1st Cavalry Division. First Lieutenant Thomas Jones, the officer cited, earned the Bronze Star medal for his role in this action.

30. Philip D. Chinnery, *Korean Atrocity, Forgotten War Crimes 1950–1953*, (Annapolis, MD: Naval Institute Press, 2000), pg. 8. The first report of soldiers captured and executed by North Koreans involved six men of the heavy mortar company of 3rd Battalion, 21st Infantry Regiment, 24th Infantry Division. The North Koreans infiltrated or enveloped 3/21 Infantry and attacked the heavy mortar company in the rear on the night of July 9, 1950. The next morning, the soldiers of that company found the bodies of six soldiers with their hands tied behind their backs. All died of bullets fired into the back of the head. This fighting took place in the vicinity of Chochi'won, South Korea.

31. William L. Maher, *A Shepherd in Combat Boots, Chaplain Emil Kapaun of the 1st Cavalry Division*, (Shippensburg, PA: Burd Street Press, 1997), pgs. 94–95. Despite the fact that he carried an M-1 carbine, it appears that no soldier of the 8th Cavalry (or any regiment) ever actually saw the chaplain fire his weapon. It still came in good use during the defense of the Pusan perimeter when the chaplain, alone and on foot on a road between the battalions of the regiment, was surprised by a North Korean officer who immediately offered to surrender, thus making Chaplain Kapaun one of the few American "men of the cloth" ever to take a prisoner in combat.

   Chaplain Kapaun was certainly working to "save his flock" a few weeks later when he became one of the few chaplains to earn a Bronze Star with ('V') Device for valor just over a week later.

   (See General Orders #82, Headquarters 1st Cavalry Division, 2 September 1950, found in RG 338, Box 41, G1 records of the 1st Cavalry Division.)

32. 8th Cavalry Message Log, RG 338, Box 27. This is the "operations order" or "division order" reported by the Associated Press as the prime evidence of orders to shoot civilians in the 1st Cavalry Division.

33. William West, interview with author, April 2001. It may be that the liaison officer of the 5th Cavalry heard the same oral exchange but was more familiar with the personality and phrasing of Major General Hobart Gay, the division commander. According to West (who was Gay's aide-de-camp at the time), Gay was extremely profane in his language and tended towards extreme statements, though he did not intend for these to be taken literally. West recounts that on several occasions Gay stated that some members of his own staff, and virtually all of the staff officers of the headquarters above him in 8th Army, should be shot. It may be that the liaison officer from the 8th Cavalry overheard a profane exclamation from Gay expressing his frustration with the problem of refugee and infiltrators and took that as a literal command.

34. William Webb, interview with author, February 2001. See also 7th Cavalry War Diary, RG 338, Box 41. The soldiers of the 2nd Battalion were delayed by a lack of rail transport and did not start moving until later that day.

35. 7th Cavalry Regiment War Diary, RG 338, Box 41. 1st Cavalry G3 Radio Log, RG 338, Box 25.

36. 1st Cavalry War Diary, RG 338, Box 25.

37. *Newsweek* reporter Harold Levine claimed in an article that appeared on August 7 that Gay apparently planned to attack in the Yongdong area. Interviews conducted by Appleman (*South to the Naktong, North to the Yalu*) and Ent (*Fighting on the Brink: The Defense of the Pusan Perimeter*) directly contradict this portrayal. Ent cites Brigadier General (Ret.) Eugene Lynch, Walker's liaison plane pilot during the war, as being an eyewitness to an exchange that occurred when an unidentified reporter asked Gay if he

was going to counterattack. Gay turned and walked away from the reporter, stating to Lynch that there was no good answer to a stupid question. According to West, Gay's aide, Gay also privately suggested at various times that reporters who asked stupid questions should be shot.

38. 7th Cavalry Regiment War Diary, RG 338, Box 41. The fact that Nist sent this missive to the division, in writing, is confirmed by its presence in the 1st Cavalry Division War Diary, (see 1st Cavalry War Diary, RG 338, Box 25), where it is listed as G3 entry #45 in the combat log of the division operations section. What is more interesting is the fact that Nist, who controlled to some degree (by inclusion) what went into the regimental diary, had this communiqué added from his personal notes into the historical record.

39. 7th Cavalry Regiment War Diary, RG 338, Box 41. See also interviews by author with De Borde, Potts, Lippincott, and Webb.

40. The 71st Tank Company was, by authorization, a battalion of medium tanks but by 1950 was just a company of light tanks. Companies of armor are not normally given a numerical designation. This was, however, a consolidation measure. When the division was at full strength, each of the three infantry regiments normally had an associated tank company from the tank battalion assigned to the division. During the reductions of 1946–1950, however, these went away, and only one company of light tanks remained for the entire division, the M-24s of the 71st Tank Company.

41. General Orders #82, Headquarters 1st Cavalry Division, 2 September 1950, found in RG 338, G-1 records of the 1st Cavalry Division.

42. 1st Cavalry Division War Diary, RG 338, Box 25.

43. G-2 Situation Overlay, Enclosure #1, G2 PR #4, Map Sheet J52T Korean 1: 250,000. RG 338, Box 25.

44. Richard Cohen, interviews with author, April-May 2001. Cohen paints a slightly different picture than that which appears in the records in the archives. According to Cohen, this group was not cut off initially but had deliberately set out on an eastward track to attempt an envelopment of the enemy blocking position that was stopping the rest of the battalion. Cohen described Field as a great leader, the best commander in the battalion, and states that this was the reason his company was selected as the base for the cross-country maneuver. He says that a lack of reliable maps and some confusing radio messages contributed to the unit's misorientation, which then led to its subsequently being cut off from the rest of the battalion and regiment.

45. Combat Log, 5th Cavalry. RG 338, Box 23, S-2/3 Journals. See also operations overlay graphics for 5th Cavalry operations, July 25, 1950, as attachment to 1st Cavalry War Diary, RG 338, Box 25.

46. S-2/3 Radio Log, 5th Cavalry, RG 338, Box 23.

47. 7th Cavalry Regiment War Diary, RG 338, Box 41.

48. 1st Cavalry Division G-3 log. RG 338, Box 25.

49. 1st Cavalry Division War Diary, RG 338, Box 25.

50. When the men of what I have arbitrarily named "Team Field" finally made it back to American lines on July 27th they were met and interviewed by *The New York Times* reporter W. H. Lawrence. (A "team" is a modern military term for a combined-arms team, a company-level unit of tanks and infantry.) His account of their trials appear in a front-page story in *The Times* on July 29, 1950 under the headline "219 Beat Way to U.S. Lines In Three-Day Trek in Korean Mud." Their story also appeared in the Pacific edition of *Stars and Stripes*. In the interview for that story, Captain Field specifically requested, "Don't call us the lost company. We weren't lost. We knew where we were going. It just took us time to get there." (*Stars and Stripes, Pacific Edition*, July 29, 1950, pg. 1.) Some veterans of Company F, 2nd Battalion 8th Cavalry Regiment remember that the infantry element of Team Field was abandoned by the four tanks of the 71st Tank Company prior to getting to the 2nd Battalion 7th Cavalry's roadblock. These veterans remember the infantry taking a cross-country route and never encoun-

tering a roadblock of any kind. My thanks to Joseph Christopher (of F Company, 2nd Battalion 7th Cavalry Regiment, 1950) for his help. This story still remains shrouded in the documents and history.

51. Several of the veterans interviewed mentioned an initial group of refugees who was allowed to pass through the lines just as the battalion arrived in position as the sun was setting.

52. Norman Matthias, interview with author, July 2000.

53. James Kerns, interview with author, July 2000.

54. Jim Crume, interview with author, February 2001.

55. Johnny Theodore, interview with author, July 2000.

56. Theodore, July 2000.

57. 7th Cavalry Regiment log, , RG 338, Box 41.

58. Ent, *Fighting on the Brink*, pgs. 96–97. The 27th Infantry Regiment did pull back that night, but they were not enveloped or defeated. Their movement did not carry them all the way to Hwanggan. The next day, July 26, 1950, the NKPA led a major attack against the left side of the 27th's line, specifically on its C Company. The company held its position not only that day but for the next three days. Final casualties for C Company alone during this fighting were nine killed, nineteen wounded and one missing. The relevant point is that the 27th Infantry held the line.

59. An alternative explanation for the events recorded in the regimental log is the possibility that the regimental war diary was modified to protect the reputation of the officers involved. This possibility is fully addressed in the afterword. If, however, we take this line of thought, it is possible that a different sequence actually took place. It may be that regiment never placed a call to battalion alerting it to a breakthrough on the right. Nothing in the division records suggests that this was the case, although the 27th Infantry Regiment was hard pressed that night. It may therefore be possible that the only thing that "hit" the 2nd Battalion 7th Cavalry was Team Field. This is plausible and fits the facts without modification. The account of a breakthrough order may have been created to save the face of the officers in charge of the battalion. Two command levels below the battalion, at the company, I can find only one witnesses who stated that his commander directly received an order originating from battalion to that effect. It may be impossible to determine the actual sequence at this point, as the breakthrough on the right order was accepted as fact by so many other historians and the memories of the veterans may well have changed to fit the "facts" that they learned in later years.

60. This report might have been a case of delayed knowledge. According to the 1st Cavalry War Diary (RG 338, Box 25, entry for July 26), the division itself pulled back from Yongdong on July 25th not because of enemy pressure, but because of the withdrawal of the 27th Infantry to the north. The records that remain do not provide the exact radio traffic that went over the division radio nets that day, but the distinct possibility exists that if Hitchner did hear something it might have been related to this event from earlier in the day.

Chapter 5: Washout

1. Marvin Daniel, interview with author, November 1999.

2. John Lippincott, interview with author, November 1999.

3. John Potts, interview with author, November 1999.

4. Johnny Theodore, interview with author, July 2000.

5. Larry Levine, E-mail to author, March 2001.

6. Leonard "Buddy" Wenzel, interview with author, March 2001.

7. Interview with anonymous soldier, G/2/7 Cavalry, November 1999.

8. Russ McKinley, interview with author, July 2000.

9. John De Borde, interview with author, November 1999.

10. Norman Matthias, interview with author, July 2000.
11. Chandler, *Of Garryowen in Glory*, pg. 276. In his history written some years after, Chandler (writing in the third person) recounted that he stopped his command when met by Major Witherspoon, the regimental S-3.
12. This report, filed by battalion headquarters to regimental headquarters and thence to the 1st Cavalry Division, is a fairly clear indication that the battalion command group had not yet linked up with Captain Chandler, who had an estimated 300 soldiers with him by that point. See also Chandler, *Of Garryowen in Glory*, pgs. 275–77.
13. 1st Cavalry Division War Diary, RG 338, Box 25, entry for July 25–26, 1950.
14. The evidence that not all of Chandler's company came through the night intact is found in the numbers and type of weapons recovered. Only H Company had heavy machine guns (water-cooled .30-caliber), and the night before, the .50-caliber guns were also attached to H Company.
15. 7th Cavalry Regiment War Diary, RG 338, Box 41.
16. G-3 message log, 1st Cavalry Division, RG 338, Box 25. At 2030, the 7th Cavalry reported to the division that although the unit seemed to be reformed (2nd Battalion), more than a hundred men were still missing at that point.
17. Message, EUSAK, found in G-3 records, 1st Cavalry Division, RG 338, Box 23.
18. G-3 Message Log, 1st Cavalry Division, RG 338, Box 25.
19. "Periodic Intelligence Report #5, July 26, 1950," G-2 Reports Annex, 1st Cavalry Division, RG 338, Box 25.
20. Ibid.
21. "Headquarters, 1st Cavalry Division (INF), Office of the AC of S, G2, Interrogation of Civilians Report, July 26, 1950," found in G-2 Reports Annex, 1st Cavalry Division, RG 338, Box 25. The four soldiers led to safety were all from the 71st Tank. Although this report was filed on July 29, it represents the situation as it existed over the preceding several days.
22. Johnny Theodore, interview with author, January 2001.
23. Johnny Theodore, interview with author, February 2001.
24. Larry Levine, interview with author, February 2001.
25. James Crume, interview with author, March 2001. Crume never headr or saw an order to shoot civilians, but opined that there must have been one.
26. Leonard "Buddy" Wenzel, interview with author, March 2001.
27. The South Korean claimants have repeatedly denied that any North Korean infiltrators were among them during this time and that only people from their own villages were with them. I believe they are correct and that there were no "North Koreans." Physical evidence, however, proves that some among them were armed with military weapons of the type used by *local South Korean communist guerillas* and that these weapons were fired in the general area of the railroad trestle.
28. Leonard "Buddy" Wenzel, interview with author, March 2001. Wenzel stated that he has never been to the U.S. National Archives and has never personally examined the files of the 7th Cavalry Regiment from that period.
29. Charles J. Hanley, Sang-hun Choe, Martha Mendoza, *The Bridge at No Gun Ri, A Hidden Nightmare from the Korean War*, (New York, NY: Henry Holt, 2001), pgs. 189–211.
30. Ibid., pg. 142.
31. S-4 (Supply) Journal, 7th Cavalry Regiment, entry for July 28, 1950. Both weapons were turned in to division.
32. Sang-Hun Choe, "Korean investigators link U.S. bullets to No Gun Ri deaths," *Associated Press*, January 10, 2001. Along with the expected .30-caliber shell casings near the former American positions, the South Korean government found Russian weapon shell casings in the area near the underpass.
33. 7th Cavalry War Diary, RG 338, Box 41. See also the S-4 (Supply) Journal for July 27.

34. Hanley, Choe, Mendoza, *The Bridge at No Gun Ri*, pgs. 251–268.
35. The Associated Press published a letter written by Mr. Chung in September 1997 in reference to his claims. See letter Eun-yong Chung, Representative of Petitioners of No Gun Ri Incident, 797-7 Kasuwon-dong, So-gu Taejon, Republic of Korea, 302-241 to His Excellency Bill Clinton, President, The United States of America, September 10, 1997.
36. Chung Gu Shik as quoted in Oh Yeon Ho, "Do You Know Our Agony?—Massacre of Villagers by the U.S. Soldiers during the Korean War" from "People's Solidarity for a Participatory Democracy" available at *http://peoplepower21.org/eng/asq2/13.html*. Accessed January 2001.
37. Department of the Army Inspector General, "No Gun Ri Review Report, Annex C, Imagery Research and Analysis," (January 2001). Anyone interested may view the actual photos themselves, either at the National Archives or in the on-line edition of the DAIG report.
38. 7th Cavalry Regiment War Diary, RG 338, Box 41.
39. See Mission #35-7 After Action Report, 35th Fighter Squadron, 8th Fighter Bomber Group and 7th Cavalry War Diary, RG 338, Box 41. The event is the same. See also Charles J. Hanley, Sang-hun Choe, Martha Mendoza, *The Bridge at No Gun Ri, A Hidden Nightmare from the Korean War*, and the supporting documents from the AP team available at its publisher's Web site at *http://www.henryholt.com/nogunri/document14.htm*.
40. Robert F. Futrell, *The United States Air Force in Korea, 1950–1953*, (Washington, D.C.: Office of Air Force History, Second Edition, 1983), pg. 59.
41. Elizabeth F. Loftus, "Creating False Memories," *Scientific America*, Vol. 227, No.3, (September 1997), pgs. 70–75. In one study, Loftus and her research partner managed to implant a patently false memory into twenty-nine percent of their test subjects with just a single suggestion from a source trusted by the subjects. This suggestion was not reinforced with multiple repetitions, but even so, when interviewed on a follow-up basis twenty-five percent persisted in believing that this implanted memory was true.
42. E. Rynearson and J. McCreery, "Bereavement After Homicide: A Synergism of Trauma and Loss," *American Journal of Psychiatry*, Vol. 150, (February 1993), pgs. 258–261 as cited in C. Brooks Brenneis, *Recovered Memories of Trauma: Transferring the Present to the Past*, (Madison, CT: International University Press, 1997), pgs. 32–33. The Rynearson-McCreery study found that seventeen of the eighteen subjects it studied for their vivid posttraumatic flashbacks (in this case the homicide of a loved one) were actually creating these memories themselves, as only one of them had actually witnessed the murder that was the cause of the distress. Brenneis also cites three other studies, one in which children suffered flashbacks to a traumatic event that they had only heard about (a school shooting) and another in which the spouses of Vietnam veterans developed flashbacks based upon what they had heard about the Vietnam War from their husbands. Brenneis conclusively demonstrates how memories, even of traumatic events, can be transferred or implanted from an outside source.
43. Sang-Hun Choe, "Korean investigators link U.S. bullets to No Gun Ri deaths," *Associated Press*, January 10, 2001.
44. In addition to the U.S. Air Force prosecuting attacks against civilians in these opening days, the U.S. Navy contributed its own share of sorties, according to U.S. Navy officers Captain Walter Karig, Commander Malcolm W. Cagle, and Lieutenant Commander Frank A. Manson in their book *Battle Report, The War in Korea, Prepared from Official Sources*, (New York, NY: Rinehart and Company, 1952), pgs. 107–112. "And thus, then, the Navy fliers reluctantly learned that the overburdened peasant family trudging towards Pusan had to be treated with the cold-blooded marksmanship accorded an armored truck . . . " and later, "So, we killed civilians, friendly civilians, and bombed their homes; fired whole villages with their occupants—women and chil-

dren and ten times as many hidden communist soldiers—under showers of napalm, and the pilots came back to their ships stinking of vomit twisted from their vitals by the shock of what they had to do."

45. Letter, Buzz Lubka to Paul McCloskey, 1989, as reproduced in McCloskey, *The Taking of Hill 610*, pgs. 21–24. This event, in contrast to an air strike brought in by a marking round ordered by McCloskey himself in an earlier mission (a strike that, coincidentally killed roughly fifty innocent villagers), took place against individuals in the open, much like the South Koreans in the open near No Gun Ri. Static targets inside buildings suffer proportionately higher casualties.

46. See Mission #35-11 and #35-12, After Action Report, 35th Fighter Squadron, 8th Fighter Bomber Group, July 26, 1950.

PART II: THE STORY OF THE STORY
Chapter 6: The Strange Tale of Edward Daily

1. Sang-Hun Choe, Charles J. Hanley, Martha Mendoza, "Ex-GIs Tell AP of Korea Killing," Associated Press wire report, September 29, 1999. This is the lead sentence of the Pulitzer Prize-winning article.

2. Martha Mendoza, "Digging Into History—AP Investigates U.S. Actions During the Korean War," *Investigative Reporters and Editors Journal*, (January-February 2000), pg. 6. Available on-line at *http://www.ibiblio.org/journalism/herschaft.html*. Accessed July 9, 2000.

3. Charles Gruntzer, "Stranded Enemy Soldiers Merge with Refugee Crowds in Korea," *The New York Times*, (September 30, 1950), pg. A1.

4. John Osborne, "Report from the Orient: Guns Are Not Enough," *Life* magazine, (August 21, 1950), pgs. 77–85.

5. Seymour Topping, E-mail to author, November 1, 2000. Topping was the administrator of the Pulitzer Prizes the year that the AP won the award. Topping was fairly clear on this point stating, "One of the things that impressed the investigative jury about the AP story was the fact that the Pentagon did not launch an investigation until the story appeared although the alleged Korean victims continued to demand it." It appears that Topping was not aware that the Office of the Secretary of Defense had conducted an investigation at the request of both the Korean claimants and the National Council of Christian Churches (NCCC). This fact was reported by the Associated Press in one of the supporting documents to its original story as well as by Victor Hsu of the NCCC in a letter to the author, February 2001.

6. Seth Mnookin, "Eyes Off the Prize," *Brill's Content*, (September 2000), pgs. 105–106. Mr. Mnookin's article appeared several months after the Pulitzer committee gave the AP the award. His research made clear the fact that the Pulitzer committees rely exclusively upon the individual news agencies and the layers of editors who exist at each to ensure that all facts are solid and all sources confirmed.

7. Robin G. Collingwood, "Who Killed John Doe? The Problem of Testimony" from *The Idea of History*, as reproduced in *The Historian as Detective, Essays on Evidence*, Robin W. Winks, ed., (New York, NY: Harper Torchbooks, 1968), pgs. 39–60. See also Pierce Middleton and Douglass Adair, "The Case of the Men Who Weren't There," also in *The Historian as Detective*, pgs. 142–180. Both essays are wonderful explanations about the nature of historical evidence, the problems with various types of historical evidence, and the strange things that people have done in the past to insert themselves into the historical record for posterity. The book in your hands stemmed from the author's fundamental disagreements with Associated Press reporters and those who followed the AP about what constitutes "proof" and valid evidence in an investigation dealing with the charge of murder.

8. Giuliana A.L. Mazzoni, Elizabeth Loftus, Irving Kirsch, "Changing Beliefs About Implausible Autobiographical Events: A Little Plausibility Goes a Long Way," draft manuscript, in the author's possession.

9. See Joseph L Galloway, "Doubts About a Korean 'Massacre,'" *U.S. News and World Report*, Vol. 128, No. 20 (May 22, 2000), pgs. 40–52; Stanley Weintraub, "Civilian Deaths in Korea Aren't News," *The Wall Street Journal*, (June 5, 2000), pg. A32; Tom Bowman and Scott Shane, "Ex-GI's Account of Korea in Doubt, Records, Memories Provide Conflicting, Spotty Evidence," *Baltimore Sun*, (May 13, 2000); Seth Mnookin, "Eyes Off the Prize," *Brill's Content*, (September 2000), pgs. 105–106; John Omicinski, "No Sto Ri in No Gun Ri Coverage," *USA Today*, (June 12, 2000); Dan Kennedy, "Battle Lines, In the Wake of the AP and New Yorker Controversies, Some Reflections on the Uneasy Relationship Between Journalism and War," *The Boston Phoenix*, (May 18–25, 2000); Michael Moss, "The Story Behind a Soldier's Story," *The New York Times*, (May 31, 2000), pg. A1; Brian Duffy, "Memory and Its Flaws, Piecing Together the Story of No Gun Ri," *U.S. News and World Report*, Vol. 128, No. 23, (June 12, 2000), pg. 22.

10. Susan Paterno, "An Ill Tailwind," *American Journalism Review*, (September 1998). There were striking similarities between the discredited case of the Tailwind fiasco reported jointly by Cable News Network (CNN) and *Time* magazine. Both relied heavily upon a central witness who was, in fact, nowhere near the actual events that he told reporters he witnessed. In both cases the reporters got in significant disagreements with the editors about the factual content of the story as well as the tone established by the writers.

11. AP original story.

12. Choe, Sang-Hun. "Korean Investigators Link U.S. Bullets to No Gun Ri Deaths," *Associated Press*, January 10, 2001.

13. Seth Mnookin, "Eyes Off the Prize," *Brill's Content*, (September 2000), pgs. 105–106. In researching his story about problems with the Pulitzer Prize process, Mr. Mnookin filed a Freedom of Information Act request. The documents he received from the National Military Personnel Records Center showed that the AP had Ed Daily's records by the first week of December 1999. The AP states that it had Delos Flint's records in the summer of 1998. See Robert Burns, "Army Extends No Gun Ri Probe," *Associated Press*, (May 12, 2000).

14. Charles J. Hanley, "Ex-GI Says He Wasn't at No Gun Ri," *Associated Press*, May 25, 2000. The Associated Press had originally identified Edward Daily as a veteran, a soldier who won a battlefield commission and was discharged as a first lieutenant. This follow-up report mentioned that Daily first started interacting with the veterans' organization in 1986. The exact date that Daily started portraying himself as an officer is not known, but many of the veterans interviewed contend that they never recalled a period that Daily did not make that claim, which would suggest that his impersonation started around 1986.

15. AP original story.

16. Michael Moss, "The Story Behind A Soldier's Story," *The New York Times*, (May 31, 2000), pg. A1.

17. Edward Daily, letter to author, November 14, 1999. See also AP story.

18. Edward Daily, interview with author, December 1999.

19. AP original story.

20. Michael Dobbs, "Shoot Them All; Half a Century After the Korean War, Members of the 7th Cavalry Regiment Had Hoped for Recognition; Instead They Are Having to Account for What Happened at No Gun Ri," *Washington Post Sunday Magazine*, (Sunday, February 6, 2000), pg. W08. See also Daily's autobiography in *From Custer to MacArthur* and *Skirmish: Red, White and Blue* .

21. Among those national news publications that cited Edward Daily extensively or conducted interviews with him were *Newsweek, Time, Los Angles Times, The Washington Post*, and *The New York Times*.

22. Eric Alterman, "How They Got the Korean War Atrocity Story, With a year's worth of digging, a team of stolid AP investigators searched records and interviewed survivors to piece together a horrifying story," *Salon.com*, September 30, 1999.

23. *Dateline NBC, with Tom Brokaw*, December 28, 1999. Over the course of fourteen months, the author made sixteen phone calls, sent more than twenty E-mails and four faxes, and mailed four letters by U.S. post to the offices of NBC, the television show *Dateline*, and Brokaw's office in an effort to give any of these elements a chance to comment on their reporting. None of them responded in any way to any of the messages or requests for interviews. The faxes were sent at the request of Mr. Brokaw's personal assistant who asked for "a request for interview in writing." Records at the National Archives suggest that NBC did not research the materials there or at the NMPRC in St. Louis.

24. See William M. Rasmussen, "Brokaw Details Media Changes," *The Harvard Crimson*, (February 27, 2001).

25. *Dateline NBC, with Tom Brokaw*, December 28, 1999.

26. Edward Daily, interview with author, October 1999.

27. The substance of this interview is buttressed by the personal account given by Daily on the NBC program *Dateline* and the graphics created by the Associated Press to explain the events.

28. Robert L. Bateman, "What We Haven't Learned," *Military Review*, Vol. LXXX, No. 1 (January-February 1999), pgs. 49–55.

29. Edward Daily, interviews with author, October, November, December 1999.

30. B. G. Burkett and Glenna Whitley, *Stolen Valor, How the Vietnam Generation was Robbed of its Heroes and History*, (Dallas, TX: Verity Press, 1998).

31. Edward Daily, interview with author, December 1999.

32. Sean Elder, "How They Got the Korean War Atrocity Story," *Salon.com*, (September 30, 1999).

33. Edward Daily, *Skirmish, Red, White, and Blue*, (Paducah, KY: Turner Publishing Company, 1992).

34. Ibid.

35. G-1 logs, 1st Cavalry Division, and S-1 logs for 7th Cavalry Regiment are accessible in the National Archives in RG 319, AG Command Reports 1949–1954, 1st Cavalry Division.

36. R. C. Gray, interviews with author, November and December 1999 and February 2000.

37. Gray now says that the only time that he could personally remember Daily specifically was in the spring of 1951 near the Hwachon reservoir. This matches with Daily's actual record, although at the time of the interview, neither Gray nor the author knew this.

38. Among the National Archives papers that both the AP and I examined, Daily's name should have appeared on the following documents: orders for promotion to corporal (July 1950); orders for promotion to sergeant (July 1950); discharge from the army for the purpose of accepting a commission (August 1950); commission to second lieutenant (August 1950); casualty reports for August 12 fight (listed as missing at least) at both 7th Cavalry level and 1st Cavalry Division G1 level; regimental diary for same; regimental and division diary and 1st Cavalry Division G2 intelligence debriefing reports for his escape and evasion from the North Koreans; 1st Cavalry Division G1 log for Distinguished Service Cross (in any month from September 1950 to February 1951); 1st Cavalry Division special orders for award of Distinguished Service Cross; 1st Cavalry Division Public Affairs Officer news release. If his personal account as according to his

autobiography had been accurate, all of these documents should have explicitly mentioned Edward Daily.

39. Daily's description of his commission as "temporary" second lieutenant is an interesting and curious sidebar. As a man familiar with the history of the 7th Cavalry and by
extension the United States Army, Daily certainly knew about two particular historical
methods of commissioning and promotion. The first is "brevet" promotions; the second is "temporary" ranks. Brevet promotions were a tool used by the United States
Army from the very beginning of its existence up through the American Civil War.
Since, at the time, no awards or medals were given in the army, the only way to
reward a man for heroism or excellence in his duties was to promote him to a higher
grade. Since, however, Congress maintained the purse strings and the ability to grant
promotions, the army could not do this summarily while on campaign. Thus the
brevet promotion was created to use with officers already commissioned. A man would
continue to be paid in his former rank, but he could wear the insignia and exercise the
authority of the rank to which he had been promoted. Robert E. Lee and Stonewall
Jackson were both notable examples of breveted officers during the Mexican-American
War. The practice continued through the Civil War, but with the creation of the
Medal of Honor in 1862 and subsequent awards below that one, brevet promotion
was slowly discontinued in favor of Napoleon's "bits of ribbon." In the First World
War, the United States Army was again confronted with a crisis of scale. The army
expanded from around 125,000 to 4.2 million in just over eighteen months, and pro-
moting officers to the ranks required to command a force of this size (almost 800 percent larger than the modern U.S. Army) required some expedient measures. This was
the genesis of the "temporary" promotion. On November 11, 1918, Dwight D.
Eisenhower was a lieutenant colonel in command of the tank training center at Camp
Colt in Gettysburg, Pennsylvania. George Patton was a colonel (O-6) in command of
the army's only combat-experienced tank brigade in France. Just afer the demobilization that followed the Armistice, both of these regular army officers reverted to their
permanent ranks. Eisenhower was a captain, and Patton was a very disappointed major.
The system was discontinued after World War I. The only vestiges applied to formerly
enlisted soldiers who held battlefield commissions in WWII, Korea, and Vietnam.
During the force reductions following these wars, those officers who had previously
been enlisted soldiers could revert to their enlisted rank with the approval of the
Department of the Army. This caveat was also discontinued in the 1980s.

40. Webb is listed in all regimental documents and division personnel documents in the
positions and at the ranks he represented to me in our initial conversation. William
Webb, interviews with author, January and February 2000.

41. Munchausen syndrome is a condition in which people feign symptoms or injuries in
order to be hospitalized and receive the attention and sympathy of the medical staff and
those around them.

42. Edward Daily, *Skirmish, Red, White, and Blue*, (Paducah, KY: Turner Publishing Company, 1992), pg. 49.

43. Leonhard F. Barnes, interview with author, March 2000. Barnes was a corporal in L
company, 3rd Battalion 7th Cavalry in 1951. See also Edward Daily, *Skirmish*, pg. 90.

44. Edward Daily, interview with author, March 2000.

45. Burkett recounts in *Stolen Valor* several experiences where television and print news
reporters demonstrated this preference for the "shaggy-dog" veterans whom they considered "real."

46. The CBS show *Sixty Minutes* has perhaps the worst record for falling for fake combat
veterans of the Vietnam War. In 1988, one episode titled, "The Wall Within," had
reporter Dan Rather interviewing six combat veterans allegedly living in the wilds of
Washington state. The *Sixty Minutes* segment was just a part of a larger one-hour CBS
special that had aired earlier. Five of the six interviewed by Rather were fakes. One of
those interviewed by Rather was a man identified only as "Steve" on camera who

claimed he was a navy SEAL in Vietnam at age sixteen. Another "combat veteran" interviewed by Rather was Terry Bradley, who "confessed" to Rather that he had personally skinned alive more than fifty Vietnamese men, women, and even babies during the war. The reality, as discovered through a check of their records, was that Steve (real name Steven Ernest Southards) was a communications repairman assigned to rear area bases. Southards had repeatedly gone AWOL during a tour in the Philippines and spent time in the brig as a result. Terry Bradley was not the fighting sergeant portrayed by CBS either. He was actually an ammunition handler, a diagnosed paranoid schizophrenic, who spent more than 300 days either AWOL or in confinement during his limited tour in Vietnam. See B. G. Burkett and Glenna Whitley, *Stolen Valor, How the Vietnam Generation Was Robbed of its Heroes and its History*, (Dallas, TX: Verity Press, 1998), pgs. 87–108.

47. B. G. Burkett, interview with author, September 1999, March 2000. See also Burkett and Whitley, *Stolen Valor*, pgs. 3–46.
48. Burkett and Whitley, *Stolen Valor*, pgs. 337, 381–383, 590.
49. Burkett, interview with author, March 2000.
50. The parallels in some aspects between Wounded Knee and No Gun Ri are fairly strong. In 1938, fifty years after the massacre at Wounded Knee, the U.S. Congress held hearings on the event. The Native American survivors, some suffering from significant problems of memory, found themselves in a media spotlight. At the same time, a host of reporters descended on the story and began printing just about anything that appeared related. In contrast, Wounded Knee did happen. It was a massacre and a tragedy.
51. Robert Gessner, *Massacre*,(1931). In Gessner's account of his interview with the "7th Cavalry veteran," he describes how the **four** battalions of cavalry rode to Wounded Knee where they surrounded the camp of Indian leader Big Foot (one battalion actually intercepted Big Foot's band some nine miles away and brought them to Wounded Knee, where they encamped for the night), and the distortions continue on and on. Even the name of the soldier, D. E. Babb, is fiction, as no such soldier was on the rolls of the 7th Cavalry from that era. Yet by relying on the fact that Wounded Knee was forty years in the past (and, in 1931, the nation was gripped by a general antimilitary sentiment) Gessner's book created a body of lies that continues to echo around the Internet to this day. The irony in this is that facts of what actually happened would have been bad enough by anyone's standards.
52. It appears that the phenomena of fake veterans is not limited to men. While the author has encountered accounts of real veterans exposing fakes as far back as the American Civil War, historians in other sub-fields of military history are discovering them as well. In March 2001, the History Channel broadcast Mindy Pomper's 1999 film, *Free A Man to Fight*, five times. This documentary discusses the role of women in the military during World War II, and it included several interviews with some outstanding women such as Colonel Mary Hallaren, General Jeanne Holm, and USCG Captain Dorothy Stratton. But three women historians saw something that set them to researching a little deeper on their own. The historians—Pat Jernigan, Margaret Salm, and Lois Beck—researched the issues raised in the film over the course of two years. As I did, they used morning attendance reports extensively. What they discovered was yet another batch of fakes riding on the coattails of some legitimately incredible women. The first of these fakes was "Johnnie" Phelps. Her unusual story includes claims to have served as a WAC (Women's Army Corp) sergeant in the Pacific and Europe, to have been a medic in the Pacific, and to have been interviewed by none other than General of the Army Dwight D. Eisenhower while she was in Europe. She was a WAC but her highest rank was corporal. Her claim to have been a medic in the Pacific is completely false since WACs did not serve as medics during World War II. According to the morning reports consulted by Jernigan, Salm, and Beck, Phelps was a clerk and truck driver who served at Langley Field, Virginia, during the war; she was

never in the Pacific and never even outside the continental United States during the war. They discovered that Phelps was briefly assigned to Germany after the war ended, in late 1946 and early 1947, during her second enlistment, but even a cursory review of World War II history points out that General Eisenhower left Germany in November 1945 to become the army chief of staff. Her claim to an interview with General Eisenhower quite simply never took place. Her tale, the most egregious female veteran's story that I have ever heard, has received widespread acceptance by people who apparently have little knowledge of World War II history, the army, or General Eisenhower. Phelps, who died in late 1998, has been widely quoted in gay and lesbian sources. However, she appears to have been the source of all quotes thus far identified. The second largely false interview in the History Channel documentary was with Ruth Karstens Helbig. Like Phelps, Helbig did serve both in the WAAC (Women's Army Air Corps) and the WAC. Her highest rank was T-4. In the film, she claimed she was assigned as the first first sergeant for the first WACs in New Guinea in the South Pacific. She claimed to have been severely injured while disembarking from a troop ship to a landing craft during the landings in New Guinea. Her record shows that she served only in the continental United States. Most of her service was at Fort Oglethorpe, Georgia. She also served several months at Fort Myer, Virginia, before her discharge in early 1946. As a junior enlisted woman (T4 was equivalent to today's sergeant), she would have been a very unlikely choice for such a senior NCO position as first sergeant even if she had gone to New Guinea.

53. Charles J. Hanley, "Ex-GI Says He Wasn't at No Gun Ri," *Associated Press*, Thursday, May 25, 2000.

54. Elizabeth Loftus and Katherine Ketcham, *Witness for the Defense, The Accused, the Eyewitness, and the Expert Who Puts Memory on Trial*, (New York, NY: St. Martin's Press, 1991), pgs. 92–124. This portion of the book is most interesting in its explanation of how an eyewitness to a certain nonviolent event modified her own memory over the course of nine months. Initially the witness, Ms. Sandra Barnes, did not see anyone at a bank machine where the cash card of the murdered victim was used a few minutes earlier. She swore oaths to that effect within weeks of the event. Over the course of nine months, as newspapers ran several dozen photos of the accused and she was repeatedly interviewed by the police and the prosecution, her memory changed. Just before the trial, she suddenly remembered that she had seen the accused at that time and place. Later evidence (including a confession) proved that this (memory) was actually a figment of her imagination. Yet it serves to demonstrate (along with thousands of other similar cases cited in records and psychology works) that human memory is subject to modification from such outside influences as maps, pictures, and questions.

55. Sean Elder, "How They Got the Korean War Atrocity Story," *Salon.com* (September 30, 1999). In this description, Mendoza must be describing a conversation with Norman Tinkler, Edward Daily, or James Kerns. As will be seen later, the AP proceeded from a position that this event occurred and that they were looking for eyewitnesses who could confirm that. Numerous veterans contacted but not cited by the AP relate this as a common thread. When called by the AP, they were told, "We understand that a large number of civilians were shot by your unit in the opening days of the war. Do you have any memory of that? Would you like to comment on that?" If the veteran stated that no such thing happened, the interview was terminated in a matter of minutes.

56. Joseph Galloway, "The Mystery of No Gun Ri," *U.S. News and World Report*, Vol. 128, No. 22, (June 5, 2000), pg. 32. See also the letter from Charles Hanley later in this chapter where Hanley explains that, according to Daily's VA therapist, his PTSD is based upon what happened at No Gun Ri.

57. Michael Moss, "The Story Behind A Soldier's Story," *The New York Times*, (May 31, 2000), pg. A1.

58. John De Borde, interview with author, November 1999. Several other veterans gave similar accounts. Daily apparently talked to every man he felt comfortable with who might have been in the area of No Gun Ri in the summer of 1950.

59. Moss, "The Story Behind A Soldier's Story," *The New York Times.*

60. Charles Hanley expressed considerable outrage to the author in the winter of 2001 because he felt that he had been quoted out of context by a reporter named Seth Mnookin and that his words had been twisted to mean something that he did not intend. To avoid any charges that I am misrepresenting him, I here include the full unexpurgated text of these letters for the reader to decide for himself what Hanley of the *Associated Press* meant when he sent them to me, a few weeks before he won the Pulitzer Prize for the quality of his investigative reporting. The original documents, along with all interview notes, are now located in the U.S. Military Academy archives, West Point, New York.

61. Ironically, given Daily's personal claims, the 2nd Battalion 7th Cavalry spent most of the time that he was with the unit as the division reserve. At no time was it likely that he ever saw combat personally. The battalion conducted one small and successful attack (actually an unopposed movement) on the morning of March 19, 1951 with no casualties. A week later, on March 25, 1951, the battalion moved up to a portion of the line (Phase Line Cairo) near Hongchon, South Korea, and conducted combat patrols but had no contact with the enemy. On March 27, 1951, the unit recorded receiving some harassing 60-mm mortar and small-arms fire, but it took no casualties. The 2nd Battalion was in the lead in movements (unopposed) northward for three days in the beginning of April 1951. The only action it would fight was in the vicinity of the Hwachon dam and reservoir where it attacked in support of a regimental objective on April 10–11, 1951. During this attack, however, Companies F and G led, with E Company in reserve. The attack stalled due to the terrain and the fact that two of three men killed were company commanders. The regiment moved into corps reserve on April 12 and remained in the area of Seoul through April 26, 1951. In the closing days of April 1951, the Chinese launched a major offensive; however, since the 7th Cavalry was well south of the main line, they saw none of this. On April 27, 1951, the regiment moved to a base northwest of Uijongbu, but made no contact in the process. The next day, two companies from the 1st Battalion 7th Cavalry did engage an attacking enemy element, but the action was short lived. The 2nd Battalion, as part of the regiment, sent out a large number of combat patrols from the regimental perimeter, but none of these resulted in close combat. Moreover, one does not take the heavy weapons of H Company out on foot patrols. They are left in the perimeter to secure the base, so it is unlikely Daily even saw an armed enemy soldier at any point. The closest Daily ever came to actual combat was in the period May 5–9 when he may have seen men from the 2nd Battalion as they returned to the base after having seen the enemy atop Hill 337 (and directing fires on same on May 6) and also on Hills 361, 158, and 213. None of these hills were actually assaulted by an infantry force as indirect (mortar and artillery) and close air support fires were used exclusively.

62. Seth Mnookin, "Eyes Off the Prize," *Brill's Content,* (September 2000), pgs 105–106. Mnookin filed a FOIA request to determine who had previously filed FOIA requests about Daily, what information those people got, and when they got it.

63. Moss, "The Story Behind A Soldier's Story," *The New York Times.*

64. Ibid.

65. Mr. Secrist (archivist at National Military Personnel Records Center, St. Louis), interview with author, May 18, 2000.

66. "AP Statement on No Gun Ri Story" by the *Associated Press,* May 16, 2000. This document was subtitled, "A statement by Jonathan Wolman, *Associated Press* executive editor."

67. "Morning Report, H Company, 7 Cav, 26 July 1950." Available through FOIA request from National Military Personnel Records Center, St. Louis, Missouri. The two soldiers from H Company listed as wounded in action and evacuated were Corporal John Mabry and Private Hector Trevino.

68. "Morning Report, F Company, 7 Cav, 27 July 1950." Available through FOIA request from National Military Personnel Records Center, St. Louis, Missouri. Ironically the morning report was somewhat off as Flint's actual service number was RA16250045, not RA6250045. The higher number indicates that Flint enlisted in the Chicago area in the 6th Army region sometime after 1945.

69. Robert Burns, "Army Extends No Gun Ri Probe," the Associated Press, May 12, 2000.

70. Brian Duffy, "Memory and its flaws," *U.S. News and World Report*, Vol. 128, No. 23, (June 12, 2000), pg. 22.

71. Moss, "The Story Behind A Soldier's Story," *The New York Times*.

72. Interview with archivists, National Military Personnel Records Center, St. Louis, Kansas.

73. This is a reasonable assumption based upon the fact that Ed Daily was very gregarious (and seemingly concerned that the "truth" finally get out) and as a result he told many of those he maintained contact with, including Robert Gray, Suey Lee, and the author, about these *Washington Post* and NBC stories within days if not hours of being contacted by both reporters. Interview with Robert Gray, February 2000; letters, Ed Daily to author, November and December 1999.

74. Louis Allen, interview with author, December 1999; letter to author, August 25, 2001.

Chapter 7: Making (Up) History

1. Martha Mendoza, "Digging into history—AP investigates U.S. actions during the Korean War," *Investigative Reporters and Editors Journal*, (January–February 2000), pg. 2. Available on-line at *http://metalab.unc.edu/journalism/herschaft.html*. Accessed July 9, 2000.

2. Bruce Cumings, *The Origins of the Korean War, Volume II, The Roaring of the Cataract, 1947–1950*, (Princeton, NJ: Princeton University Press, 1990), pg. 706.

3. The term muckraking originated at the turn of the century to describe the efforts of journalists to expose corrupt political machines such as those of New York's Tammany Hall and Chicago bosses. It was originally a derisive term applied by the politicians in their futile defense against the power of the pen. In this case, it is used due to the Associated Press's prosecutorial tone in its article and later interviews where it openly states that it believed the army had deliberately concealed the events of No Gun Ri. The AP team saw this as an expose of something that was being deliberately concealed and that in their reporting they were representing "the people" of No Gun Ri in their quest for justice. See Martha Mendoza as quoted in Miguel Espinoza, Kristin Wartman, Kathleen Haley, Katie Morris, Sommer Naffz, "UCSC Alumna Uncovers Korean War Massacre," *City on a Hill*, Vol. 34, Issue #6, Oct 28, 1999, pages 4–5. Speaking of their research Ms. Mendoza was quoted as saying, "Well, at this point we knew the Army had lied . . ."

4. For AP team self-congratulations, see Martha Mendoza's article in the *IRE Journal* where she asserts that the monolithic "U.S. military" was deliberately concealing the fact that the 1st Cavalry Division was near Yongdong and No Gun Ri. According to Mendoza, "We still didn't know whether the South Korean survivors were telling the truth. But more than ever, we realized the U.S. military had it wrong when it said the 1st Cavalry Division was not near No Gun Ri." If Mendoza or the AP team's researcher Randy Herschaft had picked up a copy of the official U.S. Army histories of the Korean War, the first volume of which is Roy Appleman, *South to the Naktong,*

North to the Yalu, and read it, they would have discovered that not only did the U.S. Army know where they were, they provided plenty of maps to illustrate their positions. Yet in her *IRE Journal* article, Mendoza claimed that the AP reporters had actually gone a step beyond that by doing archival research at the U.S. Army Military History Institute at the Carlisle Barracks in Pennsylvania where they "uncovered" thirty-seven boxes of notes from Appleman's original research for *South to the Naktong, North to the Yalu*. A single uninformed statement by a junior lawyer in a branch office in Korea became "The Military."

5. Alex Jones, "Divided Th ey Fall," *Brill's Content*, (September 2000).
6. Although several media outlets have reporters in their Washington bureaus who attend the daily Pentagon briefings, none were identified as military reporters prior to September 11, 2001. They are now so identified.
7. Fred Reed as quoted in William V. Kennedy, *The Military and the Media*, (Westport, CT: Praeger, 1993) pg. 14.
8. For an in-depth examination of the historiography of the split between the media and the military that has developed and widened over the past thirty years, see William M. Hammond, "The Press in Vietnam as Agent of Defeat: A Critical Examination," *Reviews in American History*, Vol. 17, Issue 2, (June 1989), pgs. 312–323. Hammond points out that while the simplistic vision of the "media as the enemy" portrayed in such accounts as General William Westmoreland's various postwar lectures, General Maxwell Taylor's book *Swords into Plowshares* (1972), and Colonel Harry Summers's book *On Strategy: The Vietnam War in Context* (1981) overstate the case, a considerable amount of evidence suggests that significant portions of the media were reporting badly. The critique mentions that upon occasion, especially during such events as Tet 1968, the media often took snippets of information and used them to (badly) support a point of its own creation. This does not support the contention that the media was wholly anti-military, only that as the war progressed, the media was increasingly inclined not to rely upon the official releases of the military. For a full examination of the origins of the split between the military and the media from the journalists' side of the street, see Michael Herr, *Dispatches*, (New York, NY: Alfred A Knopf, 1968); Neil Sheehan, *A Bright and Shining Lie, John Paul Vann and America in Vietnam*, (New York, NY: Random House, 1988); and Phillip Knightley, *The First Casualty, From the Crimea to Vietnam: The War Correspondent as Hero, Propagandist, and Myth Maker*, (New York, NY: Harcourt Brace, 1975).
9. Nathaniel Lande, *Dispatches from the Front, News Accounts of American Wars, 1776–1991*, (New York, NY: Henry Holt, 1995), pgs. 3–25.
10. "America's News Backbone," *Columbia Journalism Review*, (November-December 2000).
11. James M. McPherson, *For Cause and Comrades, Why Men Fought in the Civil War*, (New York, NY: Oxford University Press, 1997). McPherson's contention is based upon his examination of more than a hundred thousand documents from Civil War soldiers, both North and South.
12. Estimates place the number of reporters with the Union armies alone at five-hundred over the course of the war.
13. Harry J. Maihafer, *The General and the Journalists, Ulysses S. Grant, Horace Greeley, and Charles Dana*, (Washington, D.C.: Brassey's, 1998), pg. 91. In perhaps one of the most obviously obtuse cases of a reporter endangering his own life through his reporting, one unknown reporter managed to slip a report out of Cairo, Illinois, as Grant's command left for the attack on Forts Donelson and Henry. The report was explicit: "Sunday night, Feb. 2, the grand expedition up the Tennessee and Cumberland rivers is about to start. The last of it moves in the morning. It will attack Forts Henry and Donelson. The force to be engaged is fully 22,000 men." The dispatch appeared in the *Chicago Tribune* on February 4, 1862. Grant did not arrive at his destination with his

17,000 men until February 6. Assuming that the reporter accompanied the expedition, his reporting placed his own life in similar jeopardy as the soldiers whose movements he betrayed.

14. Lande, *Dispatches from the Front*, pgs.110–115.

15. *Cincinnati Commercial*, December 11, 1861 as quoted in Joseph H. Ewing, "The New Sherman Letters," in *Newsmen and the National Defense, Is Conflict Inevitable*, Lloyd J. Matthews, ed., (Washington, D.C.: Brassey's Inc., 1991), pg. 22. For those unfamiliar with Sherman's later military career, suffice it to say that he was a very successful commander in the war and eventually became the commanding general of the United States Army after the war.

16. Ibid., pgs 24–25.

17. Phillip Knightley, *The First Casualty, From the Crimea to Vietnam: The War Correspondent as Hero, Propagandist, and Myth Maker*, (New York, NY: Harcourt Brace, 1975), pg. 28. The "byline" was a byproduct of this. Faced with wildly inaccurate (and in some cases slanderous) reporting by anonymous reporters, Union General Joseph Hooker (who came after McClellan and Burnsides but before Meade as commander of the Union Army of the Potomac) required all reporters' dispatches and stories originating from within the Army of the Potomac to have a "by" line when published. It appears that this requirement made a significant impact.

18. Harry J. Maihafer, *The General and the Journalists, Ulysses S. Grant, Horace Greeley, and Charles Dana*, (Washington, D.C.: Brassey's, 1998), pg. 117.

19. Ibid.

20. Although Grant may well have had periods of time when he had too much to drink, he was by no means a drunk by the standards of the day. The allegations of his inebriation were based at least in part upon rumors spread by an Ohio colonel who had been relieved for cowardice during the battle of Shiloh. Ibid., pg. 123.

21. J. Douglas Bates, *The Pulitzer Prize*, (New York, NY: Birch Lane Press, 1991), pgs. 1–14.

22. "MacArthur Papers," United States Military Academy, Box 4. Major Douglas MacArthur became the censor for the United States Army in 1916 as it appeared more and more likely that the United States might enter WWI. It appears that he wanted to create extremely strict censorship, along the lines of the British and French models of the time. It is clear from this and some of his other early writings that at this point he saw the press in an adversarial role. To see the excerpts of the original statement issued by the general staff, see *The New York Times*, July 7, 1916, pg. 6. This also provides information on how the media initially reacted to MacArthur's recommendation.

23. James R. Mock and Cedric Larson, *Words That Won The War: The Story of the Committee on Public Information, 1917–1919*, (Princeton, NJ: Princeton University Press, 1939).

24. Martin Middlebrook, *The Nuremberg Raid*, (London, UK: Cassel and Co., 1973), pg. 251. The crew was British; the nationality of the reporters was not noted.

25. The literature on the current state of military-media relations is large and continues to build. Certainly one of the first works to document the process of disillusion between the institutions from the journalist's side was Michael Herr, *Dispatches*, (New York, NY: Alfred A Knopf, 1968). See also such weighty material as Neil Sheehan, *A Bright and Shining Lie, John Paul Vann and America in Vietnam*, (New York, NY: Random House, 1988) and Phillip Knightley, *The First Casualty, From the Crimea to Vietnam: The War Correspondent as Hero, Propagandist, and Myth Maker*, (New York, NY: Harcourt Brace, 1975). The military, one could argue, has become positively obsessed with understanding the fourth estate. The U. S. Army War College at Carlisle Barracks, Pennsylvania, has an annual session devoted to training lieutenant colonels and colonels about the methods and techniques of dealing with the media, complete with many editors from some of the most influential American media outlets. The byproduct is a host of books from military authors including the semi-scholarly collections of some of

the papers presented at these events in *Newsmen and the National Defense, Is Conflict Inevitable?*, Lloyd J. Matthews, ed., (Washington, D.C.: Brassey's Inc., 1991).

26. William V. Kennedy, *The Media and the Military*, (Westport, CT: Praeger, 1991), pg. 123.

27. I am indebted to David Crook of the *The Wall Street Journal*, Charles Pierce of *Esquire*, David Cay Johnston of *The New York Times*, and Richard Pyle of the Associated Press for their insights.

28. Alex S. Jones, "Divided They Stand, Journalists have less and less personal exposure to the military. That comes at a price to both professions—and to us as informed citizens," *Brill's Content*, (October 2000).

29. Alfred Thayer Mahan, "Subordination in Historical Treatment," in Mahan, *Naval Administration*,pgs. 245–272, quoted in Philip A. Crowl, "Alfred Thayer Mahan: The Naval Historian," *Makers of Modern Strategy*, Peter Paret, ed., (Princeton: Princeton University Press, 1987), pg. 454.

30. John Keegan, "Battle and the Historian," *International Security*, Winter 1978–79 as quoted in F. D. G.Williams, *SLAM: The Influence of S.L.A. Marshall on the United States Army*, (Washington, D.C.: Office of the Command Historian, United States Army, 1989), pg. 77.

31. S.L.A. Marshall, *Bringing Up the Rear, A Memoir*, (San Rafael, CA: Presidio Press, 1979), pg. 20. In his autobiography, Marshall credits sports cartoonist Tad Dorgan with realizing that Marshall's initials spelled out "SLAM." This was the name that he would most often use in both written and verbal communications. Apparently this is a fabrication as his given name was plain Samuel Lyman Marshall. It appears that Marshall added the Atwood himself to create a catchy moniker suitable for a sports writer.

32. Ibid., pgs. 1–16. This is a simplification. Actually Marshall had two brothers, both of whom died as children. Among the locations that the Marshall family lived were Killian, South Carolina, Boulder, Colorado, Niles, California, and El Paso, Texas.

33. Marshall claimed, for example, that during the fighting in Bastogne, Belguim, at the height of the Battle of the Bulge, he and two colonels had visited the outer edge of the front lines and pointed out to a private the helmet of a German soldier patrolling behind a wall just yards away. (See Marshall, *Bringing Up the Rear*, pg. 127.) Historian and WWII combat veteran Harold K. Leinbaugh doubted this improbable event when he read it in Marshall's autobiography and asked one of the colonels, then a general, if any such event had ever taken place. It had not. [See Fredric Smoler, "The Secret of the Soldiers Who Didn't Shoot," *American Heritage*, 40/2, (March 1989), pg. 42.] Marshall also claimed in the same book that his explanation to a staff officer of the "true" one-word last response of Napoleon's commander of the Old Guard at Waterloo to an offer to surrender was the genesis for one of the most famous quotes in military history—"nuts" from the commander of the 101st in Bastogne in response to the German offer to surrender. Ibid. pg. 122.

34. Ibid., pg. 15. Although Marshall carefully avoids making a direct assertion about his combat record in World War I, he gives the impression that he was in combat, leading infantry soldiers. Stenay was one of the last towns taken by U.S. troops during World War I, and the implication is obvious. Similarly, in some of the "About the Author" entries in his books, such as *Battles in the Monsoon*, Marshall claims, at 18, to be the youngest infantry company commander in the American Expeditionary Force in France.

35. See Roger Spiller, "S. L. A. Marshall and the Ratio of Fire," *The Royal United Services Institute Journal*, 133/4, (Winter 1988), pgs. 63–69

36. Susan Canedy, introduction to *SLAM: The Influence of S.L.A. Marshall on the United States Army*, by F. D. G. Williams, (Washington, D.C.: Office of the Command Historian, United States Army, 1989), pgs. 2–3.

37. Fredric Smoler, "The Secret of the Soldiers Who Didn't Shoot," *American Heritage*, 40/2, (March 1989), pgs. 37–43.

38. Williams, *SLAM: The Influence of S. L .A. Marshall on the United States Army*, pgs. 85–87.

39. S.L.A. Marshall, *Battles in the Monsoon, Campaigning in the Central Highlands, Vietnam, Summer 1966*, (New York, NY: William Morrow, 1967), pg. 298.

40. David H. Hackworth, *About Face*, (New York: Simon and Schuster, 1989), pg. 119. Hackworth did earn a battlefield commission, but he states that he never met Marshall in Korea. Hackworth was in the same company as Millett, but only after Millett had already departed the unit.

41. Marshall, *Bringing Up the Rear*, pg. 274.

42. Letter, Colonel (Ret.) David Hackworth to author, June 1, 1997.

43. Jack Stokes, Associated Press executive editor, interview with author, March 12, 2001. Mr. Stokes repeated the previously published assertion by the AP that it did not have a thesis, or an opinion, on the material presented in its story and that the story was structured to allow all sides an equal voice in its reporting.

44. Martha Mendoza, "Digging into history—AP investigates U.S. actions during the Korean War," *Investigative Reporters and Editors Journal* (January-February 2000), pg. 2. Available on-line at *http://metalab.unc.edu/journalism/herschaft.html*. Accessed July 9, 2000.

45. The lawyer, Kelley White, sent a request for information to the local history office in Korea, a request that was answered by a telephone call from a sergeant in that office. Apparently this was interpreted to mean that there was no historical basis for the claim. It is unclear at this point who, if anyone, in that "historical office" did the research that resulted in this bogus statement.

46. Martha Mendoza, "Digging into history-AP investigates U.S. actions during the Korean War," *Investigative Reporters and Editors Journal* (January-February 2000).

47. AP original story. Reprinted with permission of the Associated Press.

48. "AP Statement on No Gun Ri Story," May 16, 2000.

49. Howard Kurtz, "At The Associated Press, A Drawn-Out Battle Over Korean War Story," *The Washington Post*, (May 16, 2000), pg. C1

50. AP original story.

51. Howard Kurtz, "At The Associated Press, A Drawn-Out Battle Over Korean War Story," *The Washington Post*, (May 16, 2000), pg. C1

52. AP original story.

53. Nicole Loftus, "Pulitzer Prize winner speaks to NAU," *Northern Arizona University, Flagstaff Life*, April 12–18, 2000. According to this interview given by Ms. Mendoza shortly after she won the Pulitzer Prize, it was on the reporters' thirty-fourth interview with a "former general" that they first "hit paydirt." One obviously wonders, if they had a former general that admitted this, why did the AP not use a quote from this source? The likely answer is that Ms. Loftus did not know that "officer" is not the same as "general" and used the words as synonyms for each other, but one is never sure.

54. Charles Hanley, E-mail to author. The full text of this E-mail is in the preceding chapter, but it should be noted at this point that the AP continually fluctuated on the number of interviews conducted during its "extensive" historical research.

55. Charles Hanley, E-mail to author, March 26–27, 2000. In the full text of these E-mails (seen in the previous chapter), Mr. Hanley states that there were one hundred interviews with eighty-four veterans of the 2nd Battalion 7th Cavalry.

56. Several of the veterans interviewed in the course of the research for this book made this point. According to William Webb, the AP reporter who called him told him what the South Korean version of events was, then asked him if he recalled any such event. When he explicitly stated that no such event occurred to the best of his knowledge, the interview was abruptly terminated by the reporter. Webb believes that this reporter was Charles Hanley. The total elapsed time of the interview was approximately five minutes. John De Borde, Robert Gray, John Lippincott, John Potts, and

others recount almost the same thing: once they stated that nothing such as the events suggested by the South Koreans took place, their interviews were cut short.

57. AP original story.
58. Ibid.
59. Charles Hanley, interview with author, February 21, 2001.
60. AP original story.
61. 5th Cavalry Regiment War Diary, 5th Cavalry Radio Message Log, 8th Cavalry Regiment radio message log, RG 338.
62. There is some suggestion that this may not be quite the case. See Howard Kurtz, "At The Associated Press, A Drawn-Out Battle Over Korean War Story," *The Washington Post*, (May 16, 2000), on the editorial battles that went on at the Associated Press over this story. Charles Hanley repeatedly refused to comment on this when asked for an interview by the author. March 14, 2001.
63. AP original story.
64. Charles Hanley states that the AP conducted 100 interviews with eighty-four members of the battalion. Ms. Mendoza later claims that the AP actually conducted a total of 220 interviews. If this is a true statement, why did the AP not use some of these other sources in its story?
65. AP original story.
66. Ibid.
67. Ibid.
68. Jonathan Wolman quote appeared in Howard Kurtz, "At The Associated Press, A Drawn-Out Battle Over Korean War Story," *The Washington Post*, (May 16, 2000).
69. AP original story.
70. The Associated Press "AP Statement on No Gun Ri Story," May 16, 2000. This document was subtitled, "A statement by Jonathan Wolman, Associated Press executive editor." In this document, Wolman used the phrase "more than a year in the making" to describe the reporting effort.
71. Nicole Loftus, "Pulitzer Prize winner speaks to NAU," *Northern Arizona University, Flagstaff Life*, April 12–18, 2000. Loftus interviewed Martha Mendoza for her information.
72. Kurtz, "At The Associated Press, A Drawn-Out Battle Over Korean War Story." This article cites AP reporter Charles Hanley as saying, "The story was complete in late July of 1998, and that story was in essence and in detail the story that was released in late September 1999." If the story of the story started in South Korea where Sang Hun Choe originally reported it in April 1998, then the actual time spent reporting was not "eighteen months" or even a year, it was ninety days. See Sean Elder, "How They Got the Korean War Atrocity Story," *Salon.com*, (September 30, 1999). Elder reports the timing of the story with this lead-in: "Choe, a Korean AP reporter, broke a story in April 1998 about a group of Koreans who'd survived the massacre and had attempted to make claims against both the U.S. military and the government of South Korea." The same story notes that James Kerns had not been contracted by anyone other than Edward Daily as late as the fall of 1998.
73. Charles Hanley, E-mail to author. The author has not researched the military record of Hanley.
74. AP original story.
75. "What They Said," *U.S. News and World Report*, Vol. 128, No. 20, (May 22, 2000), pg. 52. The AP disputes this story and contends Patterson meant No Gun Ri.
76. 7th Cavalry Regiment War Diary, RG 338, Box 41, entry for July 25, 1950. See also the morning attendance reports for F Company cited and quoted in full in preceding chapter.
77. Michael Moss, "The Story Behind a Soldier's Story," *The New York Times*, (May 31, 2000), pg. A1.

78. An image of the actual letter from claimants to President Clinton, claiming that the attack started when soldiers called in an airstrike, was available on the AP's Web site for more than a year, beginning October 1999. Copy in author's possession.

79. AP original story.

80. 7th Cavalry Regiment War Diary, RG 338, Box 41. See also the morning reports for E, F, G, and H Companies, July 25–27, 1950.

81. AP original story.

82. William Webb, interview with author, March 2000 and February 2001. Most of the veterans interviewed for this book state that they were called either by Martha Mendoza or Charles Hanley in the summer of 1998 and at that time they categorically denied that there was ever any such order: or that any mass killing took place at No Gun Ri. According to several of these veterans, Mendoza or Hanley then terminated the interview after just a few minutes.

83. When the AP in the fall of 2000 illegally gained access to a list of the men interviewed by the Department of Army Inspector General (the identities of potential witnesses are protected under the Privacy Act of 1973), AP reporters interviewed two men, Larry Levine and Harold Crume, soldiers assigned to the signals section of the battalion headquarters. Although neither man heard a single thing that indicated that there were orders to fire on civilians, the AP spun the story to make it appear that these men also verified its version of events. Both Crume and Levine expressed personal opinions that there "must have been an order" (as related here in chapter six), but the AP presented this as "proof." The fact that neither man was in a position to actually hear an order, even if there had been one, was never mentioned. Instead, the AP used the men's duty positions (as opposed to actual duties on July 26, 1950) to make it appear that they were legitimate sources from "a higher command level." The lead sentence in this November 2000 article ran, "Two ex-GIs who handled radio and message traffic told Pentagon investigators that American troops had orders from higher headquarters to fire on civilian refugees at No Gun Ri in the early days of the Korean War. The sworn statements by Lawrence Levine and James Crume, who were assigned to the head-quarters of 2nd battalion 7th Cavalry Regiment, are the first from a higher command level to publicly support recollections of some other veterans that they were ordered to shoot civilians for fear North Korean infiltrators were among them." Richard Pyle, "Ex-U.S. GIs: Told To Kill Civilians," *Associated Press*, (November 21, 2000). Levine's and Crume's actual activities on July 26, 1950 were fully covered in preceding chapters of this book.

84. Charles J. Hanley and Martha Mendoza, "It's Been Good To Talk About These Things," Associated Press (September 30, 1999).

85. AP original story.

86. William Webb, interview with author, March 2001. As a member of the battalion staff (S1), Webb's place of duty was in the battalion command post. He is the only surviving officer other than Lieutenant Colonel Herbert Heyer (then the battalion commander) who would have been right there had an order to kill civilians been issued at the battalion level or passed down from the regimental level.

87. Seymor Topping, E-mail to author. Topping was at the time the administrator of the Pulitzer Prizes. In two separate E-mails, he stated that one of the most important elements that convinced the Pulitzer committee of the weight of the AP story and the quality of its reporting was the fact that the Pentagon initiated an official investigation into the matter only after the AP story broke. Mr. Topping refused further comment on the issue beyond that point.

88. Martha Mendoza as quoted in Miguel Espinoza, Kristin Wartman, Kathleen Haley, Katie Morris, Sommer Naffz, "UCSC Alumna Uncovers Korean War Massacre," *City on a Hill*, Vol. 34, Issue #6, (October 28, 1999), pgs. 4–5.

89. Roy G. Appleman, *South to the Naktong, North to the Yalu*, (Washington, D.C.: Office of the Chief of Military History, 1964), pg. 203. That last sentence, "Four enemy tanks

and an infantry force started this action by driving several hundred refugees ahead of them through American mine fields" refers to what we now know was Team Field and the events covered in detail in chapter five of this book.

90. Martha Mendoza as quoted in Miguel Espinoza, Kristin Wartman, Kathleen Haley, Katie Morris, Sommer Naffz, "UCSC Alumna Uncovers Korean War Massacre," *City on a Hill*, Vol. 34, Issue #6, (October 28, 1999), pgs. 4–5.

91. Martha Mendoza as quoted in Karin Wanless, "The Bridge at No Gun Ri," *University of California Santa Cruz Review*, (Summer 2000).

92. Martha Mendoza, "Digging Into History-AP Investigates U.S. Actions During the Korean War," *Investigative Reporters and Editors Journal*, (January-February 2000), pg. 2

93. Ibid.

94. Charles Gruntzer, "Stranded Enemy Soldiers Merge with Refugee Crowds in Korea," *The New York Times*, (September 30, 1950), pg. A1.

95. Ironically the members of the AP team eventually did find this original North Korean propaganda article in the summer of 2000. Had they been slightly less myopic in their original research and examined the archival records of the 1st Cavalry Division beyond just the few days surrounding July 26–29, 1950, they might have found this translated propaganda and made the connection in time for their original reporting. See RG 338, Box 25-30. A translation of this document floated through both EUSAK headquarters and 1st Cavalry Division headquarters in late August and early September 1950. The probable connection between Gruntzer's story and the North Korean propaganda cannot be confirmed, but given the fact that Gruntzer himself never apparently ventured forward of division headquarters for this or any story to interview troops on the actual front lines, it seems plausible that his information came exclusively through information he could gather from rear-echelon elements such as division and corps staff officers.

96. John Osborne, "Report from the Orient: Guns Are Not Enough," *Life*, (August 21, 1950), pg. 77.

97. Ibid., pgs. 84–85.

98. Perhaps the best evidence that Osborne was not in the area of the 7th Calvary Regiment on July 26–29 was the fact that several other reporters did visit the front lines of the 7th Cavalry Regiment at the time the South Koreans allege that a massacre was taking place. Their presence was noted in the regimental logs and later in the regimental war diary. In perhaps the greatest bit of irony of this whole affair, one of these reporters was none other than Tom Lambert of the Associated Press. The other reporters visiting the 7th Cavalry Regiment in that period were Davis Warner of the *Daily Telegraph and London Herald* in Melbourne and Stanley Massey of the *Consolidated Press* in Sidney. None of them filed stories about a massacre in the area. As Osborne's article illustrated, a censorship process was not yet in effect, so there was no barrier to any of them reporting such an event had it taken place. (See RG 319, Army, Adjutant General Command Reports, 1949–1954, 1st Cavalry Division, 901-INF(7), 7th Cavalry Regiment.)

99. Bruce Cumings, *The Origins of the Korean War, Volume II, The Roaring of the Cataract 1947–1950*, pgs. 705–707.

100. Martha Mendoza as quoted in Miguel Espinoza, Kristin Wartman, Kathleen Haley, Katie Morris, Sommer Naffz, "UCSC Alumna Uncovers Korean War Massacre," *City on a Hill*, Vol. 34, Issue 6, (October 28, 1999), pgs. 4–5.

101. The exact quote is, "The 1999 story, more than a year in the works, quoted a dozen U.S. veterans who said a large number of civilian refugees, many of them women and children, were shot to death under a railroad bridge at the hamlet of No Gun Ri on July 26, 1950." This statement appeared in Jerry Schwartz, "AP Responds To Questions About Prize-Winning Investigation," Associated Press, May 15, 2000. Schwartz is attributed in his byline as "AP National Writer."

102. Felicity Barringer, "A Press Divided: Disputed Accounts Of A Korean War Massacre," *The New York Times*, May 22, 2000.
103. Nicole Loftus, "Pulitzer Prize winner speaks to NAU," Northern Arizona University, *Flagstaff Life*, (April 12–18, 2000).
104. Ibid.
105. The author contacted Charles Hanley, Martha Mendoza, AP editor Jack Stokes, and the AP public relations personnel on several different occasions by telephone and E-mail asking for this information. At this time, months after the original requests, no one from the AP has responded, though they have acknowledged receipt of the requests.
106. Michael Moss, "The Story Behind a Soldier's Story," *The New York Times*, (May 31, 2000), pg. A1.
107. Martha Mendoza, "Digging Into History—AP Investigates U.S. Actions During the Korean War," *Investigative Reporters and Editors Journal*, (January-February 2000), pg. 2.
108. Edward Daily, letter to author, December 12, 1999, and interview with author, November 1999.
109. Edward Daily, letter to 1st Cavalry Division Association and 7th Cavalry Regiment Association, October 23, 1999, sent to the author by Daily in letter to author, October 29, 1999. In the author's possession.
110. Martha Mendoza as quoted in Miguel Espinoza, Kristin Wartman, Kathleen Haley, Katie Morris, Sommer Naffz, "UCSC Alumna Uncovers Korean War Massacre," *City on a Hill*, Vol. 34, Issue #6,. Oct 28, 1999, pages 4–5.
111. Martha Mendoza, "Digging Into History—AP Investigates U.S. Actions During the Korean War," *Investigative Reporters and Editors Journal*, (Jan-Feb 2000), 2.
112. Nicole Loftus, "Pulitzer Prize Winner Speaks to NAU" Northern Arizona University, *Flagstaff Life*, April 12–18, 2000.
113. Martha Mendoza as quoted in Karin Wanless, "The Bridge at No Gun Ri," *University of California Santa Cruz Review*, (Summer 2000).
114. Charles J. Hanley, Sang-Hun Choe, and Martha Mendoza, *The Bridge at No Gun Ri, A Hidden Nightmare from the Korean War*, (New York, NY: Henry Holt, 2001), pg. 272. the book says, "Then, on the thirty-fourth call, Mendoza found an ex-sergeant who described the shooting of refugees at a trestle in the first days of their deployment."

AFTERWORD

1. There is an ongoing debate in historical circles about Appleman's portrayal of the all-black 24th Infantry Regiment of the 25th Infantry Division. Some contend that Appleman was, perhaps not quite consciously, racist in his description of the regiment's behavior. In *South to the Naktong, North to the Yalu*, the 24th is very nearly the only unit described in detail as having "bugged out." As we have seen, the men of the 24th were not alone in this behavior, as the 2nd Battalion 7th Cavalry did this as well. It is also evident from the materials he left behind that Appleman knew of this episode but chose not to explain it in any depth. The 2nd Battalion 7th Cavalry was all-white at the time, as were all the infantry regiments initially committed to combat except the 24th Infantry Regiment. Other historians have discovered other units that broke apart ("bugged out") as well. Yet in Appleman's work, only one example appears—the all-black 24th Infantry Regiment.
2. These journals were preserved at the division level. They were also typewritten for the first time.
3. DAIG report, South Korean bullet analysis.
4. Sang-Hun Choe, "Korean Investigators Link U.S. Bullets To No Gun Ri Deaths," *Associated Press*, January 10, 2001.

INTERVIEWS AND CORRESPONDENCE
Alfred Clair
Alan Brister
Alexander Haig
Charles Hanley
Donald Donnelly
Edward Daily
Elizabeth Loftus
Francis Baylock
Jean Burner
James Crume
James Kerns
John De Borde
John Fatum
John Haskell
John Lippincott
John Potts
Johnny Theodore
Joseph Christopher
Larry Levine
Leonard B. Wenzel
Louis Mehl
Martha Mendoza
Marvin Daniel
Michael Moss
Norman Matthias
Robert C. Gray
Robert Alecia
Russell McKinley
Seth Mnookin
William Hoffman
William Webb
William West

PUBLISHED SOURCES

Acheson, Dean. *The Korean War.* New York: W. W. Norton & Co., 1971.

Ambrose, Stephen E. *Duty, Honor, Country: A History of West Point.* Baltimore: Johns Hopkins Press, 1966.

Bartov, Omar. *Hitler's Army, Soldiers, Nazis and War in the Third Reich.* New York: Oxford University Press, 1992.

Bates, J. Douglas. *The Pulitzer Prize: The Inside Story of America's Most Prestigious Award.* New York: Birch Lane Press, 1991.

Beech, Keyes. *Tokyo and Points East.* New York: Doubleday and Co., 1954.

Bickers, Richard Townshend. *Friendly Fire: Accidents in Battle from Ancient Greece to the Gulf War.* London: Leo Cooper, 1994.

Blainey, Geoffrey. *The Causes of War.* New York: The Free Press, 1977.

Burkett, B. G. and Glenna Whitley. *Stolen Valor: How the Vietnam Generation was Robbed of its Heroes and History.* Dallas, Texas: Verity Press, 1998.

Carlton, Eric, *Massacres: An Historical Perspective.* Aldershot, UK: Scholar Press, 1994.

Chandler, David G. *The Campaigns of Napoleon: The Mind and Method of History's Greatest Soldier.* New York: MacMillan, 1966.

Chandler, Melbourne C. *Of Garryowen in Glory.* Self published, 1960.

Chinnery, Philip D. *Korean Atrocity: Forgotten War Crimes 1950–1953* Annapolis: Naval Institute Press, 2000.

Chum-kon, Kim. *The Korean War, 1950–53.* Seoul: Kwangmyong, 1980.

Crane, Conrad C. *American Airpower Strategy in Korea, 1950–1953.* Lawrence, Kansas: University Press of Kansas, 2000.

Cumings, Bruce. *The Origins of the Korean War, Volume II, The Roaring of the Cataract, 1947–1950.* Princeton: Princeton University Press, 1990.

————. *Korea's Place in the Sun, A Modern History.* New York: W. W. Norton Co., 1995.

Daily, Edward. *Skirmish, Red, White and Blue.* Paducah, Kentucky: Turner Publishing, 1992.

————. *From Custer to MacArthur: 7th U.S. Cavalry, 1866–1945.* Paducah, Kentucky: Turner Publishing, 1995.

Dieppe, Brian W. *Custer's Last Stand: The Anatomy of an American Myth.* Missoula, Montana: University of Montana Press, 1976.

Dinter, Elmer. *Pressures Facing the Soldier in Battle.* London: Frank Cass and Co., 1985.

Du Picq, Ardant. *Battle Studies: Ancient and Modern Battle.* Translated and edited by John N. Greely. New York: The Macmillan Co., 1921.

Ent, Uzal W. *Fighting on the Brink: The Defense of the Pusan Perimeter.* Paducah, Kentucky: Turner Publishing, 1996.

Fehrenbach, T. R. *This Kind of War.* New York: Macmillan, 1963.

1st Cavalry Division, Korea, June 1950 to January 1952. No Author Cited. Paducah, Kentucky: Turner Publishing Co., 1994.

Goncharov, Sergei N., John W. Lewis, and Xue Litai. *Uncertain Partners: Stalin, Mao, and the Korean War.* Stanford, California: Stanford University Press, 1993.

Graham, W. A. *The Custer Myth: A Source Book of Custeriana.* New York: Bonanza Books, 1953.

Grossman, Dave. *On Killing: The Psychological Cost of Learning to Kill in War and Society.* New York: Little Brown, 1995.

Gutman, Roy and David Rieff, eds. *Crimes of War: What the Public Should Know.* New York: W. W. Norton, 1999.

Heller, Charles E. and William A Stofft, eds. *America's First Battles.* Lawrence, Kansas: University Press of Kansas, 1986.

Henderson, William D. *Cohesion, the Human Element in Combat: Leadership and Societal Influence in the Armies of the Soviet Union, the United States, North Vietnam, and Israel.* Washington: National Defense University Press, 1985.

Higgins, Marguerite. *War in Korea, The Report of a Woman Combat Correspondent.* New York: Doubleday and Co., 1951.

Hocking, William Ernest. *Morale and Its Enemies.* New Haven: Yale University Press, 1918.

The Howitzer, 1923. West Point, New York: Privately published, 1923.

Hoyt, Edwin P. *The Pusan Perimeter, Korea 1950.* New York: Stein and Day, 1984.

Karig, Walter, Malcolm W. Cagle, and Frank A. Manson. *Battle Report: The War in Korea.* New York: Rinehart and Co., 1952.

Keegan, John. *The Face of Battle.* New York: Harper Collins, 1986.

Kellett, Anthony. *Combat Motivation: The Behavior of Soldiers in Battle.* The Hague: Nijhoff Publishing, 1982.

Kennedy, William V. *The Media and the Military.* Westport, Connecticut: Praeger, 1991.

Knightley, Phillip. *The First Casualty, From the Crimea to Vietnam: The War Correspondent as Hero, Propagandist, and Myth Maker.* New York: Harcourt Brace, 1975.

Korean Institute of Military History. *The Korean War.* Vol. I, 1997 revision (English). Omaha: University of Nebraska Press, 2000.

Lande, Nathaniel. *Dispatches from the Front: News Accounts of American Wars, 1776–1991.* New York: Henry Holt, 1995.

Leckie, Robert. *Conflict: The History of the Korean War.* New York: Putnam, 1962.

Loftus, Elizabeth F. *Eyewitness Testimony*. Cambridge: Harvard University Press, 1979.

Loftus, Elizabeth F. and Katherine Ketcham. *Witness for the Defense: The Accused, the Eyewitness, and the Expert Who Puts Memory on Trial.* New York: St. Martin's Press, 1991.

Longstreet, James. *From Manassas to Appomattox*. Philadelphia: J. B. Lippincott & Co., 1895.

Lynn, John. *The Bayonets of the Republic: Motivation and Tactics in the Army of Revolutionary France, 1791–94.* Boulder, Colorado: Westview Press, 1996.

MacDonald, Charles B. *A Time for Trumpets*. New York: William Morrow, 1985.

Maher, William L. *A Shepherd in Combat Boots: Chaplain Emil Kapaun of the 1st Cavalry Division.* Shippensburg, Pennsylvania: Burd Street Press, 1997.

Maihafer, Harry J. *The General and the Journalists, Ulysses S. Grant , Horace Greeley, and Charles Dana.* Washington: Brassey's, 1998.

Marshall, S. L. A. *Bringing Up the Rear: A Memoir*. San Rafael, California: Presidio Press, 1979.

———. *Battles in the Monsoon: Campaigning in the Central Highlands, Vietnam, Summer 1966.* New York: William Morrow, 1967.

Matthews, Lloyd J., ed. *Newsmen and the National Defense: Is Conflict Inevitable?* Washington: Brassey's, 1991.

McCloskey, Paul N. *The Taking of Hill 610*. Woodside, California: Eaglet Books, 1992.

McPherson, James M. *For Cause and Comrades: Why Men Fought in the Civil War.* New York: Oxford University Press, 1997.

McWilliams, Bill. *A Return to Glory: The Untold Story of Honor, Dishonor, and Triumph at the United States Military Academy, 1950–1953* Lynchburg, Virginia: Warwick House Publishers, 2000.

Middlebrook, Martin. *The Nuremberg Raid*. London: Cassel and Co., 1973.

Millett, Allan R., and Peter Maslowski. *For the Common Defense*. New York: The Free Press, 1984.

Moran, Lord. *The Anatomy of Courage*. New York: Avery Publishing, 1987.

Norman, Richard. *Ethics, Killing, and War*. Cambridge: Cambridge University Press, 1995.

Osiel, Mark J. *Obeying Orders: Atrocity, Military Discipline & the Law of War.* New Brunswick, N. J.: Transaction Publishers, 1999.

Pearson, Raymond. *The Rise and Fall of the Soviet Empire*. New York: St. Martin's Press, 1998.

Register of Graduates and Former Cadets, United States Military Academy, 1995. West Point, NewYork: Association of Graduates, 1995.

Rusk, Dean (as told to Richard Rusk), Daniel S. Papp, ed. *As I Saw It.* New York: W. W. Norton and Company, 1990.

Sarkesian, Sam C., ed. *Combat Effectiveness: Cohesion, Stress, and the Volunteer Military.* Beverly Hills, California: Sage Publications, 1980.

Stone, Ian K. *Betrayals: Fort William Henry and the 'Massacre'.* New York: Oxford University Press, 1990.

Stouffer, S.A., et al. *The American Soldier, Combat and Its Aftermath, Vol. II.* Princeton: Princeton University Press, 1949.

Stueck, William. *The Korean War: An International History.* Princeton: Princeton University Press, 1995.

Sun-Yup, Paik. *From Pusan to Panmunjom.* Dulles, Virginia: Brassey's, 1996.

Terry, Addison. *The Battle for Pusan, A Korean War Memoir.* Novato, California: Presidio Press, 2000.

Watson, Bruce Allen. *When Soldiers Quit: Studies in Military Disintegration.* Westport, Connecticut: Greenwood, 1997.

Weigley, Russell. *History of the United States Army.* New York: Macmillan, 1967.

Weintraub, Stanley. *MacArthur's War: Korea and the Undoing of an American Hero.* New York: The Free Press, 2000.

Wilson, Arthur W. and Norman L. Strickbine. *Korean Vignettes, Faces of War.* Portland, Oregon: Artwork Publications, 1996.

Windschuttle, Keith. *The Killing of History: How Literary Critics and Social Theorists Are Murdering Our Past.* San Francisco: Encounter Books, 1996.

Winks, Robin W., ed. *The Historian as Detective: Essays on Evidence.* New York: Harper Torchbooks, 1968.

GOVERNMENT PUBLICATIONS

Appleman, Roy E. *South to the Naktong, North to the Yalu.* Washington: Office of the Chief of Military History, 1961.

"Crisis in Asia-An Examination of U. S. Policy." *Department of State Bulletin.* Vol. XXII. No. 551. Washington: Government Printing Office (GPO), January 23, 1950.

Department of the Army. *No Gun Ri Review.* Washington: Department of the Army Inspector General, January 2001.

————. *Table of Organization and Equipment No. 7–11N, Infantry Regiment, 21 April 1948.* Washington: Department of the Army, 1948.

————. *Table of Organization and Equipment No. 7–11N, Infantry Regiment, 20 December 1949.* Washington: Department of the Army, 1949.

————. *Table of Organization and Equipment No. 7–15N, Infantry Battalion, 15 November 1950.* Washington: Department of the Army, 1950.

Donaldson, William H., ed. *General Cullum's Biographical Register of the Officers and Graduates of the U.S. Military Academy at West Point.* Supplemental Volume VII. Chicago: The Lakeside Press, 1930.

"Foreign Relations of the United States, 1948, Vol. VI." *The Far East and Australia.* Washington: GPO, 1974.

"Foreign Relations of the United States, 1949. Vol. VII, Part 2." *The Far East and Australia.* Washington: GPO, 1976.

Futrell, Robert F. *The United States Air Force in Korea. 1950–1953.* Washington: Office of Air Force History, GPO, 1983.

Sawyer, Robert K. *Military Advisors in Korea: KMAG in Peace and War.* Washington: Office of the Chief of Military History, GPO, 1962.

Schnabel, James F. *Policy and Direction: The First Year.* Washington: Office of the Chief of Military History, 1992.

Williams, F. D. G. *SLAM: The Influence of S. L. A. Marshall on the United States Army.* Washington: Office of the Command Historian, United States Army, 1989.

PERIODICALS

"America's News Backbone." *Columbia Journalism Review.* (November–December 2000).

Barringer, Felicity. "A Press Divided: Disputed Accounts Of A Korean War Massacre." *The New York Times.* May 22, 2000.

Bateman, Robert L. "Without Malice, Without Sympathy: Civilian Antipathy for the Military, 1607–2000." *Army.* Vol. 49, No.1. January 1999.

————. "The Birth of the 'Modern' U.S. Army, A Case Study: The 17th U.S. Infantry and Columbus Barracks, 1894–1896." *The Journal of America's Military Past.* Vol. XXVI, No. 1. Spring/Summer 1999.

————. "What We Haven't Learned." *Military Review.* Vol. LXXX, No. 1 January–February 2000.

Bowman, Tom and Scott Shane, "Ex-GI's Account of Korea in Doubt: Records, Memories Provide Conflicting, Spotty Evidence." *Baltimore Sun.* May 13, 2000.

Burns, Robert. "Army Extends No Gun Ri Probe." *Associated Press.* May 12, 2000.

Choe, Sang-Hun. "Korean Investigators Link U.S. Bullets to No Gun Ri Deaths." *Associated Press.* January 10, 2001.

Choe, Sang-Hun, Charles J. Hanley, Martha Mendoza. "Ex-GIs Tell AP of Korea Killing." *Associated Press.* September 29, 1999.

Dobbs, Michael. "Shoot Them All; Half a Century After the Korean War, Members of the 7th Cavalry Regiment Had Hoped for Recognition; Instead They Are Having to Account for What Happened at No Gun Ri." *The Washington Post Sunday Magazine*. February 6, 2000.

Duffy, Brian. "Memory and Its Flaws, Piecing Together the Story of No Gun Ri" *U.S. News and World Report*. Vol. 128, No. 23. June 12, 2000.

Elder, Sean. "How They Got the Korean War Atrocity Story." *Salon.com*. September 30, 1999.

Espinoza, Miguel, Kristin Wartman, Kathleen Haley, Katie Morris, and Sommer Naffz. "UCSC Alumna Uncovers Korean War Massacre." *City on a Hill*. Vol. 34, No. 6. October 28, 1999.

Galloway, Joseph L. "Doubts About a Korean 'Massacre'." *U.S. News and World Report*. Vol. 128, No. 20. May 22, 2000.

———. "The Mystery of No Gun Ri." *U.S. News and World Report*. Vol. 128, No. 22. June 5, 2000.

Gruntzer, Charles. "Stranded Enemy Soldiers Merge with Refugee Crowds in Korea." *The New York Times*. September 30, 1950.

Hammond, William M. "The Press in Vietnam as Agent of Defeat: A Critical Examination." *Reviews in American History*. Vol. 17, No. 2. June 1989.

Hanley, Charles J. "Ex-GI Says He Wasn't At No Gun Ri." *Associated Press*. May 25, 2000.

Jones, Alex S. "Divided They Stand: Journalists Have Less And Less Personal Exposure To The Military. That Comes at a Price To Both Professions—and to us as Informed Citizens." *Brill's Content*. October 2000.

Kennedy, Dan. "Battle Lines In the Wake of the AP and New Yorker Controversies: Some Reflections on the Uneasy Relationship Between Journalism and War." *The Boston Phoenix*. May 18–25, 2000.

Kurtz, Howard. "At The Associated Press: A Drawn-Out Battle Over Korean War Story." *The Washington Post*. May 16, 2000.

Lawrence, W. H. "219 Beat Way to U.S. Lines In 3 Day Trek in Korean Mud." *The New York Times*. July 29,1950.

Levine, Harold. "Hell Country: Of Mud, Muck, and Human Excrement..." *Newsweek*. August 7, 1950.

Loftus, Nicole. "Pulitzer Prize Winner Speaks to NAU." *Northern Arizona University Flagstaff Life*. April 12–18, 2000.

Mendoza, Martha. "Digging Into History—AP Investigates U.S. Actions During the Korean War." *Investigative Reporter's and Editor's Journal*. Jan-Feb 2000.

Mnookin, Seth. "Eyes Off the Prize." *Brill's Content*. September 2000.

Moss, Michael. "The Story Behind a Soldier's Story," *TheNew York Times*. May 31, 2000.

Omicinski, John. "'No Sto Ri' in No Gun Ri Coverage." *USA Today*. June 12, 2000.

Osborne, John. "Report From the Orient: Guns Are Not Enough." *Life Magazine*. August 21, 1950.

Paterno, Susan. "An Ill Tailwind." *American Journalism Review*. September 1998.

Rasmussen, William M. "Brokaw Details Media Changes." *The Harvard Crimson*. February 27, 2001.

Schwartz, Jerry. "AP Responds to Questions About Prize-Winning Investigation." *Associated Press*. May 15, 2000.

Shils, E. A. and Morris Janowitz. "Cohesion and Disintegration in the Wehrmacht in World War II." *Public Opinion Quarterly*. No. 12. Summer 1948.

Smoler, Fredric. "The Secret of the Soldiers Who Didn't Shoot." *American Heritage*. Vol. 40, No. 2. March 1989.

Spiller, Roger. "S. L. A. Marshall and the Ratio of Fire." *The Royal United Services Institute Journal*. Vol. 133, No. 4. Winter 1988.

Sullivan, Walter. "US Movies Shown in Korean Wilds." *The New York Times*. Sunday, March 19, 1950.

————. "South Korea Fails in Guerilla Drive." *The New York Times*. Wednesday, March 15, 1950.

Wanless, Karin. "The Bridge at No Gun Ri." *University of California Santa Cruz Review*. Summer 2000.

Weintraub, Stanley. "Civilian Deaths in Korea Aren't News." *The Wall Street Journal*. June 5, 2000.

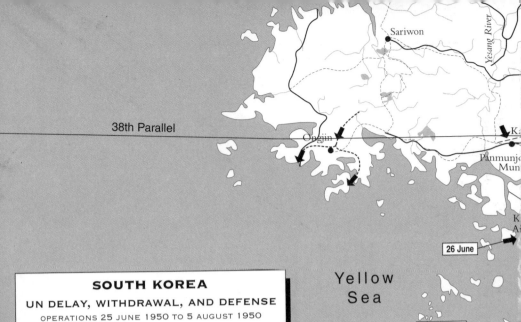

Sariwon

Yesang River

38th Parallel

Ongjin

Ka

Panmunjo
Mun

K.
A

26 June

Yellow
Sea

Task Force
Smith

Taejon falls
20 July

Light resistance
by ROK military
police units.

SOUTH KOREA

UN DELAY, WITHDRAWAL, AND DEFENSE
OPERATIONS 25 JUNE 1950 TO 5 AUGUST 1950

N

| 0 | 10 | 20 | 30 | 40 | 50 | 60 |

SCALE OF MILES

TABLE OF SYMBOLS

Company	I
Battalion	II
Regiment or Group	III
Brigade	X
Division	XX
Corps	XXX
Army	XXXX
Armor	(oval)
Cavalry	(slash box)
Infantry	(crossed box)

	ACTUAL LOCATION	PRIOR LOCATION
Troops on the March	➡	⌐⌐➤
Troops in Position	⌒	(dashed arc)
Route of March or Retreat	– ➔ – ➔	
Unit Boundary	—XX—	

WITH APPROPRIATE
UNIT SYMBOL

Area of Detailed Maps